A Concise History
of World War I

A CONCISE HISTORY
OF WORLD WAR I

PREPARED FOR
THE ENCYCLOPEDIA AMERICANA
UNDER THE ADVISORY EDITORSHIP OF

Brigadier General VINCENT J. ESPOSITO,
U.S.A. (*Ret.*)

*Professor Emeritus and former Head of the Department
of Military Art and Engineering
The United States Military Academy*

REPRINTED WITH THE PERMISSION OF THE AMERICANA CORPORATION

by
FREDERICK A. PRAEGER, *Publishers*
New York · Washington · London

FREDERICK A. PRAEGER, *Publishers*
111 Fourth Ave., New York 3, N.Y., U.S.A.
77-79 Charlotte Street, London W.1, England

Published in the United States of America in 1964
by Frederick A. Praeger, Inc., Publishers

Third printing, 1965

Printed in the United States of America

Editor's Preface

The current observance of the Centennial of the American Civil War (1861–1865), and the prevailing tensions of the Cold War between the East and the West, serve to keep the public mind focused on the subject of war. How and why the human race contrived to generate the conflicts that momentarily threaten it with virtual extinction is the predominant question.

It is in the search for an answer to this question that the true significance of World War I is revealed. The historians, who have been largely preoccupied with the more compelling events of World War II and the Cold War, now begin to see World War I in proper perspective, and the flow of literature dealing with the war is increasing sharply as the fiftieth anniversary of the advent of the war approaches. The widespread sale of publications dealing with the events of World War I also attests to the growing public interest in this phase of history.

The nature of the American Civil War indicated that future warfare, as a result of the expanding industrial revolution, particularly in transportation and communications, would no longer be restricted to the armed forces but that its horrors would soon engulf the entire national populace. This prognosis was conclusively proved during the course of World War I. The consequent sufferings and privations borne by so many peoples eventually led to a lack of confidence in existing political institutions, which, in turn, created fertile opportunities for the assumption of power by totalitarian governments, in the form of a variety of "isms." The imperialistic designs of Italian Fascism, and later of German Nazism, led directly to the outbreak of World War II; the genesis of the present Cold War lies in the Marxist doctrines of the Bolsheviks, who seized power in Russia in 1917. Hence, it would not be illogical to consider World War I, World War II, and the Cold War as one continuous conflict, interspersed with unhappy interludes of tenuous peace—or, perhaps more accurately, armed truce.

In pursuance of their standing policy of frequent revision of the articles in *The Encyclopedia Americana*, the editors, recognizing the increasing importance of World War I, decided to prepare an entirely new article on the war, presenting the most up-to-date account written by the foremost authorities. To ensure the best results, the editors decided to commission the best available historians to write the sections that concerned their respective specialties rather than to entrust the entire article to one historian. Such an approach inevitably leads to a certain amount of repetition, for the same event must occasionally be treated from different points of view.

The account of the Western Front, in Europe, is an example of the concern of the editors to enlist the most authoritative writers for the treatment not only of that crucial theater but also of other areas and periods. The events of 1914, the first year of the war, in which the role of the French predominated, are narrated by the noted French historian André Ducasse; the years 1915–1917, during which the British bore the brunt of the war on the Allied side while the French recovered from the disaster on the Aisne, are covered by Cyril Falls, one of the foremost British military historians; and the year 1918, in which the contribution of the United States to active operations in the war reached substantial proportions, is described by an American author, the undersigned. Similarly, the account of the war on the Italian Front was prepared by the eminent Italian historian Piero Pieri.

The maps and map captions in this volume—which, taken sequentially, present a chronological thumbnail account of the military events in the theaters of war—were designed by the undersigned. His basic map sketches were converted into line drawings by Mr. Edward J. Krasnoborski, cartographer of the Department of Military Art and Engineering, United States Military Academy, and into clear and attractive final production copy by Mr. L. Robert Tschirky, of *The Americana*'s art staff. The major burden of editing fell to Miss Beatrice E. Eckes, Associate Editor of *The Americana*, whose remarkable ability to ferret out inconsistencies and errors in a field of special and difficult writing foreign to women has contributed so much to the accuracy of this work. The article entered the text of *The Americana*'s 1962 edition.

The undersigned cannot close without paying warm tributes to

Dr. Lavinia P. Dudley, Editor-in-Chief of *The Americana*, and Drake de Kay, the Senior Editor. Appreciating the timeliness and importance of arranging for a complete revision of both the World War I and II articles, Mrs. Dudley set the example of earnest, selfless, and, above all, tactful management in an undertaking the completion of which demanded the wholehearted cooperation of members of the staff. Mr. de Kay directly supervised the project, patiently guided the authors and myself, and was ever vigilant in maintaining the encyclopedia's high standards.

Vincent J. Esposito

Contents

Maps

A Concise History
of World War I

1. General Survey

BY GEORGE FIELDING ELIOT

The outbreak of World War I in 1914 marked the collapse of the balance-of-power system by which the peace of Europe, and in large measure the peace of the world, had been conserved for the past hundred years. The principle of the balance of power reflected an accepted pattern of international behavior in which the nations concerned so oriented their policies as to prevent any one of them from attaining such a preponderant position as to be able absolutely to dominate the others. In terms of relatively recent European experience, this had been the principle that had underlain the series of wars between 1689 and 1814—wars chiefly directed toward curbing what William III of England had called the "exorbitant power of France," culminating in the 22-year struggle (1792–1814) to deny European domination to the wave of violence unleashed by the French Revolution and later marshaled to the brink of final success by Napoleon Bonaparte.

Pax Britannica

When, after the abdication of Napoleon, the victorious allied powers—Great Britain, Austria, Prussia, and Russia—had, with the restored Louis XVIII of France, signed the Treaty of Paris on May 30, 1814, they declared their intention of establishing "a firm peace, based on a just equilibrium of strength among the Powers." Unlike many pronouncements of good intentions, this one was to remain effective for an entire century. Its durability was favored by circumstances. At the outset none of the signatories possessed, or seemed likely to be able to acquire, such a preponderance of resources as would permit the most ambitious of rulers or politicians to dream of dominating the European scene to any such degree as Louis XIV or Napoleon had each nearly attained. In 1814, France was bled white by the sacrifices of past wars; Prussia, though a rising power within the Germanic system, was not yet master even of northern Germany; Austria, under Prince Klemens von Metternich's leadership, had enough to think of in opposing Prussian ambition, clinging to its restive Italian possessions, and keeping some semblance of order among the diverse nationalities of the

3

Hapsburg Empire; and Russia was turning its attention southward and eastward, away from unproductive forays into central Europe toward the perennial Muscovite dream of the Turkish Straits and the warm waters of the Mediterranean Sea and the Persian Gulf.

As for Britain, the policy by which the British people and Commonwealth were to prosper so richly during the nineteenth century was already taking form in the astute mind of Viscount Castlereagh, the Foreign Secretary, whose idea of a "just equilibrium" was a balance among the Continental powers while Britain remained relatively aloof and uncommitted, though vigilant against any threat to the Continental balance. In effect, the British dominated the non-European world with naval and commercial power and, from an insular position invulnerable to direct attack as long as the Royal Navy ruled the seas, held the balance in Europe by maintaining political freedom of action and avoiding long-term commitment to any Continental grouping. This was an ideal policy for British interests; it was also an ideal method of operating a balance-of-power system, since the existence of an uncommitted power element free to bring pressure wherever a dominant tendency needed to be checked gave stability to the whole system. Experience had taught British statesmen to dread the domination of the continent of Europe by a single military power. Throughout the nineteenth century and well into the twentieth, they directed the course of their own policies accordingly, and with notable success as long as there continued to exist a relative Continental balance from which Britain could remain aloof and on either side of which her weight would be decisive.

In terms more familiar to the mid-twentieth century, this was a deterrent policy. Its object was to preserve peace and security by depriving war of any reasonable prospect of gain, while keeping any hostilities that did occur confined to limited objectives not threatening to the existing equilibrium. Britain, retaining both military and political freedom of action, was capable of applying her own power in limited-objective operations when necessary, notably in preventing Russian domination of the Turkish Straits, which was regarded in London as endangering the security of British interests in India and the Middle East.

The first serious threat to this *Pax Britannica* came from two concurrent and interdependent causes. First, with the expansion of industry and the accompanying scientific progress came development of new armaments of all kinds, together with such new and rapid means of communication and movement as the telegraph, the railway, and the steamship. Military calculations became less dependent on the vagaries of wind and weather, on atrocious roads, and on wide time gaps between available information and subsequent events; military planners could count on the relatively rapid concentration of forces and on greatly increased firepower to overwhelm resistance. These considerations were likely to prove increasingly attractive to prospective aggressors.

The second danger arose out of the unification of north and west Germany under the hegemony of Prussia, an accomplishment in which King William I of Prussia, together with his master statesman, Prince Otto von Bismarck, and his chief of the General Staff, General (later Field Marshal) Count Helmuth von Moltke, made highly effective use of the new military capabilities that had become available to them. In doing so, however, they brought into being (and inevitably forced on all their Continental neighbors) the principle of universal military service in peacetime, sometimes referred to as the nation in arms. The military potentialities thus developed could be kept under dependable control only by being associated with solidly established constitutional restraints designed to that end, but, save in the militarily feeble Low Countries, Switzerland, and the Scandinavian states, such constitutional development had not yet matured on the continent of Europe. Germany, Russia, and the Hapsburg Empire remained fatally liable to the recurrence of dynastic incompetence at the summit of authority, and the kaleidoscopic republican political regime in France was to prove hardly more capable of foresighted realism. Nor did the comfortable British islanders realize until too late how dangerously the foundations of the *Pax Britannica* over which they had so long presided and which they had come to accept as their unalterable birthright had been undermined.

Deadly Timetable of Mobilization

It was an ill omen for Europe that the occasion for the appointment of Bismarck as Minister President of Prussia in 1862 should have been the determination of King William I to reorganize and expand the Prussian Army. That army had been raised by more or less hit-or-miss conscription since 1814, but the numbers called to the colors were far fewer than the number of young men who annually reached military age. Some of those not needed for the standing army went into the Landwehr, a kind of national guard; others, perhaps a majority, escaped military service altogether. William was intent on a German confederation headed by Prussia and the house of Hohenzollern, from which Austria and the house of Hapsburg should be excluded. The defeat of Austria by France and Sardinia in 1859 had demonstrated Austrian military shortcomings. In 1860, William, then Prince Regent, proposed a system of universal military service for all young men—three years in the standing army followed by four in the reserve, with reservists being used to bring units to war strength on mobilization. Men passing out of the reserve would then serve in the Landwehr, which would come under army control. Strong political opposition to these measures at once arose; it was Bismarck's agility in circumventing this opposition that brought him a firm place in the King's regard as well as the respect of Moltke.

Between 1862 and 1866 the Prussian Army was transformed. The number of regiments was nearly doubled; the officer corps was thoroughly shaken up and imbued with a new spirit and a new competence. The professional General Staff, made directly responsible to the King, began to overshadow the Ministry of War. Meanwhile, Bismarck pursued his task as the architect of German unity. His means were warlike, but his wars were carefully limited. He wrenched a province from Denmark in 1864; he crushed Austria in 1866, but he restrained the King from a triumphal entry into Vienna; in 1870, when the army reforms were bearing fruit in terms of trained reserves and Landwehr and rearmament with breech-loading rifles and artillery, he engineered a war with France, then widely thought of as the leading military power in Europe. An unbroken series of German victories, in which Prussian troops were joined by soldiers from the lesser German states, culminated in the fall of Paris and the creation of the German Empire with William as the first Emperor. From that moment onward, Bismarck directed all his efforts toward conserving the gains he had made; the central objective of his foreign policy became the preservation of the peace of Europe.

But the fate of the French professional army at the hands of the German nation in arms had taught Europe the lesson that no power could ever again feel secure that did not train all of its young men for war, establish a system of reserves, and create a general staff to prepare mobilization and war plans. After 1871 the powers of Europe—France, humiliated and vengeful; the remodeled Hapsburg Empire of Austria-Hungary; newly united Italy;

distant Russia with its peasant population but recently freed from serfdom—strove with diligence to apply this lesson to their military establishments. As a result, by 1890 all four of these powers, as well as Germany, had armies recruited on the principle of universal liability to military service, commencing at the age of nineteen or twenty. The average requirement was three years with the colors, followed by nine to fifteen years in various categories of reserve service, during which the reservists remained liable to a call to active duty and underwent periodic refresher training. First-line units of the active army were usually maintained in peacetime at 50 to 60 per cent of full war strength. Each regiment or corresponding unit was recruited from an assigned district; the reservists of this district, on mobilization, were used to bring the active regiment to full strength and also to form one or more reserve regiments. Thus mobilization could triple or quadruple the manpower strength of the peacetime army within forty-eight hours in Germany or France, which had the most efficient systems; Italy and Austria-Hungary required a somewhat longer period due to more complicated arrangements; and Russia, with its vast distances and scanty railway net, took longer yet.

On reporting to their mobilization centers, the reservists found weapons, uniforms, and equipment ready for their use and joined their units. This completed the first step in the process of mobilization for war. At this point, the war plan prepared by the General Staff took over. Every war plan made provision for the rapid movement of troops by rail to the assembly areas of the divisions and army corps, and these areas were so located as to facilitate entry into action against the assumed opponent at the earliest possible moment. Obviously a tremendous advantage was to be gained by a nation that could launch a full-scale offensive before its opponent's army was fully deployed. The precise and constantly amended general staff estimates of what each possible enemy power could do, stated in terms of so many divisions moving up to such and such a line on each day after the call to arms was sounded, constituted for each military power in Europe what may be called the deadly timetable of mobilization—deadly because to fall short of its demands in terms of countereffort was to face defeat and perhaps national ruin. Once any power set this process in motion, no potential foe or prospective victim could afford even a day's hesitation in doing likewise.

But since the fact that a mobilization order had been issued could not, in the Europe of the period 1890–1914, remain unknown to other governments for more than a very few hours (if that long), was surprise any longer a possibility, at least in the strategic sense? It was, in at least two ways: in the choice of the direction and relative weight of the main effort, and in the numbers of fully armed and trained reserve formations by which the first-line troops could be reinforced at the outset of war. The first of these was of extreme importance. German theory, indeed, held that an error in initial deployment could scarcely be corrected during the whole course of a campaign, and initial deployment obviously was governed by the whole complicated plan of rail movement and assembly of forces, a plan which had to be prepared in advance down to the smallest detail to avoid utter confusion. As to the second factor, although the numbers of first-line divisions and army corps possessed by each European power were a matter of common knowledge, the numbers of reserve units which could be thrown into action at the beginning of hostilities depended on such variables as periods of peacetime training, the training and education of reserve officers, and the theories developed by each general staff as to the employment of its reserve units in wartime. On this latter point, orthodox military judgment was inclined to hold that reservists who had returned to civilian life were likely to become unfit for front-line service except when merged into units composed largely of active soldiers; units entirely composed of reservists were, in this view, suited chiefly for occupation duty or for the garrison of fortresses. But there was clearly room for departures from orthodoxy—departures that could contain the seeds of surprise, since the details of reserve training could be kept obscure.

In one area of military theory, however, the general staffs of Europe appeared in agreement. All accepted Karl von Clausewitz' objective of decisive battle leading to the destruction of the enemy's forces. None planned for a long war. "The concept of a long war," observes Barbara Tuchman in *The Guns of August* (New York, 1962, p. 22), "could not be scientifically planned for as could the orthodox, predictable, and simple solution of decisive battle and a short war. . . . All preferred to believe, along with the bankers and industrialists, that because of the dislocation of economic life a general European war could not last more than three or four months." Recent experience seemed to lend some support to this view: Austria had been overwhelmed in seven weeks in 1866 by one decisive battle, and France in seven months in

1870–71 by a series of decisive battles. Contradictory experiences afforded by the American Civil War of 1861–65 and, when it came, the Russo-Japanese War of 1904–5 were explained away or disregarded. Rarely has a fundamental error taken such widespread hold on the minds of professional officers, or been clung to more tenaciously at greater cost in blood, treasure, and suffering.

With such a theory dominant in military thought, the compulsion of the mobilization timetable overshadowed every other consideration in periods of tension. No general staff could risk being caught napping or fail to challenge any hesitation on the part of kings or ministers with the iron imperatives of military necessity. Yet the accelerating gains of technology were even in 1890 beginning to drain validity from the concept of a short war terminated by decisive battle, as applied to anything like a general war in Europe. As the years passed, this concept became more and more inconsistent with the facts of armament and of national resources. The single-shot breech-loading rifle gave way to the magazine rifle with increased range and velocity; the machine gun with its high rate of automatic fire came slowly into use, although it was still regarded by some soldiers as merely a weapon of opportunity. Rapid-firing field artillery replaced the older types. Gasoline motors gave new mobility to armies and made practical the use of heavier types of artillery in the field than had previously been available except for siege work. These weapons and machines were the product of Europe's expanding industry, and here and there doubtful minds began to ask whether a modern industrial state could be overwhelmed and subdued in a short campaign and two or three decisive battles, since its masses of trained reserves and the output of its factories would continue to provide it with the means of further resistance. It was against the background of this emerging technological revolution that the powers continued the build-up of their military organizations and the accompanying political arrangements and rearrangements that characterized the period 1871–1914.

Polarization of the Balance of Power

Bismarck's hope was that Europe as a whole would gradually come to accept the existence of a powerful German state in the center of the Continent as more or less a matter of course and perhaps even as a contribution to European stability. To this end, he sought to establish close relations with both Russia and Austria-Hungary. Aware that the interests of these two powers must clash in the Balkan Peninsula, he hoped that Germany might play the role of mediator, and he saw that Britain's firm purpose to deny the Russians a lodgment at Constantinople (İstanbul) might cause London to take a favorable view of this Bismarckian balance-of-power policy in eastern Europe.

The other facet of Bismarck's policy was the continued isolation of France. By maintaining close relations with Russia and Austria-Hungary and by conciliating Britain, he hoped to deny France any hope of acquiring an ally. Meanwhile, the mounting German birthrate and the burgeoning industry of the Rhineland promised increased military superiority over France in the coming years. Bismarck did not underestimate the enduring quality of the French spirit of revenge, embittered by the loss of Alsace-Lorraine in 1871. He had argued in vain against pressing the demand for this territory, being overruled by the King and Moltke on the plea of military necessity, but without an ally France might hesitate to risk war.

Bismarck's system of alliances lasted with various vicissitudes through the 1880's, although in general German-Austrian relations grew closer while Russia remained relatively aloof. In 1882, Bismarck brought Italy into a Triple Alliance with Germany and Austria, and in 1887 he concluded what has been called the Reinsurance Treaty with Russia. The stated intent of all these treaties was to secure the stability of eastern Europe, especially the Balkans, where Russian, Austrian, and Italian interests were in growing opposition.

The flaw in Bismarck's statesmanship was the dependence of German policy on the personal equation. The machinery of state operated effectively under the joint direction of the outstanding personalities of Bismarck and Moltke, with the indispensable balance wheel of Emperor William's authority to reconcile occasional conflicts between them. This was a government not of laws but of men, however, and between 1888 and 1890 all three of the mainstays of German policy were swept from the political chessboard. William I died in 1888, Moltke resigned as chief of staff in that year and died in 1891, and in 1890 the weak and theatrical William II, inwardly unsure of his personal powers but jealous of prerogatives that he accounted of divine origin, found himself unable longer to endure association with his strong-willed Chancellor and dismissed Bismarck from office.

Hardly had this occurred when the Russians proposed the renewal of the Reinsurance Treaty for a six-year term. The new Chancellor, General Count Leo von Caprivi, who lacked Bismarck's vision, refused on the ground that the treaty was inconsistent with Germany's obligations to Austria. The moment was ill chosen, for the French were anxiously seeking closer relations with Russia, and the Russian reaction to Caprivi's rebuff was prompt. A French general was invited to attend the Russian maneuvers in 1891, while a French naval squadron visited Kronstadt. In August, 1892, a military convention was concluded by which each country was bound to attack Germany in case of a German attack on the other, and the mobilization of the armies of both countries was to be automatic in case any of the members of the Triple Alliance should mobilize. With the ratification of this agreement by Czar Alexander III in December, 1893, the Bismarckian security system collapsed. A new Continental balance of power came into being, with the Triple Alliance of Germany, Austria-Hungary, and Italy confronting the Dual Alliance of France and Russia, while Britain continued to retain her cherished freedom of action.

For Germany, the new grouping meant that in any future war the German Army would have to fight on two fronts, and to this problem the chief of the German General Staff, General (later Field Marshal) Count Alfred von Schlieffen, at once addressed his efforts. His plan, as it evolved, was based on mobilization time-tables which indicated that both Germany and France could complete mobilization and deployment of forces so as to be ready to begin major operations in about two weeks, whereas it was the German estimate that the Russian Army could not be ready for a major attack on Germany in less than six weeks. Therefore, the indicated German strategy called for an all-out assault on France, using every available unit except the barest minimum required to hold off any adventurous Russian thrusts (which could, it was thought, be undertaken at first only with partly mobilized units already stationed near the frontier). To crush the French in decisive battle within four to six weeks and then turn in full strength on Russia—this was the essence of the Schlieffen Plan. It was not simply a mobilization plan in which mobilization could be thought of as a precautionary measure; it was a war plan, permitting no pause for reflection if once it should be set in motion. Neither William II nor the succession of political figures who served him as chancellor had anything to do with this plan; it was the product of the General Staff, in whose decisions the Emperor and his ministers were permitted no share.

The Emperor, however, discovered another area of military activity in which his amateurish strategic imagination could have wider scope. Having read (and imperfectly digested) Alfred Thayer Mahan's *Influence of Sea Power upon History*, William II was beset by the vision of Germany's becoming as powerful on the oceans as she was on land. In this notion he was encouraged by the chief of staff of the Navy High Command, Rear Admiral (later Grand Admiral) Alfred von Tirpitz, who was eagerly supported by the great industrialists and their propaganda instrument, the Navy League, and by other "patriotic" societies. The resulting navy bill of 1900 inevitably aroused the hostility of Great Britain.

In 1900, British naval policy was based on the two-power standard of maintaining a comfortable superiority in European waters over the combined fleets of the next two strongest navies, which for years had been those of France and Russia. The Italian Fleet was a poor fourth in 1900, with Germany in fifth place. But the new navy bill proclaimed the German purpose of building a powerful fleet of battleships, cruisers, and torpedo craft which was avowedly intended to become so strong that "even the strongest naval power" (Britain) could not risk fighting Germany at sea without the likelihood of such serious losses as to leave it in an inferior position against other navies. From the moment that this pronouncement became public, Anglo-German relations began to deteriorate in proportion as the new German Fleet grew stronger. In 1902 the British Admiralty sent a memorandum to the cabinet that there was "proof that the German Navy was being constructed with a view of being able to fight the British Navy"; the short cruising radius of the new German battleships meant that they "were designed for a North Sea fleet and nothing else." British opinion ceased to regard France and Russia as possible naval enemies, and British diplomacy set about improving relations with both countries.

The Anglo-French Entente Cordiale of 1904, mutually acknowledging the special interests of Britain in Egypt and of France in Morocco, was received with charges of "encirclement" from the German press, and in 1905, taking advantage of Russian military disasters in the Russo-Japanese War, Germany demanded the dismissal of the French Foreign Minister, Théophile Delcassé, who had negotiated the entente with Britain, and French acceptance of an international conference on Morocco, with immediate war as the alternative. The German purpose was to break up the Entente by forcing the French to recognize that "the British Fleet cannot defend Paris." Delcassé resigned, but the French, sustained by firm British diplomatic support, recovered their nerve, and when the Moroccan conference met at Algeciras in 1906, the German proposals were supported only by Austria-Hungary. Early in 1907, Britain and Russia concluded a treaty adjusting their relations in the Middle East.

Thus was foreshadowed the abandonment of Britain's historic role as a stabilizing free agent. The growing power and belligerence of Germany made plainer with each passing year that a viable European equilibrium could no longer exist without the weight of British power definitely on the anti-German side of the scales. That power was expressed chiefly in terms of naval supremacy; but the shortcomings of the British Army as revealed by the South African (Boer) War of 1899–1902, coupled with emerging European anxieties, brought about the creation of a general staff in 1904, followed by the reorganization of the regular troops in the United Kingdom as an expeditionary force of six divisions ready for immediate service, supported by a small reserve and by a Territorial Army for home defense. All these forces were voluntarily enlisted, British public opinion being unwilling to accept universal service.

British opinion, indeed, was even less ready to accept the idea of any definite commitment that might bring the country into a Continental war, so that the sort of forceful warning which alone was calculated to impress the Germans was politically impossible for British statesmen to utter. The defensive power of the new Triple Entente of Britain, France, and Russia depended at first on informal preparations and discussions. To go farther would have been to risk public and parliamentary repudiation in Britain. The deterrent effect of the new arrangement was thus appreciably diminished. This was a defect which time and careful diplomacy might have corrected. But time was wanting for the crystallization of British sentiment that could have given the necessary external firmness to British policy. It was at the very moment when this need began to be felt that a new element of internal instability was introduced into the European system.

From Bismarck's time through the first years of William II, German policy had consistently sought to mediate and adjust the clashes of Russian and Austrian ambitions in the Balkans. But now Germany, demanding recognition of her "superiority" and her "right to rule" and smarting from the humiliations of Algeciras, saw only that, in her isolated and "encircled" position, Austria-

Hungary was her one dependable friend and ally. Hence Europe must be taught what it meant to be Germany's friend.

The Balkan antagonism of Russia and Austria arose from Russia's claim to be the protector of the Christian (and especially the Slav) peoples of the peninsula against Ottoman oppression, whereas Austria sought to dominate these peoples lest they become rallying points for fellow Slavs still suffering under Hapsburg oppression. Russia's end purpose was control of the Turkish Straits, and the Slavs of the Balkans were viewed as convenient instruments toward that end. As the years passed, the irreconcilable conflict between these Austrian and Russian aims had become hopelessly entangled with local blood feuds in an area where every people hated its next-door neighbor. Back in the 1870's, Field Marshal von Moltke had prophesied: "If we're not careful, the next war will start over some *dummkopfig* business in the Balkans." Now, with the Ottoman Empire visibly decaying, with those Christians still under its yoke fiercely resolved to be free and the Russians urging them on, blind German support was to be given to Austrian schemes of substituting a Hapsburg yoke for that of the Turkish Sultan. A better formula for ensuring the fulfillment of Moltke's prophecy could hardly have been devised.

But the cool and prescient statesmen of the 1870's, who had removed a Balkan threat to peace at the Congress of Berlin, were gone, and their wisdom seemed to have perished with them. Nowhere on the European scene, as the fateful year 1908 began, was there visible a monarch or a statesman who had both the vision to foresee the approach of catastrophe and the authority to make his warning listened to. Those who sought peace continued to put their trust in safeguards which had outlived their usefulness. Those who marched toward war prepared to brush these safeguards contemptuously from their path. With 1908 began a grim series of developments that made war inevitable.

The military and political developments of the period 1908–14 are examined in detail in Chapter 2, *Prelude to War*, and the occurrences immediately accompanying the outbreak of hostilities in Chapter 3, *War Declared*. Since, however, the circumstances that shaped the course and character of the war have already been set forth, this general survey may usefully be concluded by summarizing the war itself in broad perspective against the background so far developed, treating the cold-war interval of 1908–14 as introductory to the period of actual hostilities.

The War in Perspective

World War I was first and foremost a war of armies—of armies numbered in the millions. Never before had such enormous hosts been marshaled for battle. Never before had the means existed to move such numbers of troops, to arm them, to keep them supplied with food and munitions, and to direct their operations. The armies of World War I were people's armies. The proportion of professional soldiers was small; the vast majority were either trained reservists recalled from civil life, or raw replacements inducted after the outbreak of war and thrown into the fight with whatever training there was time to give them.

War was initiated by the order for mobilization. Every Continental power had a complex plan for mobilizing against the most likely opponent. Each such mobilization plan was keyed into an operational plan for deploying the mobilized troops so as to ensure their entry into action under advantageous conditions. The choice between an immediate offensive when deployment had been completed, or standing on the defensive to await hostile attack, was made in advance. Whatever the decision as to offense or defense, however, mobilization and deployment were automatic once the order had been given; subsequent changes or delays were considered out of the question. Hence the beginning of hostilities came when the military leadership was able to persuade each chief of state that military necessity demanded that he give the order to mobilize—that further delay would court defeat by allowing the opponent to gain an advantage which it might not be possible to overcome.

Once the fateful order was given (and this occurred almost, though not quite, simultaneously in all four of the great Continental powers), there was no turning back. "As a result," observes William H. McNeill in *The Rise of the West* (Chicago, 1963, p. 742), "the first weeks of World War I presented the amazing spectacle of vast human machines, complete with replaceable parts, operating in a truly inhuman fashion and moving at least approximately according to predetermined and irreversible plans. The millions of persons composing the rival machines behaved almost as though they had lost individual will and intelligence."

But the "predetermined and irreversible plans" were vitiated by a common illusion: the illusion of decisive battle under tactical and material circumstances which so favored the tactical defensive that the first loss of momentum was virtually certain to be followed by bloody stalemate. This was more definitely the case in the west, where armies totaling initially more than 3,700,000 combatants were crowded into the narrow front between neutral Switzerland and the English Channel. A western campaign of maneuver ending with decisive battle was beyond any reasonable expectation save to men who planned for war with the experiences of 1866 and 1870 as their guidelines. What they faced instead was the solidification of a fortified confrontation with unturnable flanks, and the conversion of the decisive-battle illusion into the more dreadful illusion that decision could still be achieved by the breakthrough that never came, but for which so many lives were vainly offered up. In the east, where the Russians were able to trade space for time according to their traditional practice, there was more room for maneuver, but no greater prospect of decisive battle so long as the Russian will to go on pouring human bodies into the holocaust continued to be matched by the capability of putting weapons into the hands of the new levies.

World War I stands unequaled in terms of blood sacrifice for miserable accomplishment. It remains, writes Edmond Taylor in *The Fall of the Dynasties* (Garden City, N.Y., 1963, p. 230), "the greatest trauma in Western history since the Wars of Religion," with the trench warfare of 1914–18 standing out as "perhaps the cruelest large-scale ordeal that the flesh and spirit of man have endured since the beginning of the Ice Age." And endured largely in vain. Almost all the great offensives bogged down for the same reason: The firepower of artillery could not destroy infantry and machine guns in deep shelters, and the attacking infantry could not penetrate successive trench systems defended by machine guns. Each time the planners said that they would have enough artillery preparation, that this time there would be no machine guns left. But there always were. As this process continued to absorb human sacrifices, the lives already expended weighed down governments and generals with a sense of awful responsibility to prove that these lives had not been spent in vain—by winning the next time, using the same method. Little imagination was applied to finding a different approach to the search for victory, and men whose reputations rested on justification of sacrifices already offered up bitterly assailed those who suggested trying something new.

Strategically, the Anglo-French attempted one imaginative step: the use of a sea mobility to strike with amphibious power at the Dardanelles in 1915. But sufficient resources to assure success were not made available, the advantage of initial surprise was frittered away, and subsequent reinforcements were committed in driblets. The trench-warfare commanders in France resisted the sending of troops and munitions to the Dardanelles as being an almost criminal diversion of force from the "decisive front." Yet a principal purpose of the operation was to open a direct supply line to Russia, already badly in need of weapons and munitions. These could be had only from Western industry, and only by opening the Black Sea to shipping could they have reached Russia in adequate volume. Had this been accomplished, Russia might well have fought on: A "diversion" of a handful of divisions that could keep the whole Russian Army fighting might have proved as rewarding a diversion of force as military history records.

The principal German attempt at strategic novelty was the submarine campaign, which sought to cut off the flow of war supplies from North America as well as the food supply of the British Isles. In these purposes the Germans came near success, since the Allies were slow to accept the tactical innovation, the convoy system, which defeated the submarines in the end.

Imagination was possible in land tactics as well. The tank was the answer to the machine gun, giving the attacking soldier a protected means of maneuver. But the orthodox that already had so heavy a burden of casualties to account for was reluctant to admit the possibility that there was a better way, with the inevitable inference that the better way should have been developed earlier. The tank was suggested late in 1914, designed in embryo in 1915, and committed to battle in September, 1916, in small numbers. It was not until November, 1917, that British tankers were allowed (at Cambrai) to put on a large-scale armored attack, which would have been a complete success had the High Command had the vision to follow through with reserves. Not until 1918 did the tank come into its own on the Western Front.

It was also in 1918 that airpower was first used with imagination and effect, not just for artillery spotting and reconnaissance, but in direct intervention in the ground battle with bombs and machine guns. World War I was not a true airpower war, but more could have been done with air-mobile weapons if the airmen had been listened to more receptively.

It is hard to avoid the conclusion that failure to exploit available technology, both during the war and in the peacetime years, when new weapons were appearing without appropriate changes being made in tactical doctrines and military techniques, was in large part due to the fact that military policy and planning were left mainly to professional military men. In Germany, Austria-Hungary, and Russia, supreme military authority nominally rested with the monarch, but was in fact exercised by the General Staff (in Russia by a uniformed war minister in the immediate prewar years). The growing tendency of the general staff system to separate the planning function from the troop-command function contributed to the widening gap between war planning and the realities imposed by technological progress and political factors. In France, civilian ministers of war and marine had such measure of influence on military policy as was consistent with the circumstance that the country had 42 war ministers in 45 years. In Britain, the existence after 1904 of a Committee of Imperial Defense composed of military men and eminent civilians brought about closer association between the political and the military channels of policy formulation, but even so there was a tendency for the Army General Staff and the sea lords at the Admiralty to keep their own counsel about war plans, although energetic civilian ministers such as Winston Churchill and Richard Burdon Haldane exercised much more influence on military policy than was the case with their opposite numbers in any of the major Continental capitals. Nowhere in Europe did there exist an established governmental mechanism for cross-fertilization of ideas between the military planners and civilian scientists and technicians, except where such contacts originated on military initiative in furtherance of preconceived planning objectives.

Within the structure of each of the two alliances, however, general staffs did exchange ideas with each other and even made quite definite commitments, in some cases without the knowledge of civilians nominally responsible for policy. Military plans thus exercised an increasing influence on policy and on events, an influence that proved irresistible both as war approached and in some cases during its progress.

The pattern of the war was one of two fronts in Europe—the relatively static Western Front where Germany confronted France and Belgium, with British manpower drawn more and more inexorably into the trenches, and the far more fluid Eastern Front where Germany and Austria-Hungary confronted Russia. Italy, taking advantage of Article 7 of the Triple Alliance treaty, whereby she should have been consulted before Austria-Hungary took action in the Balkans, as well as of a secret clause that relieved her of any obligation to fight Britain, was neutral at first and later joined the Triple Entente, creating an Italian-Austrian front in the Alps. Other secondary fronts were incident to Turkey's entering the war as the ally of Germany (the Dardanelles in 1915 and, later, a Salonika front and fronts in Palestine and Mesopotamia, where the British made use of considerable numbers of Indian troops). Serbia, Montenegro, and Romania were overrun by the Central Powers. Japan joined the Entente Powers, but confined her participation to acquiring German colonial possessions in the Pacific, with some competition from Australia. Australian, New Zealand, Canadian, and South African troops fought alongside the British in Europe and the Middle East. Native units under British, French, German, and Belgian command saw action in Africa.

Decision came in Europe at last, but not from decisive battles. It came from exhaustion and human attrition. Under these burdens, compounded by political collapse, the Russian war effort disintegrated in 1917 only to have the Central Powers faced in the west by a new antagonist, the United States, which the Germans had rashly challenged by declaring unrestricted submarine warfare against merchant shipping. The United States had already furnished the Allies with vast quantities of war material, which had had a substantial effect on their ability to continue the struggle. The weight of American fighting capabilities in the scales of battle proved a far more potent factor—a factor decisive to the outcome of the war. The Germans and their associates lacked the resources to meet the new armies and air fleets that the United States could put into the field. They had already expended too much of their human capital, too much of their reservoirs of fortitude and resolve.

One more factor requires mention: the command of the sea. This command remained in the hands of the western Allies throughout the war, though threatened for a time by the German submarine campaign. The German High Seas Fleet of battleships, on which vast resources had been squandered, was canceled out from the beginning by the presence of a superior British fleet on the other side of the North Sea. Only once, at Jutland, did the German Fleet offer serious challenge, and the depth of German comprehension of Mahan's precepts may be judged by the fact that they boasted afterward of a great victory because their losses had been somewhat less than those sustained by the British, although the strategic situation remained exactly the same as before. During the four years of the war the resources of the British Empire and of much of the rest of the world were made available to the Allied war effort and, relatively speaking, denied to the Central Powers. This historic principle of British sea power—that the fleet's main purpose is to preserve intact the sea communications of the British islands—was vindicated as it had been in the old wars with France. And it was by sea that the decisive intervention of the United States was finally made effective on the battlefields of Western Europe.

2. Prelude to War

BY GEORGE FIELDING ELIOT

From 1908 until the outbreak of war in July, 1914, the peace of Europe was at the mercy of events. The old title deeds of mutual security were out of date and worthless. As Barbara Tuchman states in *The Guns of August* (New York, 1962, p. 18), "Europe was a heap of swords piled as delicately as jackstraws; one could not be pulled out without moving the others." In the vacuum of political leadership, the war plans had taken charge. These impersonal, inflexible pressure forces awaited the triggering of a chance incident, a rash decision, a gesture of despair. Most potent of all was the war plan of Germany, the most powerful military nation of Europe. This was the Schlieffen Plan in its full development.

Master Plan

Count Alfred von Schlieffen had ceased to be chief of the German General Staff at the end of 1905; he was succeeded by Colonel General Helmuth von Moltke, a nephew of William I's brilliant chief of staff. The younger Moltke was not without competence, but he was inherently irresolute. He took over the Schlieffen Plan with dutiful deference, but he could not forbear tampering with its details. As outlined in Chapter 1, *General Survey*, the essence of the plan was to overwhelm France in one swift onslaught, using almost 90 per cent of the German Army for that purpose while the remaining fraction, with the Austrians, stood off the Russians. France disposed of, Germany and Austria-Hungary would be free to throw their whole weight against Russia.

Of the total force hurled against France, Schlieffen planned to concentrate about two-thirds in an immensely strong right wing. Only by striking at France through Belgium could space be found for the movement of such a mass of men, horses, and guns. The neutrality of Belgium was guaranteed by a treaty signed in 1839 by Great Britain, France, Austria, Russia, Prussia, Belgium, and the Netherlands; violation of Belgian neutrality by Germany might well bring Britain into the war as an enemy, if nothing else did. But to Schlieffen's mind, the claims of military necessity came first. France was a dangerous foe. To overwhelm her armies in decisive battle demanded that the blow be struck with lightning speed and the maximum of violence, and so directed as to roll up the French masses from this western flank. More than most German soldiers, Schlieffen respected British sea power and its weapon of blockade, but he expected to win a double victory on the Continent before the blockade could begin to count against Germany.

Consider now the "heap of swords"—Germany bound to come to Austria-Hungary's aid if the latter were at war with Russia, Russia and France mutually bound to attack Germany if either should become engaged in a "defensive war" with that country, and Germany clamped by an inflexible war plan which from the instant that mobilization was ordered would move inexorably to hurl her whole weight through Belgium against France, save for a thin defensive screen in East Prussia. Once war began, Germany could not avoid fighting on two fronts, and in a two-front war her hope was fixed on crushing France first.

By 1908, the main outlines of the Schlieffen Plan were beginning to be understood among Germany's enemies, who sought to cut their own planning cloth accordingly. The plans of the French in the period 1908–11 were for a strong defensive, both along their fortified eastern frontier, where they faced Germany directly, and along the frontier of Belgium. In the face of rising evidence that the Germans were planning to violate Belgian neutrality, military logic seemed to suggest joint defensive arrangements between France and Belgium, but the Belgians, resolved that their devotion to neutrality should remain above suspicion, would have nothing to do with joint planning.

In the annual conversations that took place between the French and Russian general staffs, French pressure steadily increased after 1908 toward inducing the Russians to promise an offensive against East Prussia in maximum force at the earliest possible moment after mobilization, and the Russians began promising more both in numbers and in timing than they could safely or effectively deliver.

From 1908 onward, moreover, Russian plans were vitiated by internal circumstances. In that year, Czar Nicholas II saw fit to relieve his soldierly cousin, Grand Duke Nicholas, as President of the Council of National Defense and to abolish the Council itself. The chief of the General Staff was thereafter to report to the Minister of War rather than to the Grand Duke, and the Minister became the only source of military contact between the army and the Czar, without whose sanction no decision of consequence could be taken.

Nicholas II himself was the weakest Czar to occupy the imperial throne in more than a century, and his wife, Alexandra, was dominated by the power-seeking monk Grigori Rasputin, who hated the Grand Duke and caused the Czarina to believe (falsely) that the Duke was plotting to usurp the throne. Inevitably, the man who became the sole arbiter of Russia's military policy, in 1908 as chief of staff and from 1909 to 1915 as Minister of War, was a crony of Rasputin's, General Vladimir A. Sukhomlinov, who was opposed to all modern advances and seems to have been guilty either of criminal negligence or of treason. A succession of chiefs of staff, lacking any real authority, served under Sukhomlinov in the period 1908–14; the promises they made to their French colleagues resulted not only in committing the Russian Army to a premature offensive in East Prussia, but to a faulty distribution of forces between the East Prussian front and the front against the Austrians in Galicia.

The French naturally hoped to diminish the force of a German attack on France by inducing the Germans to weaken it by shifting troops eastward. But the plans of the French Army were also undergoing a fundamental change. In 1911, General Augustin Édouard Michel, then commander in chief designate in case of war, increasingly convinced that the weight of the German attack would come through Belgium, proposed to build up the French defensive along the Belgian frontier by mobilizing a reserve regiment alongside each active regiment, thus increasing each infantry brigade from six battalions to twelve. This produced a violent reaction from those who were coming to believe that a furious offensive based on French *élan* was the only true doctrine for the French Army. For such a doctrine, reserve units were not considered suitable. But how could the long frontier be defended without them?

The answer that the partisans of the offensive found to this question was to deny that the Germans could or would use their own reserves in mounting an offensive through Belgium. Without the front-line use of reserves, the German Army could muster only 40-odd divisions for an initial attack in the west. If the bulk of these were concentrated in a strong right wing, the center and left would be too weak to hold fast against a French counteroffensive. On the assumption that the Germans would use only their active divisions in their offensive, it was easy to prove that the weight of the main attack could not extend west of the Meuse River without fatally weakening the rest of the front. Supported by these calculations, the partisans of the offensive secured the removal of

Michel and the adoption of Plan XVII, which called for vigorous French offensives both in Alsace-Lorraine and in northeastern France at the outset of hostilities. The Belgian frontier west of the Meuse was left unguarded save for a few reserve divisions.

But, in fact, Schlieffen had begun in 1905 to plan the development and special training of a mass of reserve divisions to supplement his active divisions in order to keep his right wing strong enough to do its work. By 1908, more than 20 such reserve divisions were at least partially in being. When war came in 1914, 28 of them were in the line of battle and proved fully equal to the demands made upon them.

While the pressures of the Schlieffen Plan were having their effect on French and Russian counterplanning, the British did not remain unaffected. Tentative contacts between the French and British army staffs had occurred as early as 1905. In 1910, these talks took on new vigor under Major General (later Field Marshal Sir) Henry Wilson, who in that year was appointed director of military operations at the War Office. By the following year, with the troubled acquiescence of the cabinet (excluding ministers of pacifist leanings), Wilson had in effect agreed with the French General Staff that in case of war with Germany the whole of the British Expeditionary Force (BEF) of six divisions would be deployed on the exposed left flank of the French battle line.

The German plan was the controlling motif of this martial symphony, not only because the German Army was the most powerful in Europe, but also because it seemed to be generally accepted that hostilities would be initiated, if at all, by a German offensive. To such anticipations, the restless, belligerent attitude of the German government and press, and at times of Emperor William II, lent a degree of unsettling realism.

Curiously, there appears little indication of any serious attempt to coordinate army and navy planning. The German General Staff regarded the Navy High Command with scorn mixed with anger that battleships should have taken money that could have given the army a half-dozen extra divisions. In Russia the navy existed, in army opinion, to protect the army's flank whenever the latter rested on a coastline. The French Navy had always been somewhat aloof and superior in attitude, though inwardly smarting from army sneers as to how little it had accomplished in the Franco-Prussian War. As for the British Admiralty, the sea lords kept their plans to themselves until in 1911 the Committee of Imperial Defense brought into ministerial cognizance the fact that the plan to move the BEF to France was not even recognized in Admiralty planning, whereupon a shake-up took place that brought Winston Churchill to the Admiralty and resulted in the creation of a Naval Staff. In 1912, Britain and France concluded an agreement by which the British were enabled to concentrate all of their battleship squadrons in the North Sea and the English Channel, facing the German High Seas Fleet, while the French battleships were concentrated in the Mediterranean. Implicit in this scheme was a British commitment to guard the French coastline along the Channel in case of war. While army-navy coordination improved somewhat, British naval opinion (and some British soldiers) continued to favor a maritime strategy, with the British Army operating independently in Belgium on the flank of the German lines of supply, or elsewhere as opportunity might offer. Churchill's mind also inclined in that direction, but the Army General Staff clung to its arrangements with the French and made its plans accordingly.

Balkan Tinderbox

In 1908 the Ottoman Empire still held more than 65,000 square miles of European territory in the Balkan Peninsula, inhabited by a population of more than 6 million, including at least 4 million Christians. Sultan Abdul Hamid II also had a shadowy claim to Bosnia and Hercegovina, which under the provisions of the Treaty of Berlin (1878) were occupied and administered by Austria-Hungary, though remaining nominally Turkish territory; and Bulgaria, while virtually independent, was also under nominal Turkish sovereignty. The inhabitants of Bosnia and Hercegovina were South Slavs (Yugoslavs), kin to the Croats and Slovenes of Austria-Hungary and also to the peoples of Serbia and Montenegro, who—having won their own freedom from Turkish rule—longed to extend that freedom to their kinsmen. The dream of Greater Serbia included in its more extreme versions all the South Slav peoples; it thus clashed with Austrian interests as well as with Turkish, and was at odds with Bulgaria over rival claims to multiracial Macedonia and with Greece over Epirus.

In July, 1908, a revolution broke out in European Turkey. A group of young Turkish officers, aided by Macedonian guerrillas, gained control of the army and forced the Sultan to restore the constitution of 1876. That constitution included specific provisions for participation in the new Parliament by representatives of Bulgaria,

Bosnia, and Hercegovina. The Bulgarians saw in this a Turkish scheme to return them to "colonial" status. The Austro-Hungarian Foreign Minister, Baron (later Count) Alois Lexa von Aehrenthal, saw a heaven-sent opportunity to put an end both to the anomalous status of Bosnia and Hercegovina and to the Serbian dream of acquiring those provinces. Russia, the traditional protector of the Slavs of the Balkans, was still suffering from the effects of defeat by Japan in 1905 and of subsequent internal disorders. Bulgaria, Russia's special protégé, was also Serbia's mortal enemy. Aehrenthal beguiled the Russians by specious negotiations while he wooed the Bulgarians by promises of recognizing their full independence.

On October 5, 1908, Bulgaria suddenly proclaimed that independence, and, on October 6, the Austro-Hungarian government informed the world that Bosnia and Hercegovina were annexed to the Dual Monarchy. "It was a bombshell," writes Winston Churchill in *The Unknown War: The Eastern Front* (New York, 1931, p. 22). "Every Chancellery in Europe recognized it as an aggressive act done in an ill-conditioned manner. Germany, who had been told nothing, was astonished, but did not withhold her support from her ally. France was cynical; Italy surprised; Russia was indignant; Turkey offended, Serbia in a frenzy and England deeply shocked." A period of rising tension followed. Serbia mobilized her small army. Austrian troops gathered on the Serbian border; others moved toward the Russian frontier in Galicia.

Abruptly, in March, 1909, an Austrian note to Serbia demanded the demobilization of the Serbian Army and public recognition of the annexation of the two provinces by Austria. Then, on March 21, the German ambassador at St. Petersburg handed an ultimatum to the Russian Foreign Minister, Aleksandr P. Izvolski. Russia would either at once recognize the annexation and herself advise Serbia to do likewise, or face immediate war with Germany and Austria-Hungary. The German moment had been well chosen. Russia was not ready for war and was uncertain of the attitude of her allies. The Czar swallowed this bitter pill of humiliation. The Serbians had no choice but to do likewise. The Germans gloated over their victory, but it was a Pyrrhic victory, for it brought all Europe to the chilling realization that Germany had been prepared to set the Schlieffen Plan in motion had Russia refused to yield. France and Russia went to work to strengthen and improve their armies and to seek closer relations with Britain. The British resolved a domestic dispute as to whether four or six dreadnought battleships should be provided for in the 1909 estimates by laying the keels of eight in that year. The bonds of the Triple Entente were measurably tightened, while Italy drew farther apart from the German-Austrian alignment. Serbian nationalists awaited a favorable moment for revenge; the Austro-Hungarian chief of staff, General Baron (later Field Marshal Count) Franz Conrad von Hötzendorf, urged unceasingly but vainly upon Emperor Francis Joseph that the safety of the empire could be assured only by launching a preventive war against Serbia while Russia was too weak to react forcibly.

Agadir Crisis

Since the Algeciras Conference of 1906, France had continued to extend her influence in Morocco. In 1911 a revolt broke out in the interior of the country; tribal forces threatened Fez, and a French expeditionary force relieved and occupied the city. The Germans fumed that they had not been consulted. On July 1, it was suddenly announced that the German Emperor had ordered the gunboat *Panther* to Agadir, where it was claimed that German interests existed which required protection. The German diplomatic attitude indicated that a challenge was intended. Germany's attitude suggested the belief that the British cabinet was so split between advocates and opponents of a firm foreign policy that France could not count on British support. In this situation, the British Chancellor of the Exchequer, David Lloyd George, theretofore counted as inclining to pacifist views, decided that plain words were needed. With the prior agreement of Prime Minister Herbert H. Asquith, he took the occasion of a scheduled speech at the Mansion House on July 21 to supply them. The reaction in Germany was stormy, but German policy turned cautious, and the Agadir crisis was resolved on tolerable terms.

Turko-Italian War and Its Balkan Aftermath

Italy had for some time sought control of the Turkish provinces of Tripolitania and Cyrenaica in North Africa. An Italian ultimatum to Turkey in September, 1911, was followed, on October 5, by the landing of Italian troops at Tripoli. The Young Turk government reacted vigorously, and prolonged military operations ensued, in which the Italians gradually took possession of the more important centers of the two provinces. Italian amphibious forces seized Turkish islands in the Aegean Sea, and the Italian Fleet threatened the Dardanelles.

Meanwhile, Russian diplomats pointed out to the Serbs, Bulgarians, and Greeks the golden opportunity of taking over the European territories of Turkey. For a brief season the Russians succeeded in inducing the Balkan states to make common cause—even to agree beforehand as to the division of the expected spoils, with the Czar of Russia as arbiter in case of subsequent disagreement. Peace negotiations between Turkey and Italy were in progress when, on October 8, 1912, hostilities against Turkey were opened by Montenegro, followed promptly by the other Balkan states. To the astonishment of most of Europe and the consternation of the Austrians, the armies of the Balkan League inflicted a series of shattering defeats on the Turks. Pressure from the powers brought peace in 1913, whereafter the victors quarreled over the spoils. Bulgaria attacked Greece and Serbia and was badly beaten, Romania joining her other two opponents. In the end, Serbia and Greece gained large accessions of territory and population, and Bulgaria far less. Austrian insistence, however, deprived Serbia of an outlet to the Adriatic Sea by inducing the other powers to recognize the independence of Albania.

Despite this accomplishment, the Balkan Wars were a setback for Austro-Hungarian policy and prestige. Serbia, far stronger than before, dreamed not just of revenge but of a South Slav union at the Dual Monarchy's expense. Romania too had blood brothers to redeem from Hapsburg rule in Transylvania. Bulgaria seethed with resentment for which no present outlet was available. Turkey in Europe—save for a corner of Thrace, the Gallipoli (Gelibolu) Peninsula, and Constantinople (İstanbul)—had ceased to exist. Voices were not lacking to prophesy that the polyglot Austro-Hungarian Empire was the next candidate for Turkey's former title of sick man of Europe. In Vienna the insistence of Conrad von Hötzendorf that only a preventive war against Serbia could save the empire from ultimate dissolution began to gain new adherents.

Preparations and Pressures

The year 1913 saw in France the embodiment of the doctrine of the offensive at all costs in a new edition of the field-service regulations. Although by this time reliable information as to the training and readiness of the German reserves made it clear that Germany would dispose of enough ready divisions to provide for a massive attack through Belgium west of the Meuse, the operations section of the French General Staff refused to listen to the warnings of the intelligence section that its plans were based on faulty information.

The government, however, did succeed in securing the passage of a law lengthening the term of service with the colors from two years to three. This meant a 50 per cent increase in the number of conscript soldiers actually under arms at the moment of mobilization in any year after 1914.

In Russia work progressed on the strategic railways being built with French loans to enable more rapid mobilization along the western frontier. Grand Duke Nicholas, as commander in chief of the St. Petersburg Military District, continued his vigorous efforts to improve the training of officers and troops and to make of his district a huge training establishment by which the efforts of Minister of War Sukhomlinov to prevent the teaching of modern doctrine might in some measure be counterbalanced.

Within the German General Staff, signs began to appear of an accumulating conviction that German strength would or could be made to reach its peak in the summer of 1914, and that time thereafter would work against Germany. This view was not without factual support. Each year from 1915 onward the French Army would have three conscript classes with the colors instead of two. Russian Army reforms would be showing results; new railways would speed deployment. Given time, a new French ministry might jettison Plan XVII, while Austria-Hungary might be weakened as a fighting ally by internal discords.

The reaction of the German General Staff to the French three-year law was a demand on the government for a capital levy to raise 1 billion marks ($238 million), which was to be spent for nonrecurrent military requirements within one year. Among the purposes to which this money was applied were immediate rather than gradual completion of the armament and equipment of the new reserve divisions and a speedup of the production of heavy artillery, especially the 42-cm. howitzers intended to overwhelm the forts at Liége, Namur, and Antwerp in case the Belgians should resist invasion. A 1914 delivery date was set for these weapons.

While the soldiers did not rule in Berlin, no one else did either. It was dangerous to the last degree for the soldiers to become convinced that time was running out for Germany, for that meant that when the next crisis came, their weight would be on the side of war now rather than at some later date. How serious this circumstance was may be understood by reflecting that no major European war could begin if the German military leadership was determined to keep the peace. Austria-Hungary dared not bring on war with Russia without definite assurance of German support. Neither France nor Russia was in any condition to attack Germany singlehanded, nor would the terms of the Franco-Russian alliance have been operative had either party to it done so. There was no authority in Germany strong enough to compel the soldiers to begin a war against their will, nor—once war had begun—to make them fight it in any other way than according to their own plans. That the military deliberately set about bringing Germany's readiness to peak level in mid-1914 is quite clear; whether or not they harbored a fixed intention of provoking a major war at that time is far less clear, but their frame of mind is indicated by a remark of Moltke to Conrad von Hötzendorf: "After this, any adjournment will have the effect of diminishing our chances of success."

On the naval side, too, the margin of British superiority over Germany in dreadnought-type battleships seemed scheduled to widen after 1914. This weighed more heavily with William II and Grand Admiral Alfred von Tirpitz than with the General Staff. The initiation of Anglo-Russian naval conversations early in 1914 produced in German naval circles some apprehension lest British aid might be applied to speeding the completion of four giant Russian dreadnoughts then under construction at St. Petersburg, with a consequent two-front problem for the German Navy as well as for the army. This problem was made less ominous, however, by the prospective completion of the widening of the Kiel Canal sufficiently to permit the direct transfer of German battleships between the North Sea and the Baltic.

A new factor now intervened. In March and April, 1914, a crisis over Irish home rule rose to dangerous proportions in the British Isles. For a time there appeared some evidence that British troops in Ireland might refuse to obey orders under certain circumstances —specifically, if ordered to use force to compel the Unionist northern counties of Ireland to accept home rule. A number of officers resigned their commissions, and feeling ran high throughout the army. There is little doubt that both German statesmen and leading German soldiers believed that Britain was hopelessly divided and not to be reckoned with in the European situation.

The British crisis was still raging when, on June 28, 1914, the heir to the Austro-Hungarian throne, Archduke Francis Ferdinand, was assassinated, together with his wife, by a Serbian terrorist while driving through the streets of Sarajevo, the capital of Bosnia. The trigger of the murderer's pistol was fated to be the trigger of the most terrible war that Europe had yet endured.

3. War Declared

BY GEORGE FIELDING ELIOT

The murder of Archduke Francis Ferdinand and his wife in June, 1914, appears to have been a by-product of the Serbian dream of South Slav unification. The exact degree of responsibility for the murders that can be definitely attached to the Serbian government, in the way of either foreknowledge or actual instigation, may never be established. At Vienna, however, Foreign Minister Count Leopold von Berchtold and General Baron (later Field Marshal Count) Franz Conrad von Hötzendorf presupposed Serbian guilt, and saw an unparalleled opportunity to dispose of Serbia and the threat that it represented to the stability of the Dual Monarchy. Conrad was all for attacking Serbia as quickly as sufficient force could be mobilized, but for that Emperor Francis Joseph's consent was necessary.

Fully conscious that Austria-Hungary could not risk war with Russia singlehanded, and that an outright assault on Serbia might well mean incurring that risk, Francis Joseph wanted to be sure of German backing before he committed himself. Count Alexander von Hoyos was therefore sent to Berlin to take soundings. As a result, Emperor William II received the Austro-Hungarian ambassador, Count László Szöyény-Marich, at luncheon on July 5 and handed him what amounted to a blank check and strong encouragement. Thereupon, William informed Chancellor Theobald von Bethmann-Hollweg and senior army and navy officers of what he had done, and departed on a yachting cruise.

The Austro-Hungarian Council of Ministers met on July 7 to frame an ultimatum to Serbia. Against the opposition of Count István Tisza, Premier of Hungary, Berchtold's proposal for an ultimatum, so worded as to be impossible for Serbia to accept, was adopted; its delivery was to be postponed until July 23, partly to allow the harvest to be completed and partly because word had come that the President and Premier of France, Raymond Poincaré and René Viviani, would arrive in St. Petersburg on July 15, to remain until July 22 or 23. It was thought better to wait until they had left their Russian allies, so that no prompt concerted reaction would be forthcoming. Indeed, it was hoped that the anticipated Serbian rejection of Austria's "just demands" could be so manipulated as to turn European opinion against Serbia. The demands which were considered certain to guarantee rejection called for the participation of Austro-Hungarian officials in the conduct of inquiries and proceedings on Serbian soil.

There now followed a time of growing tranquillity in much of Europe. The anxieties aroused by the murder of the Archduke gradually gave way to relief that nothing much was going to come of it after all. But secret communications flowed back and forth between the General Staff and civilian functionaries at Berlin and their counterparts in Vienna, revealing hidden fears that William II or Francis Joseph might have a change of heart. In each capital the military and their colleagues kept up constant pressure to avert such an eventuality. What the German General Staff expected was localized war. Serbia would be smashed by Austria-Hungary in one bold stroke; this victory would eliminate the South Slav menace and restore the prestige of the Dual Monarchy and its value as an ally. With Germany standing boldly at Austria's side, Russia would back down. France would thus have no obligation to intervene, and Britain would be happy for an excuse to stand aside.

Poincaré and Viviani left St. Petersburg on July 23. At 6 P.M., an hour after news of this event reached Vienna, the Austrian minister at Belgrade presented the ultimatum, with a 48-hour deadline attached. Accept in full, without reservations, or face instant war. So read the word from Vienna.

Like most words from Vienna in those days, this one was more sound than substance. Instant war was a commodity Austria-Hungary could not deliver. For war, even against Serbia, the creaking military mechanism of the Dual Monarchy required at least two weeks for preparation—preparation which Conrad had been denied in order not to give away the scheme prematurely. The ultimatum had been worded and reworded to make certain it would be rejected. Yet if it were rejected, the threatened action could not follow for two weeks, during which tension would be mounting throughout Europe and anything might happen. Certainly the one bold strike that the German soldiers dreamed would crush Serbia and overawe the Russians would not be forthcoming.

Chain Reaction

The deceptive repose of Europe gave way to alarm with the news of the ultimatum. Russia begged Vienna for another 48 hours' time and was refused. London and Paris consulted each other. The Serbians, having already mobilized their small army, handed their reply to the Austrian ambassador on July 25. They had brought themselves almost to complete acceptance of the humiliating terms, but refused to agree that Austrian officials should conduct semijudicial proceedings in Serbian territory. Therefore, in accordance with his instructions, the Austrian minister broke off diplomatic relations. When the news reached Vienna, Conrad insisted on the partial mobilization of eight corps, or half the active army.

On July 27, William II, fretful that the news being sent to him was being edited to keep him inactive, returned to Potsdam. Meanwhile, the text of the Serbian reply was being spread abroad, and came as a relief to those whose hopes were centered on peace and negotiation. By chance or design it did not reach William until the morning of July 28. His impulsive reaction was to annotate it: "A great moral victory for Vienna! Every reason for war is removed!" If this represented an impulse toward putting the brakes on Austria, it was too late. The delay had given time for the soldiers and ministers who feared such a reaction to bring pressure to bear on their associates in Vienna. Almost at the moment that William was penning his marginal note, Berchtold had induced Francis Joseph to sign a declaration of war against Serbia. The chain reaction had begun.

Czar Nicholas II, yielding to the entreaties of his generals, authorized a partial mobilization in the southern military districts. General Nikolai Yanushkevich, the chief of staff, found that this would upset the complicated timetable of general mobilization and begged that the latter be substituted. The Czar held back, for he was now engaged in an exchange with William II from which he hoped much. But the next day, July 29, word that the Austrian fleet on the Danube had bombarded Belgrade roused Russian tempers. The Czar wavered—he seems to have signed two mobilization orders during the day, one for general and one for partial mobilization. Germany threatened to mobilize if all Russian mobilization moves were not canceled.

This day, July 29, saw the pressures of the deadly timetable of mobilization beginning to break through the restraints of royal and ministerial hesitations much as the pressure of rising waters might seep through crevices in a leaky dam. In Russia, notification that mobilization was imminent reached the district commanders, who began local preparations. In Germany, army corps commanders were doing the same. Since travelers and telegrams could still pass freely back and forth, each government and general staff was kept well informed of what was going on in the other country. Late on July 29, the Czar's partial-mobilization order went out.

This news induced Emperor William to agree, on July 30, to a proclamation (made on July 31) of *drohende Kriegsgefahr* (threatening danger of war), which set in motion prescribed measures in preparation for mobilization. Nevertheless, on this same July 30, William and his ministers were shaken by a dispatch from his ambassador in London, Prince Karl Max Lichnowsky, conveying a proposal of the British Foreign Secretary, Sir Edward Grey, for confining the war against Serbia to the occupation of Belgrade, followed by negotiations, and implying that Britain might not be able to stand aside in a war that involved Germany and France as opponents. William, aware that if Germany mobilized, an attack on France by way of Belgium would be the immediate consequence, sent a telegram to Vienna counseling prudence. Colonel General Helmuth von Moltke, horrified at such weakness, made haste to wire Conrad von Hötzendorf, urging that Austria-Hungary mobilize immediately against Russia.

Meanwhile, the Russian Foreign Minister, Sergei D. Sazonov, had reached the conclusion that the Germans were resolved on war whatever happened. When the Czar once more refused military pleas for general mobilization, Sazonov strongly supported the generals. Late in the afternoon, the dam of reluctance that was holding back the flood waters of general war seems to have given way simultaneously at its two weakest points. The Czar finally yielded to his trusted minister. A ukase ordering general mobilization, to begin on the next day (July 31), went out that evening to every military headquarters in the Russian Empire. In Vienna, meanwhile (apparently before news of the Russian mobilization order was known), general mobilization was decided upon, also to begin on July 31.

Schlieffen Plan in Control

German reaction to the Russian mobilization was prompt. An ultimatum was sent to St. Petersburg on July 31, demanding the cessation of all "military measures" against Germany and Austria-Hungary within 12 hours. At the same time, an ultimatum was sent to Paris, demanding a statement within 18 hours as to whether France would remain neutral in the event of war between Germany and Russia. Provision was made against the slight possibility that the French might agree to abandon their ally. The German ambassador was instructed, in case the French did so, to present a demand that German troops be permitted to occupy Verdun and Toul as a guarantee of good faith. This demand no French government could possibly agree to. In the event, the Russians ignored the German demand; the French answer was simply that "France will act in accordance with her interests." Germany declared war on Russia on August 1, and ordered full mobilization to start the following day.

Earlier on August 1, the French cabinet also felt the harsh pressure of military necessity. General (later Marshal) Joseph Joffre, commander in chief designate in case of war, demanded general mobilization at once; when ministers hesitated, Joffre disclaimed responsibility for the consequences if the Germans gained a head start in the mobilization race. The mobilization order went out that afternoon, almost at the same time as in Germany. It now became of supreme importance to France to be sure of Britain's support. On August 1, neither the ministers in Paris nor their ambassador in London, Paul Cambon, were by any means sure. Grey could give Cambon little comfort. On July 31, however, he had sent telegrams to Paris and Berlin, asking assurance that the French and German governments would respect Belgian neutrality as long as no other power violated it. The French reply, affirmative, came at once. The Germans did not answer. The British cabinet met on August 1, but nothing was decided.

On August 2, the German ambassador to Belgium, Claus von Below-Saleske, received orders from Berlin to present to the Belgian government a document that·had been in his possession for several days. It was another ultimatum with a 12-hour time limit. Claiming that the French were about to attack Germany through Belgian territory, the ultimatum said that the "dictates of self-preservation" required German troops to enter Belgium to anticipate "this hostile attack." Belgium was asked to view this invasion with "benevolent neutrality." If Belgium offered resistance, she would be treated as an enemy. King Albert I and his ministers spent the night reviewing the terrible choice that faced them. The king's opening words set the tone and forecast the decision: "Our answer must be 'No' whatever the consequences. Our duty is to defend our territorial integrity. In this we must not fail." They did not fail. Belgium's "No" was handed to Below early on August 3.

Meeting that afternoon, the House of Commons listened to Grey's account of the threat to Belgian neutrality and of Britain's "obligations of honor and interest as regards the Belgian treaty." The roar of applause which followed was conclusive. The German General Staff, discounting British hostility as unimportant and pinning their faith to quick and decisive victory, had brought a united Britain into the war against them by leaving her no other honorable course. Later on August 3, Germany declared war on France. On the same day, the Italian government announced its intention of remaining neutral.

On the morning of August 4, German troops crossed the Belgian frontier and moved toward Liége. King Albert thereupon asked the other signatories of the Belgian neutrality treaty for help in defending that neutrality. The British government sent an ultimatum to Berlin demanding immediate withdrawal from Belgium. When the ultimatum expired at midnight without a reply, Britain declared war against Germany.

Collapse of Collective Security

After a century of relative peace general war had come again to Europe. What were the causes of so frightful a calamity? A principal cause was surely the decay of responsible political leadership in Germany, Russia, and Austria-Hungary at a time when technological development and industrial growth provided the nations with military forces far exceeding in size and power anything previously known. The words of Bethmann-Hollweg to the Prussian Council of Ministers on July 30 are pertinent: "All governments, including Russia's, and the great majority of their peoples are peacefully inclined, but the direction has been lost, and the stone has started rolling." Yet a distinction has to be made. Only the plan of the German General Staff was a true war plan which, once set in motion, inevitably initiated general war. While the other staffs planned for a variety of contingencies and allowed for possible reaction by opponents, the Schlieffen Plan hurled German armies immediately against Belgium and France regardless of whether or not these countries had even ordered mobilization.

It is of course true that the Austrian Plan B was based on Conrad von Hötzendorf's desire to "take and break" Serbia, but it is also true that he had for years been restrained by Francis Joseph and by a succession of ministers from setting it in motion, and was finally allowed to do so only in the frenetic atmosphere brought about by the murder of the heir to the throne, and with German encouragement and promise of support. Unhappily, the assassination took the life of the one man in the Dual Monarchy who combined some measure of political vision with personal qualities that might have arrested the process of political decay in Austria-Hungary.

It was that process, in Germany and Russia as well as in Austria-Hungary, which undermined the safeguards of European peace. In each of these countries political authority over the military resided nominally in the crown. In none had political institutions capable of exercising such authority on a constitutional basis been developed. Military objectives, defined by military men without political training, usurped the place of national or even dynastic objectives. The monarchs clung to their prerogatives without realizing that they could no longer exercise them in fact, and they resisted intrusion by strong-willed civilian advisers as jealously as they sought to stifle the development of democratic institutions. It was inevitable that the military plans should come to dominate the issues of war and peace.

The peace of Europe had been preserved for a century by a system of collective security based on a balance of power, but this system was no stronger than the national elements of which it was composed. Its survival implied the existence in the capital of each major nation of responsible political authority capable of restraint and prudence and of making itself obeyed by its military servants. Authority of that caliber virtually ceased to exist in Germany after the dismissal of Prince Otto von Bismarck in 1890, in Russia after the death of Alexander III in 1894, and in Austria-Hungary around 1900 as Francis Joseph's powers became progressively eroded by senility. Constitutional development in all three nations had by 1914 reached various stages of embryonic growth; in none of them had it acquired a real hold on the levers of decision. It is less surprising that war came at last in 1914 than that its coming was so long delayed.

4. Comparative Strength of the Belligerents

BY BRIGADIER GENERAL VINCENT J. ESPOSITO, U.S.A. (RET.)

Economic Power

By 1914, Great Britain, France, Germany, Italy, and the United States had become highly industrialized nations. Raw materials not available at home were readily obtainable in other lands, and adequate shipping had been constructed to meet transportation needs. The principal limitation to the capacity of these nations to produce armaments was a shortage of skilled workers. Japan and Belgium also had made great strides in industrialization, but Russia lagged behind and required major assistance from her allies to meet her war needs. Germany bore the additional burden of supporting her allies: Austria-Hungary required substantial aid, and Bulgaria and Turkey were almost wholly dependent on Germany for war materials.

At the outbreak of war, Germany lost her colonial empire, and, hemmed in by the Allied naval blockade, the Central Powers were in danger of strangulation. Moreover, the Allies waged intensive economic warfare to stifle the trade of the Central Powers with neutral European countries. Under these conditions, the outlook for the Central Powers was dark, but they made up most of their deficiencies through territorial expansion and the exploitation of the resources of captured Allied areas. Their offensive in Western Europe gave them control of Belgium and of the heavily industrialized area of northern France. They thereby gained the major portion of French steel, iron, coal, wool, and sugar production. Later, they acquired the resources and facilities of Russian Poland, Serbia, and Romania, and when Russia collapsed in 1917, the rich granaries of the Ukraine and the Russian Baltic provinces also came under their control. Despite the Allied blockade and measures of economic warfare, the Central Powers were therefore capable of engaging in a long war. Shortages of skilled workers were compensated for in large measure by the employment of women, who were found to be adept in many delicate phases of industrial production. The Allies also took advantage of these skills of women, but to a lesser extent. When the United States with its vast resources and industrial capacity joined actively in the war, the balance of economic power swung sharply in favor of the Allies.

MANPOWER

The greater population of the Allied countries gave them a distinct advantage over the Central Powers in the mobilization of manpower. The table below presents an estimate of the numbers of men in the standing armies and trained reserves of the various belligerents when they entered the war and of the total number of men mobilized during the war.

MOBILIZED MANPOWER OF BELLIGERENTS

Countries	Standing armies and trained reserves	Total mobilized forces
Allies:		
Russia	5,971,000	12,000,000
France*	4,017,000	8,410,000
Great Britain*	975,000	8,905,000
Italy	1,251,000	5,615,000
United States	200,000	4,355,000
Japan	800,000	800,000
Romania	290,000	750,000
Serbia	200,000	707,000
Belgium	117,000	267,000
Greece	230,000	230,000
Portugal	40,000	100,000
Montenegro	50,000	50,000
Total	14,141,000	42,189,000
Central Powers:		
Germany	4,500,000	11,000,000
Austria-Hungary	3,000,000	7,800,000
Turkey	210,000	2,850,000
Bulgaria	280,000	1,200,000
Total	7,990,000	22,850,000

* Including colonial troops.

Armament

Neither side had unusual difficulties in meeting the needs for armament and equipment for their field armies. Industrialization had not progressed far in Russia, however, and she required substantial aid from her allies. The armament of the opposing forces was generally similar. Except for the tank, no revolutionary types of infantry or artillery weapons were introduced during the war. The Germans did construct a long-range gun, known as Big Bertha, with which to shell Paris from a distance of 74 miles, but its effect was only one of harassment. Both opponents emphasized the machine gun, which, when used in conjunction with barbed wire and trench systems, was highly effective against infantry assaults. The artillery weapons of the opposing forces were largely comparable, but the French 75-mm. gun (especially when used by Frenchmen) was the deadliest weapon on the battlefield. The Germans respected it highly, and the American Expeditionary Force was equipped almost entirely with this weapon. With the introduction of the airplane on the battle scene, antiaircraft guns of up to 75-mm. caliber were developed in limited quantities by both sides.

The Germans tried to gain a decisive advantage by the employment of poison gas. When it was first used at the Second Battle of Ypres in 1915, it caused panic among the Allied troops at the front, and they fled. The German troops ran into their own gas, however, and halted the attack. Countermeasures were soon developed, and though both sides employed gas occasionally throughout the war, its use had only nuisance value.

The Allies won a decided advantage with the development and introduction of the tank by the British in 1916. It was first used in the Battle of the Somme, where the approach of the monsters caused the German troops to drop their arms and flee in terror. The results of this first tank attack were not great, for only 36 units were employed, but the potentialities of the new weapon were readily recognized, and all the major powers hastily began to build them. The production of the Germans lagged, however, and they were never able to assemble enough tanks for a decisive drive. In contrast, Allied production and improvement of the tank advanced rapidly as the war progressed. In 1918, mass attacks by as many as 500 Allied tanks were not unusual, and they exerted a decisive influence on the outcome of operations. The tank played a major role in breaking the stalemate on the Western Front and in bringing the war to an end.

AIRPOWER

Airpower was in its infancy at the beginning of the war, for the types of aircraft available were crude and limited in purpose. The Germans had about 380 planes and 30 dirigibles (also called "zeppelins" after their designer, Count Ferdinand von Zeppelin); the French had 120 planes and 10 dirigibles; and the British had a comparable small number of planes, with about 60 assigned to the British Expeditionary Force in France. Russia possessed only a few planes; and the United States as late as April, 1917, when she entered the war, had only 55 planes, all of which were obsolete or obsolescent. Originally, the military purpose of the airplane was to provide observation and reconnaissance on the battlefield. When it was found possible to synchronize the firing of an automatic gun through a rotating propeller, the true value of aircraft as a fighting weapon was appreciated, and the race for construction began. Improved designs led to planes capable of carrying heavy loads. These were converted into bombers, and large bombs were produced. Initially, the Germans emphasized zeppelins, and their heavy-bomber production lagged. Many zeppelin raids were conducted over France and England in 1915 and early 1916, but the dirigibles then became easy prey for the improved types of Allied fighter planes, and their construction was discontinued. German bomber production never equaled that of the Allies. Although German bombers struck London a few times and attacked installations on the Continent, the effect fell far short of the results achieved by the superior Allied formations. In view of the greater Allied production capacity, the Germans were generally at a disadvantage in the air on the Western Front except for occasional local concentrations in support of particular attacks. The aircraft production of Russia was small and was frequently inferior to the Germans on the Eastern Front. Toward the end of the war, Allied attacks on parts of the Western Front were supported by fleets of as many as 1,500 fighters and bombers attacking front-line troops and rear supply installations.

Many thousands of aircraft were produced during the war. Since available production figures often comprise all types of aircraft, including civilian planes, it is difficult to secure accurate statistics of the purely combat aircraft produced. As an indication of the comparative air strengths of the belligerents in combat aircraft, those with the armies at the time of the armistice were as follows: French, 3,321; German, 2,730; British, 1,758; Italian, 812; American, 740; Austrian, 622; and Belgian, 153. The planes with the

American forces were preponderantly British and French. When the United States entered the war, the Americans were urged by the French and the British to concentrate on the production of engines and bomber planes, for designs of fighter planes were changing too rapidly to initiate production of any one type. The 12-cylinder Liberty engine was accordingly designed and adapted for mass production. A superb engine, it was in great demand by the Allies, and more than 30,000 units were built during the war. The Liberty engine was the greatest single contribution of the United States to World War I aviation.

Naval Power

In 1914, Great Britain was the greatest naval power in the world, and Germany was second. The total completed tonnage of the British Navy was 2,157,850; that of the German Navy, 951,713 (if tonnage under construction is included, the figures rise to 2,714,106 tons and 1,306,577 tons, respectively.) When these figures are increased by the large navies of the other Allied powers and by the meager holdings of the German allies, it is evident that the Central Powers were hopelessly outclassed on the high seas. The relative strength in various types of warships of the British and German navies, respectively, was as follows: modern dreadnoughts and pre-dreadnoughts, 40 and 33; battle cruisers and cruisers, 116 and 54; destroyers, 218 and 142; and submarines, 55 and 28. At the outbreak of the war the preponderance of the German High Seas Fleet was in home waters, where it was quickly bottled up by the superior British Grand Fleet. The 10 German cruisers on the high seas when war broke out were rounded up and destroyed, but not before they had sunk 5 British warships and 50 Allied merchantmen. The only hope of the Germans was to catch inferior portions of the British Fleet alone and thus to whittle down the disparity in naval strength. A sortie to this end was made in 1916, bringing on the Battle of Jutland, which resulted in a moral but unproductive victory for the Germans. No further major sorties were attempted.

The Central Powers were also greatly inferior in commercial shipping. In 1914, the commercial oceangoing steamships owned by the various nations had the following aggregate gross tonnages: Great Britain, 20,100,000; United States, 2,027,000; other Allies, 7,675,000; Central Powers, 6,325,000; and neutral nations, 6,640,-000. Moreover, whereas Allied commercial shipping was free to roam the oceans, that of the Central Powers was restricted by the Allied blockade to inland waters under their control.

The submarine had been designed as an offensive weapon against major warships, and early in the war it was so considered even by the Germans. However, when it became evident that their navy was to be bottled up indefinitely by the British, the Germans turned to the use of the submarine for the destruction of merchant shipping. This was their last resort in an attempt to reduce the Allied advantage in shipping and thus to weaken the support of Allied land operations. The initial impact of the German submarine warfare was heavy, but the Allies developed the convoy system and other antisubmarine devices that proved fairly effective. Nevertheless, losses due to German submarine warfare were great, particularly in British shipping. Huge construction programs were inaugurated in British and American shipyards, and these succeeded in replacing most of the shipping destroyed.

5. Western Front, 1914:
Invasion and the Marne

BY ANDRÉ DUCASSE AND BRIGADIER GENERAL
VINCENT J. ESPOSITO, U.S.A. (RET.)

WAR PLANS

In the years before the outbreak of war in 1914, both the Germans and the Allies made plans for the struggle toward which the European tensions were leading.

German Plans

The genesis of the final German plan for the war on the Western Front was the Schlieffen Plan of 1905, compiled by Count Alfred von Schlieffen, then chief of the General Staff. He was a disciple of Karl von Clausewitz, intent not merely on defeating the enemy but on actually destroying him, and his plan reflected this philosophy. Feeling certain that the French would devote their energies to recapturing Alsace and Lorraine (which they did), he envisioned a wide sweep to get behind them and pin them against the difficult terrain of the Vosges Mountains. To gain maneuvering room for his massive encircling armies, he planned to cross the southern Netherlands and Belgium and break into France over her weakly defended frontier between Mèzieres and Dunkerque, where the French would not expect an attack because of the internationally guaranteed neutrality of Belgium. All possible strength was to be concentrated in the right-wing armies (the First and Second) of the enveloping force; the two armies on the Alsace-Lorraine front (the Sixth and Seventh) would be strategically on the defensive, but they would try to lure the French on by limited attacks, thus keeping them occupied while the encircling armies closed in on their rear. At the appropriate time, the Sixth and Seventh armies would take the offensive and close the trap on the French. To maintain the full strength of the right-wing armies, special ersatz (substitute) corps were to be organized to take over rear-area duties as the advance progressed. The campaign was to be a lightning one of only a few weeks' duration; therefore, only small forces were to be left to confront the weak Russians. Ample time to deal them a death blow would be available after the conquest of France.

Schlieffen retired at the end of 1905 and was succeeded by Colonel General Helmuth von Moltke. Initially, Moltke retained the Schlieffen Plan, but he was soon confronted by a changing international balance of power. Russia had recovered rapidly from her defeat by the Japanese in 1905 and had expanded and improved her armed forces. Germany's ally under the Triple Alliance, Italy, whom Schlieffen expected to provide troops for his left wing, showed signs of faltering. The Saar coal mines and the Rhineland industrial area became essential to the German railroads and armament industry, and their protection had to be assured. These altered factors led Schlieffen himself to recommend in 1912 that the German Army be greatly strengthened for a simultaneous attack along the front from Belfort to the sea.

Moltke attempted to modify the Schlieffen Plan to meet the new conditions. First, he decided not to violate Dutch neutrality—a laudable decision for political, ethical, and economic reasons. From a military point of view, however, this decision required the Germans to crowd their two large northern armies through the fortified bottleneck of Liége. Moltke made provision for greater forces to face the Russians and to protect the Saar and the Rhineland against the French. The net result of his modifications was that by 1914 the ratio of seven to one in favor of the right-wing armies, envisioned in the Schlieffen Plan, had been reduced to slightly less than four to one. While fault can be found with some of Moltke's changes in the original Schlieffen Plan, it was in his fumbling execution of the plan that he departed most sharply from its basic spirit, which was exemplified in Schlieffen's reported dying words, "Make the right wing strong."

Allied Plans

The Allies had no precise plan to counter an invasion by the Germans. Belgium took her neutrality seriously and would not engage in war planning with her friendly neighbors. The British had worked in close collaboration with the French since 1911, and had agreed to send a British expeditionary force to the Continent to operate on the left of the French armies.

Since shortly after the Franco-Prussian War of 1870–71, the French had been making and revising war plans to conform to changing circumstances. Plan XVI, in effect in 1911, provided for

Map 1. SCHLIEFFEN PLAN AND FRENCH PLAN XVII. The German Schlieffen Plan aimed to gain surprise by violating Belgian and Dutch neutrality; then, driving swiftly to get behind the French armies, would pin them against the Vosges Mountains. The German reserves were to follow closely and take over rear-area duties, so that the right-wing armies could remain at full strength for the coup de grâce. Count Alfred von Schlieffen's dying words are said to have been "keep the right wing strong." French Plan XVII called for drives on both sides of Metz, to liberate beloved Lorraine. It took cognizance of a possible German advance through Belgium, but it assumed that such an advance could come only east of the Meuse River. In this case, the Fifth Army was to move north of Sedan; its place in line would be taken by the Fourth Army. Note that the farther the French advanced into Lorraine, the more vulnerable the French armies would be to the German scheme.

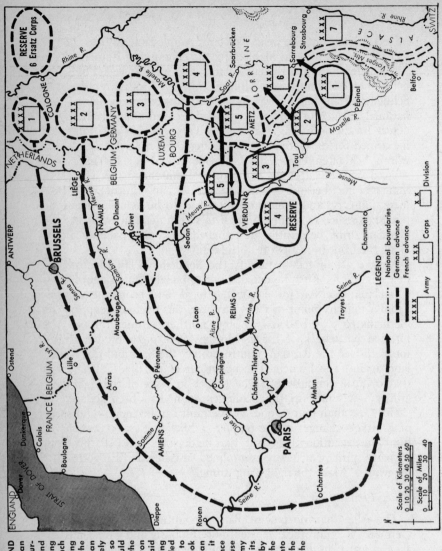

LEGEND

..... National boundaries
▬ ▬ German advance
▬▬ French advance

XXXX Army

XXX Corps

XX Division

Scale of Kilometers
0 10 20 30 40 50 60

Scale of Miles
0 10 20 30 40

an offensive into Alsace-Lorraine to recover the lost provinces. General Augustin Édouard Michel, then Vice President of the Conseil Supérieur de la Guerre, considered the plan dangerous because he believed that the Germans would advance through Belgium rather than through the difficult terrain on the Alsace-Lorraine front. He proposed a concentration on the Belgian border, between Lille and Rethel, ready to undertake a vigorous offensive to drive the Germans from Belgium when they came that way. Such a plan, however, involved the reorganization of the French Army and the possibility of unintentional violation of Belgian neutrality, and primarily for these reasons Michel's plan was rejected. He was replaced by General (later Marshal) Joseph Joffre.

Despite certain personal eccentricities, Joffre was a man of strong personality and great firmness of character. These traits enabled him to gain the confidence of four successive war ministers to the extent that his control of the army became almost absolute. Under his leadership, Plan XVII, the plan in effect when war came, was prepared. Unlike the Schlieffen Plan, it was not a complete pattern of operations. It specified only the organization and the concentration areas of the French armies and the intention to attack immediately. The First, Second, Third, and Fifth armies, in order from right to left, formed the first line. The Fourth Army was to the rear of the Third Army, ready to move to the latter's left if the Germans invaded Belgium (in which case the Fifth would move north to meet them), or to the right of the Third if the enemy moved through Switzerland. The Cavalry Corps was to be concentrated to the left front of the Fifth Army, ready to move into Belgium if the Germans came that way. The British Army, though not included officially in the plan, was to assemble on the left of the French Fifth Army, around Le Cateau, if Britain entered the war. Once the concentration was completed, two major attacks would be launched: one generally south of the Metz fortified area, and the other north of it. No further details were given as to the attacks, since Joffre preferred to allow for changes in the situation.

It is evident that the French intended to do just what the Germans thought they would, and so make themselves vulnerable to the trap of the wide German envelopment through Belgium and western France. The majority of the French High Command recognized that the Germans might violate Belgian neutrality, but they believed that German strength would not permit operations west of the Meuse River without dangerous overextension. This conclusion was based on an accurate knowledge of the strength of the German Army, but its fallacy lay in an ignorance of the fact that the German Reserve units had been so highly trained that they could operate in the first line immediately after the outbreak of war. In sum, under existing circumstances Plan XVII was unsound. Michel's plan would have placed the French armies squarely in the path of the German wheel, thus avoiding the serious situation in which Joffre's armies found themselves in early September, 1914.

THE OPPOSING ARMIES

French Army

France, with a smaller population than that of Germany, had less available manpower. In consequence, whereas the Germans took into military service 50 per cent of the men reaching the age of twenty each year, the French took about 80 per cent. The German period of reserve service was 5.5 years; the French period, 14 years. The French Territorial Army included men from thirty-seven to forty-eight years of age; the maximum age of the men in the corresponding German Landwehr was thirty-nine. As a result, the Germans had the advantages of youth and of a greater range of selection. The French Army had made tremendous strides since 1871, and by 1914, it was second only to the highly developed and precisely trained Germany Army. The French officer corps was generally devoted and highly capable, although it had become something of a political football. The Boulanger conspiracy, the Dreyfus case, and the anticlerical crusades all had affected the army, particularly the morale of the professional officers. Excessive civilian control had impelled some of them to seek promotion through political manipulation. Despite these unwholesome factors and an exceedingly low pay scale, most of the officer corps had remained true to its ideals. Years of hard work in schools, at headquarters, and with troops had developed excellent leaders and staff officers. Many of the French officers had had combat experience in colonial wars.

In tactical training the French Army lagged behind the German Army. Imbued with the philosophy of the attack (*"l'offensive à outrance"*) as preached by General (later Marshal) Ferdinand Foch, it had sadly neglected the teaching of defensive tactics. Consequently, the French were not highly skilled in field fortification, organization of the ground, and use of the machine gun and wire entanglements in the defense—areas in which German troops had received concentrated training. This do-or-die offensive spirit was to cause the decimation of the French officer corps.

In the category of artillery the French had the best weapon in the world in their 75-mm. field guns. Unfortunately, they had become so confident of this weapon that they had neglected medium and heavy artillery. When the fighting began, they had only about 300 guns larger than the 75-mm. gun, whereas the Germans had about 3,500. This discrepancy proved a serious handicap from the very first action and an even greater one when trench warfare began.

In round numbers the French armies employed in the opening campaign totaled 1.65 million men. The fighting quality and, more especially, the recuperative power of the French soldiers were to prove an unpleasant surprise to the Germans, who had held them in low regard.

German Army

At the outbreak of war the German Army was superior to other armies in organization, staff work, discipline, training, and equipment. It owed its superiority to a military tradition handed down from the days of Frederick the Great, and to the unstinted pride and support of Emperor William II and the German people as a whole. The efficiency of the army was due principally to the conscientious, hard-working cadre of regular officers and noncommissioned officers. These men, carefully selected and trained and inculcated with a tradition of thoroughness, had so developed the young men of the country that after their two years of active service they maintained a very high standard in the reserves. Reserve units were therefore able to take their place alongside regular units at the outbreak of the war, to the surprise and chagrin of the French High Command. In addition to active, reserve, and Landwehr units, the Germans formed a type called ersatz units, composed of men not suitable for the other units and designed to take over duties in the rear and on quiet fronts, thus releasing the better troops for more active employment. In round numbers the eight German field armies (including the one in East Prussia) that participated in the opening campaigns totaled 2 million men.

In tactical training the Germans believed initially, as others did, that weapons of the day gave the advantage to the attacker. They did, however, heed the lessons of the Russo-Japanese War and trained their infantry intensively in defensive measures; this was to be of inestimable value when the front became stabilized. The German Army of the day was the best-equipped army. It had specialized in medium and heavy artillery, which other armies had neglected, and had developed a mobile siege train, consisting largely of 42-cm. howitzers, that proved its worth in the opening engagement of the Western Front by battering down the formidable defenses of Liége.

British Army

The British Army in 1914 stood in sharp contrast to the Continental armies. The traditional military policy of Britain had been to have the strongest navy in the world and an army just large enough to police the colonial empire and protect the British Isles from invasion. British troops were all volunteers, Regular Army soldiers whose term of service was seven years. They were highly trained and disciplined, were commanded by well-qualified professional soldiers, and had an *esprit de corps* superior to that of any Continental troops. Backing this regular force were home guards to defend Britain against invasion during the absence of the Regular Army, but they were too poorly trained and equipped to have combat value at the beginning of the war. The outbreak of war found Britain with only six infantry and one cavalry Regular Army divisions at home, ready for war, and five divisions overseas.

Belgian Army

The Belgian Army, small and not highly trained or well equipped, was organized into one cavalry and six infantry divisions. Initially, it comprised 115,000 men in the field forces and 70,000 in garrisons. By the end of the war its numbers had increased to 267,000. It could not stem the German horde by itself, but it hoped to delay the German advance until the French and British came to its aid.

GERMAN INVASION OF BELGIUM

Moltke's decision to respect the neutrality of the Netherlands made it necessary for his huge First and Second armies, the hammer head of his wheeling movement, to pass through the narrow defile at Liége. Restricted on the north by the Dutch border and on the south by the rugged Forest of Ardennes, this defile was only a few miles wide. The valley of the Meuse and the formidable fortifications of Liége had to be overcome before the German armies could debouch into the open ground beyond.

King Albert I's plan was to assemble his entire field army along the Meuse between Liége and Namur and to hold the Germans along the river line as long as possible. His advisers, however, persuaded him not to risk the entire mobile army to annihilation at one stroke, but to assemble it behind the Gette River, a small stream about 30 miles northwest of Liége. There it could await the British and the French and complete its preparations while the forts of Liége and Namur delayed the Germans.

Liége was considered one of the strongest fortresses in Europe. The city proper was protected by 12 forts, arranged in a ring 10 miles in diameter and dominating the terrain with their guns. Its position was very strong, but its garrison of 40,000 men was not large enough to defend adequately the intervals between the forts.

The Germans had recognized the necessity of reducing Liége quickly and had made thorough preparations for the task. Selected units of the First and Second armies at full strength had been posted on the Belgian border for several years, and very heavy artillery to reduce the forts had been manufactured. The German plan was for these picked units, covered by artillery fire, to penetrate the intervals between the forts at several points, capture the city and the Meuse bridges there, and reduce the isolated forts one by one. Meanwhile, cavalry was to cross the river north of the city and attack the forts on the west side.

On the morning of August 4, the Germans assigned to reduce the fortifications crossed the frontier. The next morning, after the Belgian commander at Liége had rejected a summons to surrender, they began their attack. In attempting to penetrate between the forts, they found Belgian infantry hastily entrenched in their path. These troops fought bravely and, despite heavy losses, held the attackers to negligible gains. Meanwhile, the German cavalry succeeded in crossing the Meuse north of Liége. Realizing that the city would inevitably be encircled by overwhelming forces, the Belgian commander at Liége, General Gérard Mathieu Leman, wisely decided to send the mobile division that King Albert had left with him to join the main army on the Gette, and to fight it out to a finish with his fortress troops. The city proper fell to the Germans on August 7, but the forts continued to hold out. On August 12, the attackers belatedly brought up their heavy siege artillery. Their 42-cm. howitzers, the heaviest artillery used up to that time, were too formidable for the forts, which had been built to withstand only 21-cm. fire. One by one they fell; the last two, on

August 16. The westward march of the German First and Second armies began at once. Since the attack on Liége was made some time before German mobilization was complete and the armies were ready to move, Leman's admirable defense had not delayed the German advance for the full period August 5–16; actually, a delay of two or three days was effected.

The German First and Second armies then devoted their attention to the mobile Belgian Army under King Albert, but the latter proved elusive. By August 20, after skillful withdrawals, the Belgian Army, except for one division at Namur, was within the fortifications of Antwerp. On that day, the German First Army entered Brussels. At Antwerp, the Belgians held a flanking position that the Germans were forced to mask with one corps, thus depleting the strength of the First Army.

BATTLE OF THE FRONTIERS

Offensive in Lorraine

While the French completed their mobilization and concentration under Plan XVII, a corps of the French First Army invaded Alsace and captured Mulhouse on August 7–8. The jubilation of the inhabitants was short-lived, for a counterattack by the Germans on August 9 drove the French back to their starting point. This minor defeat caused Joffre to modify his order of battle. The Mulhouse operation had been undertaken by General Auguste Y. E. Dubail, First Army commander, who had not been able to direct it properly because of its distance from his headquarters. Foreseeing more such trouble, Joffre formed a new command, the Army of Alsace, of three corps, commanded by General Paul M. C. G. Pau, who was called from retirement. Its mission was to advance on the right of the First Army and to cover its flank.

Plan XVII was a general plan setting forth army concentration areas and declaring the intention to attack. On August 8, Joffre in his General Instructions No. 1 supplied details of the operations to come. The First and Second armies were to launch an offensive northeastward into Alsace-Lorraine. Dubail's First Army, with its right protected by the Army of Alsace, was to capture Sarrebourg and drive the enemy toward Strasbourg. General Édouard de Curières de Castelnau's Second Army was to attack on Dubail's left. Opposing the French offensive were the German Sixth Army (Colonel General Josias von Heeringen) and Seventh Army (Crown Prince Rupert of Bavaria), both armies being nominally

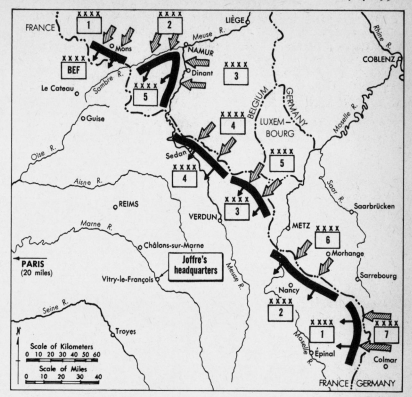

Map 2. BATTLE OF THE FRONTIERS (Aug. 14–24, 1914). This was the initial meeting of the main Allied and German armies on the Western Front. It consisted of four separate engagements: The British Expeditionary Force (BEF), rushing to the aid of the Belgians, met and was forced back by the more powerful German First Army in the Battle of Mons. Similarly, the French Fifth Army was driven back by the German Second and Third armies in the Battle of the Sambre. In the center the French Third and Fourth armies were repulsed by the German Fourth and Fifth armies in the Battle of the Ardennes. To the south, the advance of the French First and Second armies in the *offensive in Lorraine* gained initial successes, capturing Sarrebourg and threatening Morhange, but counter-attacks by the German Sixth and Seventh armies forced the French back across the border.

under the command of the Crown Prince. The latter, who was not a trained soldier, had been provided with a brilliant and forceful chief of staff, General Konrad Krafft von Dellmensingen, who was the commander except in name.

It will be remembered that Schlieffen's original plan called for a fighting withdrawal of the two German left-wing armies. Moltke had modified the plan to provide enough strength for aggressive action. The Sixth and Seventh armies were to fall back fighting to the general line Morhange–Sarrebourg–Vosges Mountains, and when the French had committed themselves against this line, the German armies were to make a converging counterattack to drive the French armies back. The battle went almost exactly as the Germans had planned.

On August 14, the French offensive began. For four days the Germans fell back slowly, delaying with rear guards and artillery fire and inflicting heavy casualties. As the planned final line of resistance was neared, the German defense stiffened. Joffre, Castelnau, and Dubail all recognized the signs of the impending counteroffensive, but they were confident of breaking it up when it came. On August 20, the German blow fell, and in very heavy fighting the French were pushed back all along the line. The First Army fell back in comparatively good order, but two corps of the Second Army were nearly routed, and only the firm stand of General Foch's 20th Corps, the so-called "Iron Corps," averted a disaster. For the next five days, the French were able to withdraw and establish themselves along the fortified heights of Nancy and behind the Meurthe River without serious German opposition.

Elated over the victory and believing the French armies to be so badly beaten that a vigorous drive would destroy them, Krafft von Dellmensingen pressed Moltke for permission to continue the offensive. Moltke agreed. In doing so, he was effecting a major change in the Schlieffen Plan, for he was trying to make a double envelopment instead of staking everything on a strong right wing. Under this new conception the German Sixth and Seventh armies were to dash themselves against the fortified heights of Nancy, the very region that Schlieffen had warned against as being unsuitable for major offensive action. Because it led Moltke into a false strategy, it may be said that the French defeat in Lorraine actually proved to be an advantage to France, for it tied down German troops and kept Moltke from sending them to his right wing, where they might have exerted a decisive influence.

Battle of the Ardennes

According to Joffre's General Instructions No. 1, while his First and Second armies attacked in Lorraine, the other French armies— the Third, Fourth, and Fifth—were to advance to the north through the Ardennes. This plan was based on Joffre's assumption that the Germans, lacking sufficient troops, would not advance to the east of the Meuse. But General Charles L. M. Lanrezac, the Fifth Army commander, was convinced that this assumption was false and kept pressing Joffre for permission to move his entire army west of the Meuse and north into Belgium to meet the German enveloping force. When, on August 15, the Germans made a strong attack on Dinant, attempting to seize the bridges there, Joffre came around to Lanrezac's view and ordered him to move north into the angle formed by the Sambre and Meuse rivers. The Fourth Army then moved upon the left of the Third Army, approximately where the Fifth had been. This change of plan reduced Joffre's forces for the attack in the Ardennes from three armies to two, the Third and the Fourth. To protect the right flank of the Third Army from any German attack from the fortified zone of Metz, Joffre formed the new Army of Lorraine, composed entirely of reserve divisions and commanded by General Joseph Maunoury.

The German Fourth and Fifth armies, forming the pivot of the great German wheel, had been moving forward slowly, regulating their advance on the speed of the hammer head, the First and Second armies. Their zones of advance were such as to bring them into collision with the French Third and Fourth armies. The clash occurred on August 22, two days after the great battle in Lorraine. The fighting took place along the narrow forest roads, where observation and liaison were difficult. The French pushed their attacks with persistence and vigor, suffering enormous losses. Finally, after three days of bloody fighting, they fell back By August 25, the Fourth Army was retiring to the west side of the Meuse, and the Third was back approximately on its starting line, with its right flank in contact with the fortress of Verdun. On the following day, the Army of Lorraine was dissolved, two divisions being sent to the west to form the nucleus of the new Sixth Army at Amiens. German general headquarters received reports of a smashing victory, the impression being given that the French Third and Fourth armies had been almost eliminated. As a matter of fact, they had been beaten and had taken frightful losses, but they were able and ready to fight again.

Battle of the Sambre

In accordance with Joffre's order of August 15, the French Fifth Army moved into the angle of the Sambre and Meuse rivers by August 20. Meanwhile, some confusion arose as to its exact mission.

On August 18, Lanrezac was advised that if the German right wing crossed in force to the west of the Meuse, his Fifth Army was to move northward to envelop it; if the enemy kept his main body east of the Meuse, the Fifth Army was to attack eastward across the river. In other words, Lanrezac was to be prepared to attack to the north across the Sambre or to the east across the Meuse, depending on where the German main forces were. Unaware of the location of the enemy, Lanrezac was perplexed. He did nothing until about noon of August 21, when he applied to Joffre for instructions. Joffre replied, "I leave it entirely to you to judge the opportune moment for starting your offensive movement." Meanwhile, Lanrezac's troops were guarding the Sambre bridges, but in the absence of orders they did not cross to the north to establish bridgeheads.

At this time, General (later Field Marshal) Karl von Bülow's Second Army was starting its wheel to the south and was headed squarely for Lanrezac's Fifth Army. The German Third Army, commanded by Colonel General Baron Max von Hausen, was approaching from the east. On the afternoon of August 21, advance units of the Second Army reached the Sambre and, finding the crossings weakly guarded, attacked. A bloody, disconnected battle, lasting all afternoon and into the night, ensued in the thickly built-up Sambre Valley. The Germans were held at some points but succeeded at others; in the end, they gained a foothold south of the river. That night, Lanrezac's corps commanders informed him that they intended to counterattack the following day and drive the enemy back across the Sambre. Lanrezac made no comment, and the attack proceeded. On the German side, Bülow directed his troops to hold their positions on August 22 and await the arrival of Hausen's Third Army on Lanrezac's right. The French attacks on that day were thrown back with heavy losses. Bülow then judged that he had enough strength to defeat the French Fifth Army without waiting for Hausen. His attack southward drove the French center and right back several kilometers by nightfall. Lanrezac then decided to attack northward on August 23 to envelop Bülow's left flank. For this purpose, he ordered his 1st Corps, which had been guarding the Meuse crossings, to move northward, leaving the crossings to be guarded by a Reserve division. Just as the 1st Corps was about to attack, its commander, General Louis Franchet d'Esperey, learned that the German Third Army had forced a crossing of the Meuse to the south. Since such a move would put it in the rear of the French Fifth Army, Franchet d'Esperey, without waiting for orders, called off his planned attack and sent advance units speedily southward to head off the Germans. They arrived in time, drove back the advance elements of the German Third Army, and temporarily stabilized the situation. That day, the Belgian division in Namur, foreseeing the fall of the city, moved out and took refuge behind the French Fifth Army.

Lanrezac correctly concluded that his army was in a serious plight and decided to withdraw—a decision that Joffre promptly approved. Bülow, believing that he was preparing a *coup de grâce*, ordered General Alexander von Kluck (whose First Army had been subordinated to Bülow) to turn against Lanrezac's left, and requested Hausen to attack with his Third Army directly westward. Kluck did not receive the order in time, but Hausen attacked to the west as Bülow had requested. When the German blow fell on August 24, it fell on thin air, for Lanrezac had withdrawn his troops the night before. This Battle of the Sambre is sometimes called the Battle of Charleroi or the Battle of Namur. It was a German victory, but the French Fifth Army, like the other technically defeated French armies, was by no means destroyed or neutralized.

The lack of decisive results for the Germans was due largely to a faulty command structure. Moltke tried to achieve coordination by subordinating the First Army to the commander of the Second Army, as he had done with the Sixth and Seventh armies in the east. This was inherently incorrect, for Bülow, concerned primarily with the operations of his own army, bent the efforts of the other armies toward its success and failed to see the picture as a whole. Hausen was not under his command, but since Bülow was a member of an ancient noble family of Prussia, the former deferred to his wishes without question. Thus far, only the Russians had solved the problem of coordinating the efforts of armies by the establishment of army group headquarters.

Battle of Mons

On August 20, Moltke's headquarters advised Bülow that the British would eventually appear in the vicinity of Lille but that "no important debarkations have thus far taken place." Actually, the British had nearly completed their concentration in the Le Cateau area and were about to begin their advance into Belgium. Based on this erroneous information, Bülow ordered Kluck's First Army to change its direction of march from southwest to south in order to assure that his own Second Army would be supported in the coming Battle of the Sambre against Lanrezac's Fifth Army. Unfortunately for the Germans, this action was unwise, for Kluck's First Army struck the British Expeditionary Force (BEF) head on at Mons, whereas if it had continued on its southwesterly course, it would have enveloped its left flank, thereby altering the course of the entire campaign.

Field Marshal Sir John French (later 1st Earl of Ypres), commander of the BEF, had moved with unprecedented efficiency. He had been instructed that, although he was not actually under Allied control, he was to cooperate with the French armies and base his strategy on theirs. On his way to Le Cateau, he visited Joffre and Lanrezac. The latter's manner irritated the British commander, generating an unfortunate relationship that was to lead to friction and lack of coordination.

On the night of August 22, the BEF took up a position at Mons. A gap of several kilometers between the British right flank and the left flank of the French Fifth Army was covered by a British cavalry brigade and by General C. C. Sordet's exhausted French Cavalry Corps. British reconnaissance planes had reported heavy columns of German troops moving toward Mons that day; and when Lanrezac suggested that the British wheel to the right and strike the flank of the German Second Army, Field Marshal French declined to do so. It was well that he refused, because such a move would have presented the British left flank to Kluck's advancing First Army.

On the morning of August 23, Kluck's advance guards struck the British position at Mons. The ensuing Battle of Mons was a series of determined German attacks running into an equally determined British defense. The British Regular Army troops, though greatly outnumbered, stood their ground and gave the Germans a sharp lesson in expert marksmanship. Attacking in close formations, the Germans suffered severely from the British fire. By the end of the day the British had been pushed back as much as five kilometers in some places but had held their ground in others. At nightfall they began to entrench their positions, intending to fight again on the next day, August 24. That night, however, French learned of Lanrezac's withdrawal and, believing it futile to stand alone, ordered a retreat that began before daybreak on August 24.

Results of the Battles

These four actions—in Lorraine, in the Ardennes, on the Sambre, and at Mons—are collectively called the Battle of the Frontiers.

The major fighting lasted only four days (August 20–23, inclusive), but French casualties exceeded 300,000, with appalling losses among the young offensive-minded officers.

Despite their heavy losses and reverses, the French soldiers maintained a surprisingly high morale. Among the general officers and higher staffs, however, the complete collapse of the French offensive plan had a demoralizing effect. But Joffre himself and his operations officer, Major General (later General) Henri M. Berthelot, maintained complete calm and confidence in ultimate victory. Now that they understood the German plan, the two generals set about to counteract it. Obviously, the BEF and the French Fifth Army were not strong enough to stop the German right wing by themselves and must therefore be reinforced. This could be accomplished by withdrawing elements from the right-wing armies, which were defending on good terrain and could spare the troops. These elements would be used to form a new army on the French left. On August 25, Joffre issued his General Instructions No. 2. The new army (the Sixth) was to assemble in the Amiens area; the BEF and the French Third, Fourth, and Fifth armies were to withdraw to the general line Somme River–Verdun, and be prepared to counterattack when they reached that line. This general plan eventually resulted in a successful counterstroke, though from a position much farther south of the Somme.

While Joffre realistically appraised the new situation and planned appropriate countermeasures, Moltke, elated by exaggerated reports of German successes, cherished the illusion that he had practically won the war. At this time, the Russians had invaded East Prussia with two armies, and the news from that front was not good. Moltke felt free to detach one corps from the Second Army and another from the Third Army and send both to East Prussia. The First Army had already been compelled to detach a corps to contain the Belgian Army in Antwerp, the Second had had to leave a corps to besiege the fortress of Maubeuge, and the Third had had to leave a division to besiege the little fort of Charlemont at Givet. Schlieffen had anticipated the necessity for such detachments, and had provided for ersatz corps to follow and take over front-line duties so that the main attack could retain its full strength. Moltke had kept the ersatz corps in Germany and eventually assigned them to the armies on the Alsace-Lorraine front. By August 26, therefore, the three right-wing armies on which a decision depended and which had entered Belgium with 16 corps, had only 11 corps. On

August 27, Moltke ordered a continuation of the general advance: the First Army to march west of Paris; the Second Army, directly on Paris; and the Third, Fourth, and Fifth armies, east of that city. The left-wing armies (the Sixth and Seventh), instead of remaining on the defensive and serving as a reinforcement pool for the right wing, were to continue the attack against the line of the Moselle River, break through, and form the eastern arm of a double envelopment.

BATTLES OF LE CATEAU AND GUISE

The resistance of Lanrezac's Fifth Army had stunned Bülow and caused him to hesitate, so that the Fifth Army had little difficulty in retreating. The British, however, were hard pressed by the iron-willed Kluck, who drove his First Army forward relentlessly. As a result, British troops were engaged daily in rear-guard actions.

Battle of Le Cateau

Kluck was under the impression that the British were based on the Channel ports of Boulogne and Calais, and kept trying to envelop their west flank to cut them off from their bases. Consequently, the left of the British line (the 2d Corps, under General Sir Horace Lockwood Smith-Dorrien) was constantly under greater pressure than the right (the 1st Corps, under General Sir Douglas Haig, later 1st Earl Haig). When the 2d Corps reached its assigned position at Le Cateau, the Germans were in close contact at many points, and the British troops were exhausted by three days of marching and fighting. Haig's 1st Corps had not been as heavily engaged at Mons as the 2d Corps and had been under relatively light pressure thereafter. It therefore occupied its prescribed position at Le Cateau on the right of the 2d Corps without difficulty.

Smith-Dorrien felt that his troops were too nearly exhausted to continue the withdrawal, and decided to stand his ground on August 26 and retreat under cover of darkness on the following night. This decision brought on the biggest battle that the British Army had fought since Waterloo.

Advance elements of Kluck's First Army, believing that they were still pursuing the fleeing British, struck the British 2d Corps position early on August 26. Meanwhile, Haig had continued the retreat, so that Smith-Dorrien's right flank was completely open and his 2d Corps had to face east as well as north. The 2d Corps held its ground well in the center, but the right flank gave way and withdrew early in the afternoon, under heavy fire and with great loss. Soon the left flank was enveloped, and the 2d Corps was threatened with disaster if it did not withdraw immediately. At this moment, Sordet's Cavalry Corps came up from the southwest, diverting the attention of the Germans and allowing the British 2d Corps to withdraw. The French corps engaged German forces of more than twice its strength, and is credited with having conducted a successful delaying action. The price was high, for it suffered casualties of 20 per cent.

Battle of Guise

During the fighting at Le Cateau, Joffre conferred with Marshal French and Generals Lanrezac and Albert d'Amade (commander of a group of French territorial and reserve divisions operating west of the British). Their reports were pessimistic and caused Joffre to doubt that the Allied forces could be organized along the line of the Somme for his counterstroke, as prescribed in his General Instructions No. 2. It began to appear that the retreat would have to continue and that the counterattack would necessarily take place much farther south. Upon his return to headquarters he received a highly exaggerated report that the BEF had "lost all cohesion" and needed "serious protection." To take the pressure off the British, he ordered the French Fifth Army to attack westward and strike in flank the German elements attacking them.

Lanrezac received these orders with dismay. His Fifth Army was facing north to hold off Bülow's advancing German Second Army. In order to comply with Joffre's order, he would have to disengage his forces and face them to the west, thereby exposing his own flank to Bülow. Nonetheless, he disposed his forces to accomplish his new mission: two corps were ordered to face west, one to hold the original army front facing north, and the fourth to remain in reserve, ready to move either to the north or to the west as developments necessitated. Lanrezac asked French to cooperate in the operation by having the British 1st Corps make a limited advance northward, but the latter bluntly refused. In French's view, the operation was designed to gain a respite for the British, and he should take advantage of it. His refusal naturally made relations with Lanrezac even more strained than before. On August 29, Bülow's army arrived and attacked from the north. Lanrezac's attack to the west was unsuccessful, for the northernmost of the two corps making the attack was struck on its north flank and its westward movement was halted. The commander of the other corps, finding himself unsupported on his right, advanced timidly and failed to push his attack home. Later in the day, he retired behind the Oise River. The heaviest fighting took place to the north, on the original Fifth Army front. Here two German corps attacked with great vigor and drove back the French troops opposing them. Franchet d'Esperey's 1st Corps, then in reserve, was thrown in, and in a general counter-attack the Germans were driven north until darkness closed the battle. This was a fine tactical success by the Fifth Army, and French morale was greatly improved by it.

Although the German attack from the north had been halted, Lanrezac's own attack to the west had failed. About half of the German Second Army and all of the First Army lay to the west in a position to envelop Lanrezac's west flank if he remained where he was. He received permission from Joffre to resume his retrograde movement, and did so on the following day. Lanrezac and his staff had done excellent work in getting the army into position for the battle, but, as on the Sambre, once it was joined, army headquarters exercised little control. If the battle is considered from a higher level, Joffre obtained substantially the results he had hoped for, although the fighting did not go as he had planned. Bülow's Second Army was so badly hurt that it stood in place for a day and a half, thus allowing the BEF and the French Fifth Army to continue their retreat without interference. A secondary result was that Kluck's First Army made a drastic change of direction of advance that was to have far-reaching consequences.

BATTLE OF THE MARNE

German Advance to the Marne

After the Battle of Le Cateau on August 26, Kluck continued the march of his First Army to the southwest, in accordance with Moltke's instructions to proceed toward the lower Seine River west of Paris. On August 30, he received a message from Bülow announcing that the French at Guise had been defeated "in a decisive fashion" and requesting Kluck to help exploit the victory by moving southeastward. (A few days earlier, Kluck's subordination to Bülow had been ended.) Kluck realized that Moltke should be consulted in this instance, but communications were so slow that several days would elapse before he could receive a reply. Meanwhile, the golden opportunity described by Bülow would have passed. Under the circumstances, Kluck decided to do as Bülow

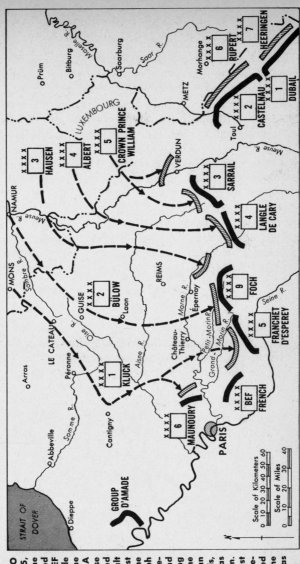

Map 3. GERMAN ADVANCE TO THE MARNE (Aug. 24–Sept. 5, 1914). After the Battle of the Frontiers, the Germans continued their inexorable advance. The BEF was overtaken, and in the Battle of Le Cateau (Aug. 26) part of the force was badly defeated. A counterattack in the Battle of Guise by the French Fifth Army caused the German Second Army to halt for 36 hours and the German First Army to change direction to come to its aid. Meanwhile, Gen. Joseph Joffre worked feverishly to regroup his forces for a stand and counterattack, and began shifting troops to the Paris area. The change of direction of the German First Army took it east of Paris, where the French Sixth Army was forming for counterattack. Gen. Alexander von Kluck, German First Army commander, left a small detachment near Paris and continued to the Marne River. By Sept. 5, the opposing forces were located as shown on the map.

wished, but when he learned that, instead of continuing the pursuit on August 31, Bülow's Second Army would remain in place for a day, he became dubious about Bülow's "decisive" victory. Nevertheless, he reasoned that if Bülow was not going to press the advantage over the French Fifth Army, someone else should do so. He therefore pushed on toward the southeast, so as to pass east of Paris.

At his headquarters in Luxembourg, Moltke was almost completely out of touch with his armies. The BEF and the French Fifth Army had been routed, the French Third and Fourth armies were falling back (according to Joffre's plan), and the pursuing Germans met only slight resistance. As a result, Moltke and his army commanders were convinced that the French had been decisively defeated. It apparently occurred to none of them that the French withdrawal might be part of a preconceived plan. Spies had apprised Moltke of the arrival of large numbers of troops by rail and of intensive fortification activity in Paris, but he failed to transmit this information to the two field commanders most directly concerned, Kluck and Bülow.

Meanwhile, events caused Joffre to change his strategic plan. The British had been so cut up at Le Cateau that they needed additional time to recuperate. Maunoury's Sixth Army (formed primarily from units transferred from the eastern French armies) was not ready. In addition, Kluck's change of direction had been observed and reported. These changes in the situation induced Joffre to move the limits of the Allied retreat southward to a huge arc extending from Paris to Verdun and curving as far south as Nogent-sur-Seine. His General Instructions No. 4, issued on September 1, outlined this plan but noted that the retreat might not necessarily go so far. It provided also that the Sixth Army assemble for its counterstroke within the entrenched camp of Paris, to be temporarily under the command of the garrison commander.

On August 31 and September 1 and 2, Kluck drove his First Army southeastward as rapidly as possible, intent on fixing and destroying the left flank of the French Fifth Army. Because of his speed and Bülow's 36-hour halt after the Battle of Guise, the German First Army was now a full day's march ahead of the Second Army. Since Kluck was proceeding to the southeast and Bülow to the south, it appeared that Kluck's army could move behind the French Fifth Army while Bülow struck it from in front. The decisive envelopment contemplated by Schlieffen would then become an accomplished fact. On the evening of September 2, as Kluck's 9th Corps reached the Marne River at Château-Thierry, he received orders from Moltke to follow the Second Army in echelon and protect the right flank of the German armies.

Moltke's order was motivated by his realization that the French forces at Paris had become formidable and that sizable forces were needed to hold them off until the German envelopment of the main French armies had been completed. Again, however, he had failed to inform Kluck of the build-up in Paris. Kluck was in a quandary. Since he was already a full day's march ahead of the Second Army, to follow in echelon meant that he must halt for two days. It appeared to him that the supreme command wanted the French driven southeastward, away from Paris. Only his army was in position to do this, for the Second Army was not in close contact with the French, and even if it had been, could only have exerted frontal pressure. Because of poor communications with German general headquarters, Kluck once more made his own decision. This was to continue his attack southward. His 9th Corps had already seized the Marne bridges at Château-Thierry and was proceeding to cross the river; Kluck directed two additional corps southward, leaving two corps (later only one corps) north of the Marne to guard against any threat from the direction of Paris. This decision was to produce grievous results for the Germans. Kluck had violated the letter of his orders, but under the circumstances he thought that he was carrying out their spirit.

German Change of Plan

Reports of the shifting of French troops in large numbers from east to west and of great activity in the Paris area finally convinced Moltke that Joffre was preparing a counteroffensive. On September 4, he concluded that the Schlieffen Plan was no longer valid, because his First and Second armies were now too weak to overpower the French in the Paris region, and substituted a new plan. This provided that these two armies would face the eastern front of Paris to hold off the French there while his other five armies sought a decision. The Third Army was to drive directly to the south to rupture the French line, while the Fourth and Fifth armies were to drive southeastward to effect a junction with the Sixth and Seventh armies, which were to push southwestward in the Nancy region. The plan had some merit, but the weakened condition of the armies, occasioned by their rapid movement, and the greatly advanced position of Kluck's army south of the Marne doomed it to failure. Kluck received these orders on September 5. From his advanced position they seemed so illogical that he believed Moltke had been given erroneous information. Again he decided that it was best to push on south of the Marne and overtake the French Fifth Army, thereby adding to the complications of the over-all German situation.

Joffre's Plan for the Counteroffensive

Joffre had determined the general pattern of his counterstroke as early as August 25, and he resolutely adhered to it despite reverses that made it impossible to launch his offensive as soon or as far north as he had hoped. Now, on September 3, conditions seemed ripe. By thrusting southeastward across the Marne, Kluck had put the German right flank in a perfect position to be struck by the French Sixth Army from the entrenched camp of Paris.

Before Joffre could order his counteroffensive, however, two difficult matters had to be resolved: The British had to be induced to participate in the operations, and the battered French armies had to be rehabilitated to regain their offensive power. The misunderstanding between Field Marshal French and General Lanrezac had caused the former to lose all confidence in the French Army and its leaders. French was convinced that his army needed a period of undisturbed rest and a complete replacement of personnel and equipment losses before it would be fit for serious action. As a matter of fact, the British units, though tired and depleted in strength, had done no major fighting since the Battle of Le Cateau and were certainly in no worse condition than most of the French troops. Impervious to Joffre's appeals, French wired the 1st Earl Kitchener, British Secretary of State for War: "I have no definite idea of General Joffre's general plan; its general result is the advance of the Germans and the retreat of the Allies." When Kitchener received this wire and others of a similar tone, he became alarmed and hastened to France on September 1 for an interview with French. There is no record of just what was said, but immediately thereafter, French wrote to Joffre, suggesting that the Allies stand and fight, and thenceforth he was consistently in favor of attacking.

The rehabilitation of the French armies proceeded rapidly, for they were now close to their supply bases and replacement centers. From the beginning, Joffre had paid particular attention to the command structure. Disregarding friendship and political factors,

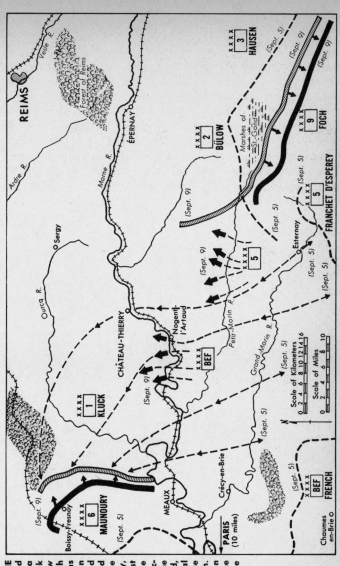

Map 4. BATTLE OF THE MARNE (Sept. 5–9, 1914). Finally apprised that the French Sixth Army was a major threat to his rear, Kluck ordered his troops to withdraw across the Marne to the French Sixth Army front. A wide gap was thus created between the German First and Second armies, defended only by weak rear guards and cavalry. Into the gap moved the BEF and the French Fifth Army, while Foch's Ninth Army held fast in the marshes of St.-Gond to the east. With the right of their Second Army forced back and the rear of their First Army threatened, the Germans began a general withdrawal to the line of the Aisne River, 40 miles to the north. The troop dispositions shown on the map are those of Sept. 9, the critical day of the Battle of the Marne.

he relieved any general officer whom he thought unfit for his job. Between August 2 and September 6, he replaced 3 army commanders, 10 corps commanders, and 38 division commanders. This weeding out naturally made many bitter enemies for Joffre, and very likely injustice was done in some cases, but the general effect of the widespread changes was good. The most controversial case was that of Lanrezac, whom Joffre replaced with Franchet d'Esperey on September 3. Lanrezac had had an outstanding peacetime record, had shown great strategic insight in divining German intentions, and had done excellent tactical planning. Some believe that he was a splendid leader, made a scapegoat to cover the derelictions of the over-all commander, Joffre. Others mark him as a man too small for his responsibilities, indecisive in action, and possessing an overbearing personality that not only bred resentment within his own command but so alienated Sir John French as to make cooperation between the French Fifth Army and the BEF almost nonexistent. His successor was a vigorous, self-confident fighter who could inspire his troops and who got along well with the British. Under the new commanders the French soldiers took heart and determined to stop the invader at any cost.

On August 26, Joffre appointed General Joseph Gallieni governor of Paris. While Joffre prepared his mobile forces for the decisive battle, Gallieni looked to the defenses of the capital. He was a dynamic and distinguished veteran of the Franco-Prussian War and the colonial wars. With energy and determination rare in a man of his age, he put the neglected defenses of Paris in order, strengthening forts and building field fortifications in the intervals. Maunoury's Sixth Army entered the fortified area on August 30 and was put under his control. Gallieni constantly prodded Joffre to set the army in motion eastward and stop the retreat. On September 3, the French government departed for Bordeaux, leaving Gallieni in complete control of Paris, where his dash and enthusiasm heartened the people.

Joffre's plan for his counterattack, as outlined in his General Instructions No. 6, was simple. The Sixth Army, moving out of the entrenched camp of Paris, was to advance north of the Marne and cross the Ourcq River early on September 6. At the same time, the BEF and the other French armies were to attack with determination on their respective fronts. If this great counterblow failed, little would be left to the French to carry on the war. Fully realizing this fact, Joffre for the first time issued a direct appeal to his men. It began: "As we engage in the battle upon which the safety of our country depends, all must remember that the time for looking backward has passed. . . ." His brief message was greeted with eager response in all ranks, and the French Army steeled itself for a supreme effort.

Battle of the Ourcq

Maunoury's Sixth Army marched eastward on September 5, so as to be in position to cross the Ourcq the next day. At the same time, General Hans H. K. von Gronau's 4th Reserve Corps of Kluck's army was advancing southward along the west bank of the river toward Meaux. Soon Gronau received reports of strong French patrols and of several strong columns of all arms. He realized that something important was taking place to his right, but he lacked aviation and was weak in cavalry for scouting purposes. Deciding that there was only one way of learning the significance of the French activity, he ordered an attack to the west by his entire corps. Maunoury was not expecting to fight on September 5, and initially his leading elements were thrown into confusion. They soon recovered their poise, however, and a violent fight ensued. The Germans gained the upper hand and pushed the French back all along the line. By dark it was clear to Gronau that he was dealing with no mere reconnaissance force, and he therefore withdrew his exhausted troops to a strong defensive position six miles eastward.

Notified of the battle, Kluck reluctantly started his 2d Corps northward to help Gronau. Neither the French nor the German higher commanders seem to have appreciated the importance of this fight. Gallieni reported it as "a small successful engagement," while Kluck sent only the 2d Corps to intervene. During the next day (September 6), Maunoury engaged all the troops he had available, attacking frontally and also endeavoring to envelop the enemy's north flank. Each attempted envelopment was met by another German unit from south of the Marne. Kluck, still unconvinced of the seriousness of the engagement on the Ourcq, sent only the 4th Corps north during the day in response to appeals from the commanders on the Ourcq, and refused to move his other two corps, which were under fierce attack south of the Marne. However, when a copy of Joffre's attack orders was picked up by the Germans on the battlefield, it became clear that Maunoury was conducting a major offensive, and Kluck ordered his two corps on the Marne north to the Ourcq. Although their movement widened an already existing gap between the German First and Second armies, Kluck was confident that the British did not present a serious threat to the Germans. He admired the fighting qualities of the British troops, but since Le Cateau they had not paused in their hasty retreat, and he reasoned that they were unlikely to make a dangerous thrust at this time.

Meanwhile, Maunoury pressed his attacks vigorously on September 7 and 8. Gallieni rushed reinforcements to him from Paris, including two regiments of infantry sent in taxicabs.* Possessing numerical superiority, the French retained the initiative despite the arrival of Kluck's other two corps, but they gained little ground. On the evening of September 8, Kluck ordered a coordinated attack for the following day, stating: "The decision will be obtained tomorrow by an enveloping attack on the north wing. . . ." At the same time, Maunoury, having committed all of his troops and knowing that additional German forces had arrived, ordered the Sixth Army to pass to the defensive on September 9, and secretly directed his senior subordinate to prepare plans for a step-by-step retreat toward Paris. Victory seemed about to reward Kluck's fighting spirit and iron determination, but events elsewhere had already made German failure inevitable.

Battle of the Two Morins

Franchet d'Esperey's Fifth Army, beginning its advance on September 6 as scheduled, encountered Kluck's two corps south of the Marne. Fighting raged from noon until dark, when the Germans broke contact and withdrew to the line of the Grand-Morin River. Meanwhile, Franchet d'Esperey's right corps advanced unopposed to its objective for the day, but it was then struck by one of Bülow's corps and driven back. The first day's fighting by the Fifth Army thus was indecisive: Franchet d'Esperey now ordered a general advance for September 7. On that day, Bülow, fearful for his exposed right flank, ordered it behind the Petit-Morin River. The French followed up the withdrawal and attacked the new line unsuccessfully on September 8. By that time, Kluck's last two corps had moved northward to the Ourcq and were no longer supporting Bülow. His afternoon attack having failed, Franchet d'Esperey decided to attempt an attack that evening. The night attack was a

* Contrary to the popular impression at the time, this spectacular movement did not have an important influence on the battle, but it was significant in that it was the first movement of troops to a battlefield by motor transport.

complete success, piercing Bülow's line and forcing him to withdraw about six miles to a position facing west.

This movement so widened the gap between Kluck and Bülow that it could not be closed. Only two cavalry corps, aggregating about 10,000 men, were available to defend the gap. The British moved forward on September 6, but since they had retreated so far, their advance began from a position considerably behind the point from which Joffre had hoped they would start. Field Marshal French seemed in a position to strike a fatal blow to the Germans through the gap on his front between their First and Second armies, but his advance was slow. While the troops were eager to fight, their commanders, remembering Mons and Le Cateau, were overcautious. The small German cavalry forces were handled with great skill, and it took the British three days to cover 25 miles. By the evening of September 8, the British had advanced to within artillery range of the Marne; that afternoon, Kluck's last two corps, the 3d and the 9th, crossed to the north of the Marne en route to the Ourcq.

The British advance into the gap, though much too slow, had put the Germans in a critical position. The British troops were nearing Kluck's rear, while Franchet d'Esperey's Fifth Army was in a position to envelop Bülow's right flank. For the Allies to exploit this favorable situation, however, it was necessary for Maunoury's Sixth Army to hold its own against Kluck's attacks on the Ourcq and for Foch's Ninth Army to prevent Bülow's left and Hausen's Third Army from breaking through.

Battle of the Marshes of Saint-Gond

Foch's Ninth Army (newly created from units of the eastern French armies) was scheduled to participate in Joffre's general offensive by attacking northward, but during most of the battle it was compelled to stand on the defensive because from the outset it was attacked by superior forces. In order to face Paris, as prescribed in Moltke's new plan, Bülow had to pivot on his right. In so doing, his two left corps ran into Foch's left and center. Hausen, driving his Third Army southward in accordance with Moltke's orders, ran into Foch's right. The French Ninth Army thus found itself in the path of the main efforts of two German armies. Its position was strong in the center, fairly good on the left, and weak on the right. On September 6, Foch was fully occupied on his left and center with Bülow's troops. The French left held, though only with difficulty; the center, under fierce attack, was forced south of the marshes, where it then held. On September 7, Bülow resumed his attacks and Hausen joined him against Foch's right, but the Ninth Army remained firm. The fighting was bloody and bitter all along the line; in the open terrain on Hausen's front, the French light artillery was especially effective. Although Foch had considerable cause for concern, he held on.

Hausen decided to avoid the devastating French artillery fire by making a large-scale surprise night attack. Such an attack was a highly unconventional procedure at this stage of the war, and most of the German commanders thought it foolish. Nonetheless, Hausen attacked with four divisions at 3 A.M. on September 8, moving the infantry forward in the moonlight with fixed bayonets, unloaded rifles, and no artillery preparation. This innovation was a huge success. The attack swept three miles forward, throwing three French divisions into confusion and capturing 28 pieces of artillery. It seemed that the Ninth Army was crushed, especially when Bülow renewed his attacks against its left and center. Foch met the emergency by peremptorily ordering his hard-pressed troops to attack, which served to eliminate the possibility of retreat from their minds. French determination and German exhaustion, caused by two days of bitter fighting following weeks of hard marching, finally brought the enemy advance to a halt. It was at this critical time that Foch purportedly sent his famous dispatch to Joffre: "Hard pressed on my right. My center is yielding. Impossible to maneuver. Situation excellent. I attack."

Foch's Ninth Army had another hard day on September 9. Hausen, assisted by Bülow's left corps, launched violent and repeated attacks throughout the morning, determined to crush the French. Foch's troops were gradually driven back along most of the line, but, inspired by a series of imperative orders for local counterattacks and by news of successes gained by the French armies to the west, they held, though almost at the breaking point. Franchet d'Esperey lent some troops from his Fifth Army to Foch, and with these the latter was able to fill gaps in his line where necessary and to counterattack. Nonetheless, defeat still seemed imminent. At this critical juncture the German attacks lessened and then ceased. The German High Command had decided to withdraw from the Marne. Foch's stand is a classic example of self-sacrifice without hope of gain in order to make victory possible elsewhere.

Fighting to the East

While the BEF and the French Fifth and Ninth armies engaged the Germans in the critical area of the Battle of the Marne, the French First, Second, Third, and Fourth armies to the east played their parts well in the over-all plan. General Fernand L. A. M. de Langle de Cary's Fourth Army, after its defeat in the Battle of the Ardennes, had retreated step by step. On September 5, when it received Joffre's order for battle, it was between Foch's Ninth Army on the left and General Maurice P. E. Sarrail's Third Army on the right. There were large gaps on both sides of the Fourth Army, which Langle de Cary lacked the troops to close. His primary task, therefore, was to prevent the Germans from exploiting the gaps. Opposing him directly was the German Fourth Army under Albert, Duke of Württemberg, and to the east of the latter was the Fifth Army under German Crown Prince William.

The battle opened on September 6 and for three days raged furiously. The German attacks were mainly frontal, and the French succeeded in stopping them; on the other hand, Langle de Cary's troops could not advance. Albert and the crown prince debated about which gap on Langle de Cary's flanks should be exploited. Moltke was requested to settle the dispute and, apparently not wishing to become involved between the two princes, replied: "It is desirable that the Fourth and Fifth armies lend each other mutual support." While these discussions were being held, reinforcements arrived from Lorraine, and the gap on Langle de Cary's left was closed. The princes then decided to attack the gap on his right, but Langle de Cary's right corps had stretched its front eastward so that the German attack became frontal. Being overextended, this corps was forced gradually to give ground, although it fought tenaciously. Relief came on the night of September 10, when the German Fourth Army broke off contact and withdrew to the north.

Sarrail's Third Army had retreated from the Ardennes until, on September 6, it occupied a position facing northwest with its right wing resting on the fortress of Verdun. When it moved forward that day to attack as Joffre had directed, it encountered the German Crown Prince's Fifth Army. Fierce combat continued for four days, during which time William tried unsuccessfully to exploit the gap between Sarrail's and Langle de Cary's armies. He then attempted to cross the Meuse south of Verdun in order to take Sarrail in the rear, but he could not subdue the little forts at the crossing points. On September 10, he returned to his attacks west of Verdun, but failed there also and withdrew northward.

The fighting on the front of the French First and Second armies was almost continuous from the opening of the Battle of the Frontiers to the end of the Battle of the Marne. After the Germans smashed the great French offensive in Lorraine on August 20, they followed up slowly and, on August 24, launched a drive that they hoped would carry them across the Moselle to penetrate the French lines. The French First and Second armies had recovered rapidly from their initial defeat, however, and in a counterattack not only stopped the Germans but hurled them back. There was a lull in the fighting from August 28 to September 3, during which time Joffre moved out large bodies of troops to bolster his threatened left. On September 4, in conformity with Moltke's revised plan, a strong German attack was directed against the heights of Nancy. Determined attacks were made until September 10, but to no avail, for the French, though inferior in strength, were in excellent defensive positions. Moltke finally realized that Schlieffen was right in that Lorraine was not a suitable area for major operations. He called off the attacks and began to move the Seventh Army to his weakened right on the Aisne, as the Sixth Army withdrew toward the frontier.

German Retreat

When Moltke learned that Joffre had ordered a general offensive for September 6, he was pleased, because he was confident that if the French would only stand and fight, his armies could destroy them. On September 4, he had issued directives describing how the Allied forces were to be destroyed. All he could do now, he felt, was to rest at his headquarters in Luxembourg and wait for his orders to be executed. Communications between headquarters and the front were inefficient, and it was not until September 7 that he learned of the gap developing between his First and Second armies. Since it was obvious that general headquarters would now have to intervene, Moltke sent his chief of intelligence, Lieutenant Colonel Richard Hentsch, to the right-wing armies to secure a complete picture of the situation. Moltke recognized that one or more of his strong-minded army commanders might already have begun a retreat, and he therefore authorized Hentsch to issue in his (Moltke's) name such orders as might be necessary to coordinate the withdrawal, close gaps in the line, or halt the rearward movement at a strong defensive position. These instructions were not reduced to writing, a fact that has caused much controversy.

On September 9, at Bülow's headquarters, Hentsch was informed that the German Second Army was in a precarious position (as it was) and would retreat behind the Marne and then behind the Vesle. He next traveled to Kluck's headquarters, about 50 miles away. Kluck was in the midst of his attack to envelop Maunoury's northern flank, and the attack was progressing well, but Kluck's southern flank had to be drawn back to avoid its envelopment by the advancing British. Hentsch invoked his authority and ordered that a retreat begin before the First Army was trapped. The attack was then halted.

When Moltke received Hentsch's personal report on the afternoon of September 10, he immediately ordered the right-wing armies (First, Second, and Third) to fall back and the others to halt. On the following day, he decided to visit the front, for the first and only time during the campaign. The impressions he gained on this trip were so unfavorable that he ordered a retreat to the general line Noyon–Verdun, which was to be fortified and defended. The German withdrawal was effected with little interference from the Allies. Severely tried by their marching and fighting, the latter failed to make a vigorous pursuit, thereby losing many of the fruits of victory. By September 14, the German armies were organizing their new prescribed positions for defense, and the Marne campaign was at an end. On that day, Moltke was relieved of his command by William II and was replaced by General Erich von Falkenhayn. This change was kept a secret because it amounted to an admission of failure. To prevent the news from spreading, Moltke was required to remain at general headquarters until November 1, when his replacement was announced openly.

CONCLUDING OPERATIONS OF 1914

First Battle of the Aisne

Although their pursuit was so slow that they lost contact at many points, when the Allies arrived before the new position on the Aisne, they attacked with vigor. The German position was on high ground about two miles north of the river. Spurs ran from this ground to the Aisne, giving the Germans surveillance of the river crossings. The Allies crossed the Aisne on September 13 against little resistance and the next day began a general offensive, with the British making the principal effort. Bitter fighting continued with minor gains until September 18, when Joffre stopped the attacks.

This battle marked a transition from the open warfare that had preceded it to the stabilization of the front that ensued. It was the first battle in trench warfare and the forerunner of many such battles to come. The Germans had chosen and skillfully organized one of the strongest positions on the Western Front. Here they reaped the full reward of their prewar defensive training. Their skill with grenades, machine guns, and field fortifications gave them a great advantage in this type of fighting. Artillery came into its own in the battle. In such a stabilized situation, the artilleryman had ample time for registration, and he developed great accuracy. Adjustment of artillery fire by airplane later became commonplace, and the consumption of ammunition reached rates unforeseen by prewar planners. The lack of medium and heavy artillery counted strongly against the Allies, for many targets in the rough hill mass before them could not be reached by their light, flat-trajectory field guns.

Fall of Antwerp

Stabilization of the main battlefront on the Aisne left the Germans with their west flank near Noyon open and vulnerable. Behind them lay Antwerp with the entire Belgian Army of approximately 150,000 men. In order to relieve this dangerous situation, Falkenhayn ordered the city reduced at once. The Allies, especially the British, were anxious to hold Antwerp, hoping that the main line of battle eventually could be extended to include it, but it was difficult to send help. Actually, they had little to send, and they could not move what they had up the Schelde (Scheldt) by ship, for the neutral Netherlands controlled the mouth of the river and would not permit them to adopt this course.

The city had been considered one of the strongest fortresses in Europe, but the forts were easy prey for the heavy siege guns of the Germans, which knocked them out one by one. On October 6, King Albert moved out with the mobile army. Three days later, the city fell despite the efforts of Winston Churchill, First Lord of the Admiralty, who arrived with the Royal Naval Division, consisting of a brigade of marines and two brigades of naval Reservists. Two divisions of trained British Army troops had reached the vicinity of Brugge (Bruges) on October 6, and had started up the coast to lend their assistance at Antwerp. Meeting the retreating Belgians and Royal Naval Division, they fell back with them toward Ypres (Ieper).

Race to the Sea

The successive operations that took place in September and Oc-

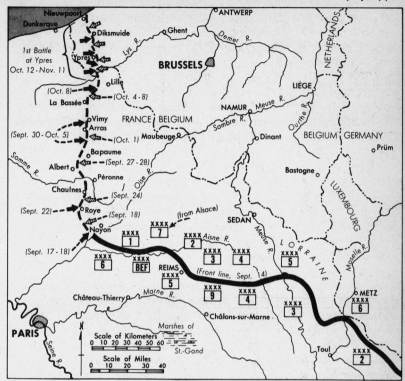

Map 5. FIRST BATTLE OF THE AISNE AND THE RACE TO THE SEA. After the Battle of the Marne the Germans withdrew to formidable positions along the Aisne. When their repeated frontal attacks against these positions failed, the Allies attempted to envelop the German flank on the north. This initiated a series of enveloping maneuvers by both sides, each determined to outflank the other, without significant success. Meanwhile, the front extended farther and farther north. The final clashes took place between the Lys River and the English Channel coast in the First Battle of Ypres (October 12–November 11). The Germans and Allies strove desperately to succeed in this last opportunity for envelopment. Fighting was bitter and bloody; heavy losses were sustained by both sides, but gains were insignificant. Exhausted, the opponents began to dig in and strengthen the positions held; trench warfare, which was to frustrate the Allies and Germans alike for almost four years, had begun.

tober, 1914, are commonly called "The Race to the Sea," but the title is misleading. Neither contestant was trying to reach the sea; each was attempting to envelop his opponent's flank. In mid-September, when the Aisne front began to be stabilized, each side began to shift troops from east to west in an effort to envelop the other. Each attempt was successfully repulsed by the enemy, and

the result was a series of bloody battles extending successively northward as the newly arrived forces collided. In the course of this maneuvering, the BEF began a movement from the Aisne front to the
vicinity of Ypres in Flanders.

First Battle of Ypres

When the left flank of the Allied forces reached the sea, Falkenhayn decided to penetrate their lines in the vicinity of Ypres before
they could organize their positions properly. This seemed an opportune time, because the front at Ypres and to the south was only
lightly held pending the arrival of the bulk of the BEF, which was
then moving up from the Aisne. On October 12, Falkenhayn threw
his full strength against the Allied position at Ypres, hoping to
drive through to the Channel ports. For nine days he pressed his
attack with vigor. On several occasions it seemed that the thin Allied line would break, and Joffre sent Foch to Flanders to coordinate the defense. While Foch had no command authority over the
Belgians or the British, he did control the French reinforcements
that were being sent to the north as rapidly as possible. His strong
personality and determined fighting spirit soon gave him such influence over Field Marshal French that he was, practically speaking, able to direct operations as an Allied commander. This development was fortunate, for a firm coordinating hand was essential.
The Germans had great superiority in numbers and artillery, but
they were finally stopped.

On the left flank, the Belgians opened the sluice gates in an effort to halt the Germans. An area two miles wide extending from
Diksmuide to the sea was inundated to a depth of three or four
feet, halting the German advance. The fighting there was bitter,
however, and the Belgians lost 35 per cent of their strength.

By October 20, the German attacks had been entirely stopped.
Foch and French reasoned that the enemy must be exhausted, and
since the entire BEF had now been assembled together with many
French units, the Allied commanders decided to attack in their
turn. This proved to be a costly error, for heavy rains were setting
in, and the low-lying plain of Flanders was rapidly becoming a
swamp. Furthermore, the Germans had brought up reinforcements
and were in the process of bringing up more. The Allied attacks
persisted with frightful losses until October 28, when Foch halted
them.

On the following day, Falkenhayn, who had amassed a superiority of about six to one at the point of attack, resumed the offensive. A breakthrough was achieved in the British line southeast of Ypres on the third day of the offensive, but, by throwing in all of their reserves, the Allies managed to hold firm. Falkenhayn kept pressing his attacks to no avail until November 11, when heavy rains and snow finally brought them to an end.

The fighting at Ypres left the British in an unfavorable defensive position. This was a salient six miles deep, with the town of Ypres at the center of its base. The Germans held positions on the surrounding hills that gave them excellent observation over the entire salient. The area was so low that construction of entrenchments was difficult, ground water being struck in many places at a depth of one foot. A far better defensive position would have been one extending north and south just behind Ypres, giving up the salient and the town. But Ypres had become a symbol of Allied resistance, and the effect on public opinion of withdrawing would have been unfortunate. Accordingly, the troops held on to the town year after year.

Stabilized Front

Ypres was the last major battle on the Western Front in 1914. Both sides dug in, and trench warfare began to take on the form that was to become so familiar in the next four years. In the autumn of 1914, however, the elaborate systems of field fortifications that were developed later were unknown. Over most of the front, the trench system consisted of an irregular ditch with a depth equal to the height of a man and another such ditch 200 or 300 yards to the rear. The forward trench was called the front line, and the one in the rear the support line. The area between the opposing positions was known as no man's land; it might vary in width from 30 to 800 yards. From the beginning, the German defenses were superior to those of the Allies. They generally had been located with due regard for terrain, fields of fire, and observation, whereas the French and British front line was simply the place where the foremost troops had dug in at the end of an attack. The Allied policy was that ground once gained must never be given up (a good enough principle in its place), and this policy was vigorously enforced. As a result, the Allied positions, as at Ypres, were often poorly sited in sectors where excellent positions existed a short distance to the rear.

From the crude beginnings of 1914, both sides eventually evolved elaborate defensive systems, the German defenses usually being better than those of the Allies. With typical thoroughness the Germans constructed deep belts of wire entanglements, large dugouts where platoons and companies could find shelter from the heaviest bombardment, concrete pillboxes, and telephone and electric-light systems.

When no major attacks were in progress, life in the trenches varied from extreme misery to passable comfort. Mud and cold brought great hardship, especially during the first winter, because neither side had yet learned the techniques of trench living. On the British front, the offensive spirit was kept alive by constant patrolling, raids, mine warfare, and sniping. Except during offensives, the French were more inclined toward the tacit encouragement of a policy of live and let live, while the Germans adapted themselves to their opponents.

The breakthrough of enemy positions was to remain a dream for nearly four years. The line established in November, 1914, did not move as much as 10 miles in either direction until February–April, 1917, when the Germans voluntarily withdrew to the Hindenburg Line. Innumerable attacks, costing hundreds of thousands of lives, were to be launched with little or no result.

1914 IN RETROSPECT

The Schlieffen Plan and Plan XVII both failed completely. Under prevailing circumstances, Plan XVII was unrealistic and never had a chance of success. An erroneous estimate of the number of mobile German troops available caused General Joffre to minimize German capabilities for major operations west of the Meuse. The French attacks were directed over terrain highly unsuited for major offensive action. Moreover, an unreasonable faith was placed in the deeply inculcated French offensive spirit; 80 per cent of the infantry officers were either killed or wounded during the first five months of the campaign. Joffre was responsible for the disastrous Plan XVII, but when his preconceived ideas collapsed in the Battle of the Frontiers, he did not lose his head or show signs of discouragement. Instead, he faced the situation calmly and shifted forces to the left wing for a counterblow. His control of his armies was close and intimate throughout the campaign. He had good communications and used his liaison officers freely. As a result, he was always familiar with the situation, and his subordinates were never in doubt as to what he wanted done.

The Schlieffen Plan depended for success on close control, speed of execution, and a strong encircling right wing. It failed primarily because of General von Moltke's lack of direction and control, for which inadequate signal communications were partly to blame. It is difficult to understand why the Germans, ordinarily precise and well prepared, neglected this vital field of military support. Moltke remained aloof in his headquarters far to the rear and let his subordinates have their own way. As a result, they not only failed to cooperate with each other but did not follow the strategic plan. All German commanders fell into the error of interpreting their successes at the frontier as decisive victories and the planned French withdrawal as a rout. The exaggerated reports of success prejudiced the German operations in many ways. They led Moltke to give way to the importunities of Prince Rupert and General Krafft von Dellmensingen, and allowed them to hurl large numbers of Germans against small numbers of Frenchmen in good positions in the difficult terrain of Lorraine and the heights of Nancy, so that Joffre could assemble superior power on his left wing. Considering how close the French came to breaking on the Ourcq River and at the Marshes of Saint-Gond, it seems reasonable to suppose that the additional strength provided by a resolute adherence to the original plan would have enabled Kluck, Bülow, and Hausen to gain a decision.

The Battle of the Marne proper was a great strategic victory for the Allies. It turned back the invader and eventually proved to be the turning point of the war. But it was not a great tactical victory. The German troops were not demoralized, as they soon demonstrated. Only about 15,000 German prisoners were taken.

Losses on both sides during the constant and heavy fighting were huge. By the end of 1914, the French had lost 380,000 killed and 600,000 wounded, prisoners, and missing in action; the Germans, because of their better training in defense, suffered to a slightly smaller extent.

6. Western Front, 1915–17: Stalemate

BY CYRIL FALLS

The war in 1914 had been open fighting insofar as that term can be applied to the Western Front before March, 1918, and its fluctuations had covered great distances. Only at the end of the year had it become trench warfare rather than warfare waged from scrapings in the ground where the forces on either side had halted. Now this state of affairs was to be changed, though it was not until 1916 that defenses were perfected, above all in the famous line named after Field Marshal Paul von Hindenburg, to which he withdrew from the battlefield of the Somme. Even the trenches of 1915, however, altered the whole character of the war, especially in winter.

OPERATIONS IN 1915

British Expansion

At the opening of 1915, the BEF had been expanded from the original 6 divisions to a total of only 10, but in the course of that year its strength was raised to 37 divisions. While these included 2 Canadian divisions, the forces of Australia and New Zealand had been sent to Africa to oppose the Turks in Egypt. In South Africa, General Louis Botha had to suppress a brief but painful revolt before he could fight the Germans in German Southwest Africa. The strength of the French on their own soil was 107 divisions, and that of the Germans 94. The majority of the remaining 65 German divisions were in Russia. Thus, the main burden of the war in the west was being carried by France, and Britain, as the junior partner, was not able to make her voice heard in strategic matters.

Reorganization of British arms production began on June 9 with the formation of a Ministry of Munitions, of which David Lloyd George was the first head. His vigor and persuasiveness in office coincided with a great improvement in organization and output, for which he was accorded the credit by popular opinion. While his work was undoubtedly invaluable, the foundations had been well laid by the master general of the ordnance at the War Office. Of the guns issued to the army, 1,638 were from Woolwich Arsenal, 1,406 from the United States, and 25,512 from private armament firms. Of 55,000 aircraft, 1,502 came from Royal Aircraft Establishment factories.

German Plans

The extremely able chief of the German General Staff, General von Falkenhayn, decided to make the east the principal theater of war, buttress the Austrians there, and administer to the Russians a defeat that, if it did not remove them entirely from the war (he did not believe this was possible), would render them innocuous for a long time to come. This policy accounts for the shift of German forces eastward and for the fact that Falkenhayn himself moved to a position of proximity with the Austrian High Command. It was all the more essential that he do so because he found it necessary to keep General Ludendorff, Hindenburg's chief of staff, and Lieutenant Colonel (later Major General) Max Hoffmann, his director of military operations, under observation. These two generals intrigued against him and urged Hindenburg to oppose him, and it was only the implacable will of Falkenhayn and the loyalty with which Emperor William II supported him that enabled him to prevail.

Battle of Neuve-Chapelle

The northern fringe of the Forest of Ardennes lies about 90 miles east of Arras, and the southern fringe about 25 miles north of Verdun. The Germans could avail themselves of only one first-class rail line south of the forest, and those lines which passed through it were inadequate for the supply of their southern front. The main burden was therefore borne by the fine railway system north of the Ardennes, and most of these lines passed through the bottleneck of Liége, between the forest and the salient formed by Limburg Province of the neutral Netherlands.

For his next offensive north of Arras to capture Vimy Ridge, Marshal Joffre had called on the British to relieve the two French corps still in the salient formed at the First Battle of Ypres in 1914. Field Marshal French believed that after the relief he would be unable to afford any adequate assistance to the Artois offensive of his allies, and his solution of the problem was therefore to attack before the relief. His First Army commander, General Sir Douglas Haig, with his brilliant staff officer, Brigadier General John Edmond Gough, made excellent preparations for the attack.

The assault on Neuve-Chapelle, which was launched on March

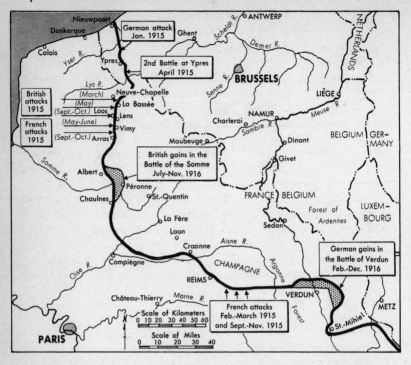

Map 6. OPERATIONS ON THE WESTERN FRONT, 1915 AND 1916. During 1915 the Germans concentrated their efforts against Russia while defending themselves on the Western Front. The Allies made a series of limited attacks, as shown, but without success. At the Second Battle of Ypres the Germans introduced poison (chlorine) gas to modern warfare. By the end of the year the line had not changed more than three miles at any point. In 1916 the Germans launched the bloody battle of attrition at Verdun, and the Allies undertook their equally costly offensive on the Somme.

10, won complete surprise, opening a gap in the enemy's front. The Germans were unable to launch a counterattack, and such reserves as reached the scene (four battalions from four different regiments) were entirely engaged in efforts to patch holes in the line. On the following day, however, British progress had scarcely begun when the Germans, who in the course of the night had assembled 16,000 men for the purpose, launched a belated counterattack. Only at a few points did it recover any ground, but it achieved its ends by bringing the British advance to a halt, and the battle ended on March 13.

Second Battle of Ypres

Falkenhayn was now tempted to make use of his "secret weapon," poison gas. At 5 P.M. on April 22, after a fierce bombardment, Algerian *tirailleurs* were seen in headlong flight toward Ypres, some pointing to their mouths and croaking the word *gaz*. The commander of the British Second Army, General Sir Horace Lockwood Smith-Dorrien, issued orders for the re-establishment of the front, but the first troops available consisted only of the reserve Canadian brigade. Though a second gas attack on April 24 inflicted heavy casualties on the Canadians, they succeeded in halting the Germans.

On April 27, Smith-Dorrien decided that the time had come for a voluntary withdrawal to the outskirts of Ypres. When the order reached headquarters, French told him to turn over his command to Lieutenant General Sir Herbert C. O. Plumer (later 1st Viscount Plumer). The latter issued precisely the same orders as had Smith-Dorrien, however, and this time French accepted them. The withdrawal began on May 1, and the battle came to an end after a new German attack on May 24–25. British losses at Ypres amounted to 60,000, or almost twice the German total of 35,000. For the next two years the burden of holding the reduced Ypres salient became almost intolerable.

Second Battle of Artois

On May 9, the French launched their long-planned attack in Artois. Their troops were their best and were inspired by traditional French *élan*. Their optimism was justified at the start, when they secured a foothold on the crest of Vimy Ridge, but this was lost, and the battle ended in a deadlock on June 18. French losses totaled 100,000, and those of the Germans 75,000.

Autumn Offensives

A series of offensives in the autumn of 1915 fared little better. One in Champagne (which became known as the Second Battle of Champagne) was postponed until September 25 because General Victor L. L. d'Urbal in Artois estimated that his preparations could not be completed earlier. The Second Army of General (later Marshal) Henri Philippe Pétain and the Fourth Army of General de Langle de Cary broke the German lines, but Falkenhayn's perspicacity and his immediate arrival on the scene stopped the deep withdrawal contemplated by his subordinates and restored the front. The battle ended on November 6. The Artois offensive (known as the Third Battle of Artois), which lasted from September 25 to October 15, was even less successful, as was that portion of it fought by the British at Loos.

OPERATIONS IN 1916

Battle of Verdun

The aim of Falkenhayn in 1916 was to lower French morale, which he suspected had already been weakened by defeatist propaganda. He chose for the front of attack the region of Verdun because he was confident that the French would be induced by the prestige of its name to fight for it to the last man, and his object was to bleed France white. The second reason was the corollary of the first: Verdun was a self-contained slaughterhouse, the flanks of which need not be extended. The attack was to be made by German Crown Prince William, commander of the Fifth Army.

The French commander at Verdun was General Pétain. He had no responsibility for any lack of preparedness, for he had been summoned by Joffre only four days after the launching of the offensive on February 21, but his calm and methodical nature was ideally suited to making the best use of the assets and remedying the deficiencies, the chief of which was the lack of adequate railways. The main artery was a narrow secondary road from Bar-le-Duc, 40 miles to the south, which held out against constant German shelling because of widening, first-class organization, and incessant repairs. The French came to call it la Voie Sacrée (the Sacred Road).

Both sides fought with equal bravery, and the Germans with extraordinary tactical skill. The manner in which they were able to cancel assaults in a few minutes when a company commander on patrol noted that the French were particularly on the alert was astounding. They were equally quick and clever in shifting the weight of an attack from a strong to a weak point of resistance, and their handling of their artillery was masterly. The French had no opportunities for such nicety of tactics because they were limited to straight counterattacks, but two commanders earned exceptional reputations. These were General Robert Georges Nivelle, who came in as a corps commander and succeeded Pétain in command of the Second Army, and Major General (later General) Charles Mangin, who commanded the 5th Division and somewhat later was promoted to the command of a corps. The French were, however, plagued by a series of panics, which involved unnecessary

Map 7. BATTLE OF VERDUN (Feb. 21–Dec. 18, 1916). Knowing that the French would defend Verdun to the last, the Germans attacked with a view to inflicting heavy casualties and thus altering the manpower balance on the Western Front. In heavy and vicious fighting the Germans made the moderate gains shown. In the period October–December, the French counterattacked, recaptured Fort Douaumont and Fort de Vaux, and advanced almost to Ornes. Fighting stopped on December 18, after the French had suffered about 550,000 casualties, and the Germans 450,000.

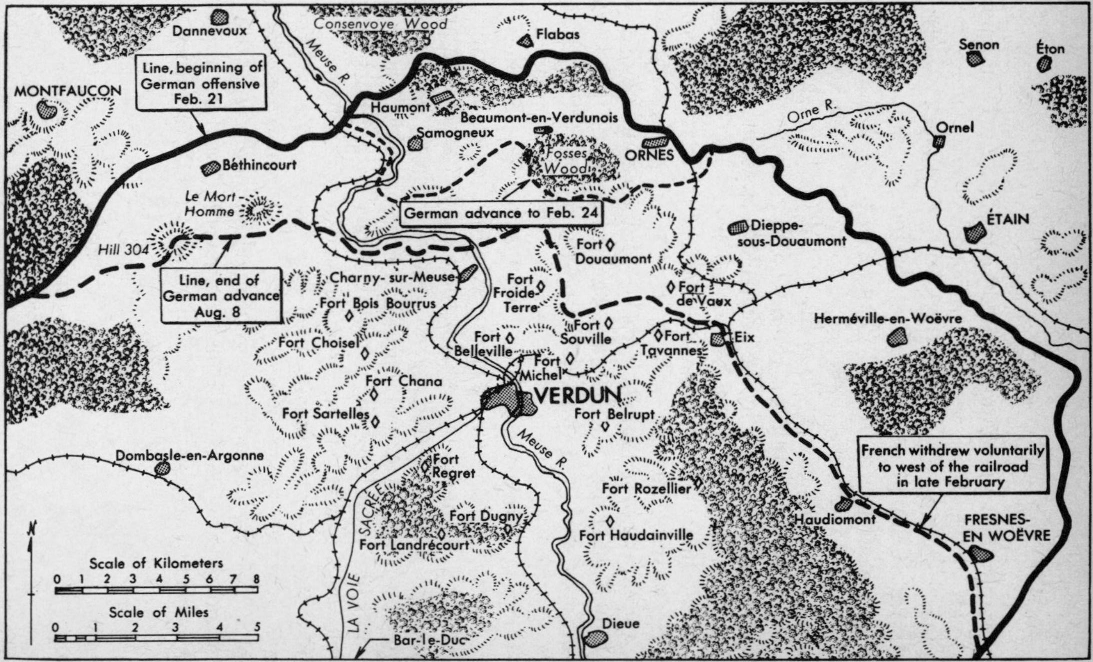

withdrawals. These did not include the loss of Fort Douaumont on February 25, because it was ungarrisoned and was taken by a single German company. Here, too, the situation changed speedily. On April 10, a German assault south of the fort was shot to fragments, and as a consequence the best German corps commander, General Bruno von Mudra, was replaced by General Ewald von Lochow. The French artillery was also brilliant. The German giant howitzers in very many cases were destroyed, and throughout the battle they were harried mercilessly by the French long 155-mm. guns.

In the final phase of the Verdun offensive the Germans slowed down still further, but they gained one more outstanding success on the right bank of the Meuse River. Pétain had realized the falsity of the prewar doctrine that the forts of Verdun should be dismantled and their guns used in the field. He had done all that lay in his power to remedy the situation by providing the forts with permanent garrisons of about 300 men each. On the German side, the crown prince's resolute chief of staff, General Konstantin Schmidt von Knobelsdorf, obtained permission to attempt the capture of Fort de Vaux and, if successful there, of Forts Souville and Tavannes as well. The defense of Vaux by Major Sylvain Eugène Raynal was heroic. After the fort had been completely surrounded, he fought on desperately repulsing attack after attack and surrendering only when the water supply gave out on June 7.

For the attack on Souville and Tavannes on June 21, the Germans used the lethal green-cross gas shell but were completely routed. Although the fighting continued until July 11, this was the real end of the offensive. Its only achievement had been to reduce the French contribution on the Somme. French casualties totaled 315,000; German casualties, 280,000.

Later, on October 24 and December 15, Nivelle and Mangin launched two successful attacks at Verdun. These won back a large proportion of the ground lost and almost all that counted.

Battle of the Somme

Once more, General Haig had the experience of fighting a battle in the wrong place, since the Somme Valley was barren of major strategic objectives. The terrain was poorly watered, and the population was sparse. The toil of excavating dugouts in the chalk, which had begun early in the year, was immense.

The assault was launched on July 1 under the command of General Émile Fayolle and General Sir Henry Seymour Rawlinson

Map 8. BATTLE OF THE SOMME (July 1–Nov. 18, 1916).
In conformity with their over-all strategic plan for 1916
—and to relieve the pressure on Verdun—the Allies
launched an offensive astride the Somme River against
what were perhaps the strongest German defenses on
the Western Front. Immense preparations were made for
the attack, including a seven-day bombardment. The
British Fourth Army, making the main attack, advanced
in dense formations and suffered many casualties. The
Allies gained some territory but no particular strategic or
tactical advantage. The battle developed into an even
greater struggle of attrition than Verdun. The Germans
lost 650,000 men; the British, 420,000; and the French,
195,000. In this battle, the British introduced the tank to
the battlefield.

(later 1st Baron Rawlinson), who were opposed by General Fritz
von Below. Fayolle could muster only five divisions in the first line
astride the Somme, but he was much stronger than the British in
heavy artillery. His success was complete. The British 13th Corps
on the French left did equally well, but this was the end of suc-

cess. The British suffered overwhelming defeat and great casualties, the loss for that day amounting to 57,450. There was nothing Haig could do but confine the attack to the area on which ground had been won. He formed a new army, the Fifth, under Lieutenant General Sir Hubert de la Poer Gough, for a holding operation on the Ancre River. The Germans did likewise, putting General Max von Gallwitz in command of a new army south of the Somme.

The fortunes of the battle fluctuated in succeeding weeks. Haig had adopted the policy of attrition as completely as Joffre had, while General Ferdinand Foch, the army group commander, had never believed in the Battle of the Somme except as a means of relieving the pressure on Verdun. On August 29, Falkenhayn was dismissed by the Emperor. Hindenburg, his successor as chief of staff, came west with General Ludendorff.

On September 15, the British launched a general attack on a 10-mile front. For the first time they used 36 units of the weapon of the future, the tank, with considerable success. Haig has been criticized for disclosing the new weapon prematurely and thereby losing the element of surprise, but this verdict is of doubtful validity in view of the fact that he had available almost precisely the same number of tanks at Arras in the following spring. What is indisputable is the widespread impression that both Haig and Joffre wasted lives on the Somme. Joffre was regarded in France as being immersed so deeply in petty problems, harassed so greatly by the task of placating politicians, and at the same time presiding over what amounted to a ministry of war at Chantilly, as to be out of date. Premier Aristide Briand made every effort to save him by bringing in a new fighting subordinate and leaving Joffre in general control. It could not be done. The part played by the new man was honorable, but Nivelle was destined to the supreme command. In December, 1916, Joffre and Foch were both retired.

Meanwhile, the Battle of the Somme ended on November 18. The casualty figures, which have been much disputed, were as follows: German, 650,000; British, 420,000; and French, 195,000. In all, 95 German divisions (including those that entered the battle more than once), 55 British divisions, and 20 French divisions were engaged.

OPERATIONS IN 1917

The year 1917 opened with several promising peace proposals. First came that of President Woodrow Wilson. On December 18,

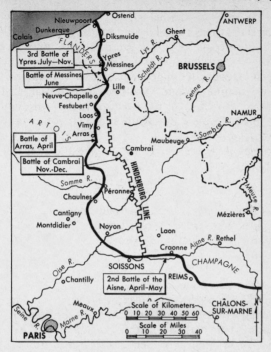

Map 9. ALLIED OFFENSIVES IN 1917. The principal Allied offensive of 1917 was to be a great French attack on the Aisne, preceded by a British attack in the Arras area to draw German reserves away from the river. The Germans, apprised of the plan, withdrew voluntarily to the Hindenburg Line. The French attack on the Aisne was repulsed with such enormous losses as to cause widespread mutiny in the French Army. Primarily to occupy the Germans while the shattered morale and confidence of the French were being rebuilt, the British launched successive offensives at Messines, Ypres, and Cambrai. These attacks made moderate gains and succeeded in preventing a German offensive against the disorganized and weakened French.

1916, he had addressed circular notes to the American diplomatic representatives accredited to the belligerent governments. These were not offers of mediation but requests for statements of terms; in fact, the governments of the Central Powers did not venture to disclose their terms, while those of the Allies sent Wilson wholly inacceptable terms that included the division of the Austro-Hungarian Empire. On January 22, 1917, Wilson addressed to the Senate a speech that called on the belligerents to accept "a peace without victory," and reached its apogee in its delineation of the American people as peacemakers. Only 10 weeks later, however, the President led the United States to war. This change of view was due to the German decision, announced on January 31, to reintroduce unrestricted submarine warfare. Another peace appeal, that of Pope Benedict XV, also failed, as did that of the new Austrian emperor, Charles I, made through the medium of his brother-in-law, Prince Sixte (Sixtus) of Bourbon.

The British people hoped that the aid of the United States would be instant and overwhelmingly strong, but the government and the fighting forces were well aware that this was impossible. The one powerful and immediate military aid that the United States could afford was naval. By June 5, thirty-four American destroyers were based on Queenstown (now Cobh), from which they joined in the antisubmarine warfare in the Atlantic.

The most important event of the year by far was the revolution in Russia. The Petrograd Soviet of Workers' and Soldiers' Deputies, formed on March 12, compelled Czar Nicholas II to abdicate. He was replaced by a provisional government in which Aleksandr Kerenski became Minister of War and, later, Prime Minister. Kerenski was determined to maintain the war against the Germans, Austrians, and Turks. He found General Aleksei Brusilov, the best of the Russian generals, ready to become commander in chief and confided to him all the most reliable troops, especially the Siberian. The offensive, which was launched on July 1, began with a heartening success, but the process of demoralization had gone too far, and the bulk of the troops were soon streaming homeward. The end came with the Bolshevik Revolution of November 6–7, and the accession of Lenin and Leon Trotsky to power. Armistice talks with the Central Powers opened at Brest-Litovsk (now Brest) on December 3. Russia had been driven from the war in the same year that the United States entered it, but Russia was armed and, unfortunately for the Allies, the United States was not.

Nivelle's Offensive

Meanwhile, Nivelle had put into operation plans differing vastly from Joffre's cautious program. His theory was that what could be and had been done on a small scale could be done on the greatest scale yet envisaged in the war. The chief component of his tactics was lightning speed, but his gunner's eye showed him exactly how

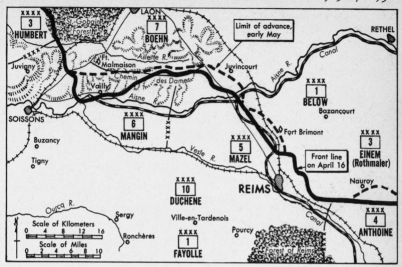

Map 10. SECOND BATTLE OF THE AISNE (April 16–May 9, 1917). In the area chosen by Gen. Robert Georges Nivelle for his great offensive, the French armies would have to attack across three steep ridges, including the formidable Chemin des Dames, cut by ravines covered by woods and heavy undergrowth. Since Nivelle had publicized his coming offensive the Germans had had ample time to convert these natural barriers into a veritable fortress. The offensive was poorly organized and fell into confusion from the start, and by nightfall of the first day it was evident that the attack was a failure. Nonetheless, Nivelle persisted in ordering successive futile and costly attacks. By early May, widespread mutiny had broken out in the French armies.

far he must go in the first rush after his colossal bombardment was over: the line of the enemy's field batteries. The second component was surprise. Such reserves as the enemy could bring into the breach were to be destroyed, after which the huge French reserve would push forward.

There must, however, be a single great diversionary attack, and this was allotted to the British. Through a secret agreement with the French government, made at Calais without the knowledge of his own commander in chief, the new Prime Minister, Lloyd George, had arranged to place Haig under Nivelle's orders. Nivelle interpreted this as making Haig no more than an adjutant and quartermaster general, looking after his troops and serving as an intermediary between the British government and the French commander. This arrangement was subsequently modified so that Haig retained absolute command of the British Army and had the right to appeal against French orders if he considered that they placed him in peril, but he remained suspicious.

Everything else that could possibly go wrong did so. The retreat of the Germans to the strong defensive position of the Hindenburg Line, which was completed by April, was disregarded by Nivelle, although it placed at their disposal large reserves. Carelessness that involved the German capture of two vital documents in trench raids revealed the exact boundaries of the attack between Reims and Soissons. The army group commander, General Joseph Alfred Micheler, who had been chosen by Nivelle because Pétain disapproved of the plan, finally disapproved of it just as heartily.

Nevertheless, the attack, in what became known as the Second Battle of the Aisne, began on a grand scale on April 16. The troops of Generals Mangin and Olivier C. A. A. Mazel dashed forward with gallantry and confidence, but German machine guns soon called at least a partial halt to the advance. This had been a commonplace in previous battles, but it was fatal to the new theories of Nivelle. Moreover, many of the 200 French tanks were destroyed. On the following day, Nivelle achieved a substantial success when the enemy was driven from the Fort Malmaison salient for a gain of two and one-half miles; and though this could be described as a voluntary withdrawal, it involved the loss of a great quantity of German artillery. Finally, however, the continuation of the offensive was postponed by the French cabinet until May, when it failed again. Meanwhile, on April 29, Pétain was appointed chief of the General Staff, and on May 15 he superseded Nivelle, being himself replaced by Foch, who came out of retirement to serve as chief of staff.

There has been much dispute about French losses in the offensive, Nivelle's bitterest opponents alleging that they were actually twice as large as the figures announced. The probability, however, is that they were not much higher than those listed in the French official history, or 96,000. The Germans lost 163,000 men. Their gains and the French losses were augmented by the destruction of French morale in widespread mutinies. The number of verdicts of guilty was 23,385, but only 55 men were shot. The French Army was out of action for a considerable time.

Battle of Arras

Haig began 1917 as a field marshal, secure in the confidence of George V, who wrote after the Calais conference: "The King begs you to dismiss from your mind any idea of resignation. Such a

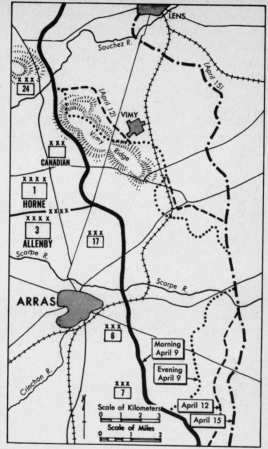

Map 11. BATTLE OF ARRAS (April 9–May 3, 1917). The German withdrawal to the Hindenburg Line had invalidated the Allied plan for their 1917 offensive; nevertheless, Gen. Robert Georges Nivelle, the French commander, persisted in going ahead with the attack on the Aisne. The plan provided for an initial British offensive at Arras to draw German reserves away from the Aisne. This offensive had great initial success, but was soon halted by stiffening resistance. The only important gain was the capture of Vimy Ridge by the Canadian Corps, which provided a firm northern anchor for the British in the first great German drive of 1918.

course would be, in His Majesty's opinion, disastrous to his Army and to the hopes of success in the coming struggle." The offensive to which he was pledged in support of Nivelle extended from approximately eight miles south of Arras to seven miles north of it, and was to be carried out by the Third Army of General Sir Edmund Allenby (later 1st Viscount Allenby) on the right and the First Army of General Sir Henry Sinclair Horne (later 1st Baron Horne) on the left. The whole of the German front was under the command of General Baron Ludwig von Falkenhausen. The initial attack was to be made by 14 divisions, but for the first time the British were not undergunned and had at their disposal 2,800 pieces. The Germans had six divisions in the line, but they also were in the novel situation of possessing abundant reserves—another six divisions.

The attack began successfully on April 9, in squally, snowy weather, even though the tanks were an almost complete failure, all of them being either ditched before they went into action or speedily maimed when they did so. The advance immediately north of the Scarpe River was the deepest made by any belligerent since trench warfare had frozen the Western Front. Here Lieutenant General Sir Charles Fergusson's corps breached the German third line, captured the village of Fampoux, and covered a distance of three and one-half miles. Horne's army prospered as greatly as Allenby's did, but the Canadian Corps of four divisions, which bore the main burden in the assault, had not far to go on the muddiest part of the front to the crest of Vimy Ridge. The ridge was not completely secured by nightfall, but little was left for the following day.

That day provided a rude shock. Allenby's simple telegraphed order overnight to pursue a beaten army was issued under a misapprehension. The army was indeed beaten, but there was another of equal strength in the rear. Falkenhausen had disobeyed orders so that he could keep his reserves out of range, and they were on the average 15 miles farther east than they ought to have been. Now they were ready to fight, while the original British divisions were exhausted. Nothing serious could be attempted until April 23, when in a two-day battle the British outfought the enemy but made small progress. The last phase of the battle was the single day of May 3, when Haig permitted the attack to proceed solely in the hope of aiding Nivelle to keep the French fighting. Intervention by Gough's Fifth Army on the right at Bullecourt led to the terrific slogging described in detail in Volume I of the present writer's official work, *Military Operations: France and Belgium, 1917.**

* (London, 1940.)

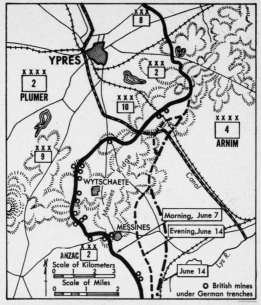

Map 12. BATTLE OF MESSINES (June 7–8, 1917). With the French armies almost prostrate on the Aisne, the main weight of the war fell on the British. At the same time, the collapse of Russia made it necessary to strike a vital blow on the Western Front before German strength could be transferred from the Eastern Front. The British chose the Ypres area, where a breakthrough would outflank the entire German defensive system; but first the Messines Ridge, which gave the Germans perfect observation over the British lines south of Ypres, had to be cleared. In a brilliant, well-planned, and perfectly executed operation (in which hundreds of tons of mines were placed under the German position) the ridge was quickly captured.

Battle of Messines

Haig now turned to Flanders and the operation that had been in his mind since February: the clearance of the Flemish coast, the only place where a flank could be found and rolled up. He was already under heavy pressure from Pétain to keep the Germans off the French, and from the British Admiralty to root out the submarines based on Brugge and making their sorties from Oostende (Ostend) and Zeebrugge. The first part of the program was the capture of the Messines (Mesen) Ridge, the steepest approach; after this had been accomplished, the main advance was to be made toward Rouselare (Roulers) and Thourout (now Torhout). The most remarkable feature of the battle was a great chain of mines, the earliest of which had been begun two years before, which had been driven into the bowels of the ridge, two of the galleries being 2,000 yards long. At zero hour, 3:10 A.M. on June 7, the mines were exploded with tremendous effect. The nine divisions of Plumer's Second Army swept through to the crest of the ridge. Crown Prince Rupert of Bavaria immediately ordered all troops to fall back behind the Ypres-Comines (Komen) Canal.

For the main battle, Haig had brought up Gough and the headquarters of the Fifth Army to divide the command with Plumer. Feeling that the moment was appropriate for displaying greater dash than was likely to come from this cautious veteran, he allotted the main role to Gough, though Plumer had not left the Ypres salient since he superseded Smith-Dorrien and knew it well. The result was a delay caused by the adaptation of Plumer's methods to Gough's, and this was accentuated by a slow concentration of the small, elite French First Army, commanded by Major General François Paul Anthoine.

Third Battle of Ypres

The interval since the assault on the Messines Ridge had been one of cloudless hot weather, and this continued on July 31, when the Third Battle of Ypres began. The attack did well and, even after Gough's left had been robbed of a considerable amount of ground by fierce and gallant counterattacks, retained a maximum advance of two miles. That evening the weather broke. The Battle of Langemarck (now Langemark) was fought on a dry day on August 16, but remission for a day or two no longer counted. The shell holes were filled to the brim with water. Every round of ammunition had to be carried over the final stage on pack saddles, and many mules and a considerable number of men were drowned. Haig had to reverse once more the roles of his two army commanders, and the sideslipping required for the purpose wasted still more time.

Plumer had determined to act with extreme deliberation, securing the Ypres Ridge with divisions closed down to 1,000-yard frontages, often with two of the three brigades in support and reserve, tremendous barrages, and very limited objectives, in three separate thrusts. The skilled and devoted work of the Royal Engineers in constructing plank roads and laying duckboards enabled him to

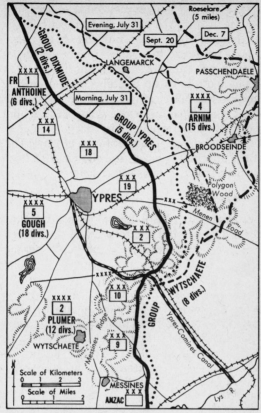

Map 13. THIRD BATTLE OF YPRES (also called Battle of Passchendaele; July 31–Nov. 6, 1917). With the Messines Ridge cleared, the British launched their Ypres attack. A 10-day preliminary bombardment churned up the sticky clay, thereby slowing the advance. Nevertheless, the first day's objectives were captured despite German counterattacks. Then a 14-day heavy rain bogged down guns and transportation. Tactical success was no longer possible, but, with the French armies demoralized, continued British pressure on the Germans was essential to prevent disaster. Plodding along in the mud and subjected to mustard gas, which was added to the horrors of the battlefield by the Germans, the British finally captured Passchendaele on November 6, and the battle ended.

assault in maximum strength, and he was also helped by miraculous good fortune. The first two battles, Menen (Menin) Road Ridge (September 20–25) and Polygon Wood (September 26–October 3), were actually fought in clouds of blinding dust, and though the rain had started again on October 3 before the third battle, Broodseinde, the ground was still in excellent condition. This time, however, it had to be taken for granted that the weather had broken for good, and it was now autumn.

The last phase of the battle (October 26–November 6) resulted in the name of the village of Passchendaele (now Passendale), which covers a single final incident, having been expanded in popular parlance to cover the whole Third Battle of Ypres. The losses associated with it also led to bitter criticism of Haig. The British loss for the entire battle was 240,000, and the German loss almost precisely the same; 37,000 prisoners were taken.

French Victories

Pétain was eager to contribute all he could, both to aid the British offensive and to test the recovery of the French Army and encourage its self-confidence. The first of these experiments was the victorious blow struck by General Marie Louis Adolphe Guillaumat and his Second Army on August 20 near Verdun. It was an invaluable effort, but the anxiety it created in German minds was brief, though Ludendorff for the next month or so expected the foe to try again. The second and more famous episode was delayed until the end of the main battle on October 23 and was carried out by the Tenth Army, commanded by General Paul André Marie Maistre. By November 1, the attack had recaptured Fort Malmaison and secured 12,000 prisoners.

Battle of Cambrai

As the year 1917 drew to its end, Haig realized that at most one more offensive would be possible before he and the French faced the full flood of the German divisions set free by the Russo-German armistice. By the end of October, he was doubtful whether even that much would be possible. Between October 24 and November 11, Austro-German forces won a brilliant victory over the Italians in the Battle of Caporetto (now Kobarid). The rout ended on the Piave River after 11 Franco-British divisions had been sent to Italy from the Western Front, but before they had been in action.

Meanwhile, Haig's problem was that he was still unsure of how many troops he would have to send to Italy (actually, the British contingent was reduced to five divisions, whereas the French sent the original quota of six). The anxiety was, however, mild by comparison with his satisfaction that tanks were at last to be used as

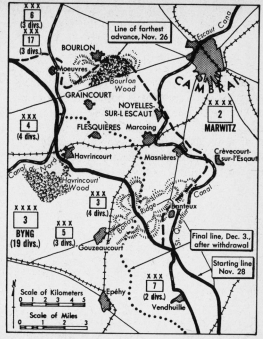

Map 14. BATTLE OF CAMBRAI (Nov. 20–Dec. 3, 1917). As a possible solution to the breaking of the stabilized front, the British launched a massed attack of almost 500 tanks at dawn on November 20. Cavalry followed closely to exploit the hoped-for breakthrough. The attack gained spectacular initial successes, but by nightfall the tanks and cavalry had become stalled along the difficult Saint-Quentin Canal. For the next few days bitter fighting took place in Bourlon Wood; by November 26, the advance had progressed only to the line shown. On November 30, an overwhelming German counterattack drove the British steadily back. By December 3, they had stabilized their lines, retaining some ground gained in the center, but losing an equal amount of their original holdings to the south. This first massed tank attack had failed, but it indicated great promise for the future.

their creators had foreseen, and that he could allot the Third Army of General Sir Julian H. G. Byng (later 1st Viscount Byng) 324 tanks, as against the 48 in action at Arras. Moreover, owing to new artillery methods, especially sound ranging and flash spotting, every German battery could be pinpointed, a preliminary bombardment could be dispensed with, and complete surprise could be achieved for the first time.

At 6:20 A.M. on November 20, the fire and the advance of the tanks began simultaneously. By evening the advance exceeded three miles, and it might have been far greater but for the one calamity of the battle at Flesquières, where a single German field battery knocked out tank after tank as they breasted the rise, while the supporting infantry could not force a way through the wire of the Hindenburg Line as long as it remained uncut. The battle now resolved itself into a fight for the height surmounted by Bourlon Wood, which was taken and retaken.

Ludendorff saw exactly what was required. He massed his reinforcements on the flanks of the bulge between Banteux and Moeuvres and directed General Georg von der Marwitz, commanding the Second Army, to eliminate it by convergent thrusts. Marwitz struck at 8:30 A.M. on November 30, after an all-night bombardment, and on the southern flank won a great victory. The German infantry had never fought with greater enthusiasm or tactical skill. Disdaining the heights that commanded the valleys, it made use of these to paralyze the defense. The attack not only smashed the British array on the new front, but captured the original position farther south on a frontage of three miles. The Guards Division recovered Gouzeaucourt, however, and brought the enemy's advance to a halt.

The same tactics were employed on the northern flank, but on more open ground with better observation they did not meet the demands of the situation. The guns were firing over open sights, shooting the successive waves to fragments, and when the accompanying batteries strove to unlimber, they laid out the horses so that the guns were thenceforth stationary. Prince Rupert and Marwitz called off the battle on the night of December 1. Between December 4 and 7, Haig had to yield a few more of his gains in order to obtain a defensible front based on the Hindenburg Line. His losses totaled 43,000 men, including 6,000 prisoners taken on the first day of the counteroffensive; the Germans lost 41,000 men, 11,000 of them prisoners. The British public, which had listened to the premature ringing of church bells, was bitterly disappointed by the reversal of fortunes and staggered by the loss of guns: 158, as contrasted with 138 taken from the Germans.

The most interesting feature of Cambrai was its significance for the future. The tactics and strategy of World War II were first developed in this battle, and the victories of 1918, beginning with the reduction of the Amiens salient on August 8–September 3, depended on it to an equal extent.

7. Western Front, 1918:
The Year of Decision

*BY BRIGADIER GENERAL VINCENT J. ESPOSITO,
U.S.A. (RET.)*

At the beginning of 1918 the Allied situation was critical. Though General Pétain had succeeded in quelling the mutinies that followed the disastrous attacks of General Nivelle on the Aisne River in April, 1917, French morale had not been completely restored. Three years of bitter offensive fighting had so depleted France's manpower that much of her infantry now consisted of men too young or too old to be the most effective fighters. The British personnel problem was also acute. Infantry units were composed mostly of replacements, but their morale was much better than that of the French, and they could be depended on to fight. Prime Minister David Lloyd George, however, fearing that Field Marshal Haig would repeat his costly and futile attacks of 1917, refused to send large reinforcements to the Continent. Haig was forced to reduce the battalions in his divisions from 12 to 9, thereby generating resentment among the officers and men whose units were disbanded.

The Italian disaster at Caporetto in October, 1917, had necessitated the dispatch of 11 precious Allied divisions to bolster the faltering Italians, who even by 1918 had not fully recovered. Russia and Romania had been knocked out of the war by the Germans, and American troops were slow in arriving. On March 1, 1918, nearly a year after she had entered the war, the United States had only six divisions in France; of these two lacked combat experience, and the other four had served only in quiet sectors. The only recourse for the Allies seemed to be to hold fast on the Western Front until American forces arrived in sufficient strength to launch a general offensive. The French and British accordingly took up a defense in depth over most of the front (similar to the defensive system developed by the Germans in 1917) and braced to meet the German onslaught, which was sure to come. Haig and Pétain agreed to assist each other promptly in case of attack, but there was no unity of command to guide the Allied effort forcibly. The Supreme War Council, with no troops under its control, could act only as an advisory body. A plan to form a 30-division general reserve under the council's control had been vitiated by Haig's contention that he could not spare any divisions and still retain responsibility for his front.

The general situation of the Germans was little better than that of the Allies. Although submarine warfare had greatly reduced Allied shipping, it had failed to starve Great Britain or to halt the flow of American troops across the Atlantic. Conversely, the Allied blockade, coupled with the inefficient use of the internal transportation system, was causing hunger and discontent among the German people. Germany's allies were faltering: Austria-Hungary, through popular pressure, refused to send troops to the Western Front, preferring to concentrate her forces against the Italians; Turkey's armies had been futilely expended in Mesopotamia and Palestine; and Bulgaria was war-weary. Nevertheless, the German manpower situation was more favorable than that of the French and British, for the collapse of Russia had released sizable German forces from the Eastern Front. Many of these divisions, having seen little fighting for almost a year, were fresh, and their troops were eager to fight.

General Ludendorff, through his string of victories, keen intellect, and strong personality, had by now overshadowed Emperor William II and the successive German chancellors, and the decision as to the next major German move was his to make. A victory was needed to bolster Germany's prestige among her allies; moreover, the Americans were arriving in increasing numbers and would make their strength felt by summer. Ludendorff concluded that decisive action was mandatory on the Western Front in the spring of 1918, and plans were prepared accordingly. Troop transfers from the Eastern Front gave him a 10 per cent advantage in combat personnel in the west, but he lacked reserve strength, since the reservoir of German youth had been almost drained by heavy demands in previous years. This deficiency made it imperative that the initial attack be decisive, for if its impetus were retarded, there would be little left to engage. Ludendorff, however, was confident of the effectiveness of his numerical superiority and of the success of new German offensive tactics.

Three areas were considered for the offensive: Verdun, Flanders, and the Somme. The Verdun area was rejected because of the difficult terrain and the lack of a major strategic objective. The Flanders area was the best, for a breakthrough there would lead to the Channel ports, which were vital to the British on the Continent, but the wet ground in the area precluded an attack before April. While there was no critical terrain feature in the Somme area, a breakthrough to the sea would separate the French and the British and would crowd the latter into a pocket in which they might later be destroyed. Thus the Somme area was chosen of necessity. Since it had been devastated in the 1916 battles, the speed of the German advance would be reduced; on the other hand, it was the most lightly held sector of the three considered. Ludendorff selected the British as his primary target because he believed that the defeat of Britain would bring a favorable peace. Moreover, he considered the French troops the more skillful (if less tenacious) in defensive operations, and the expert French artillery was much to be feared. His staff had urged two limited offensives at different points to throw the Allies off balance, but Ludendorff, experienced only in successful single crushing offensives on the Eastern Front, decided that he had enough troops and guns for only one major offensive. In order to deceive the Allies and facilitate other attacks if these should be found desirable, preliminary preparations, such as the stockpiling of ammunition, were begun at two places in Flanders: opposite the Ypres salient and to the south of it. In addition, simulated preparatory bombardments were planned at other places along the front.

German Drives of 1918

Though surprise was an essential element in the German scheme, Haig had developed a fair estimate of Ludendorff's plan. Pétain, however, had concluded that the attack would come in his sector, in the Reims area. The British and the French each attempted to organize a deep defensive zone, but because of manpower shortages and the negligence of subordinate leaders, neither zone was completed in time.

Ludendorff expected to break the deadlock on the Western Front by the large-scale application of the new Hutier tactics, which had been developed by General Oskar von Hutier and his staff at Riga and had been tested successfully at Caporetto. These tactics made radical changes in the employment of artillery and infantry. Instead of a lengthy bombardment designed to obliterate the defenses within a limited zone, such as the 19-day shelling in

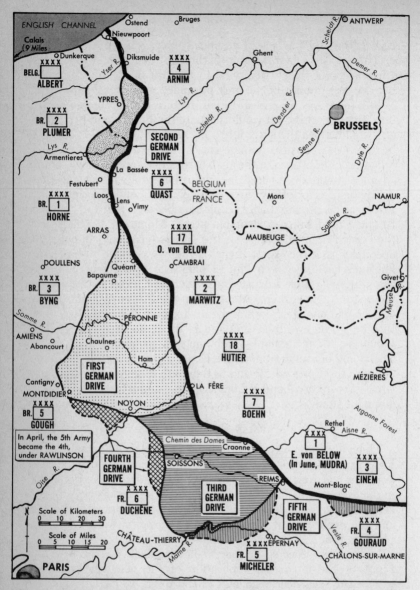

Map 15. GERMAN DRIVES OF 1918 (March 21–July 17, 1918). Russia's collapse enabled the Germans to gain numerical superiority on the Western Front. It was decided to make a supreme effort to defeat the French and British before the Americans could arrive in sufficient numbers to intervene effectively. Five separate drives were made: in March, April, May, June, and July. Two—the first and third—won spectacular tactical success, but they did not achieve a breakthrough to split the Allies and gain a strategic victory. These tremendous but unsuccessful efforts cost the Germans 800,000 casualties and seriously depressed the morale of the German troops. Exhausted, the Germans were forced to surrender the initiative to the Allies.

the Third Battle of Ypres in 1917, only a short preparation was fired. It included a high proportion of gas and smoke shells and was designed to put out of action for a short period the enemy gun positions, headquarters, machine guns, observation posts, and trenches. After this preliminary bombardment, the artillery began to fire a rolling barrage that started on the enemy front line and moved forward at a predetermined rate. The rate varied with the terrain and the opposition expected, but was usually one kilometer per hour. The infantry followed the rolling barrage as closely as possible. The advance of each unit was planned in great detail by higher headquarters so as to infiltrate between known hostile centers of resistance. When the barrage reached the limit of its range, full control of the various units reverted to the regimental and battalion commanders, and the troops advanced as fast and as far as possible in a given general direction, no objectives being specified. When strong resistance was met, leading units bypassed it and moved speedily ahead, disregarding the security of their flanks and leaving the reduction of resistance to follow-up units. Each assault battalion had its own light artillery; infantry troops were formed into small battle groups, each of which was built around the light machine gun (formerly the bulwark of defense but now considered by the Germans the principal infantry weapon in the attack).

The new tactics demanded exceptional standards of training and physical fitness, especially on the part of the infantry. The operations at Riga and Caporetto had been conducted on a moderate scale against enemies of low morale; the contemplated Somme operations were to be on a gigantic scale and would require dozens of highly effective shock divisions. These were pulled out of the line early, filled with selected men at the expense of the other divisions, and extensively trained. Since the Germans had few tanks, this weapon was to play little part in the attack, but special air units were formed to provide low-level bombing and strafing in support of the ground attack.

First German Drive (Somme Offensive), March 21–April 4

The plan for the Somme offensive was simple. Three German armies were to break the British front from Arras to La Fère: the Seventeenth Army, under General Otto von Below, in the north; the Second Army, under General Georg von der Marwitz, in the center; and the Eighteenth Army, under Hutier, in the south. The Second and Seventeenth armies belonged to the army group commanded by Crown Prince Rupert of Bavaria; the Eighteenth Army, to that of German Crown Prince William. Ludendorff engaged these units of two army groups so that he could exert greater overall control and ensure that the resources of both groups would be used to the maximum extent. Initially, the three armies were to advance straight ahead on their respective fronts: the Seventeenth to Bapaume, then northward toward Arras; the Second to Péronne, then northwestward to Doullens; and the Eighteenth to the Somme River, where it would protect the south flank of the general offensive against probable French counterattacks. The ultimate object of the attacks was to separate the British from the French and drive them to the sea.

Haig was expecting a strong attack on the front of his Fifth Army, commanded by Lieutenant General Gough, late in March. Gough's 15 divisions were deployed sparsely to cover a 41-mile front. The southern 14 miles of his front had recently been transferred by the French through political machinations. Not only was his army overextended, but the area turned over by the French had been organized for defense in a manner different from the British system and was not suited to British defensive tactics. The British Third Army, consisting of 14 divisions and commanded by General Byng, held the northern sector. These 29 British divisions on the line had the task of stemming the assaults of 71 German divisions —Below, 25; Marwitz, 21; and Hutier, 25. In addition, the German divisions individually were stronger than those of the British. While Haig had expected the German attack, he and the other Allied commanders were completely surprised by its power, ferocity, and tactics.

At 4:40 A.M. on March 21, German artillery (6,000 cannons and 3,000 mortars) began a five-and-one-half-hour bombardment with gas, smoke, and high-explosive shells. At 9:40 A.M., 32 German divisions, followed closely by 28 additional divisions, began the attack in a dense fog. This fog did not hamper the German artillery, which was firing by map, but it affected British defensive fires, especially those of the infantry. During the first day, the British front was shattered throughout the zone of attack. By the evening of the second day (March 22), the entire Fifth Army had been forced from its battle position; on the following day, Gough ordered it to retire behind the Somme. Byng's Third Army had lost part of its front line, but since it was defending a deep zone, it was able to hold the German Seventeenth and Second armies to moderate gains. Ludendorff had expected these two armies to make rapid progress while Hutier's Eighteenth Army guarded their south flank. Now he changed his plan to capitalize on Hutier's unexpected success. His armies were directed to drive along both banks of the Somme to the sea, fanning out north and south to strike both the French and the British. He reasoned correctly that the primary concern of the French would be the defense of Paris and that of the British the safety of the Channel ports, and that these divergent interests would prevent cooperation between the Allied forces.

On March 23 and 24, the German advance continued with great speed, particularly in the Fifth Army sector. Gough's rapid retreat exposed the south flank of Byng's Third Army, but the gap was soon filled by British cavalry. By March 26, Amiens, the major link between the British and the French, was in peril. These successes caused Ludendorff to expand his plan again by driving northward, first striking Arras; 20 German divisions were thrown toward the town, using the new tactics that had created the initial breakthrough. A number of divisions had to be employed that were not well trained in these tactics, however, and this time there were no fog and no surprise. Byng's army now included some of the best British units, and it was posed in an excellent position. The German attack toward Arras was completely repulsed without denting the British line.

Meanwhile, Hutier continued his advance south of the Somme, while French units arrived in driblets to help Gough, who was fighting a good delaying action. On March 25, General Émile Fayolle assumed command of the mixed French and British units south of the river. By this time, six French divisions had arrived, but as Hutier advanced, they tended to fall back to the southwest as if to cover Paris. And this might well have been Pétain's reason for sending even this weak assistance, for he still was convinced that the Germans were about to attack his front between Soissons and Reims and kept most of his reserves disposed to meet such an offensive. On March 27, Hutier captured Montdidier, but his divisions were becoming exhausted, and supplies were not reaching the troops. In the center, Marwitz drove toward Amiens, but he was met near Abancourt by a hastily improvised force of rear-area service troops (which included two companies of American engineers) designated as Carey's Force after its commander, Brigadier General George Glas Sandeman Carey. For three days (March 28–30), the Germans repeatedly assaulted the old trenches in which Carey had posted his modest force, but to no avail. Ludendorff made two other futile attacks—one on March 30, between Montdidier and Noyon; and the second on April 4, near Albert—and then stopped the offensive.

The first German drive was a brilliant tactical success, having achieved an advance of about 40 miles in eight days. The Germans captured 70,000 prisoners and 1,100 guns and inflicted nearly 200,000 casualties. In a strategic sense, however, the drive was a failure. The British armies had not been destroyed or separated from the French. German manpower losses approximately equaled those of the Allies, but most of their losses had been sustained by the highly trained shock divisions. Moreover, the losses could not be replaced, whereas American troops were arriving at an accelerated pace to join the Allies on the Western Front.

Allied Unity of Command

One important result of the first German drive was that it forced the Allies to adopt a system of unified command. The Italian disaster at Caporetto had made it clear that better coordination of the Allied effort was essential, and the Supreme War Council had been formed in November, 1917. Lloyd George and Premier Georges Clemenceau wished to give the council control of a general reserve of 30 divisions, but Haig, contending that he could not spare his quota, devised with Pétain an arrangement for mutual assistance if necessary. "I can deal with a man but not with a committee," said Haig. The arrangement failed in the acid test of the first German drive. As the Germans pressed forward, Haig called on Pétain for help; Pétain agreed to send a few divisions. Haig wanted more, but the French commander refused because he expected a German attack near Reims. Furthermore, he announced that, in the event of a retreat, his troops would withdraw to the southwest to cover Paris. This decision alarmed Haig, for such a move would create a large gap between the French and British forces that would invite disaster. He reported to the British Secretary of State for War, Viscount Milner, that the Allies would be defeated unless "Foch or some other determined general who would fight" was placed in supreme command of the Allied forces in France.

On March 26, the Allied leaders assembled at Doullens. Clemenceau suggested that General Ferdinand Foch be "charged with the coordination of the action of the British and French armies in front of Amiens." Haig and Pétain called attention to the inadequacies of such an arrangement and urged that Foch be given authority over all the British and French operations on the Western Front. This course was finally approved as an emergency measure during the crisis; on April 3, Foch was given authority over the American forces as well, and, on April 14, he was formally made commander in chief of all the Allied armies in France. Foch thereafter led the Allies to victory, but not so much by legal authority as by military acumen, determination, and force of personality.

Second German Drive (Lys Offensive), April 9–29

Though his first drive had failed, Ludendorff hoped that one more blow would shatter the BEF. The Germans still had reserves that could be used in an attack, and preparations had been made for one near Ypres as a deceptive measure to cover planning for the first drive. These preparations and an excellent rail network would permit a rapid regroupment and an attack in Flanders, although it could not be made on the scale of the Somme offensive. General Sixt von Arnim's Fourth Army was to attack north of Armentières and General Ferdinand von Quast's Sixth Army south of the town. Only 35 divisions were available for the two attacks, and they were much inferior to those employed in March. There were no cratered fields in the zone to hinder an advance, but the country was cut up by hedges, canals, dikes, and small streams, which would facilitate a British delaying action.

At 8:45 A.M. on April 9, after an intensive bombardment consisting largely of gas shells, eight divisions of the German Sixth Army struck south of Armentières, where three divisions of the British First Army of General Henry Sinclair Horne held the front. The center division was a Portuguese unit that was occupying not only its own sector but also that of another division, pending relief by two British divisions on April 10. The German blow sent the overextended Portuguese fleeing to the rear and crushed the British division on their left. Within three hours, Quast's troops had passed through the entire trench system and were in the open, and by day's end they had advanced five miles. The next day, Arnim's Fourth Army attacked north of Armentières, concentrating four divisions against a single British division sector on the front of the British Second Army, commanded by General Sir Herbert Plumer. This attack succeeded largely because British reserves had been drawn southward by Quast's attack of the previous day. On April 11, the two German armies joined forces and advanced westward.

By the morning of April 12, the BEF was in extreme danger, and preparations were made for evacuating Calais and for flooding the countryside. Meanwhile, Haig rushed all the reinforcements he could find to the scene and pleaded with Foch for more. The supreme commander had been trying to scrape together reserves for a major Allied counterattack. Since the First Battle of Ypres, Foch had admired and developed great confidence in the British soldier's tenacity on the defensive. Despite Haig's angry protests, he therefore sent only relatively small forces. His faith in the British soldier was vindicated, for in some of the most heroic fighting of the war the British, with the help of such French troops as Foch sent, stopped the German offensive.

Ludendorff had again achieved a brilliant tactical success and a strategic failure. The drive had cost him 350,000 men to acquire a vulnerable salient; the British lost 305,000 men. The German commander now scraped the Eastern Front for men, while American reinforcements more than compensated for the Allied losses.

Third German Drive (Aisne Offensive), May 27–June 6

Ludendorff believed that the British were overstrained, and that one additional heavy blow would defeat them. Accordingly, preparations were made for two new attacks in Flanders. Appreciating the fact that the French and British reserves then in that area could probably stop the attacks of his depleted forces, however, he decided to make a thrust elsewhere to draw the reserves away before launching the two attacks. The area selected for the diversionary attack was the Chemin des Dames, a highway along the Aisne between Soissons and Reims. This was precisely the area in which Pétain had feared an attack in March. None having come, it was presumed that the Germans considered the position impregnable, and the garrison had been severely reduced. Since Foch considered the junction between the French and the British in the Amiens area the critical point in the Allied line, most of his reserves were posted there. Knowing that the Allies were alert for another attack, the Germans prepared the Aisne offensive with the greatest secrecy. Two weeks before the actual attack, the American intelligence service had predicted its location, but the prediction was ignored by Foch and Pétain. On May 26, definite information was obtained from two German prisoners that the attack would take place on the following day. It was then too late to do more than alert the Allied front-line units. Although eight Allied divisions were started down from the north, they could not arrive in time.

On the morning of May 27, two German armies—General von Below's First Army and Colonel General Max von Boehn's Seventh Army—attacked with 17 divisions in the line and 13 in the rear. Approximately 4,600 guns supported the offensive. General Denis Auguste Duchêne, who was in charge of this sector of the Allied front, had been loath to relinquish the high ground of the Chemin des Dames in the front of his position. To ensure its retention, he had placed most of his infantry in the forward defenses, thereby abandoning a defense in depth. The German attack broke through his defenses and by night had raced 13 miles to Fismes, across the Vesle River. Ludendorff had planned to stop there and begin his offensive in Flanders, but his troops were moving rapidly against little resistance, and he could not withstand the temptation to let the attack run its course. Three days later, the Germans were on the Marne at Château-Thierry, within 37 miles of Paris.

Pétain now asked General (later General of the Armies) John J. Pershing for an American division to hold the Marne crossings. Pershing had been firm in his intention of engaging American troops as a separate army, but the situation was critical, and he assigned the American 3d Division to the task. The division had never been in action and was then 110 miles away in a training area. A hurried movement by rail and motor brought it to Château-Thierry on June 1. For the next three days the Germans strove to cross the Marne, but the Americans threw them back repeatedly and kept them on the north bank of the river. Meanwhile, other German forces advanced west of Château-Thierry on the road to Paris. The American 2d Division was thrown across the road and in bitter hand-to-hand fighting stopped the foe. Ludendorff now halted the German offensive. It was his greatest tactical success on the Western Front, but its net result was to leave the Germans in a salient more unfavorable than the two formed in the previous drives.

On May 28, the second day of the German Aisne offensive, an operation took place that was important not so much for its military impact as for its psychological effect. It was the capture of the village of Cantigny by the American 1st Division, the first offensive operation undertaken by an American division in the war. Cantigny stood on high ground, a factor that gave the Germans good observation over the Allied lines and concealed their own rear-area activities. The offensive was a success in every way. To the Germans, who had been scornful of American fighting ability, this success brought great discouragement, but to the formerly skeptical

British and French this display of the fighting potential of American troops was a great encouragement.

Fourth German Drive (Noyon–Montdidier Offensive), June 9–13

After his third drive, Ludendorff found himself in a dilemma. His advance had created a salient that was extremely vulnerable to Allied counterattack. The proper course was to withdraw to a safer military position, but such a move would adversely affect the morale of the German troops and the home front and, simultaneously, would bring joy to the Allied countries. Yet if he did not withdraw from the salient, he would not have enough troops for his Flanders offensive, for which the third drive had been undertaken as a diversionary operation. It was imperative that he not surrender the initiative to the Allies; therefore, he decided on a smaller two-pronged offensive. One thrust would drive southward from the Noyon–Montdidier sector; the other, westward from Soissons. Ludendorff's purpose was to extend the front forward between the Amiens and Aisne salients in order to facilitate supply operations and to threaten Paris. Again he hoped that the threat to Paris would draw reserves from Flanders so that he could undertake his ultimate object: the destruction of the British in that area. On June 9, Hutier's Eighteenth Army attacked from the Noyon–Montdidier sector and Boehn's Seventh Army from Soissons. This time there was no surprise, and the French under Fayolle were well prepared. They had adopted a deep-zone defense against which the German offensive gradually wore itself out. After a tortuous advance of nine miles, the Germans were stopped by French counterattacks. Fighting ceased on June 13. For unimportant gains the Germans had suffered heavy losses, while French losses were light.

Fifth German Drive (Champagne–Marne Offensive), July 15–17

A month of comparative quiet followed the fourth drive. Many German leaders favored making peace overtures, but Ludendorff was resolute. Nonetheless, German troops had shown signs of slackening discipline during the rigors of the Lys offensive. Now, poorly fed and in a weakened condition, they were easy prey for the worldwide influenza epidemic that struck in June. Between 1,000 and 2,000 men in each division had developed the disease. Allied propaganda leaflets, designed to alienate the troops and the people from their leaders, were sent across the lines by balloons. United States troops were arriving in such numbers that, for the first time in 1918, Allied infantry strength on the Western Front exceeded that of the Germans. Foch was busy assembling forces and preparing for his counteroffensive.

Despite the unfavorable situation, Ludendorff strove to retain the initiative and to gain final victory by two great attacks. One was to capture Reims; the other, on a much larger scale, was to take place 10 days later in Flanders (this was his final plan to destroy the BEF, which was never to be carried out). In the Reims offensive, Boehn's Seventh Army was to attack southeastward from the Marne salient toward Épernay; General Bruno von Mudra's First Army was to attack southward to capture Châlons-sur-Marne; and, to the east, Colonel General Karl von Einem's Third Army was to attack to cover the flank of the First Army. In this stroke, 52 German divisions were to be employed; 36 Allied divisions confronted them—23 French, 9 American, 2 British, and 2 Italian.

Through aerial photography and German deserters (the last drives had been signaled by a marked increase in the number of German deserters on the eves of the offensives), Foch learned of the German plans in detail and took proper countermeasures. He anticipated the German preliminary bombardment with one of his own, which caught the Germans in close formations and inflicted severe losses. The Seventh Army attack toward Épernay was frustrated; that of the First Army gained initial successes, but was finally stopped by a heroic Allied defense. The psychological impact of this setback on the German troops was great. Ludendorff had designed the operations as a diversion to draw Allied reserves from Flanders, but the German troops had called it *Friedensturm* (peace offensive) and had expected it to produce decisive results. This was the last offensive Ludendorff could launch, for Foch had now gained the initiative. During the five drives the Germans lost more than 800,000 men.

REDUCTION OF THE GERMAN SALIENTS
*Aisne–Marne Offensive, July 18–August 6**

As early as May 20, Foch had planned a counteroffensive to seize the initiative from Germany. His opportunity came with the failure of the fifth German drive. In preparation for a general offensive, he planned to reduce the three prominent German salients

---

* This offensive and the Champagne–Marne offensive of July 15–17 together are often referred to as the Second Battle of the Marne.

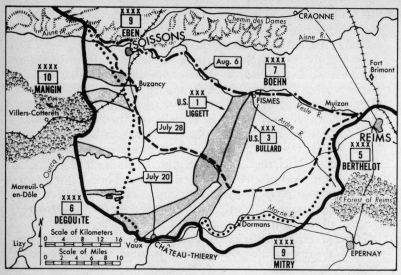

Map 16. REDUCTION OF THE MARNE SALIENT (Aisne-Marne offensive; July 18–Aug. 6, 1918). Gen. (later Marshal) Ferdinand Foch planned to launch a general offensive as soon as the German drives had spent themselves. First, however, it was necessary to reduce several salients, occupied by the Germans, which restricted Allied lateral communications along the front. The Marne salient, created during the third German drive, was attacked by Allied forces, predominately French, from three sides in July. In a brilliant operation the Allies forced the Germans back to the Vesle and Aisne rivers, thus straightening the front.

so as to improve lateral railway communications along the Allied front and facilitate future operations. The three savients were the Marne salient, created during the third German drive; the Amiens salient, formed during the first German drive; and the Saint-Mihiel salient, formed in the autumn of 1914 and relatively quiet ever since. Foch's first objective was the Marne salient, although it was difficult to assemble promptly the means for an offensive there. Haig was called on to provide some of his reserves and responded generously despite the objections of the British cabinet, which was fearful of reducing British strength in Flanders to a dangerous level.

Foch's plan was to attack the Marne salient from all sides. Four French armies were to engage in the offensive; in counterclockwise order these were General Charles Mangin's Tenth and General Jean M. J. Degoutte's Sixth armies, in the western half of the salient; and General Marie Antoine Henry de Mitry's Ninth and General Henri M. Berthelot's Fifth armies, in the eastern half. Included in these armies were 8 American, 4 British, and 2 Italian divisions. Mangin was to make the main assault. Early on July 18, he struck with 20 divisions (including 2 American and 2 British) and 350 tanks. An hour later, Degoutte joined the attack on Mangin's south flank, and by nightfall the Tenth and Sixth armies had advanced from two to five miles. (This was the greatest and most successful use of tanks by the French during the war.) On July 19, Mangin continued to advance toward Soissons and the Soissons–Château-Thierry road, the vital artery of the German salient, although more difficult terrain and mechanical failures were beginning to render the tanks less effective. Modest gains were made by other French armies on this day.

Alarmed by Mangin's threat against the key communications center of Soissons, the Germans decided to withdraw from the Marne salient. The withdrawal was conducted skillfully and in good order. The Germans delayed at successive positions, defending each resolutely while evacuating supplies and equipment to the rear, until the pressure of the Allied attacks compelled them to retreat. By August 3, they had withdrawn to a strong position at the base of the salient behind the Vesle and Aisne rivers, where they held fast. On the morning of August 6, two American divisions attacked this position. Minor gains were scored, but it was not broken. The Marne salient had been eliminated; the French had gained a glorious victory, but they did not forget to express their gratitude for the help of their British and American allies. This, the first significant Allied success of the year, brought relief in the Allied homelands; Paris was jubilant. On August 6, Foch received his baton as a marshal of France.

The largest American contingent thus far had participated in the operation. For the first time, American divisions were formed into corps. Near the end of the battle the American 1st and 3d corps held the entire front of the French Sixth Army. American divisions had been used as spearheads in the offensive and had performed in a manner to gain praise from their allies. A total of eight American divisions had been engaged in the offensive, but the number does not indicate the true magnitude of American participation. Each division, comprising 28,000 men, had twice the infantry strength of a British, French, or German division. The organization of the American division has been criticized by many (including Americans), but its huge size did give it integral power for sustained operations, thereby necessitating fewer shifts of divisions between front and rear—a distinct advantage in the warfare of the times in France.

German losses in the Aisne–Marne offensive were heavy but not ruinous. What was more important, the initiative had now passed to the Allies, where it would remain until the end of the war. Ludendorff's cherished Flanders offensive had become a dream, and it was clear that his hope of crushing the Allies before the United States could put a large force in the field would not be realized.

Reduction of the Amiens Salient, August 8–September 3

In mid-July, plans were developed for operations against the Germans in the Amiens salient, and preparations were begun. The main attack was to be made almost directly eastward from Amiens by the British Fourth Army of General Sir Henry Seymour Rawlinson; assisted on the right by General Marie Eugène Debeney's French First Army. General Georges Louis Humbert's French Third Army was to exert pressure against the southern face of the salient. Rawlinson amassed on a 10-mile front a powerful striking force: 17 infantry divisions (including 1 American division and two of the best fighting corps on the Western Front—the Canadian Corps of 4 divisions and the Australian Corps of 5 divisions); 3 cavalry divisions; about 600 tanks, the majority of which were a new and much-improved type; 2,000 guns; and 800 fighter and bomber aircraft. Debeney had 10 divisions but few tanks; he was to be supported by 1,100 aircraft. To oppose this avalanche the Germans had two armies—Marwitz's Second and Hutier's Eighteenth—totaling 20 divisions, mostly of dubious quality, supported by few tanks and less than 400 aircraft.

Because of the disparity in numbers of tanks, the attacks of the British Fourth and the French First armies were to differ. Rawlinson was to use the tactics that had proved so successful at Cambrai in November, 1917. There, the tanks, followed by the infantry, had advanced under the cover of a rolling barrage. Since surprise was essential in this type of attack, no artillery preparation was to be used. Debeney, lacking tanks, had to attack conventionally. His offensive was to be delayed about an hour in order to allow for artillery preparation and yet not jeopardize the surprise of the British attack.

At 4:20 A.M. on August 8, the British Fourth Army struck in a helpful mist, and Debeney joined in the attack at the appointed time. Although Ludendorff had taken special precautions to

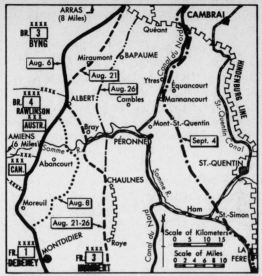

**Map 17. REDUCTION OF THE AMIENS SALIENT (Aug. 8–
Sept. 3, 1918).** The Amiens salient was created during the
first German drive. In August, Allied forces, predominately
British, strongly supported by tanks, forced the Germans
to give way and drove them back to the Hindenburg
Line, from which they had started their first drive in
March.

strengthen this important part of the front, it now collapsed. The
German infantry could not stand up against the British tanks, and
six divisions, considered battleworthy by Ludendorff, gave way at
once. It was not the effectiveness of fire from the tanks that demoralized the Germans (this was wobbly and erratic), but the
inexorable advance of the steel monsters against infantrymen who
had no defense against them. (Advancing against artillery fire,
tanks usually suffered about 25 per cent casualties a day in an
attack.) Within two hours, the British had taken 16,000 prisoners
and 200 guns; by noon, tanks and armored cars, as well as cavalry,
were nine miles to the rear of the German lines. Debeney's advance
had not been as spectacular as that of the British, but it progressed
successfully. This great Allied victory caused Ludendorff to call
August 8, 1918, the "black day" of the German Army, since for the
first time entire units collapsed. Retreating troops called out to
reinforcements marching toward the front: "You're prolonging the
war."

By August 10, the Canadian and Australian corps and the Cavalry Corps had advanced 12 miles and were close to the strong German Roye–Chaulnes position. The French First Army was rapidly catching up, and Humbert's Third Army was successfully driving northward. Foch urged Haig to exploit these successes and drive straight east to the Somme, but Haig insisted that the Roye–Chaulnes position was too strong to be broken without extensive preparations, including the moving up of heavy artillery. Instead, he wanted to suspend the attack and to open a new one with Byng's Third Army on the north flank of Rawlinson's Fourth Army. Foch finally agreed to this plan, and Haig shifted his reserves to the north for the new drive, which was to be opened on August 21. The Germans conducted a zone defense before Byng's attack, falling back three miles to their main position. From there they counterattacked on August 22. The crafty Haig had foreseen this maneuver, however, and had engaged only part of his force on the first day. Hence he was able to beat off the counterattack and maintain his momentum. On August 23, he ordered a general advance along a 30-mile front. The increasing pressure in the north caused the Germans to evacuate the Roye–Chaulnes position, as Haig had predicted. In brilliant operations, the Australians captured the dominating heights of Mont-Saint-Quentin on August 30–31, and two days later the Canadians broke the elaborate German switch position east of Arras. The Germans then withdrew to the Hindenburg Line, whence they had started their first drive five months earlier. The Amiens salient had been wiped out.

The mounting German disasters brought on during August a crown council, at which governmental and military leaders discussed their future actions. Ludendorff offered his resignation, but it was refused. The decision was made to fall back fighting and to maintain a foothold in France as long as possible. Peace negotiations were to be opened through the mediation of neutrals, but, as it turned out, little was done for some time.

Saint-Mihiel Offensive, September 12–16

By early July, 25 United States divisions were in France; of these, 12 were trained and had engaged in or were ready for combat. On July 24, General Pershing ordered the formation of Headquarters, United States First Army, with himself as commander, to be effective on August 10. It had been planned to have this headquarters assume control of the American 1st and 3d corps, then engaged on the Vesle. When the situation was stabilized there, Pershing ob-

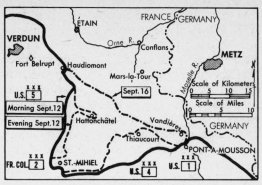

Map 18. REDUCTION OF THE ST.-MIHIEL SALIENT (St.-Mihiel offensive; Sept. 12–16, 1918). The St.-Mihiel salient was created during the initial German offensive in 1914 and had been practically dormant ever since. The task of reducing the salient was given to the United States First Army (with one French corps attached) as its first operation as an independent army. Appreciating their vulnerability in this exposed salient, the Germans had begun to evacuate heavy equipment and materials before the attack was launched. German resistance to the American attack was not determined, and the salient was reduced in four days.

tained Foch's permission to take over the Saint-Mihiel sector instead, leaving three or four divisions on the Vesle under French command.

The Saint-Mihiel salient hampered rail communications between Paris and Lorraine, and its reduction was necessary before Foch's final offensive could be undertaken. In addition, it was important to the Germans, since it covered Metz and the Briey iron mines; for these reasons, this naturally strong position had been carefully fortified. The severe fighting earlier in 1918 had made great inroads in the Germans' manpower, however, and had forced them to economize wherever possible. To further this purpose a step-by-step withdrawal from the Saint-Mihiel salient had already been ordered, and the removal of heavy materials and some relatively immobile artillery pieces had begun on September 11, the day before the American attack.

By the end of August, Pershing had nearly completed his plans and preparations for the Saint-Mihiel offensive. Now Foch, elated by the success of the Aisne–Marne and Amiens offensives, planned to reduce the scope of the Saint-Mihiel offensive and to divide the American forces into three groups to operate in different areas. A heated controversy ensued between Foch and Pershing. The latter saw the advantage of pressing the enemy and of giving him no respite, as Foch proposed; but he saw no valid reason for splitting his own forces. When Foch insisted, Pershing remained adamant, replying, "While our army will fight wherever you may decide, it will not fight except as an independent American army." Finally, a compromise was reached: the U.S. First Army would remain intact, the ob'ective of the Saint-Mihiel attack would be limited to capturing the base of the salient, and the First Army would then take over the Meuse–Argonne sector as its major role in the final offensive.

The plan for the Saint-Mihiel offensive provided for attacks by three American corps (1st, 4th, and 5th) on the flanks of the salient, while the French 2d Colonial Corps drove against its nose. As an army, the U.S. First Army was decidedly unbalanced. During the dark days of the early German drives, the British and French had pleaded for American infantry and machine-gun units to fill their most pressing needs. Priority had accordingly been given to the shipment overseas of these types of units. Now the First Army found that it was dependent on the British and the French for heavy support. This was cordially given: Most of the 3,000 guns to support the attack were provided by the French; the 267 light tanks to be employed also were French, some being manned by French crews and some by American; and the air force of 609 American planes was increased to nearly 1,500 by the attachment of French, British, Italian, and Portuguese units.

The battle opened at 1 A.M. on September 12 with an intensive artillery preparation, and at 5 A.M. the infantry jumped off. Resistance was generally light, and by day's end most of the American units had reached their second-day objectives. By evening of September 13, all objectives had been taken, and the salient had been reduced. A much greater advance could probably have been made, but since Pershing was committed to the impending Meuse–Argonne operations, the Saint-Mihiel attacks had to be halted. French units began relieving the American divisions so that the latter could be moved immediately to the Meuse–Argonne area.

The Saint-Mihiel operation was a well-executed limited offensive. It was not a hard fight, but American commanders and their staffs there displayed their competence to handle a large operation, as American troops had proved their fighting qualities in the Aisne–Marne offensive.

Foch's Plan

Since June, Foch had been contemplating a general offensive in September, but he apparently did not believe that such an offensive would be decisive at that time, for he continued to urge the British and the Americans to strengthen their forces for a decisive effort in 1919. Nevertheless, the Aisne–Marne and Amiens victories had clearly demonstrated the superiority of the Allied armies. To Foch, this ascendancy seemed to justify an attempt to gain the victory in 1918. The British cabinet was reluctant to permit Haig to engage in such an enterprise, believing that the final drives could not be made before 1919, but the general went to London and persuaded the cabinet to accept Foch's view.

Foch realized that his offensive could be frustrated by a rapid withdrawal of the Germans to the frontiers, combined with the thorough demolition of roads and railways in their wake. Such a retreat would compel the Allies to build new communications as they advanced, and it would probably be impossible for them to make a major coordinated attack against the German frontiers before the spring of 1919. However, a rapid German withdrawal would necessitate the abandonment of vast stores of supplies and equipment that had been built up in France and Belgium, and the German General Staff could not reconcile itself to this sacrifice. Understanding all of these factors, Foch is said to have remarked: "The man could still escape if he did not mind leaving his luggage behind." The keystone of Foch's offensive plan accordingly became the prevention of orderly, step-by-step evacuations by the Germans.

The German armies depended for supply (and would have to depend for evacuation) primarily on the railroad running from Cologne through Liége, Namur, and Maubeuge. Another line ran from Koblenz up the Moselle Valley to Luxembourg and Virton, and a third ran southward along the west bank of the Rhine River to Strasbourg and thence northwestward to Metz. The great lateral railroad was the Brugge–Gent–Maubeuge–Mézières–Metz line, from which branches ran to the fighting front. The key rail junctions were Aulnoye and Mézières, and the loss of these places would deprive the Germans of their principal capabilities for withdrawal. Foch's general plan, then, was to capture both junctions rapidly by means of two major converging offensives. One offensive, mainly British, was to drive eastward to Aulnoye; the other, mainly American, was to drive northward to Mézières and Sedan.

For his final offensive, Foch had 220 divisions: 102 French, 60 British, 42 American, 12 Belgian, 2 Italian, and 2 Portuguese. Besides having twice as many infantry troops as the other divisions, the American divisions were at full strength, while the other Allied divisions were below strength. On the line were 160 divisions; 60 were held in reserve. To oppose the Allied offensive the Germans had 197 divisions: 113 in line and 84 in reserve. Only 51 of these divisions were classified by the Allies as effective fighting units, however, and all were under strength. News from a disillusioned home front further depressed the already low morale of the German troops. Ludendorff braced his forces as best he could for the impending blows. Special counterattack divisions, composed of selected men and better armed and equipped than the other divisions, were kept in reserve to counter any Allied breakthrough.

Though Foch intended a sort of pincers operation with a British–French pincer moving from the west and an American–French pincer moving from the south, his plan provided for aggressive action by all of the 160 front-line divisions. *"Tout le monde à la bataille"* ("Everyone in the fight") was his expressive description of the offensive. Fully aware of the scarcity of the German reserves, he planned to stagger his attacks in order to confuse the enemy and keep him off balance. Should the German reserves be directed to counter one Allied attack, subsequent attacks elsewhere might find easy going. Foch had employed this scheme of staggered attacks in the Aisne–Marne offensive with excellent results.

The offensive was to be initiated on September 26 by the southern pincer (the American First Army, with the French Fourth Army on its left), with Mézières–Sedan as its objective. The western pincer would begin its attack toward Aulnoye on September 27 with the British First and Third armies. The British Fourth and French First armies, to the south, would join the attack on September 29, with the French First Army on the right. The French Fifth and Tenth armies were to advance in the center between the French First and Fourth armies in order to maintain pressure on that front and prevent the movement of German troops to other sectors. It was hoped also that these troops would be trapped by the converging pincers. In the Flanders area three armies—the Belgian, French Sixth, and British Second—under King Albert I would attack toward Gent on September 28. The British Fifth Army was to cover the gap between King Albert's and Haig's army groups. The remainder of the Western Front, south of the U.S. First Army, was

Map 19. ALLIED FINAL OFFENSIVE (Sept. 26–Nov. 11, 1918). The obstructive salients having been reduced, Foch launched his general offensive on September 26. His objective was to capture the key rail junctions of Aulnoye and Mézières, thus preventing an orderly withdrawal by the Germans and leaving them vulnerable to destruction. To execute the plan, a Franco-British pincer was to advance rapidly to Aulnoye from the west, and a Franco-American pincer to Mézières from the south. The Germans prevented the pincers from closing and withdrew in fair order, though suffering heavy losses. Recognizing the hopelessness of their cause against the massive and relentless Allied offensive, the Germans asked for an armistice. It was granted, effective November 11.

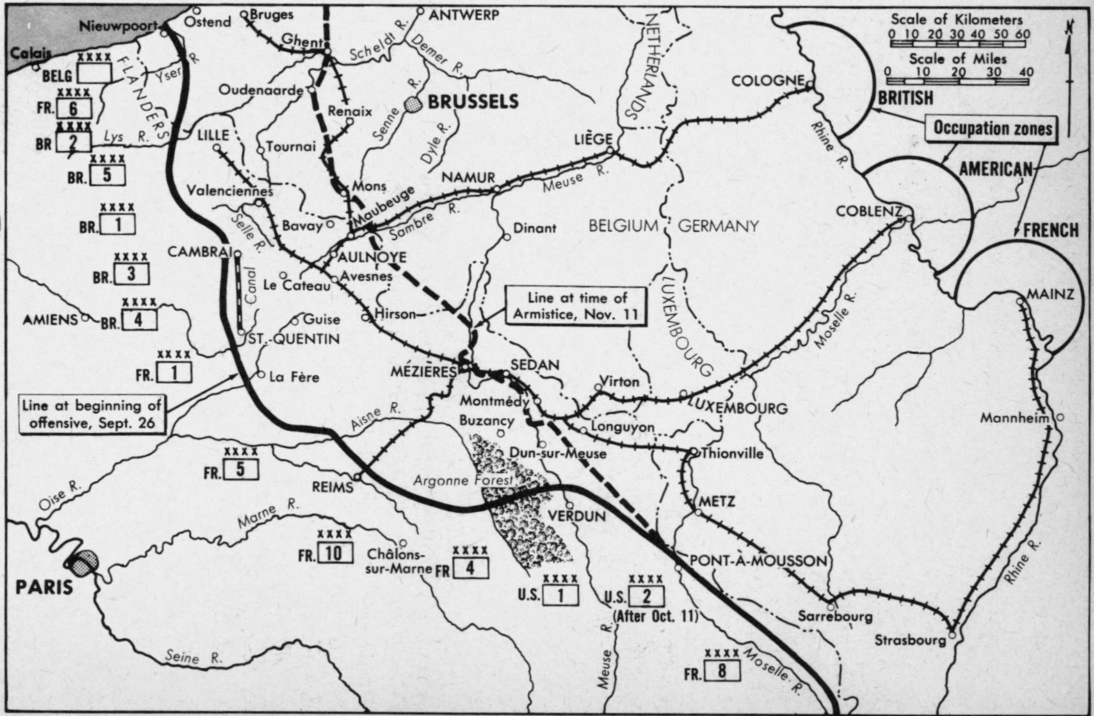

held by General de Castelnau's French army group, with the French Eighth Army adjacent to the Americans. Castelnau's forces were to play only a defensive role in the offensive.

The grouping of forces for the final offensive indicates the degree of mutual confidence and cooperation among the Allies under Foch. French troops served enthusiastically under British, Belgian, and American command; British, under French and Belgian command; and Americans (six divisions), under French and British command. In fact, there was greater harmony among commanders of different nationalities than among those of the same.

For simplicity and continuity in tracing the complex operations of the many Allied armies, they are classified here into four groupings. From north to south these are the Flanders offensive, the western pincer (Cambrai–Saint-Quentin), the operations of the French center, and the southern pincer (Meuse–Argonne). The operations are further divided into two time periods: September 26–October 31 and November 1–11.

Operations, September 26–October 31

Southern Pincer (Meuse–Argonne). The mission of the U.S. First Army, as stated by Foch, was to drive the enemy behind the Sedan–Mézières rail line before winter weather made offensive operations difficult. The French Fourth Army would attack on the American left. Both armies would effect a junction north of Grandpré, at the northern end of the Argonne Forest. Before the offensive could be launched, 220,000 men of the French Second Army had to be moved from the Meuse–Argonne sector, while 600,000 American troops moved in from the Saint-Mihiel front and from the rear. Through remarkable staff work, the move was accomplished smoothly and expeditiously. Because of the short interval between the end of the Saint-Mihiel offensive and the contemplated final drive, however, most of the experienced American divisions could not be brought up in time to lead the Meuse–Argonne attack. Consequently, of the nine divisions that were to take part in the initial attack, five had not been previously engaged in combat and four did not have their own artillery.

An advance in the Meuse–Argonne sector posed a serious threat to the entire German position on the Western Front. The Germans therefore had carefully fortified the zone during the four years they had occupied it. Three main lines of defense had been thoroughly organized, and almost every wood and village between them had been fortified as a strong point. In addition, every possible route of advance was covered by Germans on dominating ridges, and the rugged and thickly wooded hills of the Argonne Forest themselves provided strong obstacles.

At 5:25 A.M. on September 26, after a preliminary bombardment, General Henri J. E. Gouraud's French Fourth Army advanced, and five minutes later, Pershing's U.S. First Army moved forward. The French advance was hampered by mine craters and shell holes, which had been created during the operations of previous years, and by strong German positions on the commanding heights. It had progressed only three miles by the evening of September 27; by October 1, after three days of bitter fighting, Gouraud had advanced six additional miles; by October 9, his offensive had gained only another mile and a half. Meanwhile, the American assault on September 26 had encountered only four German divisions on the front line. By evening, the surprised Germans had been beaten back five miles along the Meuse but only two miles in the difficult Argonne Forest. The advance continued until October 1, but meanwhile German resistance had stiffened. Although the first two German positions had been broken, the American effort spent itself before reaching the third position. After the relief of units and reorganization, the attacks were resumed on October 4.

The next four weeks saw a grueling series of frontal attacks, during which the Americans beat their way through the third German defensive position as casualties mounted rapidly. Meanwhile, Pershing launched an offensive across the Meuse to clear the heights on the east bank. This sector was turned over to the newly formed U.S. Second Army, under Lieutenant General Robert L. Bullard. Lieutenant General Hunter Liggett was given command of the First Army, and Pershing thereafter acted as army group commander. By October 31, the Argonne Forest had been cleared, and the Americans had advanced 10 miles beyond their starting line of September 26. Gouraud's Fourth Army had broken through the desolated area on its front into open ground, and by October 31 had reached the Aisne River, 20 miles from its starting points.

The slow though steady progress of the U.S. First Army during this phase of the battle was highly unsatisfactory to Clemenceau, who suggested to Foch that he try to have Pershing relieved of command. Foch, however, had "a more comprehensive knowledge of the difficulties encountered by the American Army," and declined to support such action. As a matter of fact, the U.S. First

Army was accomplishing far more than its limited territorial gains indicated. The threat of its slow but persistent advance had alarmed Ludendorff, who eventually sent 27 of his precious reserve divisions to the American front, thereby facilitating the progress of the other Allied offensives.

Western Pincer (Cambrai–Saint-Quentin). Four Allied armies were poised to move eastward on the Cambrai–Saint-Quentin front. From north to south these were the British First (Horne), Third (Byng), and Fourth (Rawlinson) armies and the French First Army (Debeney). The British First and Third armies were to attack on September 27, one day after the attack of the southern pincer; the British Fourth and French First armies would move out on September 29, in consonance with Foch's plan of staggered attacks. Between Haig's armies and their objective, Aulnoye, lay canals, rivers, and German defensive positions, including in the southern sector the formidable Hindenburg Line with its three deep defensive positions. At dawn on September 27, the British First and Third armies began their offensive without preliminary bombardment in order to gain surprise. The attacks progressed according to plan but not as rapidly as had been anticipated; by the night of September 28, they had broken through the German defenses to a depth of six miles. This success, plus the American early successes on the Meuse–Argonne front, convinced Ludendorff of eventual German defeat. On the night of September 28, he reported to Field Marshal Paul von Hindenburg that there was no chance of an improvement in the German situation and that efforts to obtain an armistice should be begun. The following day, Hindenburg reported to his government that "the situation demands an immediate armistice in order to avert a catastrophe." On October 4, German and Austrian notes proposing an armistice were forwarded to President Woodrow Wilson.

Meanwhile, on the morning of September 29, Rawlinson's Fourth Army joined the attack, with Debeney's First Army advancing on its right as flank protection. An intensive bombardment had been started on the night of September 27 along the Fourth Army's front, and it had been continued through the night of September 28. This lengthy bombardment was necessary because the attack had to be made across the Saint-Quentin Canal, and tanks could not precede the infantry in the assault. Artillery had to be employed to soften the German defenses, preparatory to forcing the canal. The effect of this sustained bombardment was to drive the Germans deep into their shelters and to prevent the delivery of food and ammunition to the front-line troops. Moreover, since most of the German troops on the line were either new conscripts or recent arrivals from the Eastern Front, the demoralizing effect of the bombardment was great. In a determined attack, British, Australian, and American troops hurled themselves at the tunnel defenses and swam the canal. The ferocity of the attack panicked the Germans, who abandoned their machine guns and positions and fled to the rear. By nightfall the Fourth Army had captured the advanced position of the Hindenburg Line and a good part of the second position. All three British armies were now engaged in a slow but inexorable advance. On September 30, Cambrai was enveloped on the north and south, but the Germans were not cleared from the town until October 9. Saint-Quentin was flanked by the Fourth Army, evacuated by the Germans, and occupied by the French First Army on October 1–2. By October 5, the third and last position of the Hindenburg Line was in British hands. With his front giving way, Ludendorff withdrew his forces to a new position along the line of the Selle River. His special counterattack divisions had proved ineffective, not only because they were too few in number, but also because the front-line troops in assaulted areas would not hold positions long enough to permit their arrival.

The Allies moved to the line of the Selle, and on October 17 the British Fourth and French First armies attacked the German positions from Le Cateau southward. The German troops, exhorted by appeals to hold fast in defense of the fatherland, fought well, but after two days of bitter combat they withdrew before the two Allied armies. At 2 A.M. on October 20, the British First and Third armies attacked the northern sector of the Selle position. The infantry crossed the river and, assisted by tanks, assaulted the high ground along the east bank. Again the Germans fought stubbornly, but they were eventually driven off. The three British armies and the French First Army on their right continued the advance through seas of mud, hampered by German mines and demolitions. By the end of October they had reached the next German position, which lay behind the Schelde River and extended southward to the vicinity of Laon.

Flanders Offensive. King Albert's army group was to attack on

September 28, the day between Haig's assaults of September 27 and 29. The offensive of his three armies (from north to south, the Belgian, French Sixth, and British Second armies) began well despite persistent heavy rains. By October 1, the advance had progressed eight miles and had succeeded in recapturing the Ypres Ridge. The grave threat of Haig's attack to the south had influenced Ludendorff to send reserves to that area. These were few, and, forced to make a choice, he decided to draw troops from the Flanders front. Some five German divisions were left in Flanders, and these, their commander said, would "no longer stand up to a serious attack." The principal obstacle to the Allied advance in Flanders was rain, which made the limited road net almost impassable and bogged down supply and transportation systems. The impasse lasted for two weeks, and it was not until October 14 that serious operations could be resumed. On October 20, the Lys River was reached. By October 28, the successes of Haig's armies in the Selle battles had forced a general German withdrawal, and Albert's armies advanced that day without serious opposition to the German position on the Schelde. Though not as strenuously engaged as the troops in the two principal offensives, the King's army group played its role well in the execution of the over-all plan.

Operations of the French Center. Four French armies participated in the offensive in the sector between Haig's British and Pershing's American armies. The role of the French First Army at the right of the British advance and that of the French Fourth Army on the American left have been described. Between these two armies the line was held by the Fifth and Tenth armies, whose task was to harass the enemy on their fronts, prevent their movement to other fronts, and hamper their withdrawal so that they might be trapped by the British and American pincers. This relatively passive assignment was an odd one for Frenchmen who had been imbued with Foch's philosophy of *"l'attaque, toujours l'attaque"* ("keep on the offensive")—a philosophy that, under General Joseph Joffre's skillful guidance in 1914, had turned the tide at the Marne after two heartbreaking weeks of retreat and had led the French to a brilliant victory; and which, conversely, in the hands of the obstinate and pompous Nivelle, had led brave Frenchmen to disaster at the Aisne in 1917, with consequent demoralization and mutiny in the French Army. Nevertheless, the French played their unusual role well, but the pincers did not close, and by October 31 the Germans in the center had withdrawn to a shortened line. This shortening of the line required fewer French troops in this section of the front, and some were withdrawn and formed into a new Tenth Army (the old Tenth Army remained in position, but was renamed the Third). The new army was sent to the Lorraine front, to the right of the Americans, where, with the French Eighth Army, it was to engage in an offensive northward on both sides of Metz. This offensive was scheduled for November 15, but the armistice on November 11 made it unnecessary.

German Situation

On October 31, the Germans in the north held the line of the Schelde. This position had not been fortified as strongly as the Hindenburg Line or the defenses of the Selle, for the Germans had had great confidence in the impregnability of their forward defenses. In the south, in front of the French Fourth and U.S. First armies, they still held the greater part of the formidable Kriemhilde Line and the Bourgogne Wood, just north of the Argonne Forest. The setbacks of the past month, however, had lowered the morale of the German troops to the danger point. German sailors had already lost their fighting spirit, and on November 3 they mutinied at Kiel. Within a few days, revolutionary councils of soldiers and workers, like those of the Bolsheviks in Russia, had been established in a number of German cities. These uprisings, combined with the collapse of Germany's allies in late October, created serious unrest, but the military press agencies (through which all military information now passed) continued to try to deceive the people with favorable reports of activities at the front, describing reverses as planned withdrawals to stronger positions.

Nevertheless, Ludendorff was confident of German capabilities to effect an orderly withdrawal to the line of the Meuse, using the time thus gained to secure better armistice terms. President Wilson's reply to the German request for an armistice had not been to Ludendorff's liking. It had prescribed the acceptance of Wilson's Fourteen Points, the cessation of submarine warfare, and the evacuation of all occupied territories as preliminary requirements. The German government, however, was convinced of the hopelessness of the situation, and on October 20 signified its acceptance of Wilson's terms. The President then referred the matter to the Allies jointly.

The Reichstag suggested that "the defeated general [Ludendorff] should offer his resignation and retire." Instead, on October 25, Ludendorff issued an order of the day to the troops in which he described the armistice terms as unacceptable. On October 27, the Kaiser informed Ludendorff of his intention to consult other generals, whereupon Ludendorff tendered his resignation; the Kaiser hastened to accept it. General Wilhelm Groener, who replaced Ludendorff, realistically considered the lack of reserves, the morale of the troops, and the near collapse of the railway system. Each day he reported progressive deterioration; finally, on November 6, he urged that an armistice be effected not later than November 9 to avoid chaos. Soldiers' councils had already been formed at the front; and on November 8, a large group of senior officers, called from the front for a conference with the Chancellor, Prince Max of Baden, agreed that the army could not be relied on if it were ordered to quell uprisings at home. By now the longing among the civilian population for peace had become the paramount consideration. Almost all Germans turned against the Kaiser as the one who prolonged the war solely to perpetuate his regime. On November 9, Prince Max announced William's abdication, and a German Republic was proclaimed.

Allied Operations, November 1–11

By November 1, the Allied armies had consolidated their positions, put their supply lines in order, and brought up ammunition and supplies for a continuation of the offensive. Foch's plan of operations for this final phase of his general offensive was substantially the same as his initial plan. The major thrusts would be delivered by the British in the west and the Americans in the south, both being aided by the French armies on their flanks. The British would force the line of the Schelde, advance to Maubeuge, and press on to capture crossings of the Meuse from Namur to Dinant. If these crossings could be captured before the Germans withdrew from Flanders, they would be pressed against the Dutch border and captured. In the south, the rapid seizure of Mézières and Sedan by the U.S. First and French Fourth armies would, it was hoped, isolate the Germans facing the French center armies.

Allied Attacks from the South. On November 1, in cold, wet weather (which continued along the entire Western Front until the end of hostilities), Liggett's American First and Gouraud's French Fourth armies attacked astride the Bourgogne Wood. On that day, they advanced five miles; on November 2, they drove six miles farther, the Americans capturing Buzancy. Constant pressure affected the already low morale of the German troops, who finally broke, offering little resistance. On November 3, the Americans drove five miles through the German lines and joined forces with the French Fourth Army beyond the Bourgogne Wood. This advance brought the rail line running southeastward from Sedan within range of American artillery, and it quickly pounded the rail centers of Montmédy and Longuyon, through which the Germans were attempting to withdraw troops and supplies. By November 7, the American 1st Corps had pushed back German rear guards and reached the heights of the Meuse overlooking Sedan, for an aggregate gain of 21 miles since November 1. Gouraud's troops, confronted with the task of breaching strong defenses, and with a greater distance to go, reached the Meuse opposite Mézières on the evening of November 10. At this juncture, Foch shifted the left boundary of the American First Army to the east of Sedan to allow the French to capture that city, and thus erase the stigma of the disastrous defeat by the Germans there in 1870. The two armies closed up to the Meuse before the armistice on November 11 halted operations.

As the offensive moved northward, the American 3d Corps crossed the Meuse to the east and occupied Dun-sur-Meuse on November 4. Subsequently, three French corps on the left wing of the U.S. Second Army advanced through the hills east of the Meuse, and at the time of the armistice these American and French troops were within six miles of Montmédy. On November 10, the U.S. Second Army began an offensive toward Briey which was halted by the armistice after slight gains had been made.

Allied Attacks from the West. The British also began their final phase of the offensive on November 1. Haig's first task was to force the German defenses of the Schelde. To avoid the difficult terrain and intricate dike system immediately in front of his forces, he made his principal attack south of Valenciennes, using elements of the British First and Third armies. By the night of November 2, the Canadian Corps had captured the town. On November 4, Haig launched a general offensive on a 30-mile front, which by evening had advanced five miles beyond Valenciennes. On the British right, Debeney's French First Army advanced to the north of Guise. The fighting had been bitter, but the Schelde position had definitely been turned, and German resistance collapsed. Meanwhile, south of Gent, French and American units of King Albert's force drove the Germans back from the Schelde, and the Americans captured Oudenaarde (Audenarde).

The Germans withdrew all along the line, hampered by blocked roads, traffic snarls, a shortage of rail equipment, and Allied air attacks on their retiring troops and transport. On the other hand, the Allied pursuit was slowed because of lengthening supply lines and the methodical demolition of supply routes by the Germans as they withdrew. On November 7, the British entered Bavay; on November 8, Avesnes; and on November 9, Maubeuge. The French armies, following up the advance of the British and Americans on their flanks, took Hirson on November 9. King Albert's troops joined in the pursuit, which now extended along the entire front. Tournai and Renaix (Ronse) were occupied, and a Canadian division entered Mons a few hours before the armistice.

THE ARMISTICE

The Allies had left the details of the armistice terms to be arranged by their military leaders. Pershing objected to granting an armistice at all, preferring to continue the attack until the German forces were obliged to lay down their arms in the field. Foch's view was that additional bloodshed was unnecessary if the terms of the armistice were sufficiently rigorous to deprive Germany of the ability to continue the war, and they were so made.

Actually, though the German armies had been beaten, the Allied armies were in no position to administer a *coup de grâce* before winter put an end to serious hostilities. The advance of November 1–11 had strained their logistical support systems to the breaking point. Despite concentrated efforts to repair and operate the railroads, supply railheads lagged behind the troops by 50 to 100 miles. Motor transport had to be used to haul supplies for these intervening distances over roads strewn with mine craters and blown bridges. Under such conditions, vehicles broke down in large numbers. Foch had urged his commanders to make final efforts to destroy the retreating Germans, and Rawlinson, Debeney, and Pershing had organized pursuit forces. It is unlikely that any but small pursuit columns could have pressed forward on November 11, and these could have had only minor local effects in a withdrawal of such magnitude. If the Germans could prevent the collapse of the home front and the disintegration of their armies, there was little to prevent them from establishing a position behind the Meuse. In this case, the war would have continued into 1919.

Occupation of Germany

The Allied armies paused on the armistice line for almost six days, ostensibly to allow the Germans time to begin an orderly withdrawal, but also to permit the solution of their own logistical problems. Early on November 17, the movement toward Germany began. The advance was conducted slowly and without enemy interference; only about one-fourth of the Allied armies participated. Nevertheless, the general advance was almost halted in early December because supply trains had fallen far behind schedule. In addition to supplying the troops, it was now necessary to provide food for the millions of civilians in the liberated areas who were on the verge of starvation. Moreover, the Germans released large numbers of prisoners as they withdrew, and these also had to be cared for.

On December 1, the Allied armies marched into Germany proper. Later that month, in accordance with the armistice terms, bridgeheads with a radius of 30 kilometers were established east of the Rhine around Cologne (occupied by the British), Koblenz (occupied by the Americans), and Mainz (occupied by the French). Subsequently, the occupation forces were reduced, despite Foch's protests. The Americans withdrew the last of their forces in January, 1923; the British, in December, 1929; and the French and Belgians, in June, 1930.

Attitude of the German Army

When it became clear to the German military leaders that victory was no longer possible, they made every effort to escape the blame. No military leader participated in the armistice discussions. Though several admitted defeat to Allied leaders, the situation was portrayed differently to the German people. The theme adopted was that the war had been terminated to prevent further bloodshed and to raise the blockade so that the sufferings of women and children might be alleviated. Returning troops were received as conquering heroes and marched in holiday fashion through gaily decorated streets. When this myth began to be exploded, the German Army accused the home front, charging that its disloyalty and lack of support had caused the catastrophe. Ludendorff heard the phrase "stabbed in the back" and took it as his slogan. Later, Adolf Hitler was to adopt this theme in his exhortations to his Nazi followers. Nevertheless, the facts prove without question that the German Army had been decisively defeated in 1918.

GENERAL COMMENTARY

American Participation in the War

The importance of American participation in the war has often been exaggerated in the United States and minimized in Britain and France. At the time of the armistice there were more American troops in France than British troops, and they held a wider front. The American Army was still growing rapidly, and munitions production in the United States was reaching great heights. If the war had lasted until 1919, American troops would undoubtedly have struck the principal blows. While the United States can scarcely claim to have played the major role in the war, it may fairly be said that it could not have been won without American aid.

To participate effectively in the 1918 battles, the United States Army required substantial support from its allies. A little more than half of the 2 million American troops shipped to France were transported in British vessels. Divisions arriving overseas before July 1, 1918, had to be equipped with the French automatic rifle and machine gun; those arriving thereafter had the new American Browning automatic rifle and machine gun, considered the best in the world at the time. Almost complete reliance had to be placed on the French for artillery: of the 2,250 artillery pieces used by the Americans in action, only about 100 were of American manufacture. On the advice of her allies, the United States concentrated on producing aircraft engines and observation-bomber planes. The 12-cylinder Liberty engine, developed and put into mass production, was a superior engine, in great demand by the British and the French. By the end of the war, 45 American squadrons were operating at the front, but only about a fourth of them were equipped with American-built aircraft. American battle casualties during their brief role totaled 257,404—a very small number compared with the millions suffered by each of the other Allies during four years of bitter war.

Developments in Warfare

World War I saw an increasing tendency toward the subordination of man to the machine. The growing importance of armament meant that a nation's industries exerted a decisive influence on its military operations. The bravest and most skillful fighting man, if improperly armed, might find himself helpless in combat. Logistics was transformed from a relatively simple business to a vast field of endeavor equal in complexity and importance to the control of operations. The proportion of noncombatant soldiers needed for the great logistical machines would have astounded Frederick the Great or Napoleon, though it did not approximate the proportion that was to be required in World War II.

The introduction of new methods, based upon the design and production of new equipment, was an outstanding feature of the war of 1914–18. Except for the atomic bomb, almost every major development of World War II was foreshadowed in World War I. The tactical effect of the increased power of the machine gun and the modern artillery piece gave an ascendancy to the defense that baffled commanders on both sides for a long time.

The tank was undoubtedly the war's most remarkable development in the field of ground combat. Despite its slowness, limited operational radius, and mechanical unreliability, it achieved some spectacular results in 1918; and even the brilliant Ludendorff was unable to find any adequate means of coping with it.

The airplane became an important weapon. Though the results attained by airpower during the war were hardly decisive, its potential was clearly demonstrated. By war's end, strategic bombing had passed its infancy. German dirigibles and aircraft had bombed London, and British aircraft had frequently bombed Rhineland towns. Had the war lasted another week, British bombers would have attempted to bomb Berlin with one-ton bombs.

Gas warfare was employed on a large scale by both sides—initially, with serious effects. Countermeasures were promptly developed, however, and poison gas became a harassing rather than a decisive weapon.

The warring nations undertook psychological warfare on a systematic basis. The Germans harassed Paris with their long-range gun, and propaganda "hate" campaigns and subversive leaflets were used by both sides. Many of these efforts were amateurish by later standards, but they had considerable effect.

Throughout the war the development of battle tactics centered on the basic problem of breaking through a strong defensive position without prohibitive casualties and such loss of time as to make the breakthrough useless. What was accomplished by the capture of a trench line if it took so long that the defender had time to construct another a mile or so in the rear? In his first three drives of 1918, Ludendorff solved the initial breakthrough problem by achieving surprise and by creating a highly efficient body of troops. He gained great local successes, but he could not win a strategic decision because he had no powerful, highly mobile force capable of extended operations to exploit a tactical breakthrough. The Allies, however, were never able to force tactical breakthroughs comparable with those achieved by Ludendorff.

In a military sense, the net result of World War I was that the Allies became convinced of the superiority of the defense and made their future plans and preparations accordingly; the Germans, having been frustrated by the lack of a strategic exploiting force, sought ways to build one. They found an answer in the tank-airplane team, the heart of the blitzkrieg, which in 1940 achieved in three weeks what the Germans could not do in the four years of World War I.

8. Eastern Front

BY GERALD FREUND

Russian and German strategy and tactics on the Eastern Front were determined largely by the terrain. In the middle of the line was the Polish salient, at this time a part of Russia, comprising an area 230 miles long and 210 miles wide and leading directly into Germany. On the broad Vistula River, which crossed the salient, was the fortress city of Warsaw. Warsaw had important defensive value, but it could also serve as a base for a Russian offensive westward into the rich mining and industrial area of Silesia.

Russia could not make a direct advance against Silesia and Berlin, located only 180 miles from the western extremity of the salient, without first safeguarding the flanks of East Prussia to the north and Galicia to the south. If the Germans in East Prussia and the Austrians in Galicia launched converging attacks across the flat land against Brest-Litovsk at the center of the salient, Russian forces west of the Vistula could be cut off. To defend themselves against such attacks, the Russians built a series of fortresses along the Nieman and Narew rivers and at Lublin and Kholm (now Chelm). No Russian troops were stationed in the area west of Warsaw, which was kept without railroads and roads in order to prevent a rapid German advance.

To defend East Prussia the Germans constructed fortifications on the upper Vistula and a forward line in the lake district east of Allenstein (now Olsztyn), while in Galicia the Austrians built a fortified defensive barrier along the Carpathian Mountains centering on Lemberg (now Lvov) and running from Kraków to the Romanian border. Thus the Polish salient was hemmed in and threatened from both north and south. Russia proper was divided from the salient by the Pripet Marshes, a region of swamps, forests, and few roads. To the north, south, and east stretched vast areas that could swallow whole armies.

Railways played an important role in the strategy of the Eastern Front. Germany had 17 lines leading to the Russian frontier, with a capacity of 500 troop trains daily, enabling her to concentrate a vast force on the border within a few days of a declaration of war. Piercing the Carpathians were seven Austrian rail lines, permitting a flow of 250 trains daily from Hungary into Galicia. Both the German and Austrian railway systems also had numerous spurs branching off from the trunklines and running parallel to the frontiers. These facilitated rapid deployment and redeployment to repel attacks or to mount offensives. On the Russian side, six trunklines, several of which were double-tracked, radiated from Warsaw to the interior. All the military strength of the Russian Empire could be drawn up along the lines passing through Kiev, Moscow, and Saint Petersburg (renamed Petrograd in 1914), but there were few spur lines. The relative lack of north-south lines prevented the Russians from rapidly shifting men along the front to mount surprise attacks or to counter German tactics. These shortcomings in railway transportation (and in the road network) later handicapped the Germans as they penetrated Russia east of the Polish salient.

WAR PLANS

The initial events of the Eastern Front were dominated by German strategy in the west. Germany had long prepared for a war on two fronts. In 1890, Field Marshal Count Helmuth von Moltke had devised a plan to defend the Western Front and throw Germany's main strength against Russia before concentrating on the defeat of France. This strategy was subsequently reversed by Count Alfred von Schlieffen. According to the celebrated Schlieffen Plan, Germany's entire strength was to be directed against France, leaving virtually no forces in the east. The French armies were to be captured or destroyed within six weeks, and the troops then shifted to the Eastern Front for a full-scale drive against Russia.

This plan assumed that Russian mobilization would be slow and that it would therefore be safe initially to leave German territory in the east undefended. By 1913, however, it was clear that this premise was no longer valid, for Russia was enlarging and improving her army and building military railways. Colonel General Helmuth von Moltke, nephew of the field marshal, therefore modified the Schlieffen Plan. He realized that Russia was bound by treaty to take the part of France and would mobilize rapidly from the first sign of hostilities. Since Austria-Hungary would remain on the defensive if she were not assisted by Germany, the net effect of the Schlieffen Plan would be to give Russia complete freedom of action to occupy East Prussia and Galicia and march toward Berlin. For these reasons, Moltke decided to station an army in East Prussia and support it with strong garrisons at Germany's eastern

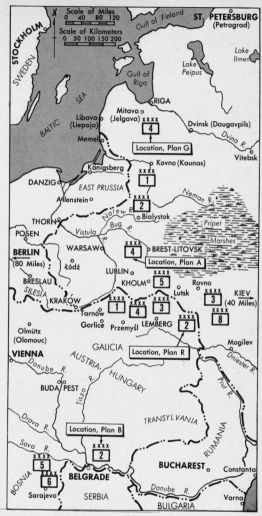

Map 20. WAR PLANS; EASTERN FRONT. Germany's plan provided for its Eighth Army to hold the Russians until France had been defeated; then full German power would be turned against Russia. Russia's plans were based on two contingencies: Plan G, an offensive plan, if Germany's main effort was directed against France; and Plan A, a defensive plan, if the effort was directed against Russia. The only difference in troop dispositions was the location of the Fourth Army. Similarly, Austria-Hungary provided for war against Serbia alone (Plan B) and for war against both Russia and Serbia (Plan R).

fortresses. As will be seen, Moltke's modifications of the Schlieffen Plan played a key role in the repulse of the initial Russian offensive and in the German victory in the campaign around Tannenberg (now Stębark).

Austria-Hungary and Russia each had two war plans. One Austrian plan assumed a war with Serbia alone, which would be invaded by three armies, while the other three Austrian armies guarded the Russian front in Galicia. The second plan assumed a war with both Serbia and Russia. In this case, four armies would be thrown into battle against Russia, and two would invade Serbia. Of the Russian plans, one was wholly defensive and assumed that Germany would make her first major effort in the east. The army groups in the north and south would retreat eastward until a counteroffensive could be organized. The second plan, which was actually effected, was offensive. It envisaged the main German attack against France and provided for Russian drives against East Prussia and Galicia in order to safeguard both flanks of the Polish salient in preparation for an invasion of Silesia. When war was declared in August, 1914, the French, fearing an all-out German drive in the west, urged an early Russian offensive to divert German forces to the east. Much to their regret, the Russians succumbed to their ally's insistence.

OPERATIONS IN 1914

Tannenberg Campaign

Russian mobilization proceeded rapidly after the outbreak of war and was accompanied by great enthusiasm. The people considered the struggle a defensive war against German imperialists, who had long threatened Russia and exploited her economically. By mid-August, the commander in chief, Grand Duke Nicholas, and the chief of staff, General Nikolai Yanushkevich, had nearly 2 million men on the front line. Although this was only a third of the potential fighting force, and although logistical support for an offensive was lacking, the Russians heeded the pleas of their French ally and ordered converging attacks to start on August 13 from the east and southeast against East Prussia. General Pavel Rennenkampf's First Army and General Aleksandr Samsonov's Second Army, both under the over-all command of General Ivan Zhilinsky at Warsaw, immediately moved their troops into advance positions for the attack. Rennenkampf crossed the border on August 17, five days before Samsonov was scheduled to do so. The

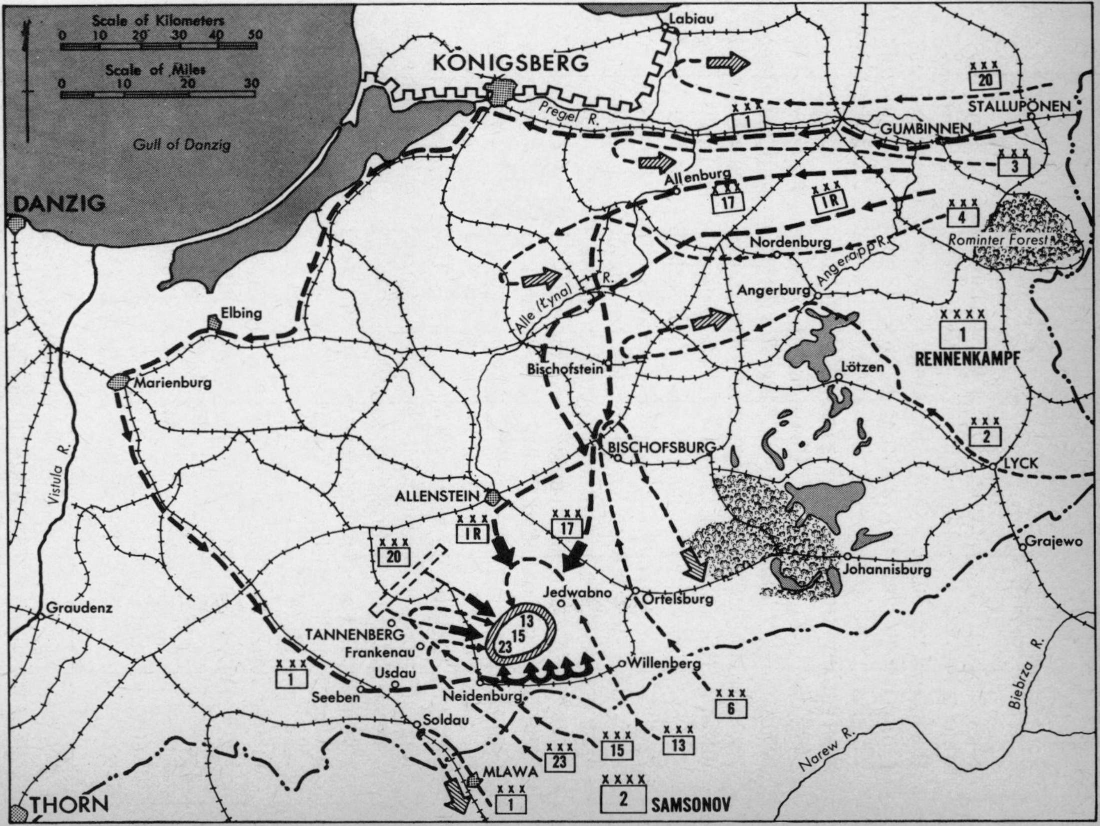

Map 21. TANNENBERG CAMPAIGN (Aug. 17–29, 1914). Germany having made its main effort against France, Russia immediately launched its offensive Plan A against both East Prussia and Austria in accordance with its agreement with the French, although its forces were only partially mobilized. The First Army advanced from the east and engaged elements of the German Eighth Army at Stallupönen and Gumbinnen without material results. Meanwhile, the Second Army entered East Prussia from the south to trap the German Eighth Army. In a brilliant operation the Germans shifted front to engage the Second Army, encircled three Russian corps, and virtually destroyed the Second Army. The Russian First Army, which had made a halfhearted effort to assist the Second, then turned about and withdrew.

plan was to draw German forces north and east, enabling Samsonov's army to envelop their rear. This strategy failed because of the lack of adequate information about German troop dispositions, faulty liaison, and the fact that Rennenkampf did not carry out Zhilinsky's orders to weight his north flank so as to drive the German garrison from Königsberg (now Kaliningrad).

At his headquarters in Allenstein, the German Eastern Front commander, Colonel General Max von Prittwitz, ordered three corps to the Angerapp (Węgorapa) River area, to guard against invasion from the east, and his fourth corps to the Tannenberg area, to guard the southern border. Although he was authorized by the high command to withdraw to the Vistula if necessary, he knew that he was expected to use the terrain and the railroads to organize a defense against anticipated successive Russian blows. By means of spies and intercepted radio messages, which the Russians habitually sent uncoded, Prittwitz had obtained information concerning Zhilinsky's battle orders. What he did not know was that the headstrong commander of his 1st Corps, General Hermann von François, had moved forward independently to Stallupönen (now Nesterov) on the border, where he was prepared to fight to prevent Russian violation of Prussia's "sacred soil." When a Russian corps approached, François counterattacked, inflicting heavy casualties on the invaders. Tactically, his action was sound, but it upset Prittwitz' carefully planned strategy. Time was important to the German commander, for he had only five days to defeat Rennenkampf before he would have to turn his armies south to stop Samsonov's anticipated attack. Prittwitz therefore planned to lure Rennenkampf westward into a decisive battle on the Angerapp River. François' counterattack delayed the Russian advance to the contemplated major battlefield.

Fortunately for the Germans, Rennenkampf did not appreciate the danger to his forces. He continued his advance for two days, approaching but not reaching the Angerapp. By this time, François had consolidated his forces at their designated position around Gumbinnen (now Gusev), but he urged Prittwitz to order an immediate counteroffensive. Over the objections of his brilliant operations officer, Lieutenant Colonel Max Hoffmann, who wanted time to bring up two corps entrenched west of the river, Prittwitz gave in and ordered a full-scale attack for August 20.

As Hoffmann feared, the German attack was made piecemeal and achieved little success. Along the greater part of the front the

German troops were repulsed. The result was a stalemate, but Prittwitz needed a decisive victory. He had to make up his mind whether to resume the attack or to withdraw toward the Vistula. Later on August 20, news was received at his headquarters in Allenstein that Samsonov's Second Army had already entered East Prussia. Prittwitz thereupon telephoned Moltke that he would withdraw to the Vistula, but that he would need reinforcements to hold the Russians even there. Moltke's immediate reaction was to relieve Prittwitz of his command, and by August 23, his successor, General Paul von Hindenburg, called from retirement, reached the front with his chief of staff, Major General Erich F. W. Ludendorff, who had already distinguished himself in the fighting on the Western Front.

While Hindenburg and Ludendorff were to be credited with reversing the tide of battle and achieving a German victory at Tannenberg, Hoffmann actually developed a new strategic plan before they arrived at the front. Between August 20 and 23, he moved a division and a corps from the front against Rennenkampf to face Samsonov's advancing Second Army, which was threatening to cut off the German troops by a drive northwestward to the Gulf of Danzig. Two additional German corps were moving westward and were ready to turn south if Rennenkampf did not press his advance. Hoffmann's plan was approved by Hindenburg and Ludendorff. The German forces were now concentrated against Samsonov's slow-moving offensive, with only a cavalry division and a brigade left in the north to delay Rennenkampf. The shift was a daring maneuver, but the Germans could well afford it. Inadequate railroads and roads, virtually nonexistent logistical support, and dissension between Zhilinsky and Samsonov slowed the Russian advance. These difficulties, as well as the day-to-day tactics of the Russians, were well known to the Germans, because they were broadcast in plain language by Zhilinsky's headquarters and by Rennenkampf and Samsonov in the field. The lack of trained code and communications personnel proved a major handicap to the Russians.

On August 24, the middle of Samsonov's line met entrenched German opposition at Frankenau, and heavy fighting broke out that lasted all day. Since Samsonov still thought the Germans were in flight to the west, however, it was announced on his radio that August 25 would be a day of rest.

The Germans did not rest. Assured that they would have time to concentrate their strength against Samsonov before Rennenkampf was able to intervene, Hindenburg, Ludendorff, and Hoffmann set their trap. The 20th Corps at Frankenau was withdrawn northwestward and dug in at Tannenberg. To the south, garrisons transported from Königsberg and the Vistula prepared a breakthrough at Usdau (now Uzdowa); and at Bischofstein (now Bisztynek), to the northeast of Allenstein, German forces diverted from the front against Rennenkampf were detrained to strike a decisive blow at the Russian rear. On August 26, François' 1st Corps, which had been moved south, took Seeben. On the same day, the Russian 6th Corps was routed by the German 17th and 1st Reserve Corps just north of Bischofsburg (now Biskupiec), and the envelopment of Samsonov's northern flank began. The Russian 6th Corps escaped across the border south of Ortelsburg (now Szczytno), as did their 1st Corps via Mława; but the three central corps (13th, 15th, and 23d) were threatened with encirclement by the four German corps.

Samsonov does not seem to have realized the full measure of the disaster until the morning of August 29, when the Russian retreat had become general. During the day the Germans forced the three fleeing Russian corps into a pocket that constantly grew smaller. On August 30 and 31, the Russians tried to break through François' lines, but they succeeded only in retaking Neidenburg (now Nidzica), which they had to evacuate again the following day. All escape routes were now tightly sealed. The Germans captured 125,000 men and 500 guns in the Tannenberg pocket, whereas their own losses for the whole campaign totaled between 10,000 and 15,000 men. There are no accurate figures on the Russians killed and wounded, but the losses were staggering. Defeated and despondent, Samsonov committed suicide.

The Tannenberg campaign thus ended in a great German victory. Rennenkampf's army in the north was still intact, however, and Hindenburg, Ludendorff, and Hoffmann now made plans to dispose of these remaining Russian invaders.

Masurian Lakes Campaign

Rennenkampf had been ordered by Zhilinsky to come to the aid of the Second Army, but his troops did not have time to reach the battlefront. On August 30, the First Army commander learned of the catastrophe at Tannenberg and turned his own forces back. With his right flank on the Baltic Sea, his left flank extending to the Masurian Lakes, and a corps protecting the Lötzen (now Giżycko) Gap, Rennenkampf felt secure against a German offensive.

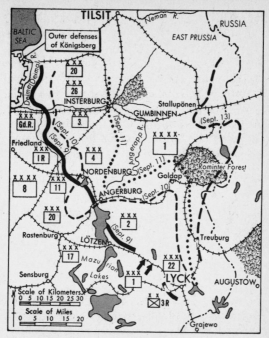

Map 22. MASURIAN LAKES CAMPAIGN (Sept. 9–14, 1914).
After Tannenberg, the German Eighth Army, now augmented by reinforcements from the Western Front, concentrated its efforts against the Russian First Army. A
successful German envelopment on the south flank made
the position of the Russians untenable and forced them to
withdraw. To cover the withdrawal, they launched a
strong counterattack in the center, which deceived the
Germans and allowed sizable forces to escape. Nonetheless, the Russian First Army was decisively defeated
and expelled from East Prussia with large losses.

Again the Russians miscalculated. Zhilinsky reinforced the remnants of Samsonov's army in anticipation of a German offensive
against Warsaw. Although the Austrians, who were in difficulties
in their Galician campaign, urged the Germans to attack Warsaw,
Hindenburg and his staff considered Rennenkampf's force their
first objective. On September 9 and 10, the Germans secured the
southern flank by Lyck (now Ełk) and Augustów. An attempt to
break through the Lötzen Gap was repulsed by Rennenkampf, but
he had to commit all of his reserves to do so. Then the German
1st Corps forced the Russian 2d Corps to retreat, clearing the
route toward Gumbinnen. Fearing another Tannenberg, Rennen-

kampf ordered his army to withdraw. Meanwhile, to protect his retreat, he simultaneously launched a counterattack between Nordenburg (now Krylovo) and Angerburg (now Węgorzewo). The losses suffered by the German corps facing this attack alarmed Ludendorff, who curtailed the advance of his right flank. The enveloping movement was therefore not so deep as he had planned originally, and Rennenkampf was able to save most of his army by forced marches of as much as 55 miles in 50 hours. Nevertheless, the Russian First Army sustained losses estimated as high as 145,000 men. German losses were in the neighborhood of 10,000 men.

Thus, in three weeks, Hindenburg, Ludendorff, and Hoffmann had cleared East Prussia of the enemy. Zhilinsky, who complained to headquarters of Rennenkampf's deficiencies, was himself relieved of his command on September 17 in favor of General Nikolai Russki, who had scored successes on the southern flank of the Polish salient in Galicia.

Galician and Polish Campaigns

While Zhilinsky's forces were being driven from East Prussia, other Russian forces under General Nikolai Ivanov fought the Austrians under Field Marshal Count Franz Conrad von Hötzendorf in Galicia. Conrad von Hötzendorf's indecision jeopardized the Austrian position from the first days of the war. Initially, he committed three of his six armies against Serbia. Subsequently he withdrew part of one army, but it arrived too late to affect the outcome of the first Galician battles.

To make matters worse, Conrad von Hötzendorf decided that the Russians would probably concentrate their forces in the Lublin–Kholm area, and he deployed two armies in that direction, retaining only one for the defensive line southward from Lemberg. Ivanov also misjudged his enemy. Anticipating the major Austrian attack from Lemberg, he directed his own main attack in that area, while a weaker force moved down from the north through Kraśnik, Zamość, and Komarov. Reconnaissance on both sides was poor. On August 23, the Russian Fourth and Austrian First armies collided unexpectedly at Kraśnik. The Russians were forced back by August 25, and Conrad von Hötzendorf, prematurely elated, ordered his troops to attack at Zamość and Komarov, drawing reinforcements from the Lemberg front for the purpose. The Austrians scored limited gains in the Battle of Komarov (August 26–September 1),

Map 23. GALICIAN BATTLES (Battles of Kraśnik, Komarov, and Gnila Lipa; Aug. 23–Sept. 1, 1914). The Austrian and Russian offensives collided along the Galician border. On the left the Austrian First and Fourth armies drove back the Russian Fourth and Fifth armies in the battles of Kraśnik and Komarov. On the right the Austrian Third Army advanced to the Gnila Lipa, where it was forced to retreat by the Russian Third and Eighth armies.

but they were wholly unprepared for the major Russian thrust at Lemberg, which also was launched on August 26. In the ensuing Battle of the Gnila Lipa (now Gnilaya Lipa), the Austrians were routed, and Conrad von Hötzendorf, failing to see that he might still save the situation by ordering an enveloping drive on the Russian flank and possibly scoring a stunning victory against Ivanov's main force, ordered instead a general retreat. By September 8, the Austrian First Army had fallen back to the south of Kraśnik, while the Second, Third, and Fourth armies were endeavoring to consolidate their hold on the Lemberg front. This development opened a huge gap through which the Russian Fifth Army poured. Tired and disorganized from days of entraining and detraining, the Austrians gave ground. This engagement is known as the Battle of Rawa Ruska (now Rava-Russkaya). The battle lines on September 26 show that the Austrians had withdrawn 100 miles; they had suffered 350,000 casualties.

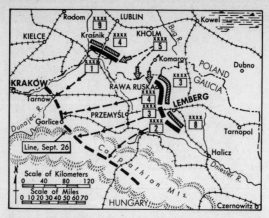

Map 24. GALICIAN BATTLES (Battle of Rawa Ruska, Sept. 5–11, 1914). The Austrians sent their Fourth and Second armies (the latter rushed from the Serbian front) to assist their stricken Third Army. In its movement the Fourth Army left a wide gap in the line in the Komarov area through which the Russian Fifth Army poured. Threatened with encirclement from the north, the Austrians withdrew to the line of the Carpathian Mountains, leaving 100,000 men in the fortress of Przemyśl, all of whom were lost when the fortress subsequently surrendered to the Russians.

Ivanov scored a decisive victory in Galicia. The way was now open for the Russian forces to enter Silesia unless the Germans could stop them. Following their defeat in the First Battle of the Marne, the Germans could not afford to transfer troops from the Western Front, however, and Hindenburg was compelled to rush troops from East Prussia to help the Austrians. On September 28, a newly constituted German Ninth Army detrained at Chenstokhov (now Częstochowa) for this purpose.

The imminent Russian threat to Kraków made immediate action imperative. Hindenburg's goal was to seize crossings on the lower Vistula preparatory to an advance on Warsaw. The Ninth Army reached the river on October 9. Intercepted Russian radio messages gave Hindenburg a clear picture of Ivanov's strategic plan to encircle the German left flank, but the Germans continued on their course, and by mid-October they were within 12 miles of Warsaw, the high-water mark of their offensive. Then Russian pressure, combined with Austrian weakness on the southern flank, forced them to withdraw, and by November 1, they had fallen back to the starting line of September 28.

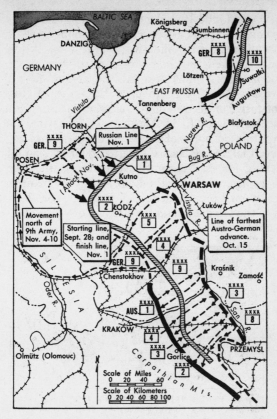

Map 25. **GERMAN NINTH ARMY IN POLAND** (Sept. 28–
Nov. 24, 1914). The Germans formed the Ninth Army in
southern Poland to bolster the Austrians after their defeats in the Galician battles. The Russians, meanwhile,
prepared to launch a huge offensive into Germany. To
forestall this offensive, the Ninth Army attacked toward
Warsaw, supported by the Austrian armies on the right.
The attack was turned back at the gates of Warsaw by
superior Russian forces, and the Germans and Austrians
withdrew to their original starting line. The Ninth Army
then shifted rapidly to the Posen-Thorn area, drove between the Russian First and Second armies, and almost
succeeded in enveloping the Second Army in the Battle
of Łódź. These operations of the Ninth Army definitely
stopped the proposed Russian invasion of Germany.

Meanwhile, the French again besought their Russian allies to
invade Silesia via Warsaw and Posen (now Poznań) in order to relieve German pressure on the Western Front. Since Silesia's min-

eral resources and industrial plant were vital to their war effort, the Germans could be expected to withdraw troops from the west to combat an all-out Russian offensive. The Russians acquiesced, but Hindenburg blocked their plan for a drive straight through the Posen-Thorn (now Toruń) area and was able to move the Ninth Army into position in time to parry the expected Russian blow with an offensive of his own. On November 11, the German forces under General (later Field Marshal) August von Mackensen's command attacked north of Łódź; in four days they advanced 50 miles. Nevertheless, the Russians started their Silesian offensive on November 14, not realizing until November 16 that their Second Army was being encircled in the Łódź area. They managed to extricate their troops from Hindenburg's trap, but the cost was great; Łódź fell to the Germans, and the Russian drive into Silesia had to be abandoned.

Map 26. WINTER BATTLE OF MASURIA (Feb. 7–21, 1915). The plan of the Central Powers for 1915 was to drive Russia from the war. It envisioned an offensive from East Prussia by the Germans and a simultaneous advance by the Austrians in the Carpathians. The Germans secretly concentrated their Tenth Army on the Neman River, attacked, and overwhelmed the Russians. The 3d, 26th, and 3d Siberian corps escaped, but the 20th Corps was encircled in the Forest of Augustów, and more than 100,000 prisoners were taken. This was a great tactical victory for the Germans, but the Austrian attack in the south failed, so that the over-all strategic gains were nil.

OPERATIONS IN 1915

Winter Battle of Masuria

In January, 1915, Hindenburg and Ludendorff persuaded Emperor William II that an effort should be made to knock Russia out of the war. An Austrian offensive on the edge of the Carpathians in February failed, but the German Tenth Army, driving southward from the Nieman River, forced a Russian corps to surrender in the Forest of Augustów. Although three other corps escaped, the Russian casualties totaled 200,000 (of these, half were prisoners). The winter Battle of Masuria thus resulted in a major victory for the Germans, but their over-all plan to eliminate Russia from the war did not succeed.

Gorlice–Tarnów Breakthrough

By March, war weariness had set in in Russia. On the home front, food shortages in the cities, incapacities of administration, and corruption had created a desire for peace that was voiced by both left and right. On the fighting front, the armies were too

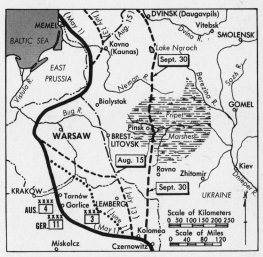

Map 27. GORLICE-TARNOW BREAKTHROUGH (May 2–4, 1915). The critical Russian shortage of weapons and munitions led the Germans to believe that another offensive would eliminate the Russians from the war. The Eleventh Army (from the Western Front) attacked in conjunction with the Austrian Fourth Army, gained surprise, and practically destroyed the Russian Third Army. Continued German and Austrian attacks compelled the Russians, whose logistical problems were now acute, to withdraw to the line shown.

weak to launch a major offensive; clothing and ammunition were often in short supply. Meanwhile, the Germans were secretly developing an offensive base in the Gorlice–Tarnów area. Infantry and artillery were brought in from the Western Front to reinforce the Fourth and Eleventh armies for an attack. The offensive was launched on May 2 behind a barrage utilizing 950 artillery pieces. Taken completely by surprise, the Russians fled in panic. A complete breakthrough was scored two days later, and by June 22, the German juggernaut had rolled over Lemberg. Turning north, the Germans took Warsaw on August 4–5 and Brest-Litovsk on August 25. By the beginning of October, German armies had penetrated deep into Russian territory, the front running from just west of Dvinsk (Daugavpils) in the north southward through the Pripet Marshes to Kolmea (now Kolomyya).

The Gorlice–Tarnów breakthrough and subsequent campaigns in 1915 cost the Russians 2 million casualties, half of whom were prisoners. Meanwhile, on September 5, Czar Nicholas II assumed command of the Russian armies.

OPERATIONS IN 1916

Winter and Spring

Following the losses of the Gorlice–Tarnów breakthrough, the Russians tried to rebuild their armies in preparation for a summer offensive. French entreaties for a diversion at the time of the German Verdun attack in February, 1916, once again caused them to act prematurely. In March, the Russians attacked near Lake Naroch, but their drive was soon halted by stiff German resistance and by mud from the spring thaws. The Eastern Front then remained dormant while both sides got ready for the summer campaigns. The Czar, no strategy genius, planned a July offensive north and south of the Pripet Marshes with the capture of Vilna (Vilnyus) by the West Army Group as its first goal. In May, however, the Austrians launched an attack on the Italian front, and now it was Italy's turn to appeal to Russia for assistance. The Czar agreed to create a diversion. The Russian commanders north of the Pripet Marshes felt unprepared to advance the date of the projected summer offensive, but the commander of the Southwest Army Group, General Aleksei Brusilov, volunteered to attack alone, starting on June 4.

Brusilov's Summer Offensive

Alone among high-ranking Russian officers, Brusilov had carefully studied German tactics. He concluded that it would be advantageous to forgo concentrations of superior manpower for the

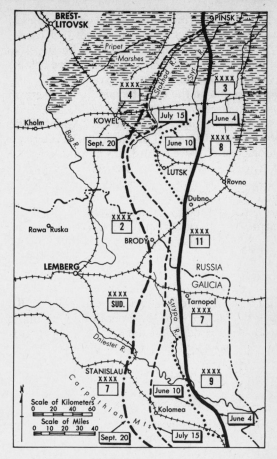

Map 28. BRUSILOV OFFENSIVE (June 4–Sept. 20, 1916).
Gen. Aleksei Brusilov launched a gigantic offensive to relieve Austrian pressure on the Italian front. The attack
surprised the Austrians and gained striking initial successes. Through use of their superior rail net, however,
the Germans shifted troops from the north and halted the
Russian offensive. Losses totaled more than 1,000,000 men
on each side. The strategic results of the Brusilov offensive
were far reaching. Austrian losses were so great as to
preclude further offensive action, and the Austrian offensive in Italy had to be halted; 15 German divisions had to
be transferred from the Verdun front to the Eastern Front;
Romania entered the war on the side of the Allies; and
Russia's huge losses started her on the road to revolution.

surprise to be gained through a rapid, highly mobile attack prepared in complete secrecy. Once his forces had been drawn into position and his officers carefully briefed, he struck quickly and hard. His efforts were not in vain: The offensive achieved Russia's greatest success of the war.

The Austrian line on the Dniester and Strypa rivers was breached within a week. Brusilov's troops then took Lutsk and threatened the rail junction at Kowel (now Kovel). Again Hindenburg was compelled to come to the aid of the Austrians, but although German reinforcements slowed Brusilov's advance, they were unable to stop it. The advisory editor of this volume, Brigadier General Vincent J. Esposito, has written that the battle "became a race between the excellent German–Austrian lateral communications and the inferior Russian railroads. The Germans won."* The battle lines of September 20 show that Brusilov's offensive had carried the Russians to the Carpathians in the south and along a line running west of Stanislau (now Stanislav), Brody, and Pinsk. The drive had exacted a tremendous toll, however, and it collapsed because of the exhaustion of the troops and the lack of ammunition.

The Brusilov offensive had raised great hopes in Russia, all of which were now dashed, and the groundwork was laid for the revolution. It also had major consequences for the Germans. By weakening their position on the Western Front and helping to influence Romania to enter the war on the Allied side, the offensive contributed to the eventual German defeat.

REVOLUTION AND MILITARY COLLAPSE

When the Brusilov offensive ended without success and with huge losses, morale in the Russian Army quickly deteriorated. Ammunition supplies had run out, many soldiers lacked shoes and sufficient clothing; adequate food supplies had long ceased reaching the front; and to the soldiers it seemed that the leaders callously ignored the loss of lives. The Czar refused to countenance the governmental reforms demanded by the left and alienated what little support remained for his rule among the liberal middle class. The slogan "Peace and Bread" reflected an overwhelming Russian desire. Rebellion broke out in Petrograd on March 12, 1917, and three days later the Czar was forced to abdicate. A liberal provisional government headed by the socialist Aleksandr Kerenski was swept

* The West Point Atlas of American Wars (New York, 1959), Vol. II, opposite Map 36.

Map 29. COLLAPSE OF RUSSIA (March, 1917–March, 1918). After the abdication of Czar Nicholas II on March 15, 1917, the Russian armies rapidly disintegrated. A last desperate attack was made—the Kerenski offensive—in July, 1917. It met with some initial success, but the Russians were soon driven back. In September, 1917, the Germans attacked the city of Riga to hasten Russian capitulation; on March 3, 1918, the Treaty of Brest-Litovsk was signed, under which the Germans occupied the area shown.

into office, but real power in the capital was exercised by the Petrograd Soviet of Workers' and Soldiers' Deputies.

At first, the overthrow of autocracy seemed a great advantage for the Allies, for Russia appeared wholeheartedly to have joined the democracies of the West. But appearances were deceptive. The Petrograd Soviet's Order No. 1, designed to create a more democratic army, in fact caused the dismissal of the best and most experienced officers, and, with the abolishment of capital punishment, soldiers deserted by the thousands. The Germans realized that Russian demoralization would be exacerbated by inaction. No offensive was launched, but in April the High Command brought Vladimir Lenin and his Bolshevik lieutenants east by sealed train from their exile in Switzerland. Hindenburg and Ludendorff expected that increased Bolshevik propaganda, the lack of discipline in the army, and the growing desire for peace in Russia would soon leave the Germans virtually unopposed on the Eastern Front.

Kerenski's undoing was that he tried to uphold Russia's obligations to her allies. The remaining Russian commanders—Russki, Brusilov, Lavr Kornilov, Vasili Gurko—insisted that the new government must not heed the popular desire for a separate peace with Germany. Kerenski gave in and authorized Brusilov to attempt a new offensive against Lemberg. On July 1, Brusilov led a force composed chiefly of Finns, Siberians, and Poles (the most reliable elements left in the Russian Army) against remnants of the collapsing Austrian Army. They registered gains of as much as 30 miles before a German counteroffensive sent them reeling back to the Galician frontier. The attack was a futile effort and the last Russian offensive of the war.

END OF THE WAR ON THE EASTERN FRONT

Hindenburg and Ludendorff calculated that one more successful German offensive would cause the overthrow of the Kerenski government and remove Russia from the war. On September 1, the German Eighth Army assaulted Riga, capturing the city two days later and driving beyond it. The Kerenski government fell, and on November 6–7 (October 24–25, Old Style), Lenin seized power in Petrograd. The next day the new Soviet government adopted a peace decree. This was interpreted by Leon Trotsky, on November 21, as a request for an armistice. Hostilities on the Eastern Front were suspended on December 2, and the next day delegates of Russia and the Central Powers met at Brest-Litovsk to arrange terms. The armistice negotiations were succeeded on December 22 by a peace conference.

Trotsky, who became the head of the Soviet delegation in January, 1918, haggled and played for time, hoping that the Bolshevik Revolution would sweep Germany and keep Russia from having to sign that power's severe peace terms. Pressed hard by the chief German delegate, General Max Hoffmann, he tried an audacious maneuver. On February 10, he announced that Russia refused to sign the German terms and unilaterally declared the state of war to be ended. This amounted to a declaration of "no war–no peace." The reaction of the Germans was furious and immediate. They denounced the armistice, and, at dawn on February 18, their troops poured across the lines, meeting no resistance. They captured Dvinsk in the north and Lutsk in the south. The next day, German headquarters received a telegram from Lenin accepting the peace conditions offered at Brest-Litovsk, but the advance continued to Lake Peipus and Narva in the north, where it directly threatened Petrograd. In the south, German troops swept through the Ukraine. Finally, on March 3, a peace treaty was signed at Brest-Litovsk. By its terms, Germany was to occupy a large expanse of Russian territory. If it had not been superseded by the subsequent armistice on the Western Front and by the Treaty of Versailles, Russia would have lost a third of her population, a third of her agricultural land, and more than half of her industry.

The war on the Eastern Front was over, and Russia lay defeated and racked by poverty and civil war. Victory came too late for the Germans, however, for the long struggle had prevented them from ever concentrating all of their strength in the west.

9. Italian Front

BY PIERO PIERI

Italy declared war on Austria-Hungary on May 23, 1915, and began active operations the next day. The initial Italian strategic plan, which had been developed early in April, envisioned operations in conjunction with the Russians, Serbs, and Montenegrins to break into the plains of Hungary and force the collapse of the Austro-Hungarian Empire. At that time, the Russians had advanced to the foot of the Carpathian Mountains, deep in Austrian territory. Early in May, however, an Austro-German counterattack drove the Russians back and crumpled their Southern Front. Now, on May 24, the general situation, which had looked so promising for the Allies a month before, was dark indeed. Stalemated on the Western Front, frustrated in Gallipoli, and with Russia in serious straits, they were grateful for Italy's decision to join them. With the principal attention of the world focused on the titanic Western Front, the part played by Italy in the war has generally been underestimated. Some of the bitterest fighting under the most difficult conditions took place on the Austro-Italian front, and events there exerted considerable influence on the conduct of the war as a whole.

The general course of the war on this front is simply told. Restricted by topographical considerations to offensive action on the single narrow front of the Isonzo River, the Italians launched 11 ferocious attacks there between June, 1915, and September, 1917. The resulting territorial gains were meager, but the attacks succeeded in so wearing down the Austrians that large German formations had to be rushed to the front to prevent a collapse. Meanwhile, an Austrian offensive from the mountainous Trentino in mid-1916 to relieve the pressure on the Isonzo front had failed. In the autumn of 1917, a combined Austro-German offensive on the Isonzo caught the Italians unprepared and brought on the debacle of Caporetto. Forced back to the Piave River, the Italians, bolstered by Allied units, held firmly and repulsed all attempts to dislodge them. The sting of Caporetto brought a resurgence to the Italian home front that excited the admiration of the world. Factories hummed, and all hands turned with determination to preparations for the final victory. In the fall of 1918, these efforts culminated in the glorious Battle of Vittorio Veneto, in which the Austrians were eliminated from the war.

Strategic Considerations

Nowhere has terrain exerted a more decisive influence on strategy than on the Austro-Italian front. Unfortunately for the Italians, this influence was for them predominantly adverse. The frontier, 484 miles in length, was divided into three distinct sectors: the Trentino (part of the South Tirol) on the west, the Dolomites and the Carnic Alps in the center, and the line of the Isonzo River on the east. The Trentino, which then belonged to Austria, formed a deep wedge into northern Italy. It was a rough, mountainous area, which the Austrians had converted into a veritable fortress. Any major advance in the Trentino would have to be made up the Adige Valley, where it could easily be stopped in the fortified Trento (Trent) defile area or at the Brenner Pass farther north. Even if successful, such an advance would lead to no strategic objective of consequence. The Trentino pointed straight to the heart of northern Italy, and an Austrian offensive there would threaten to cut off Italian troops at the Carnic and Isonzo fronts. The area was detached from Austria proper, however, and it was served by only one railroad, which could not supply forces of the size necessary to ensure success. Furthermore, an excellent rail net enabled the Italians to shift troops rapidly from other fronts to counter an offensive in the Trentino.

The Carnic Alps in the central sector were forbidding. Mountain passes suitable only for Alpine troops were often situated at altitudes of over 6,500 feet. A breakthrough here might lead to the cutting of the rail line from Austria proper to the Trentino, but the great number of Italian Alpine troops needed for such a venture was not available, and the operational season in the mountains was only of a few months' duration.

The only area in which a decision could be reached by either side was the Isonzo front, and from the Italian point of view this front was less formidable than the others only by comparison. The Austrians controlled all the crossings of the Isonzo and the dominating mountains and high areas to the east, and any Italian attempt to cross the river was therefore subject to withering artillery and infantry fire. As one analyst described the Italian dilemma, "the river could not be crossed until the mountains had been seized, and the mountains could not be seized until the river had been crossed." The principal features of the Isonzo front were the strongly fortified Gorizia (Görz) area in the center, the rugged Bainsizza (Bansizza) Plateau to the north, and the rocky, barren Carso (Karst; Kras) Plateau to the south, with its precipitous slopes rising as high as 900 feet above the sea, and dominated by two towering mountains, Monte San Michele and the Hermada. In short, fighting by the Italians along the frontier would be consistently uphill and against strong defenses.

OPERATIONS IN 1915

Initial Operations

At the time of Italy's entry into the war, the Austrians had joined with the Germans in highly successful operations against the Russians, and for the time being they elected to pursue these operations and to maintain a purely defensive posture on the Italian front. The Austrian chief of staff, Field Marshal Count Franz Conrad von Hötzendorf (often referred to as Conrad), had assembled 14 divisions on the Southern Front. In addition, although Germany and Italy were not then at war, the Germans had provided their *Alpenkorps* (a crack mountain unit of about division strength) for employment in the mountains of the Trentino. The Italian commander, General (later Marshal) Count Luigi Cadorna, had at his disposal 35 divisions. This would seem to indicate a better than two-to-one superiority over the Austrians, but since the training, equipment, and artillery of the Italian troops were not complete and the Austrians occupied extremely strong defensive positions, the combat strength of the two opponents was approximately equal.

On the first day of war, Cadorna launched a general offensive along the entire front. His First Army struck the nose and southeastern face of the Trentino salient as the Fourth Army attacked the northeastern face, hoping to break through to the railroad and cut off the Austrians in the Trentino. The Fourth Army would then advance eastward down the valley of the Drava River, join the Carnic Corps as the latter broke through on its front, and move toward Villach. Meanwhile, the Second Army would capture Caporetto and its environs, and the Third Army would advance to the Isonzo between Gradisca and Montfalcone. It was an ambitious enterprise, but the 23 divisions allotted to the three principal offensive armies were not sufficient to accomplish the many tasks

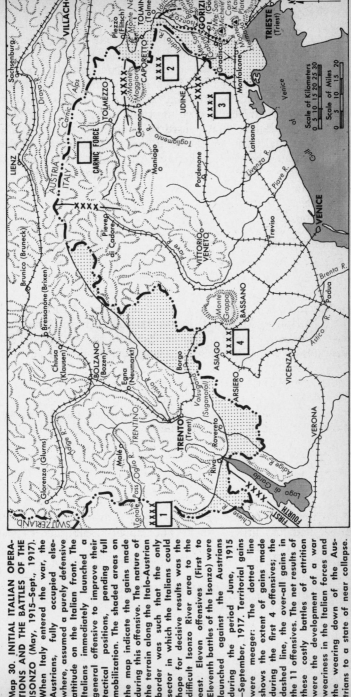

Map 30. INITIAL ITALIAN OPERA-TIONS AND THE BATTLES OF THE ISONZO (May, 1915–Sept., 1917). When Italy entered the war, the Austrians, fully occupied else-where, assumed a purely defensive attitude on the Italian front. The Italians immediately launched a general offensive to improve their tactical positions, pending full mobilization. The shaded areas on the map indicate the gains made during this offensive. The nature of the terrain along the Italo-Austrian border was such that the only sector in which the Italians could hope for decisive results was the difficult Isonzo River area to the east. Eleven offensives (First to Eleventh battles of the Isonzo) were launched against the Austrians during the period June, 1915 –September, 1917. Territorial gains were meager: The dotted line shows the extent of gains made during the first 4 offensives; the dashed line, the over-all gains in the 11 offensives. The net results of these costly battles of attrition were the development of a war weariness in the Italian forces and the wearing down of the Aus-trians to a state of near collapse.

assigned. Nevertheless, by June 16, when the initial operations were halted, significant gains had been made up to the Austrian line of resistance *à outrance*, and the Italian positions for subsequent tactical operations had been greatly improved. It had become clear, however, that the war on the Austro-Italian front was to be a war of deliberate siege of strong defenses and of bloody attrition. The Italians now paused to complete their mobilization, move additional troops to the front, and prepare for a new drive. As the Italian official account stated, ". . . the strengthened barrier which the enemy has prepared with skill and feverish activity against our irruption will require a series of attempts to wrest the strengthened positions, beginning on June 23 with the first battle of the Isonzo."

First Four Battles of the Isonzo

On June 23, 1915, the Italians began the First Battle of the Isonzo, which lasted until July 7. It was followed in rapid succession by the Second Battle (July 18–August 3), the Third (October 18–November 3), and the Fourth (November 10–December 2). These battles were attempts by the Italians to break through the strong Austrian defensive positions from south of Tolmino (Tolmein; now Tolmin) to the sea, the major efforts being made in the Gorizia area and against the Carso Plateau. Lacking heavy artillery, blocked by stubborn defenders in well-prepared positions, and plagued by heavy autumn rains and winter cold, the Italians paid dearly for the small gains they scored. Courage and untold sacrifices abounded, and the Italian infantry won the admiration of the enemy. In fact, one may read in the Austrian military report on the war: "The front-line official reports are emphatic on the magnificent valor of the Italian infantry and particularly on the conduct of its officers in the field." It should be mentioned that the Italian officers were of the educated classes, while the troops were drawn from the masses of peasants and workers with whom the former had had little contact. The rapport established between these divergent groups by the common struggle and by common sacrifices proved to be one of the greatest revelations of the war.

OPERATIONS IN 1916

Fifth Battle of the Isonzo

By the end of 1915, Italian losses had aggregated 66,000 men killed, 190,000 wounded, and 22,500 taken prisoner; Austrian casualties had totaled about 165,000. The Italian Army was close to exhaustion, but the Austrians were fortunately not aware of its state. Meanwhile, Austrian strength on the front had been increased to 22 divisions. During January and February, 1916, demands for operations in Albania and rescue work for the Serbs served to accentuate the poor condition of the Italian forces. When the Germans launched their determined attack against Verdun in February, Marshal Joseph Joffre urged Italian diversionary aid by means of an attack on the Isonzo front. Cadorna responded with a hastily prepared offensive: the Fifth Battle of the Isonzo (March 9–17, 1916). Directed to the north and south of Gorizia, the offensive bogged down in fog, rain, and snow and served only to further exhaust the Italian troops. Cadorna, learning of an impending Austrian attack from the Trentino, halted the offensive and prepared to meet the new threat.

Austrian Asiago Offensive (May 15–June 17)

Since his days as a young officer, Conrad had considered an attack from the Trentino as the best method of defeating the Italians. Now he believed the time ripe for such an offensive. German aid was requested, but General Erich von Falkenhayn, understanding better than Conrad the implications of large-scale operations in the Trentino, refused the Austrian request. Nevertheless, Conrad decided to proceed with his *Strafe* (punishment) expedition with the forces available—14 divisions and 4 *Kaiserjäger* regiments, which had replaced the German *Alpenkorps* in October, 1915. He planned to compensate for his deficiency in troops by assembling huge quantities of medium and heavy artillery.

The objective of the offensive was to drive into the northern Italian plain, capture the key rail center of Padua (Padova), and thus effectively cut off the Italian Carnic and Isonzo forces. The commander of the Italian First Army on the Trentino front, General Roberto Brusati, had been instructed to organize a position in depth to hold off any Austrian offensive moves there. Instead, he engaged in interminable local actions to improve his position, so that when the Austrian blow fell on May 15, 1916, he was caught off balance. Conrad's offensive made good initial gains and captured Arsiero and Asiago, gateways to the northern plain. Here the momentum of the attack declined because of lack of strength, difficult terrain, and the resistance of Italian reinforcements transferred from the Isonzo front. Under the pressure of an Italian coun-

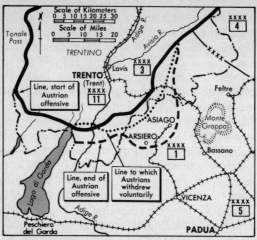

Map 31. AUSTRIAN ASIAGO OFFENSIVE (May 15–June 17, 1916). The Austrians attempted to get behind the Italian main forces on the Isonzo front by an offensive from the Trentino to capture the key rail center of Padua. Difficult terrain, lack of strength, and the timely shifting of Italian forces from the Isonzo front over the excellent rail net in northern Italy all joined to stop the Austrian attack. In June a successful Russian offensive in Galicia (Brusilov offensive, Map 28), caused the Austrians to dispatch forces from the Trentino and to assume a strictly defensive attitude on the Asiago front.

teroffensive and the necessity to shift troops to Galicia, where a Russian attack was impending, Conrad drew his forces back almost to their original positions in the Trentino. The Asiago offensive ended on June 17: Conrad's pet scheme had been tried and found wanting. Losses on each side totaled about 100,000.

Sixth to Eleventh Battles of the Isonzo

After the failure of the Austrian Asiago offensive, Cadorna rapidly began to return his troops by rail and motor to the Isonzo front. The Austrians, who had to move from the Trentino over a longer, less efficient route, were at a disadvantage. As a result, when Cadorna launched the Sixth Battle of the Isonzo (also known as the Battle of Gorizia; August 6–17, 1916), his operations met with immediate success. Both Gorizia and the bastion of Monte San Michele, dominating the northern section of the Carso, were captured. Threatened now from the north, the Austrians on the Carso fell back. Stiffening resistance and the lack of adequate reserve to force a real breakthrough, however, brought the offensive to a halt. This battle had given the Italians their first real gains of the war; nevertheless, nothing decisive had been achieved.

Subsequent Italian military actions took on political aims to aggravate the "moral crisis" of the Dual Monarchy through a relentless wearing down of its forces that might eventually lead to internal collapse. Since Austria considered the retention of Trieste (Triest) vital, the Italians saw in the capture of that Adriatic city the opening wedge toward the downfall of the Hapsburg Empire. The plan was to reach the city, which lay only 30 miles behind the front, by a succession of well-timed, energetic, limited-objective attacks punctuated by well-planned respites to prevent unnecessary losses, thus approaching the major objective by bounds. To this end the Seventh (September 14–17), Eighth (October 10–12), and Ninth (November 1–4) battles of the Isonzo were initiated. The theory was sound, but in practice (and in large part due to the growing insufficiency of artillery) the attacks developed into the same drawn-out and bloody affairs that had formerly characterized fighting on that front. Notable local successes were achieved, but not much progress was made toward the larger goal. The three offensives did disturb the Austrian commander on the Isonzo front, General (later Field Marshal) Baron Svetozar Boroević von Bojna, who requested reinforcements, adding, "The last three battles have shown that the enemy has learned his lessons well and is taking advantage of all past experience in utilizing to the full modern techniques of war." For the Italian soldiers, who knew little of the tremendous strain under which the Austrians were operating, however, these battles seemed disproportionate in terms of results and sacrifices, of victories and losses, and of the means employed and the results attained.

Efforts to refurbish the Italian Army in the autumn of 1916 and the succeeding winter brought imposing results. A total of 16 new divisions were put in the field, and 6 additional divisions were being made ready; medium artillery was doubled, and heavy artillery was increased fourfold; the number of machine guns, which at the start of the war had been only 600, was brought to 8,200; a gigantic acceleration in the production of bombs was being spurred; and military aircraft, which had numbered 382 in 1915, were now increased to 3,860, with great improvements in speed, striking capacity, and logistical potential. Early in 1917, Cadorna felt confident enough to resume offensive operations. It had been agreed by the

Allies that their efforts in the spring of 1917 would be coordinated. Accordingly, the British attacked at Arras on April 9; the French drove forward on the Aisne on April 16; and the Italians took the offensive in the Tenth Battle of the Isonzo on May 12. This offensive was planned as two coordinated flanking attacks, first against the Bainsizza barrier and later against the Carso. The operations developed into the same exasperating pattern as had the engagements of the preceding autumn. After great losses, the battle was halted on May 28. On June 4, a surprise Austrian counterattack deprived the Italians of a number of hard-won positions; the battle ended on June 8.

Cadorna now turned to a limited offensive on the eastern face of the Trentino salient, between the Valsugana (Suganatal) and Asiago, where he employed 12 divisions and 24 Alpine battalions on a 10-mile front. Under the misnomer of the Battle of the Ortigara, the engagement lasted from June 10 to 29. The battle turned into a Carso-like struggle of attrition waged at an altitude of 6,500 feet. There were initial and occasional brilliant successes, but no major results were attained, and Italian losses were enormous.

This might have been the moment to suspend operations to permit the troops to recoup their strength. The Allies kept pressing for a new offensive, however, and Cadorna was eager to gain a better defensive line, at least on the Isonzo. Concentrating on the river such a mass of men and matériel as had never been seen on that front (51 divisions with 5,200 pieces of artillery), he launched the Eleventh Battle of the Isonzo (August 19–September 12). The Second Army was to gain the Bainsizza Plateau, officially described as "a transitional objective and zone of maneuver opening the way to the capture of the Ternova [Tarnova] Plateau." The Third Army was to attack the Carso and seize the dominating Hermada and the surrounding plateau. Diversionary actions were planned for the north as far as Tolmino.

The Third Army attack came to nothing, and, on September 4, a powerful Austrian counterattack hurled the Italians once again down the slopes of the Hermada. The Second Army attack failed in its principal purpose through the intransigence of its commander, General Luigi Capello, who converted the diversionary action against Tolmino into the main attack and obstinately continued it even after it had failed. Since the reserve had been allotted for his use, it was lost to the general action. Instead of a single, coordinated offensive with alternating pressures and judicious use of the reserve, three separate and distinct actions had resulted: at Tol-mino, for the Bainsizza, and on the Carso.

The Italian offensives of 1917 had gained notable local tactical successes, including a five-mile penetration into the strongest Austrian defenses. Nevertheless, the pivotal points of the Austrian defense line remained in enemy hands: Tolmino, Monte San Gabriele, and the Hermada. Italian losses had been staggering; once again, and to a greater extent than ever, fatigue, weariness, and frustration gripped the Italian troops, making them prey to an unscrupulous neutralist and defeatist propaganda mercilessly exploited at home and abroad.

BATTLE OF CAPORETTO, 1917

After the Eleventh Battle of the Isonzo, the Austrians on that front were at the point of collapse and might well have succumbed to another offensive. Emperor Charles I now requested the replacement of Austro-Hungarian troops on the Russian and Romanian fronts by Germans, so that he might throw the entire weight of his armed forces against the Italians. The German High Command felt, however, that the war would be decided on the Western Front. An offensive against Italy at this time would be justified only if it could definitely knock her out of the war; otherwise, it would merely lead the Austrians to abandon their present excellent defensive positions and perhaps necessitate redeployments to less favorable ones. Nevertheless, the Germans agreed to intervene on the Italian front with a limited number of crack troops fully supported by artillery, air forces, and logistical services. A quick, resolute blow was envisioned that would throw the Italians back beyond the Isonzo and, if possible, behind the Tagliamento, in order to afford the Austrians some respite and time to prepare for a victory offensive at a future propitious moment. For this purpose the Austro-German Fourteenth Army was organized from seven German divisions (including the powerful *Alpenkorps*) and eight Austrian divisions. General Otto von Below, of Western Front fame, was given its command.

By September 18, Cadorna had become convinced that an Austro-German offensive was impending on the Isonzo. On that date he ordered his Second Army (General Capello) and Third Army (Emmanuel Philibert, Duke of Aosta) to assume defensive positions in depth and brace for attack. Having issued the order, he took no measures to supervise its execution, as is incumbent on a

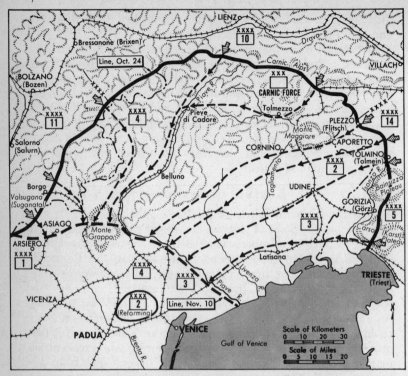

Map 32. BATTLE OF CAPORETTO (October 24–November 12, 1917). German troops were sent to the Isonzo front, and a combined Austro-German offensive was launched. Using new tactics, the Germans quickly shattered the front of the Italian Second Army, whose commander, even though apprised of the coming offensive, had failed to take adequate defensive measures. The Italians were forced into a general withdrawal and succeeded in reorganizing on the line of the Piave River after suffering 320,000 casualties. This disastrous defeat, however, not only failed to demoralize the Italian troops and home front but engendered greater unity and determination to prosecute and win the war.

commander in chief, nor did he issue any directive for the defensive battle. Meanwhile, the offensive-minded Capello dreamed of a counteroffensive in the Tolmino area and neglected to prepare his defensive position. Cadorna, who spent the time until October 19 inspecting other fronts, was generally out of touch with the activities of his forces on the Isonzo. When he and Capello finally bestirred themselves to reinforce the left flank of the Second Army, it was too late.

Before dawn on October 24, 1917, an intense and effective bombardment fell on the Italian lines. First gas and then high-explosive shells were used. The Italian gas masks offered little protection against the gas, and panic seized the troops. At 8 A.M., the Fourteenth Army moved forward on a line from Tolmino to Plezzo (Flitsch; now Bovec), concealed by a heavy mist that blanketed observation from the heights. Capello had 25 divisions with which to oppose Below's 15 divisions, but they were under strength, poorly distributed, and in inadequate defensive positions. Using their new tactics of infiltration and relentless pressure, the Germans shattered the front of the Italian Second Army. By evening of October 25, it was clear that a retreat was imperative; Cadorna did not issue the order until October 27, thereby losing two precious days. It was anticipated that at least a temporary stand would be made behind the Tagliamento, but when the enemy crossed the river near Cornino to the north the Tagliamento position became untenable. On November 4, Cadorna ordered a further withdrawal to the Piave. Many troops had been cut off, particularly those of the Carnic Corps, but the Isonzo forces, covered by an excellent cavalry rear guard, reached the strong line of the Piave by November 10. This Caporetto disaster (sometimes called the Twelfth Battle of the Isonzo) cost the Italians 320,000 casualties in killed, wounded, and prisoners and several thousand guns.

Meanwhile, General Cadorna was replaced by General (later Marshal) Armando Diaz. The line of the Piave was organized with the Fourth Army on the left and the Third on the right, while the broken Second Army attempted to reorganize in the rear. A force of 11 Anglo-French divisions, hastily rushed from the Western Front to Italy, constituted a general reserve, which Cadorna had so sadly neglected. Of the 65 Italian divisions available prior to Caporetto, only 33 divisions were now at full efficiency (4 or 5 others were still partially serviceable). Pitted against them were 50 Austro-German divisions and 4,500 cannon. As the so-called "law of Clausewitz" (originated by the Prussian Karl von Clausewitz) had foreseen, however, the Austro-German offensive had been reduced in power as it advanced in space. The very speed of the advance had outstripped the capacity of the bridge engineers and other essential logistical services.

The Austro-German forces persisted in their efforts to force crossings of the Piave and destroy the Italian Army until December 26, but they were consistently repulsed. Particularly fierce attacks were thrown against stubborn Italian defenders on Monte Grappa but to no avail. Regarding the fight on the Grappa, General Konrad Krafft von Dellmensingen, German chief of staff of the Fourteenth Army, later wrote: "Thus our offensive was brought to a standstill short of its objectives, an offensive which had been so rich in expectations and hopes, and the Grappa became the 'Sacred Mountain' of the Italians. They can be rightly proud that they held it against the heroic efforts of the best troops of both the Austro-Hungarian Army and their German comrades."

The resurgence of the Italian Army and the home front after Caporetto was truly remarkable. The disaster strengthened the determination of the Italian people; the entire nation at last began to support the war effort. In a few months, industry replaced all of the artillery matériel losses, and the supply of munitions was considerably increased. The army proved to be still sound, and during the winter of 1917–18 it further recovered its strength with marvelous speed. The place of the Second Army was taken by the Fifth Army, which for the moment at least served as the chief reserve of the supreme command. In the meantime, measures were taken to minister to the physical needs and restore the battered morale of the Italian soldier. General Diaz possessed a more humane sense of the soldier's life than Cadorna did, for under the uniform he saw the man and the citizen. New organizational methods for defense and offensive were developed which sought maximum results with a minimum loss of life. Greater emphasis was placed on the use of airpower; intelligence and information services were overhauled; and a central agency was formed to engage in counterpropaganda against the enemy.

The other important result of the Caporetto affair was that high Allied officials gathered in conference at Rapallo and agreed to form an Allied Supreme War Council to coordinate the activities in all the theaters.

BATTLE OF THE PIAVE, 1918

In the spring of 1918 the Germans began a series of five drives on the Western Front designed to win the war before American forces could effectively intervene. Locked in a death struggle, each side asked its ally on the Austro-Italian front to attack. The Germans urged an all-out Austrian attack to drive Italy from the war, so that Austrian troops could be transferred to the Western Front (the seven German divisions in Italy had already been shifted); Foch wanted an Italian offensive on the Trentino front to circumvent such a move. In March, six Anglo-French divisions in Italy

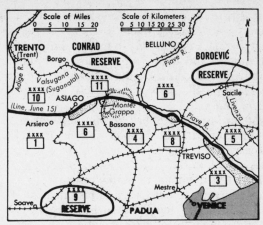

Map 33. BATTLE OF THE PIAVE (June 15–24, 1918). In June, 1918, after the failure of their first three drives on the Western Front, the Germans were in desperate need of manpower. They therefore urged the Austrians to attack to put Italy out of the war, so that Austrian troops could be sent to the Western Front. The Austrian offensive against the Italian position on the Piave failed because of the dispersion of effort and the well-planned Italian defense.

were sent back to the Western Front; the other five were moved to the mountains of the Trentino front in preparation for an offensive there. In April, two Italian divisions went to France. Diaz saw no advantage in an offensive against the Trentino and vetoed the idea; the Austrians proceeded to attack.

In all, 58 Austro-Hungarian divisions were assembled for the drive; Diaz had 57, including the 5 Anglo-French divisions. Conrad, demoted after his abortive Asiago offensive, commanded in the Trentino; Boroević, on the Piave front. Because of conflicts of personality and inadequate lateral communications, the Austrian forces, including reserves, were divided almost equally between the two sectors, thus denying the possibility of a concentrated effort anywhere on the front. On June 13, a diversionary effort was launched at Tonale Pass to the west of the Trentino; on June 15, the main attack began. By evening, minor gains had been made in the Trentino, but these were wiped out by counterattacks and heavy artillery fire on the next day. Boroević had better initial success in the Piave River sector. Crossings were effected at three points; at one, an advance of three miles was made. For eight days the Austrians and Italians struggled fiercely in attack and counterattack. Aircraft and artillery struck at the Austrian floating bridges, and the Piave rose sharply to further threaten their destruction. With supplies and ammunition beginning to run out and harassed by Italian counterattacks, Boroević ordered his troops back across the Piave on the night of June 22–23; the movement was completed on June 24.

Foch, who on July 1, 1918, had become supreme commander of all Allied forces, urged Diaz to exploit this victory and to launch a general offensive in coordination with an Allied offensive against the Soissons salient on the Western Front, scheduled for mid-July. He judged the Austro-Hungarian Army to be in a state of collapse and ripe for a final push, but Diaz and his principal aide, General (later Marshal) Pietro Badoglio, thought otherwise. Diaz pointed to the Austrian failure in the river operations and was doubtful of Italian success in repeating the venture in reverse, particularly with his armies in their present state, for the Battle of the Piave had been hard fought. He preferred to reorganize, re-equip, and launch a deliberate offensive when he was fully prepared.

Battle of Vittorio Veneto, 1918

For his final offensive, Diaz had 57 divisions (51 Italian, 3 British, 2 French, and 1 Czechoslovakian, plus the U.S. 332d Infantry Regiment), and his artillery numbered 7,700 guns. Opposing him were 58 divisions and 6,000 guns. The main attack of the offensive was to be made in the center by the Eighth Army of 14 Italian divisions under General (later Marshal) Enrico Caviglia, supported on the right by the Tenth Army of two British and two Italian divisions under British Lieutenant General (later Field Marshal) Frederic Rudolph Lambert, the 10th Earl of Cavan, and on the left by the Twelfth Army of one French and three Italian divisions under French General Jean César Graziani. The plan was subsequently changed so that the Fourth Army (on the left of the Twelfth) would make the initial attack of the offensive on the massif of the Grappa in order to draw the Austrian reserves away from the front of the main attack. The ultimate object of the offensive was to split the Austrian armies and roll them up on the flanks. On the morning of October 24, 1918, Diaz launched his offensive.

Meanwhile, the Allied final offensive on the Western Front was making good progress, and the Germans were withdrawing under great pressure. Convinced of eventual defeat, the German Reichs-

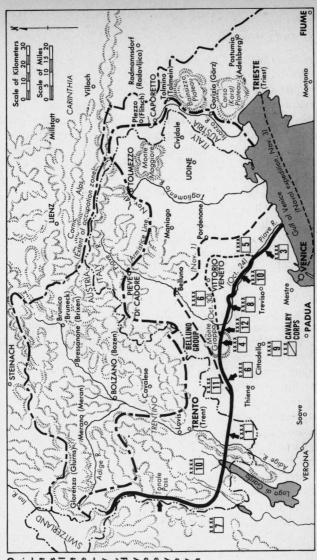

Map 34. BATTLE OF VITTORIO VENETO (Oct. 24–Nov. 4, 1918). The Italians made great preparations for a final offensive to defeat the Austrians. In October, 1918, as Marshal Ferdinand Foch's general offensive on the Western Front pushed back the Germans, the Italians launched their all-out offensive. The main attack, made by their Eighth and Tenth armies, penetrated the enemy position, and the Austrians broke. The Cavalry Corps, held in readiness for the purpose, rushed through the breach to exploit the success. By November 4, when an armistice became effective, approximately 500,000 Austrians had been taken prisoner.

tag had signified on October 20 its acceptance of President Woodrow Wilson's Fourteen Points as part of a basis for an armistice. Earlier, on October 4, the Austrians had appealed to the President and had begun to assemble an armistice commission.

If the political leaders of the Central Powers were in a mood for an armistice and peace, this attitude was not as yet reflected at the fighting front on the Piave. For three days the Austrians resisted the attacks of the Italian Fourth Army on the Grappa in a fierce, determined manner reminiscent of the early battles of the Isonzo. Territorial gains were minimal on both sides, but the Fourth Army succeeded in its objective of attracting the Austrian reserves from the front of the main attack. In the meantime, the Eighth, Tenth, and Twelfth armies began crossing the Piave on their fronts. By October 27, Italian, French, and British contingents had established three small bridgeheads, but until noon of October 28 the situation appeared to be grave all along the line. On the afternoon of that day, however, the situation changed; part of the Eighth Army broke through over bridges opened by the Tenth Army and advanced toward Monticano. At that moment the Austrian Sixth Army, on the Italian Eighth Army front, received orders to retire to its second line of defense. October 29 proved to be the day of decision, as Austrian resistance began to falter before the determined advance of the three central armies. In some places, the Austro-Hungarians stood their ground fiercely; in others, they made a halfhearted stand; and in still other sectors, they crumbled. The real dissolution occurred among the Austrian reserves; some refused to counterattack, while others mutinied.

The final collapse began on the night of October 30–31, when the struggle turned into a series of isolated encounters, of Austrian units cut off, pursued, captured, and overtaken by advance troops. In these operations after the breakthrough the Italian Cavalry Corps played a splendid role. On the afternoon of November 3, Trento was occupied, and a few hours later a naval expedition landed Italian *Bersaglieri* at Trieste. In the early evening the armistice was signed at Villa Giusti, near Padua. Approximately 500,000 Austro-Hungarian prisoners were taken in this final Italian offensive.

GENERAL COMMENTARY

The political and psychological crisis that had gripped the Austro-Hungarian Army in the final phase of the war should not obscure the fact that the Italian victory was the result of more than three years of arduous struggle that had cost the lives of 650,000 Italian troops and the maiming of almost 1 million others. Moreover, the Italian contribution was not limited to the Austro-Hungarian front. The Italian 2d Army Corps was sent to the Western Front, where it participated with distinction in the Second Battle of the Marne. Approximately 100,000 Italian workers were employed in French war industries; at the same time, they constituted the manpower pool from which the ranks of the 2d Corps were replenished. An Italian division of 35,000 men fought with the Allied Salonika armies in Macedonia, and five Italian divisions were engaged in Albania. Italy mobilized a greater percentage of her male citizens than did any other Allied nation except France.

The activities of the Italian Army had been fully supported by those of the Italian Navy. Though the Italian Fleet was superior to that of the Austrians in many respects, it operated under the handicap of a lack of adequate bases on the Italian side of the Adriatic Sea, while the Austrians possessed numerous excellent and strongly defended ports on their side. Nevertheless, the Austro-Hungarian Navy, except for occasional minor sorties and raids, was kept virtually bottled up within its well-protected harbors. An especially arduous and valiant feat performed by the Italian Navy was the rescue of the bulk of the Serbian Army, which had been driven from its homeland by an overwhelming German-Austrian-Bulgarian offensive to the coast of Albania, on the Adriatic. Faced by continual threats from nearby major Austrian naval bases, the Italian Fleet transported in safety to Corfu 260,895 men, 10,153 horses and other animal stock, 68 cannons, and much equipment during the period November 22, 1915–March 4, 1916.

10. Colonial and Japanese Campaigns

BY BRIGADIER GENERAL VINCENT J. ESPOSITO,
U.S.A. (RET.)

In 1914, Germany possessed a vast colonial empire with territories in Africa, Asia, and the Pacific. Its area exceeded 1 million square miles, and its population was about 15 million. Less than 25,000 of the inhabitants of the various colonies were German nationals, and these were mostly administrators and settlers. In Africa the colonies were Togoland, the Cameroons (Kamerun), German Southwest Africa, and German East Africa; in Asia, Kiaochow, a protectorate in China's Shantung Province; and in the Pacific, the Bismarck Archipelago, Western Samoa, Kaiser-Wilhelmsland (northeastern New Guinea), the Caroline, Marshall, and Mariana Islands (except Guam, a United States possession), and part of the Solomon Islands. Although the eventual fate of these colonies would depend on the outcome of the war in Europe, the Allies could not allow them to remain unmolested, for they provided excellent bases for German warships and commerce raiders and had long-range wireless communications systems. The Germans had a grand plan for the mastery of central Africa from coast to coast, including the Belgian and Portuguese possessions. This aim was to be furthered as the fortunes of war in Europe permitted.

African Campaigns

The nature of the military campaigns in Africa differed sharply from those in other areas. Roads and trails were few and poor; whenever possible, operations were conducted either along the rivers, receiving their support by boat, or along the few railroad lines. Logistical support of overland operations was provided primarily by native carriers, who generally far outnumbered the combat troops they supported. (The tsetse fly abounded in many areas and quickly killed any transport animals or cattle brought in.) The military forces on both sides consisted chiefly of trained natives formed into companies officered by Europeans, with, on occasion, a leavening of white units. Native police forces of the German colonies had received some military training and were employed at times. Advances were of necessity difficult and slow; the relatively

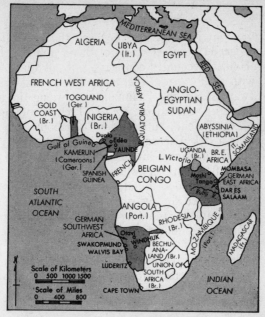

Map. 35. German possessions in Africa in 1914.

small forces operating in the vast tropical areas could evade each other easily; and disease killed and incapacitated far more combatants and carriers than battle did.

Togoland

Togoland (now divided between Ghana and the Republic of Togo) had a maximum width of 90 miles and extended inland for 330 miles from the Gulf of Guinea. About 100 miles from the coast, the Germans had installed a powerful wireless station that gathered information from the other German African colonies and relayed it to Berlin. On August 7, 1914, British and French forces attacked Togoland from the west and east, respectively. The small garrison of 200 Germans and about 1,000 native troops withdrew before the advancing Allied forces toward the wireless station at Kamina, where, on August 26, it was penned in and surrendered after destroying the wireless facilities. A Franco-British administration was set up, and in a few weeks normal peace conditions again prevailed.

Cameroons

The Cameroons (now divided between the Republic of Cameroon and Nigeria) occupied 200,881 square miles in the Gulf of Guinea. Inland, the country consists mostly of forest, bush, and grassland, with a hilly area in the north. The coastal strip, with its mangrove swamps and heavy rainfall, was among the most pestilent areas in Africa. On August 20, two French columns (including a Belgian contingent) entered the Cameroons from the southeast, beginning a trek that was to extend for more than 300 miles through desolate and forbidding territory; and between August 25 and August 27, three British columns crossed the Nigerian-Cameroons border. After modest initial gains, German counterattacks in early September forced the British back across the border in great disorder. The complete failure of the attack is attributed to inadequate preparations, topographical ignorance, and the rainy season then in progress.

A Franco-British naval-military expedition up the Wouri River was then organized. Better prepared, it met with greater success than the land attack. On September 27, Duala (now Douala), 20 miles up the river, was captured, although most of its garrison escaped. The Allies pursued the Germans southeast for 35 miles, to Edéa, which they occupied on October 26. After an unsuccessful counterattack on Edéa, the main German forces withdrew toward Yaunde (now Yaoundé), 100 miles to the east, where their munitions facilities were located. It was their plan to hold out on this high ground until the soon-expected German victory in Europe.

The Allies' plan was to converge on Yaunde from all directions, but it was to be more than a year before they reached the town. The advance was conducted under the most demoralizing conditions. Swamps, forests, and tropical heat impeded progress; columns had to travel great distances without transportation and communications; small German detachments harassed the troops in guerrilla operations and hostile natives set up ambushes, making it necessary to build and garrison blockhouses every 20 miles; the rainy season intervened to halt the advance completely for a long period; and tropical diseases, principally dysentery, thinned the Allied ranks. On January 1, 1916, the British entered Yaunde from the north, only to find the town evacuated; the German forces had begun a 125-mile march to neutral Spanish Guinea in the south. Efforts to cut them off failed, and they were interned safely by the Spaniards. Oddly enough, marching and fighting far apart and without communications for almost a year and a half, the Allied columns converged on their objective, Yaunde, within a few days of each other. By mid-February, 1916, the last of the small isolated garrisons had been captured. White prisoners were sent to England, and natives to their homes. A joint Franco-British administration was established.

The maximum German strength in the Cameroons reached 8,000 white and native troops; in the final advance the Allies employed 24,000 troops (10,000 French, 8,000 British, and 6,000 Belgian), in addition to 40,000 native carriers. Battle losses were small on both sides; disease exacted the major toll, particularly among the native carriers.

German Southwest Africa

German Southwest Africa (now South West Africa) covers 317,725 square miles on the Atlantic coast of the continent. Primarily desert and bush, it has few rivers and meager rainfall. In 1914, it had a population of about 15,000 whites and 100,000 natives, chiefly Hottentots, Bushmen, and Bantu. Most European powers had shown little interest in the area, although the British occupied the fine port of Walvis Bay and annexed it to Cape Colony in 1878. Germany took over the territory in 1884 primarily because it would look imposing on the map. Later, the territory was found to be rich in minerals, particularly diamonds. Railroads ran several hundred miles inland from the German ports of Swakopmund and Lüderitz. The capital, Windhuk (now Windhoek), lay 170 miles inland on high ground. There a powerful wireless station had been installed.

Allied operations against the German colony were assigned to the troops of the Union of South Africa (now the Republic of South Africa). Originally, it was intended only to capture the German ports to prevent the supply of naval surface raiders. On September 19, Lüderitz was captured, but further operations were brought to a halt by the defection of two of the South African military leaders, Brigadier General Christiaan F. Beyers and Lieutenant Colonel Solomon G. Maritz. Beyers fanned the smoldering disaffection among segments of the Afrikaners, and Maritz joined the Germans, threatening an invasion of South Africa. Approximately 30,000 troops were needed to quell the widespread uprisings. Then, in January, 1915, operations in German Southwest Africa were resumed with vigor under General Louis Botha. A force of 20,000 men, which Botha commanded personally, landed at Swakopmund and proceeded toward Windhuk; one of 25,000 advanced inland from Lüderitz; another of 8,000 moved in from the south; and a fourth of 2,000 crossed the eastern border. More than half of the troops were mounted. Logistical support presented great problems, for all supplies and much of the water had to be brought from Cape Town and conveyed inland by oxcarts, mule wagons, and automobiles. Large groups of natives were employed day and night to shovel shifting sand from the railroads. All of the native tribes united with an eager desire to help the South African troops against their former masters. They were not permitted to fight, but were employed as scouts and transport drivers.

The advance was slow but inexorable. Once driven from the railroads, the hopelessly outnumbered Germans were forced to flee, for they could not establish defensive positions in the desert wastes. On July 1, 1915, they made a final stand at Otavi, at the end of the railroad. Cut off from further retreat to the north by Botha's cavalry, 3,500 Germans surrendered unconditionally on July 9 (1,500 others had been captured previously). The Union of South Africa was assigned the administration of the territory.

German East Africa

German East Africa (now Tanganyika), the greatest and richest of the German colonies, covers 361,800 square miles. Its western border is mountainous; lakes abound in the west, and rivers in the east. In 1914, the colony was sparsely settled by a population of about 8 million, including 5,500 whites. The road net was fair by tropical standards, but few roads were fit for motor transportation. One railroad traversed the middle of the territory, and another joined the port of Tanga with the key base of Moshi.

The German garrison, initially small, never exceeded 3,500 white and 12,000 native troops even when augmented. It was commanded by Lieutenant Colonel (later Major General) Paul von Lettow-Vorbeck, a determined and crafty leader. At the beginning of the war, the British forces in the adjacent colonies were almost negligible. Since the forces of the Union of South Africa were occupied in conquering German Southwest Africa and in suppressing rebellion, a call was made for India to send troops. Meanwhile, the British enlisted whatever natives they could and assembled them to defend the vital Uganda Railway, which paralleled the border and in places was 50 miles from it.

Hostilities began on August 8, 1914, when British landing parties destroyed the wireless station and floating dock at Dar es Salaam. Lettow busied himself with border raids in Rhodesia while preparing for an invasion of British East Africa to the north. Indian troops arrived just in time to repel a German attempt against the Uganda Railway in September. In October, an advance against the key British coastal port of Mombasa was similarly halted. Additional Indian troops arrived in November and attempted to capture Tanga. A landing was made on November 2, but, constantly attacked and harassed by the Germans (and swarms of wild bees), the troops were forced to return to their ships on November 4 after suffering severe losses. Sporadic and indecisive fighting took place along the lakes and frontiers until the end of 1915. By then the British had been ejected from German territory, and Lettow held stretches of British East Africa, including a portion of the Uganda Railway north of Moshi.

The fall of German Southwest Africa in July, 1915, had permitted the transfer of South African troops to the east, and in March, 1916, the British, under Lieutenant General Jan Christiaan Smuts, launched an offensive. The Germans were driven from the Uganda Railway on March 9, and four days later their base at Moshi was captured. Then followed a long series of operations designed to outflank and capture Lettow, in which Belgian troops from the Belgian Congo and Portuguese from Mozambique joined. Lettow proved elusive, however, and by the end of 1916 had fallen back south of the Rufiji River. It had become clear to Smuts that the Indian and white South African troops, highly vulnerable to disease and roadbound in their tactics, were unsuited to the prevailing guerrilla type of operations. They were replaced by Nigerian troops, who could better match Lettow's forces in bush fighting. In January, 1917, Smuts left for an imperial conference in London and was succeeded by Major General Sir Jacob Louis van Deventer, a South African. In July, when the rainy season ended, van Deventer took the offensive vigorously. Lettow's principal force of 5,000 troops was surprised and captured just south of the Rufiji on November 28. Meanwhile, Lettow and his remaining small force crossed into Mozambique. Portuguese and British troops pursued him down and up the length of Mozambique, then back into German East Africa, and finally into Northern Rhodesia—a distance of 1,600 miles. It was not until November 25, 1918, almost two weeks after the armistice in East Africa, that Lettow surrendered his force of 1,300 men. It had been his plan to wend his way across Africa to Portuguese Angola.

Lettow's campaign in East Africa is a classic of guerrilla warfare. With only a handful of men, he kept 300,000 enemy troops busily engaged during most of the war at a cost to Britain alone of about $350 million. He inflicted about 15,000 battle casualties, but casualties among Allied troops and transport followers caused by disease acquired in the pursuit totaled almost 700,000.

PACIFIC CAMPAIGNS

Kiaochow

The German colony of Kiaochow occupied about 200 square miles on a sheltered bay in the Chinese Province of Shantung. The city of Tsingtao, at the head of the peninsula, was a naval station garrisoned by about 4,000 German marines, which had been developed into a strong fortress at a cost of $100 million. Heavy guns covered the coast, and three strong and deep defensive zones, extending across the neck of the peninsula, guarded the base proper. Tsingtao's excellent harbor made an ideal base for the German Far East Squadron, which sailed for the high seas at the outbreak of war in 1914. On August 15, Japan delivered an ultimatum to Germany, demanding the evacuation of Kiaochow. The Japanese declared war on August 23, and opened the campaign by occupying the islands outside the harbor four days later. On September 2, Japanese troops landed at Lungkow, 110 miles north of the fortress, with the object of isolating and attacking it from the landward side. Heavy rains thwarted this project, and the Japanese turned to aerial bombardment of ships in the harbor and military installations. On September 18, another landing was made, this time closer to the outer defense line. British forces from Hong Kong landed on the seaward side on September 23, and joined with the Japanese to form a cordon across the peninsula. Lacking sufficient troops to hold them, the Germans withdrew from the two forward positions; the British-Japanese forces followed to within five miles of Tsingtao. Noncombatants were permitted to leave the town on October 15 and were conducted through the Allied lines.

The Japanese now began a relentless and deliberate advance, using the methods of regular siege warfare. On October 31, they opened a bombardment of the German defenses with heavy howitzers, while the British and Japanese warships pounded key German defensive installations. By November 6, Japanese siege parallels had reached to within 300 yards of the main German defenses. That night a general assault captured the last infantry redoubts, and early the next morning the Germans surrendered. They had suffered 700 casualties; the remainder of the 4,000 garrison troops were taken to Japan as prisoners. The Japanese had employed 23,000 troops, and the British 1,500; their casualties had been 1,800 and 70, respectively. Administration of the German colony was assigned to the Japanese, effective until the end of the war, when they were to open negotiations with China.

German Pacific Islands

There were very few German nationals in the Pacific island colonies, and these were primarily civilians. Unable to be reinforced from the homeland, the islands were easy prey for Allied forces. The principal German possession in the Pacific was Kaiser-Wilhelmsland, situated in northeastern New Guinea. It covered 69,700 square miles and had a population of about 500,000, of whom 300 were Germans. The large number of German-held islands in the Bismarck Archipelago to the northeast, including Neu Pommern (New Britain), Neu Mecklenburg (New Ireland), Neu Lauenburg (Duke of York Islands), the Admiralty Islands, and Neu Hannover (Lavongai), were populated by 200,000 natives and 300 Chinese and Germans. The Solomon Islands to the east were partly German and partly British. The Western Samoa group (the other German South Sea possession) contained about 500 Europeans (chiefly British and German), 1,500 Chinese, and 15,000 natives. Farther out in the Pacific lay the Carolines, the Marshalls, and the German islands of the Marianas chain.

While Australian, British, and Japanese warships patrolled the Pacific hunting for German cruisers in 1914, Allied forces undertook the capture of the German islands. A New Zealand force of 1,500 landed at Apia on Upolu Island on August 29 and took possession of Western Samoa without opposition. On September 11, an Australian expeditionary force of 1,500 landed unopposed on Neu Pommern. It took possession of Kaiser-Wilhelmsland on September 17, and subsequently occupied the adjacent island groups. Meanwhile, the Japanese captured the outlying islands.

By the terms of the Treaty of Versailles, Germany was deprived of all her colonies. France and Great Britain were instructed to make a joint recommendation as to the future of Togoland and the Cameroons. Mandates for the rest of the colonies were apportioned as follows: German East Africa, Great Britain; German Southwest Africa, the Union of South Africa; Western Samoa, New Zealand; other former German Pacific possessions north of the equator (the Marshall, Caroline, and Marianas groups), Japan; other former German Pacific possessions south of the equator, Australia (Nauru, assigned to the British Empire, also was actually under Australian control).

11. Turkish Campaigns

BY CYRIL FALLS

At the outbreak of World War I, Turkey was politically and militarily in a state of transition. The Young Turk regime was thoroughly established, but it was not united, nor had it recovered from the crushing defeat suffered in the Balkan Wars of 1912–13. The army was being restored and rearmed by a German military mission. At the same time, Britain was endeavoring to carry out a similar task for the navy, with poor prospects by comparison, since whereas the army contained magnificent fighting material, the navy was largely antiquated. The division of sentiment in the Turkish government was represented by Ahmed Djemal Pasha, the Navy Minister, and Enver Pasha, the War Minister. The former was an old-fashioned Pan-Turk who was prepared to keep out of war if possible, though he was by no means as wholehearted in this resolve as the grand vizier, Mehmet Said Halim Pasha. Enver, on the other hand, had adopted and in part invented the creed of Pan-Turanism, which sought to embrace all speakers of Turanian (Ural-Altaic) languages, and he was indifferent to the fate of the Turkish possessions in the purely Arab countries. He was determined on war.

On August 2, 1914, a secret treaty providing for the subsequent entry of Turkey into the war on the side of the Central Powers was signed with Germany. At the last moment, the government had misgivings because the forces of the Allies were making a better showing than had been expected, but Enver pressed for Turkish belligerency. In this he had the collaboration of German Vice Admiral Wilhelm A. T. Souchon, whose determination had enabled him to escape the powerful fleets of France and Britain in the Mediterranean Sea and to bring the battle cruiser *Goeben* and the light cruiser *Breslau* safely through the Dardanelles. The arrival of a modern battle cruiser at Constantinople (now İstanbul) transformed Turkey's naval position and threatened the Russian Black Sea Fleet, which included no warships of the dreadnought type nor any with the *Goeben*'s speed. The two ships were nominally embodied in the Turkish Navy; on October 29, Souchon led the combined fleet in the bombardment of the Black Sea ports of Novo-

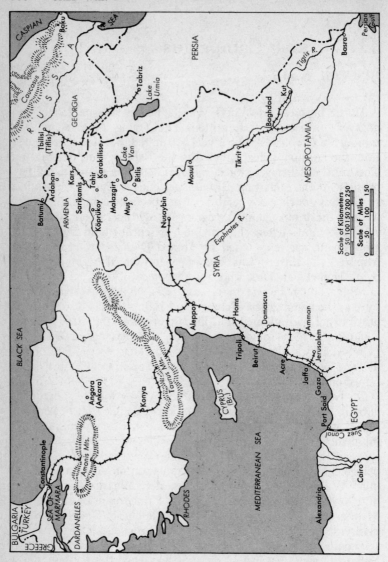

Map 36. Turkish Empire in 1914.

rossisk, Feodosiya, Sevastopol, and Odessa, thus ensuring war with Russia. Russia declared war on Turkey on November 1, and Britain and France followed suit on November 5.

Meanwhile, Turkey had mobilized 36 divisions by the end of September. The head of the German military mission, General Otto Liman von Sanders, was a man of ability, energy, and integrity, and all the work that he was able to supervise was admirably done. The situation in Turkey's Arab possessions was another matter. The Baghdad Railway included great gaps, which were covered by execrable roads over which all supplies had to be borne because the tunnels through the Taurus and Amanos mountains had not been pierced. Moreover, on the east side of the mountains the railway extended only halfway between Aleppo (Haleb) and Mosul, the terminus being Ras el 'Ain. For these reasons, it was impossible to make nearly as good progress east of the Taurus as west of it. The garrison at Yemen, in southwestern Arabia at the southern extremity of the Ottoman Empire, seemed useless, although it actually proved a sharp thorn in the British flank by maintaining a siege of Aden throughout the war. The reinforcement of the Turkish garrison in Syria was paralleled and indeed proportionately exceeded by that of the British garrison in Egypt. The regular infantry brigade and the regiment of cavalry stationed there at the beginning of the war were sent to fight in France, but they were replaced by two Indian and two British Territorial divisions under the command of General Sir John Grenfell Maxwell, who had a long experience of the country.

OPERATIONS IN 1914

In the Caucasus

Throughout the war the Caucasian theater was to a great extent divorced from the conflict at large and even from the main Russian front. The Turks were able to put their finest troops into the area, whereas the Russian High Command consistently drained it to fill gaps in other Russian theaters of operations. The area with which the Caucasian theater became most closely connected was the British theater of Mesopotamia (now Iraq), where a slender Russian spearhead joined it through Persia (now Iran). While the Russians in Asia Minor created troops as good as all but the best that they lost, drawing them from such local peoples as the Armenians, in the beginning the odds favored the Turks, who could put into the field 150,000 men to the Russian 100,000, and those

distinctly the better trained. The opposing armies were commanded
by Hassan İzzet Pasha and General Myshlayevski.

On the Turkish side, however, Enver himself was the strate-
gist, and Hassan İzzet the tactician who had to implement the
minister's plans and remedy his errors, a task that proved beyond
this hard-fighting and devoted man. Enver was a professional
soldier, but he did not know how to conduct a campaign, although
he saw himself as a Hannibal or a Napoleon. He could deduce
from the map that everything depended on the roads, but he could
not assess the handicaps. His aim was to draw the main body of
the Russians forward and then by a lightning stroke put an overwhelmingly strong Turkish force between them and their main
bases, Ardahan and Kars. He was confident that by this means he
could destroy the bulk of their Caucasian army and complete his
victory by the invasion of Georgia, where the Turanian peoples
would rise against Russia. Enver's plan might have succeeded in
summer, but in midwinter the troops had to live on the country
because their trains could not reach them through the heavy snow.
Night temperatures regularly fell to $-20°$ F., and winds rose to
gale force on the higher ground.

While Turkish forces in the Caucasian theater totaled 150,000
men, Hassan İzzet's army numbered only 95,000, although it was
still in a proportion of three to two against Myshlayevski's. Both
sides fought bravely, and death came swiftly and mercifully to the
wounded. One Turkish division started its march 8,000 strong, and
after four days in the mountains was reduced to 4,000 men. In the
deployment phase of the campaign alone, Hassan İzzet lost 25,000
men from a combination of frost and desertion. The great Russian
victory was won at Sarikamiş, 33 miles southwest of Kars, between
December 29, 1914, and January 2, 1915. By mid-January, the force
of 95,000 Turks had fallen to 18,000. One brilliant soldier was revealed in the campaign. He was Nikolai Yudenich, who served as
senior staff officer to Myshlayevski and was later in command of
an army corps.

In Mesopotamia, October–November

British operations in Mesopotamia during the war developed
from a minor protective measure into a big and costly operation.
At the end of September, 1914, the India Office suggested that a
reinforced brigade be sent to the head of the Persian Gulf. The
main object of the expedition was to protect the installations of

Map 37. OPERATIONS IN MESOPOTAMIA, 1914–15. In December, 1914, the British advanced northward from Basra. They seized Ahwaz in May, 1915, thereby driving the Turks from the important oilfields and pipeline. In July, the Turks were ejected from Nasiriya. Maj. Gen. Charles V. F. Townshend, commanding the main British column, advanced along the Tigris River and seized 'Amara in June, Kut in September, and Al 'Aziziya in October. In November, he ran into the Turks entrenched at Ctesiphon and was badly defeated. He then retired to Kut; the Turks followed and besieged the city.

the Anglo-Persian Oil Company (later, Anglo-Iranian Oil Company) on Abadan Island, at the end of its pipeline. It was also expected to confirm the sheikhs of Kuwait and Mohammereh (now Khurramshahr) in their allegiance to Britain.

After the expedition reached Bahrein on October 23, the British government gave its approval to an advance to Basra, which was suitable as a base. The city was taken on November 22 after relatively hard fighting in which British and Indian casualties were by far the heaviest of the year in Mesopotamia, totaling 489. Once the force had made a ceremonial entry into Basra and the Union Jack had been hoisted, a proclamation of extreme subtlety was read in Arabic by the chief political officer, Sir Percy Cox, later to become a figure of world celebrity. It must be recalled that Britain had treated Turkey in a spirit of friendship up to the moment when she was maneuvered into the war against the will of her

wisest ministers, hoping to the last that she would succeed in maintaining her neutrality. This spirit was maintained in the proclamation, though it was addressed to Arabs and Kurds:

> Let it be known to all that from of old the British Government has
> had many millions of Mahomedan subjects, more than any other
> power in the world, more even than Turkey.
>
> As is well known, Great Britain has in the past always displayed
> friendship and regard for Turkey; and a few months ago, when war
> broke out between certain of the powers of Europe, the British Gov-
> ernment urged most strongly on the Sublime Porte that the Otto-
> man Government should on no account join in the conflict, as such
> a course was opposed to the best interests of Turkey. Furthermore,
> in this connection Turkey was assured that so long as she refrained
> from participation in the war the British Government and her allies
> would guarantee the maintenance of her independence and integrity.
> Unfortunately the Turkish Government did not accept or attend to
> the advice of the British Government in this regard, for the reason
> that she was misled and tricked by German intrigues to such an ex-
> tent that she committed numerous acts of hostility which forced the
> British Government into a state of war with her.
>
> The British Government has now occupied Basra, but though a
> state of war with the Ottoman Government still exists, yet we have
> no enmity or ill-will against the population, to whom we hope to
> prove good friends and protectors. No remnant of Turkish adminis-
> tration now remains in this region. In place thereof the British flag
> has been established, under which you will enjoy the benefits of
> liberty and justice, both in regard to your religions and your secular
> affairs. . . .

The statements in the proclamation were very much to the
point, but from another aspect the expedition was typical of the
private wars initiated by the India Office and the Colonial Office,
which barely consulted the War Office until they needed its help
in extricating themselves from untenable situations. To some extent, this state of affairs endured throughout the war.

OPERATIONS IN 1915

In the Caucasus

The peril of the invasion of Russian territory from Asia Minor,
which had been averted at Sarikamiş at the beginning of 1915, became even more pressing in the course of the year, especially after
the Austro-German victory on the Eastern Front, which started
with the Gorlice–Tarnów breakthrough. Turkey itself was not seri-

ously engaged in other areas until the grip of the Gallipoli campaign began to be felt. The German staff at Constantinople reconstituted the shattered Turkish divisions and created new ones, and in the course of the year Turkish strength rose from 500,000 men in 40 divisions to a peak of 800,000 men in 52 divisions.

Meanwhile, the staff of the corps commanded by General Yudenich, relying on reports that were unconfirmed by strong fighting reconnaissance, estimated the strength of the Turks in the hills north of Lake Van as three or four divisions, whereas there were actually eight. Yudenich directed his subordinate, General Oganovski, to drive the enemy from the hills by a rapid advance. Not even the very strong resistance encountered warned Oganovski immediately of his danger, and when the warning came, it was too late. The Turkish commander, Abdul Kerim Pasha, advanced with odds of three to one in his favor and caught the Russians just as they thought they had reached a refuge at Malazgirt, which covered the only north-south road for some miles. In his distraction, Oganovski submitted no adequate report, and Yudenich did not learn the full truth until he sent a staff officer to Malazgirt. Within a week, the remnant of Oganovski's force was in flight, having lost all its artillery and transport. Enver ordered Abdul Kerim to drive the Russians across the frontier, but the latter suspected that his communications might be attacked and advanced with caution.

Though his resources were slender, Yudenich assured the viceroy in Tbilisi (Tiflis) that there was no cause for concern. The force that he was able to scrape together numbered little over 20,000, of whom a fair proportion were cavalrymen, and he assembled it between Köprükoy and Tahir, where the road to Karakilisse (now Karaköse), which the Turks had reached, branched off the main road to Kars. He placed this force under the command of General N. N. Baratov and ordered him to drive across the enemy's lines of communication and sever them. The Turks hastily retreated, while Baratov's Cossacks captured a great number of guns and much food in the blocked streets of Karakilisse. The Turks were reported to have lost 10,000 killed and wounded, and they left 6,000 prisoners in Baratov's hands. It was a notable victory, but Yudenich lacked the means to exploit it.

In Southern Mesopotamia

The British force in Mesopotamia moved north from Basra and captured Al Qurna on December 9, 1914. It now received orders to take 'Amara, nearly 70 miles farther up the Tigris. Moreover, whereas all the earlier operations had been conducted astride the Shatt-al-'Arab or the Tigris, the force was now directed to secure Nasiriya on the Euphrates River and Ahwaz on the Karun River and the pipeline. Although there were good arguments in favor of these fresh advances, they represented another instance of the policy of taking steps without any clear conception of where they were to lead, but giving the impression that they were designed to force the hand of the British government and induce it to attempt the capture of Baghdad. At this time, only 21 river steamers and tugs were available for operations.

Meanwhile, another brigade and supporting artillery had arrived in Mesopotamia, and it had been decided that a senior officer of the Indian Army, General Sir John Nixon, should set up a corps headquarters to command the two infantry divisions and the cavalry brigade now in the country. The Turks were very weak on the Tigris, in contrast to their left wing of 8,000 men near Ahwaz and their right wing of 18,000 men on the Euphrates, which together constituted two divisions and a cavalry brigade, or exactly the strength of the total British force. The Turks' center consisted merely of a detachment of gendarmerie, and their east-west communications, though much better in the drought of spring and summer than in the floods of winter, took some time to pass between the two wings.

Major General (later Sir) Charles V. F. Townshend advanced up the Tigris and, after a series of minor operations, on June 3 seized 'Amara at small cost. The task of Major General (later Sir) George F. Gorringe proved more arduous. He suffered at least one sharp check and had some trouble in seizing Ahwaz, but the difficulties of his two months' advance were due almost entirely to lack of sufficient transport and grilling heat. Strategically, this was the most valuable operation since the original landing, because the enemy was driven from the oilfields, which were not threatened again during the war. Gorringe went straight to the next undertaking and took only half as long to capture Nasiriya, which he occupied on July 25.

Advance on Kut

It would have been well if Gorringe, who was a steady, painstaking soldier, had been entrusted with the next venture, an advance up the Tigris to Kut-al-Imara. Townshend, the commander

to whom it was allotted, was of a very different type. Already celebrated for his achievements in the North-West Frontier Province
of India, he was very much a showman. He would be certain to
support any form of forward policy and perhaps to move in advance of orders, as he can be said to have done when he pushed on
from Kut, which he took on September 28, 1915, to Al 'Aziziya.
His force at this period was short of physicians and medical equipment, and as soon as it became engaged in the first heavy fighting
of the campaign, the medical system broke down, and a great
number of unnecessary deaths occurred.

Townshend reached Al 'Aziziya without difficulty on October 5,
but then he was delayed by a fall in the depth of the Tigris. To
supplement the riverboats, a motley assortment of camels, horses,
mules, and asses were assembled. Townshend had been forbidden
by Nixon to advance any farther, but the British cabinet, anxious
to regain popular support, which it was losing because of the now
inevitable collapse of the campaign in Gallipoli, on October 23
sent to the viceroy of India the following telegram: "Nixon may
march on Baghdad if he is satisfied that the force he has available
is sufficient for the operation." This put the blame for failure on
Nixon, who was doubtful about the venture, and the credit for
success on the government.

For the first time, the Indian troops, hitherto steady and reliable,
showed signs of discouragement when they saw the heavily fortified position at Ctesiphon, only 20 miles southeast of Baghdad.
The assault on November 22 was a complete failure and cost 4,500
casualties out of a total strength of 14,000. Townshend halted at
Ctesiphon until his sick and wounded had been evacuated to Kut,
but he followed them on December 3 and decided that he must
stay there in view of the fatigue of his troops. He had a food supply
that he reckoned would last two months, and was confident of
relief well within that time. The Turks soon followed Townshend
and began the investment of Kut with the care they always applied
to siege warfare. It was small consolation that Baratov's Cossacks,
sent by Grand Duke Nicholas to Persia after the victory of Karakilisse, had reached Hamadan on December 14, since they were
230 miles from the scene of operations and were such a small and
lightly armed force that they could have no effect on the campaign
in Mesopotamia. Of greater interest was the report of the arrival in
Baghdad of the veteran General (Field Marshal in the Turkish
Army) Baron Kolmar von der Goltz, the best pupil of Field Mar-

shal von Moltke. His reputation and his knowledge of Turkey were thoroughly established in the military world, and his British admirers took serious note of his advent, which was likely to make the relief of Kut still more difficult than they had expected. Almost simultaneously with Goltz' arrival, a Turkish commander named Halil Pasha also reached the Mesopotamian capital. He was a bold soldier, and the combination of experienced age and enterprising youth was likely to prove formidable.

The British and Indian governments had created and embraced their own difficulties, and the risks embodied therein, in the hope of providing their own people and those sections of the Moslem world that backed them with a victory to counter the disaster of Gallipoli. In war, however, a clear purpose is an indispensable element of good strategy.

GALLIPOLI CAMPAIGN, 1915

Origins of the Campaign, January–March

On January 2, 1915, a message from the Russian commander in chief, Grand Duke Nicholas, was delivered in London. Its contents may seem insignificant when it is considered how immense were the consequences, for it asked no more than that a demonstration be mounted against the Turks in order to induce them to withdraw troops from the Caucasus. Once the victory of Sarikamiş had been won, however, the Grand Duke withdrew his plea, and it is certain that the Russian government would at that time have been sorry to see its allies in the Bosporus. This does not alter the fact that the conception of the 1st Earl Kitchener, the Secretary of State for War, and Winston Churchill, the First Lord of the Admiralty, to open communications with Russia by forcing a passage through the Dardanelles, was good strategy from the Russian point of view as well as from the British and the French.

Before the land forces of the Allies reached the scene, their naval forces tried to do the job by themselves. The first efforts, from mid-February to mid-March, were on the whole successful; after the outer forts had been thoroughly pounded, landing parties were able to blow up the guns. The intermediate forts covering the Narrows were expected to be more difficult to reduce, but the naval commander, Rear Admiral Sir John de Robeck, and his staff officer, Commodore Roger J. B. (later 1st Baron) Keyes, were optimistic.

It is still a moot point whether or not their optimism was justi-

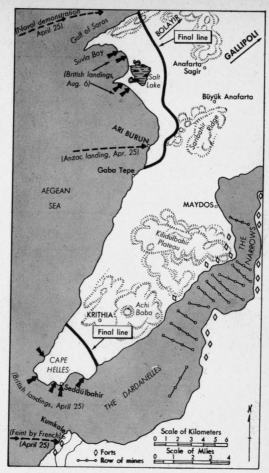

Map 38. GALLIPOLI CAMPAIGN, 1915. On March 18, 1915,
British and French naval units attempted to force their
way through the Dardanelles, but withdrew after several
battleships were lost in the minefields. On April 25, a well-
planned amphibious Allied attack, accompanied by demonstrations and feints to deceive the Turks, was launched.
Landings were made at Cape Helles and Ari Burun, but
the advance inland was stopped by the Turks after
meager gains. In early August, a second attempt was
made. The main landings in Suvla Bay were to be supported with offensives by the forces already ashore at
Cape Helles and Ari Burun. The Suvla Bay landing was a
success, but the advance ashore was stopped after a gain
of only a few miles. The supporting offensives at Cape
Helles and Ari Burun accomplished little. During the period Dec. 10, 1915–Jan. 9, 1916, the British and French
completely evacuated the Gallipoli Peninsula.

fied. When the attack was made on March 18, a French battleship, a British battleship, and a British battle cruiser were sunk on a newly laid minefield that was undiscovered and unswept; two other ships had to be beached; and a sixth was put out of action by the defense. On the other hand, it is now fairly well established that the Turks were at the end of their resistance, mainly for want of ammunition. Keyes sensed this and urged Robeck to renew the attack, but the Admiral understandably declined to do so in view of the terrible losses in ships and men already sustained. General Sir Ian Hamilton, who had arrived in the area in advance of his troops, refused to advise a resumption of purely naval efforts for the same reason.

Landings on the Gallipoli Peninsula, April–May

The force made available to clear the way for the passage of the two navies consisted of four British divisions, including the Anzac (Australian-New Zealand) Corps, and one French division. The French were to make a feint landing on the Asian shore at Kumkale, where some thought the main operation should be conducted.

The Turkish commander, Liman von Sanders, had two more divisions than Hamilton had. He posted one at Cape Helles, the toe of the Gallipoli (Gelibolu) Peninsula; one at Maydos (now Eceabat), just north of the Narrows; two on the Asian side; and two at Bolayir (Bulair), 40 miles north of Helles at the narrowest point of the peninsula, where it was defended by the Bolayir lines. On the map this appeared to be the most favorable place for the main British landing, but Hamilton had ruled it out because of the strength of its fortifications. Hamilton had arranged that one of his assault divisions should demonstrate in front of Bolayir before being transferred to its next duty, and Liman von Sanders intended to send the two divisions there to Cape Helles or to any intermediate point on the peninsula where the need was urgent. It may thus be said that the two generals' conceptions of the right way to attack and hold the peninsula coincided and may be considered sound.

On the British side, the obverse to the potential advantages of the naval attack must be examined. The attack had put Liman von Sanders on the alert, which he cannot be said to have been before it. Much criticism was therefore directed at Churchill, the chief sponsor of the operation, and allegations that he ruined the chances of the expedition were often repeated in later years. In point of fact, Liman von Sanders was deceived by the spectacle of ships and landing craft lying off Bolayir on the morning of April 25. He mounted his horse, galloped up to the town, and spent the night there. The Russian Black Sea Fleet bombarded the Bosporus forts and thus increased the illusion of an attack on Bolayir, though the bombardment was in fact a second example of the jealous policy of the Russian government where the straits were concerned. Russia was determined that if Constantinople was to be occupied by her allies, her troops should be on the spot. It was a junior Turkish divisional commander, Mustafa Kemal (later celebrated as Kemal Atatürk), who saved the situation by engaging his whole division without authorization against the Anzacs and holding the heights that were their objective.

The Helles landings were a tragedy. Of four landings, one was repulsed altogether after sickening slaughter in the sally ports of the *River Clyde*, a collier grounded to act as a landing ship, and one was abandoned in panic; but a firm foothold was secured eventually. In the Anzac landing, an error in navigation put the troops a mile north of the planned beach in an area backed by steep ridges, but the determined attackers fought their way into a defensible position. At home, the reaction was the formation of a coalition government on May 25 and the removal of Churchill from the Admiralty two days later. Then the tide turned in favor of the campaign, which was strongly backed by the new government and was given priority over the Western Front for ammunition supplies. The Mediterranean Expeditionary Force was raised to a strength of 13 divisions, 2 of them French, against the 16 divisions of the expanded Turkish force.

Landings at Suvla Bay and Evacuation of
Gallipoli, August, 1915–January, 1916

The new plan was to land two divisions at Suvla Bay; these were to surprise the enemy and then march eastward together with the Anzac Corps, thus cutting off the main Turkish force. The landings at Suvla on August 6 were virtually unopposed, but the initial advantages were wasted because of the inexperience of the troops, who indulged in picnics and bathing parties, and the inertia of the senior officers, including Hamilton. Liman von Sanders had ample time to move two divisions from Bolayir and repulse the attack. Despite great efforts made by supporters of the enterprise to keep it going, this was the end of the campaign. Kitchener visited the peninsula and cabled to London on November 22 that the Anzac and Suvla beachheads should be evacuated. Meanwhile, Hamilton had been ordered home. He was succeeded by General Sir Charles Carmichael Monro, who had the over-all command at Gallipoli and Salonika, where a new campaign was beginning; Lieutenant General (later Field Marshal) Sir William Riddell Birdwood, the Anzac Corps commander, was placed in command on the peninsula itself. The evacuation was completed when the rear guards were taken off early on December 20 without the loss of a man. No such good fortune was expected at Helles, but the same result was achieved early on January 9, 1916. For the entire campaign, the British alone had a casualty list of 214,000, a colossal figure.

It is safe to say that no other campaign was so ill conducted by Britain during the war. Each landing provided an admirable opportunity of securing the passage of the Dardanelles, and each opportunity was wasted. The final decision to withdraw was then inevitable for two reasons. First, the piers were too fragile to withstand winter gales. Second, German, Austrian, and Bulgarian forces had routed the Serbs, driving them from the Baghdad Railway and enabling munitions to be delivered to the Turks in great quantities and at speed over a direct line.

Operations in 1916
Campaigns Against the Senusi and in Sinai, 1915–16

The British had won freedom of political action in Egypt in December, 1914, by deposing the Khedive, Abbas II Hilmi, an extreme pro-Turk who was living in Constantinople. He was succeeded by his uncle, Hussein Kamil, a moderate and sensible man who ascended the throne with the title of sultan, afterward changed to that of king. On February 2, 1915, a Turkish force of 20,000 men under an able German officer, Colonel (later General) Baron Friedrich Kress von Kressenstein, approached the Suez Canal halfway between Lake Timsah and the Great Bitter Lake. Its march across the Sinai Peninsula had been in the best Turkish tradition, for the main body disdained the coast route and followed the almost waterless track through Nakhl, dragging pontoons through the deep sand. Three boatloads of soldiers actually crossed the canal, but the force was mercilessly pounded by British and French warships and had to withdraw by the way it had come. The British had not as yet assembled enough camels for a pursuit.

The evacuation of Gallipoli raised the question of whether it

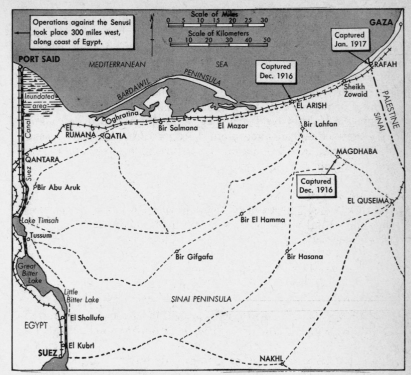

Map 39. CAMPAIGNS IN SINAI, 1915–17. In February, 1915, the Turks attacked the Suez Canal in force and actually got some troops across, but they were finally driven back. After subduing an uprising of the Senusi in Egypt, the British began an advance through Sinai to the Palestine frontier. The rate of advance was governed by the progress of construction of a railroad and a water pipeline, needed to support the troops in the desert wastes. The British entered the desert in May, 1916, brushed Turkish resistance and attacks aside at several points, and reached Rafah, on the Palestine border, in January, 1917. They now prepared for operations against the Turkish stronghold at Gaza.

would further Turkish designs against Egypt. Some exaggerated estimates were made of the number of troops that could cross the desert, with the result that a major fortification of the canal was undertaken, and 14 divisions were assembled in an Imperial Strategic Reserve, which included divisions from France and the United Kingdom as well as those from Gallipoli. This force was speedily dispersed, however, 10 of the divisions having left Egypt by the middle of the year.

The chief activity in the Egyptian theater was that directed against the Nile Delta by Ahmad al-Sharif, head of the powerful sect of the Senusi, with whom Enver Pasha's half-brother, Nuri Bey, was residing. Ahmad gave the British of General Maxwell's command much trouble by his elusiveness, time after time escaping in a series of running fights. At the Battle of the Wadi Majid, fought on Christmas Day, 1915, the skilled young Turkish commander of his forces, Jafar Pasha, put more than 2,500 men into action. At Halazin on January 23, 1916, Jafar carried out a fine counterattack and inflicted more than 300 casualties on the small British force. At Agagiya on February 26, however, Jafar was wounded and captured, and, without him, Senusi activities declined almost to nothing. Maxwell, having completed his task of rendering Egypt secure from the west, returned to England. By this time, Lieutenant General Sir Archibald Murray had taken over the bulk of the troops on the Suez Canal and in the Nile Delta. He now included under his authority all those in the theater of war, and the title of Mediterranean Expeditionary Force was exchanged for that of Egyptian Expeditionary Force.

Advance into Sinai

At the beginning of 1916 the command in Egypt was committed to an advance into Sinai toward the Palestinian frontier. The advance was to be extremely deliberate, being accompanied step by step by a railway and a pipeline to provide water, though General Murray's numerous yeomanry and Australian and New Zealand cavalry were expected to range ahead in order to protect the main body of troops and the Egyptian workmen against a surprise attack. In April, however, this screen was itself subjected to an attack by the enterprising Kress von Kressenstein, who secretly led a Turkish force of 3,500 men to the oases of Oghratina and Qatia and routed their garrisons.

In the latter part of May, Murray moved an infantry division east to El Rumana, which was now established as the railhead, though the pipeline lagged behind. The division had to be supplied with water either by trucks from El Qantara on the Suez Canal or from the pipehead by camel convoy. Then the situation changed dramatically, for Kress was active again. On July 19, an aircraft discovered a force of about 2,500 Turks in a depression 20 miles southeast of the railhead; later, it was found that 16,000 men were on the march. These included the German personnel of four batteries and two trench mortar companies.

Murray could bring a considerable numerical superiority to bear —in fact, one measured almost entirely by the water supply, in which British needs were several times as large as those of the Turks. He realized at a glance that Kress would not dare to attack the railhead defenses frontally, and that, since the British left lay on the sea, he must try to envelop the right. This in its turn would afford an opportunity to take the Turks on their flank. To add to Kress' confusion, Murray proposed to establish a false flank. He was an experienced staff officer, and in the prewar period this type of defense had been emphasized in military training. A position four miles long was selected but left unvisited and untouched, except that telephone lines were laid down. Natural gullies in a patch of hard sand provided adequate defense. The false flank was entrusted to two brigades of the Australian Light Horse, with strong reserves behind it, and to this force was given the task of holding the Turks until they could be outflanked by the reminder of the mounted troops.

The Turkish attack was launched early on August 4, and it was soon evident that the Turks were not only fulfilling their destined role but doing it with great ardor and pluck. The situation of the cavalry became precarious, but frontal attacks on the defenses of El Rumana caused the British infantry no concern. Finally, as darkness gathered about 7 P.M., the reserves brought the enemy's advance to a halt. At daybreak on August 5, the British, including an infantry brigade, assaulted with bayonets. The brave Turkish rear guard was forced to surrender; 1,500 prisoners were taken, most of them in an agonizing condition for want of water. The mounted advance captured many more Turks, but its efforts soon slackened as the shortage of water affected it also and prostrated the majority of the troops. The morale of the main body of Turks never broke, but Turkish losses totaled 6,000, of whom 4,000 were prisoners as against a British casualty list of 1,130.

Siege of Kut

There was small likelihood that the Turks would take Kut by assault so long as the British garrison could stand on its feet. The sack of the Tigris bend in which the town lies is less than two miles long and not much over a mile wide. After Townshend had fortified the open northwestern end of the sack with three lines of trenches, there was nothing left for him to do but send out his cavalry brigade before he was completely invested and await relief.

The first attempt at relieving him, made by Lieutenant General Sir Fenton John Aylmer in January, 1916, was abortive, the Battle of Shaikh Sa'ad costing 6,000 casualties. Aylmer tried again in March, by which time the Turks were well dug in, and he failed to take the Dujaila redoubt despite the gallantry with which his assaults were pressed, losing nearly 3,500 men, including 500 killed and 500 missing. By this time, Townshend had resolved to kill 1,100 horses and mules to keep the garrison alive.

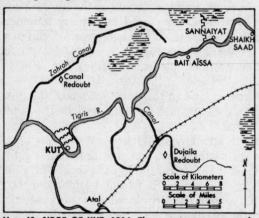

Map 40. SIEGE OF KUT, 1916. Three attempts were made to rescue Townshend and his British troops besieged in Kut. The first was turned back in an abortive battle at Shaikh Sa'ad. The second, in March, also failed. In April, a third attempt was made with some initial success, but it bogged down in front of the strong Turkish trenches at Sannaiyat. The British garrison of Kut surrendered on April 29, after having suffered great privations and many deaths.

Aylmer was now succeeded by Gorringe, who in April was to make what was generally recognized as the final and decisive attempt at the relief of Kut. Acting with skill and vigor, Gorringe succeeded in breaking the Turkish front at Bait Aïssa on the right bank, and hopes of relief soared. This, however, entailed another assault on the left bank and penetration at Sannaiyat of a heavily fortified gap between the Tigris and a marsh. On April 22, Gorringe made the attempt, was repulsed, and reported that his troops had for the time being reached the end of their offensive powers. Lord Kitchener then authorized the command to open negotiations for surrender. These were carried out by Townshend and Halil in a Turkish launch, and the surrender took place on April

29. Goltz had died of cholera on April 19, but not before he knew that Kut was doomed to fall. The prisoners were barbarously treated, being flogged across the desert by their mounted escort. The people of England took the catastrophe hardly, but it had curiously little effect in the Arab lands.

In August, General Sir Frederick Stanley Maude succeeded Lieutenant General Sir Percy H. N. Lake, who had only six months earlier succeeded Nixon. Maude was a strong advocate of a forward policy and won the support of General Monro, who visited him en route to take up his new appointment as commander in chief in India. The war cabinet took the two generals' side against that of the War Office, but the latter then withdrew control of the Mesopotamian campaign from India and assumed it itself. Maude now had five divisions at his disposal, four of them in two corps on the Tigris and the fifth on the Euphrates. He was by far the best soldier engaged in this hitherto luckless theater, but his resources were also much superior to those of his predecessors. Including cavalry and troops on the lines of communication, his forces totaled 340,000 men, although only 166,000 of them were fighting troops (107,000 Indian and the remainder British). Turkish fighting strength was estimated at 42,000, half that number being stationed on the Tigris and the remainder on the Euphrates and at Baghdad. The Turkish Army was riddled with disease, and reinforcements never equaled the wastage from this source plus the battle casualties. Nevertheless, the Turkish soldier was nearly as formidable as ever in a prepared position, and unless he could be maneuvered from it, gains could be secured only at great cost. Maude began his advance northward on December 13.

Operations in the Caucasus

The destination of the Turkish divisions that had fought on the Gallipoli Peninsula was a source of anxiety to the Russian General Staff early in 1916. It was to be expected that a fair number would be dispatched to Syria and Mesopotamia and a few to Europe, but a majority would certainly be moved eastward in Asia Minor against the forces under the command of Grand Duke Nicholas. A Russian defeat there might be deadly, though it did not count as a main theater of war.

The grand duke, formerly the Russian commander in chief, was playing a minor part now as viceroy of Transcaucasia. His subordinate, General Yudenich, studied the problem of the Gallipoli

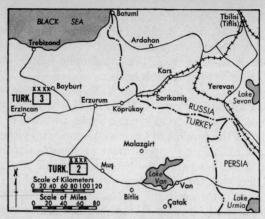

Map 41. OPERATIONS IN THE CAUCASUS, 1916. Anticipating that the Turks would take the offensive in the Caucasus with the troops released by the British evacuation of Gallipoli, the Russians struck first. In January, they took Köprüköy; in February, Erzurum; and in April, Trebizond. The Turkish Gallipoli divisions tried to recapture Erzurum in May and Trebizond in June, but without success. The Russians continued their advance, capturing both Bayburt and Erzincan in July, practically destroying the Turkish Third Army in the process. To the south, the Turkish Second Army took Mus and Bitlis in mid-August, but the Russians recaptured the two towns a week later.

divisions in detail and concluded that none of these forces was likely to appear before late March. The Russians should therefore anticipate the Turkish offensive, which would inevitably be launched as soon as possible after that. Yudenich prepared his plan and its material components, and only after that had been accomplished went to Tbilisi to lay them before his chief. Yet the grand duke could never be a cipher, and with any lieutenant but Yudenich he would have intervened far more comprehensively.

The latter must have recalled the Battle of Sarikamiş, fought at the same time of year as that in which he now proposed to attack. He provided his troops with fur caps, thick shirts, and felt boots for marching in the snow. His offensive at Köprüköy on January 17 took the Turks by surprise and, though complete envelopment failed, forced Abdul Kerim into retreat at the best pace he could muster, with a loss of about 25,000 men, largely from frostbite.

On February 12–16, Yudenich exhibited great skill and daring in storming Erzurum—a notable feat for an army without siege artillery—by his swift infiltration between the forts. Simultaneously, he sent General Lyakhov westward along the coast in a combined operation with the Black Sea Fleet against Trebizond (Trabzon). By systematically bombarding the steep valleys running down to the shore and convoying two brigades from Novorossisk, the fleet put Lyakhov into the best roadstead on the north Anatolian coast on April 17.

Meanwhile, Enver made ambitious plans for the Gallipoli divisions, which were to engage the Russians on a wide front south of the Black Sea and simultaneously to turn their flank at Bitlis, near Lake Van. Yudenich did not want to await the attack passively, but in view of the enemy's superior strength he had to choose his opportunities carefully. At the end of May, without awaiting the arrival of the bulk of the reinforcements on their way, the Turkish Third Army attacked west of Erzurum, but its offensive soon collapsed. In June, Enver, angry that the Russians should retain Trebizond, to which they were steadily sending troops, ordered its recapture, but once more his lieutenant failed him.

Meanwhile, Yudenich had completed his deliberate preparations. His main blow, on July 2, was struck through Bayburt, located south-southeast of Trebizond at the apex of a triangle of which the base ran from Erzurum to Erzincan. As was his general practice in this country of few roads, he planned to split the enemy's front and not to turn his flank. The shock was tremendous and led to a crushing Russian victory and the capture of the road center of Erzincan on July 25. Harried by the Cossacks, the Third Army was removed from the war. It had lost 17,000 men in killed and a like number in prisoners taken by the Russians. To these figures must be added an unknown number of deserters who had settled in the villages. On the Turkish right wing, the Second Army did not launch its attack until it had received all the reinforcements allotted to it, but also not until Yudenich had been able to send southward troops that had fulfilled their mission at Erzurum. While this attack achieved some success, the only sector where it could be said to have been substantial was on the right flank, where Mustafa Kemal, now a corps commander, captured Muş and Bitlis on August 15. Kemal's achievement showed what a fine commander could do at the head of a seasoned, well-trained army, proud of its victory at Gallipoli, but even the very moderate army commanders employed in Asia Minor might have accomplished much more if they had been placed under any commander but

Enver. In any case, Yudenich was able to recapture Muş and Bitlis on August 24.

Arab Revolt and Campaign on the Palestinian Frontier, 1916–17

On June 5, 1916, Sherif Husein, ruler of the Hejaz under Turkish control, began a successful revolt against his overlords, and on June 10, after three days' street fighting, captured the summer garrison at Mecca. He next turned his attention to Taif, where the main body of the Hejaz garrison was installed according to custom, and, with the aid of two Egyptian mountain batteries under their own Moslem officers, forced it to surrender. This time the Arab commander was Husein's second son, 'Abdullah, later Emir of Transjordan and King of Jordan. By then the Arabs had captured more than 5,000 prisoners, but this was the last of their good fortune for a long time. Feisal, Husein's third son, failed completely in an attempt to capture Medina, which was held by the Turks until the end of the war. The British had prepared trouble for themselves by the secret Sykes-Picot agreement of May 16, which allotted Syrian territory to France without regard to British pledges to Husein. It was a case of the left hand, Sir Mark Sykes, not knowing what the right hand, Lord Kitchener, had promised the Arabs.

By December, 1916, the British forces in Sinai had reached the neighborhood of El Arish (al-'Arish), 27 miles from the frontier of Palestine. Murray was being urged by Prime Minister David Lloyd George, through the medium of the doubting chief of the Imperial General Staff, General (later Field Marshal) Sir William Robertson, to invade Palestine as soon as possible, a task for which he did not believe he had the necessary strength. Nevertheless, after occupying El Arish on December 21, he cleared out the two Turkish outposts south of the frontier. The first was Magdhaba, where, on December 23, 1,300 prisoners were taken for a British loss of 146, and only a handful of the garrison escaped. The second was Rafah, which was captured on January 9, 1917, by five brigades of light horse, yeomanry, and camelry, after a much more fiercely contested struggle. This time the number of prisoners was a little larger, 1,600, but the British losses were not far short of 500.

OPERATIONS IN 1917

Capture of Baghdad

General Maude's orders to capture Baghdad depended for their fulfillment on supply. In this he was fortunate because he had been provided with 45 (later 64) river craft, but it was not until March, 1917, that he considered himself able to furnish support for four infantry divisions and a cavalry division of two brigades as far north as Baghdad. Meanwhile, beginning on January 9, he was engaged in hard-fought actions as a result of which Kut changed hands for the third time. As in 1916, Sannaiyat proved difficult to take, and Maude's assault on February 17 was thrown back in disorder, but this mishap was repaired five days later. On February 25, Kut was found deserted and in ruins.

Maude pressed on at high speed, but had to make a brief halt at Al 'Aziziya. He estimated the Turkish force in the whole theater at about 35,000, as against his own fighting strength of 120,000. The next Turkish stand was made on the Diyala River, which enters the Tigris 10 miles below Baghdad. Maude, whose land artillery was admirably seconded by the Royal Flying Corps and a flotilla of gunboats, laid down a crushing bombardment on the enemy's position. Under its cover he established a pontoon bridge and passed his two brigades of cavalry and a strong force of infantry over to the left bank. Thus outflanked, the enemy was unable to withstand the shock of his attack on the Diyala and abandoned Baghdad. Maude entered the city on March 11. This time he took 9,000 prisoners.

Halil Pasha, who had creditably held together his weary, sick, and underfed army, led it to a strong position 50 miles above Baghdad, with its right flank bent forward to Ramadi. He had received two more divisions of 7,000 men each, but his forces were perilously strung out, his left facing on the Persian frontier a Russian force inclined to break up as a result of the revolution. Maude had still to consider whether any substantial additional forces of Yilderim (Lightning) troops would reach the scene, but that danger passed, and he had been promised two more divisions from India. In any case, he did not intend to move while the baking summer heat lasted.

On November 18, less than two months after an impressive victory at Ramadi (September 29), in which the majority of the garrison was captured, the commander in chief died in the house in Baghdad that had seen the end of Goltz, and like him of cholera. Maude's death came as a shock to the people of Britain, for whom he had become by far the most popular soldier of the war. In the first place, he had transformed the life of the troops with the aid of supplies from home and of the work of a remarkable administrative officer, Major General Sir George Fletcher MacMunn. Chicken farms and kitchen gardens provided fresh eggs and fresh vegetables to supplement the abundant local fruit, and chilled meat became plentiful even for troops in the front line. Electric fans were installed in the hospitals. Secondly, Maude had wiped out the shame of the 1916 surrender at Kut. He was succeeded by his senior corps commander, Lieutenant General Sir William Raine Marshall, who made a good start by driving the Turks out of Khanaqin on December 9.

General Robertson was, however, no better pleased with the prospects than before. He had divined that Mesopotamia was becoming more and more of a political theater. The oil wells to the north attracted the British government, somewhat to the chagrin of the French, who saw no such interesting prospects for themselves and considered that Britain was failing to do her share. Late in 1917, Robertson had Marshall's best Indian division transferred to Allenby's command in Palestine, where he felt it would find more useful occupation.

First Battle of Gaza (March)

In the spring of 1917, General Murray, though deprived of one of his four divisions, was directed to invade Palestine, starting with the capture of Gaza. His chief subordinate was now Major General Sir Charles Macpherson Dobell, to whom he delegated the operation in its entirety. Dobell decided to form a wide screen of mounted troops, in which he was exceptionally strong, to hold off outside Turkish intervention, and within it to storm the town from the south. As in previous campaigns, the key to the situation was the water supply, for it was doubtful whether Major General Sir Philip Walhouse Chetwode's cavalry force of two divisions, known as "the Desert Column," could water horses numbering more than 10,000 anywhere except at the wells of Gaza.

The starting line was the bed of the Wadi al-Ghazze, now nearly dry, from a point six miles south of the town. Gaza was a very formidable objective. Although the garrison totaled only about 4,000 men and a few trenches had been dug, dense and virtually indestructible cactus hedges thick with thorns made the town a natural fortress.

On the morning of the attack, March 26, there was a very heavy fog, but it did not seriously interrupt the envelopment of Gaza by the mounted troops, who used compass bearings. In general, the infantry also defied the fog and made satisfactory progress, gal-

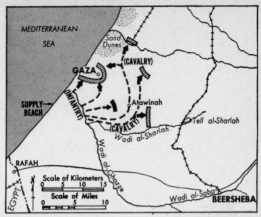

Map 42. FIRST BATTLE OF GAZA (March, 1917). As an initial step in the invasion of Palestine, the British attempted to drive the Turks from their positions at Gaza. The town itself was a veritable fortress. Reliance was placed on the cavalry to isolate the town while the infantry assaulted and carried its defenses. Just as success was within reach, the cavalry was recalled through poor staff work, and the battle was called off.

lantly capturing strong positions on the ridges three miles south of the town.

The rest of the battle was badly managed. The cavalry was ordered to withdraw for lack of water at a time when it had actually found some fair-sized pools and had watered a number of its horses. The crowning positions just captured were abandoned because of an error by Chetwode's staff, and though they were retaken the next day by a fine attack carried out by tired troops, the success came too late. The mounted troops and the right flank of the infantry were pressed sharply by the force driven westward by Kress von Kressenstein. To cap the confusion, Murray sent a misleading telegram to the chief of the Imperial General Staff, hoping to be able to repair the situation before his superiors learned of the reverse. Robertson naturally urged him to make a fresh effort. The British losses were 4,000, and the Turkish 2,400.

Second Battle of Gaza (April)

The situation was now entirely different, because the Turks had deployed and dug themselves in along the Gaza-Beersheba road. General Dobell, again left largely uncontrolled by Murray, decided to attack this new position mainly with a single division on a two-mile front beginning two miles southwest of Gaza. He was asking a great deal of his troops, for the gentle ascent there was a veritable glacis. Despite the dauntless courage with which the attack was conducted on April 17–19, it was a complete failure, costing 6,500 British casualties as against 2,000 Turkish. This disparity was too great for Lloyd George and Robertson, though they may not have realized the fact that Murray had remained aloof from responsibility to the extent that his headquarters had become merely a military secretariat. They recalled Murray in June and sent in his place General Sir Edmund Allenby (later 1st Viscount Allenby), hitherto commanding the Third Army in France.

Map 43. SECOND BATTLE OF GAZA (April, 1917). In April, the British launched another attack against the Turks at Gaza. By now the Turks had strongly entrenched their position from Gaza to Beersheba. The British attack, delivered directly against the trenches, was driven back.

Allenby, known as "the Bull" because of his height, bulk, and explosive temper, was welcomed even by the very democratic Australians and quickly restored the morale of a depressed army. In such circumstances, a new commander immediately demands reinforcements and gets them. Two divisions were forming in the country from dismounted yeomanry units which had served in the Gallipoli campaign and from other troops available. Two more divisions from Macedonia and Mesopotamia raised Allenby's total strength from three to seven divisions, and he formed two corps, commanded respectively by Chetwode and Lieutenant General (later Sir) Edward Bulfin.

Third Battle of Gaza and Advance into Palestine
(October–December)

Allenby's plan was to attack both at Gaza and at Beersheba. The attack at Gaza was to be a holding operation, while Beersheba and its vital wells were to be captured from the east by Australians and New Zealanders with the aid of two infantry divisions attacking from the west. The whole Turkish front along the road to Gaza was then to be rolled up. For the Gaza attack, Allenby was sent eight tanks, the only ones used outside France in the war.

In the attack on Beersheba on October 31, Allenby had un-merited good fortune. Everything hinged on capturing the wells in-

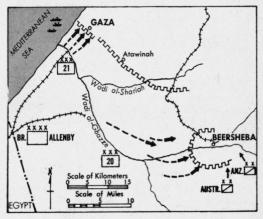

Map 44. THIRD BATTLE OF GAZA (Oct.–Nov., 1917). Heavily reinforced, the British, under Gen. Sir Edmund Allenby, again attacked the Turkish Gaza position. The initial attack was made against Beersheba, to capture the water wells and, from there, to roll up the Turkish line. The Beersheba attack was successful, and Allenby now struck directly at Gaza, supported by naval gunfire. The Turkish defenses were overpowered, and Gaza captured on November 7.

tact, for without them the cavalry would have to withdraw. In a prolonged fight the local Turkish command had ample time to destroy the wells but failed to do so. Thus the rolling-up process could begin in good time, and it proved most successful. The same could not be said of the exploitation of the cavalry, which was not concentrated quickly enough, although it did inflict heavy losses on the enemy. Allenby now turned his efforts to the coast, made the Gaza feint the real attack, broke through the Turkish defenses with the powerful aid of British and French naval guns, and thrust northward up the coastal plain. Gaza was occupied on November 7, and Jaffa on November 16.

Meanwhile, a grandiose project fathered by Enver, to send a Turkish army of 14 divisions and 6,000 German troops under General Erich von Falkenhayn to retake Baghdad, had proved impracticable because of the impossibility of transporting such a force to Mesopotamia or of feeding it if it got there. Falkenhayn himself hurried to Palestine, and the first of the Yilderim divisions arrived in time to take part in the Battle of Gaza. Falkenhayn missed no opportunity of harassing Allenby's open flank, but he lacked the strength to do more.

The German general gave more trouble when Allenby wheeled into the Judaean Hills, launching a number of successful counterattacks and blocking the British project. By Allenby's direction, Bulfin had made his thrust seven miles north of Jerusalem in order to avoid the risk of damage to the Holy City, but the commander in chief could no longer maintain this policy. He brought up Chetwode's corps for a direct drive across the Jaffa road, and after very hard fighting received on December 9 the surrender of Jerusalem, which had been handed over to the municipal authorities by the Turks. Allenby made his entry on December 11, on foot and with the greatest modesty, in accordance with instructions from Lloyd George.

Falkenhayn made an attempt to recover Jerusalem on December 26–30. The Turks once more gave of their best, but the venture was hopeless in the face of Chetwode's strength and preparedness; in fact, Chetwode counterattacked and drove the enemy back to the safe distance of eight miles from Jerusalem. The victory was complete but costly. Turkish losses in the campaign to date were approximately 25,000, of whom 12,000 were prisoners of war. The losses of the Egyptian Expeditionary Force totaled 18,000.

The activities of the Arabs were not of major importance during 1917, but they strained Turkish resources by means of raids on the Hejaz Railway and held out great promise for the future. They had been enlivened by the influence and exploits of an extraordinary young genius, T. E. Lawrence, who was consistently supported by both Murray and Allenby. Lawrence allied himself in particular with Husein's son Feisal.

End of the War in the Caucasus, 1917–18

The campaigns of Yudenich and his hard-fighting troops in the Caucasus ended tragically. On the whole, these forces, especially the Armenians, resisted the summons of Vladimir Lenin and Leon Trotsky to return to their homes rather more strongly than did the troops on the Eastern Front. Nevertheless, the command was quickly paralyzed by insubordination, and soon it and the hierarchy of officers lost all authority. The Cossacks led the rush back to the farms, which were, as they believed erroneously, to become their personal property as free peasants. Yudenich also went home and later distinguished himself in the civil war.

The Turks now enjoyed a favorable situation, which was to continue until the autumn of 1918, when their collapse in Syria and that of the Germans on the Western Front reversed it. They had already perpetrated abominable massacres of the Armenians while engaged in fighting the Russians in 1915, and now the massacres were resumed. Estimates of the number of Armenians who were killed or died of starvation during the war vary, but the deaths amounted to at least half a million. In addition, the lives of such communities as the Georgians were gravely disrupted.

OPERATIONS IN 1918

Palestine, Transjordan, and Syria

Immediately after the operations for the capture and consolidation of the Jerusalem–Jaffa line, Palestine suffered unusually heavy rains and floods, which delayed Allenby's contemplated advance. In March, 1918, he did carry out a large-scale operation, which he considered promising, for the destruction of the Hejaz Railway at Amman. The operation was in many respects well conducted, and on March 30 the town was ringed on all sides but the east. The attacking force was not strong enough to tip the balance, however, and in the afternoon orders were issued for a general withdrawal after trifling damage had been done to the railway. The great viaduct, which had been the principal objective, had not been reached. A second raid into Transjordan was nullified on April 11 by a brilliant counterattack across the British communications in the Jordan Valley in which the Australians lost nine guns. The perilous retreat to Palestine was safely accomplished.

By this time the great German offensive of March 21 had been launched on the Western Front. The War Office, spurred by a sense of guilt at having left too many first-class troops in Palestine, recalled all that it safely could. In April the Lys offensive led to further demands. Allenby's Yeomanry Mounted Division was reconstituted with Indian regiments from the Indian cavalry divisions in France, and they sufficed with the yeomanry to form an entirely new cavalry division, of which he now had 4. In all, Allenby sent to France 2 infantry divisions, 9 yeomanry regiments, 23 infantry battalions, and some heavy artillery, aggregating almost 60,000 men. He retained 4 cavalry and 7 infantry divisions, including a second division from Mesopotamia, but most of the Indian troops were raw.

The Turks, in addition to a German contingent represented by a small but heavily armed division, had received some reinforcements, but they never attained a strength of 30,000 even if the troops on the Hejaz Railway north of Ma'an were included, whereas the British forces were well over twice as large. They had a new commander in chief in Liman von Sanders, who had replaced Falkenhayn in March. The change in leaders brought about a change in strategy and major tactics, from defense by maneuver to defense by resistance in trenches.

Meanwhile, the exploits of Lawrence, now a major, had been outstanding. Perhaps the high point was reached at El Tafila in southern Transjordan, which may be described as a classic operation. Falkenhayn had sent two strong columns, which compelled the Arabs to evacuate the village, but in the end it remained in their possession after changing hands five times. Allenby's aid was generous. The Arab Northern Army, which now included small regular sections, was the nucleus of a far larger force of Bedouins and villagers who could be called out as needed. The attacks on the Hejaz Railway were increased until Medina was cut off because the supply of spare rails had been exhausted.

Allenby's plan was to mass his infantry in the coastal plain, wheel to the right, and open a gate for his Desert Mounted Corps of three cavalry divisions. The assault in what became known as the Battle of Megiddo began on September 19. Here and there Turkish resistance was determined, but demoralization soon appeared, and the gate was open. Bombing by aircraft was highly effective, blocking traffic for long periods. The two leading cavalry divisions went forward at 7 A.M. One, emerging the next morning into the plain of Esdraelon (Jezreel), reached the Jordan at Beisan (now Beit Shean), having covered 70 miles in 34 hours. The other

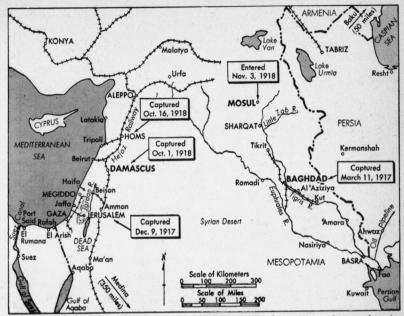

Map 45. THE TURKISH COLLAPSE, 1918. *Palestine*—After the capture of Jerusalem in December, 1917, the British conducted unsuccessful operations against the Hejaz Railway until March, 1918. Then many of the troops were transferred to the Western Front to help stem the German offensives. Operations in Palestine were resumed in September, 1918, when the British routed the Turks in the Battle of Megiddo, bringing their forces to the point of disintegration. The British pressed the pursuit, captured Damascus on October 1, Homs on October 16, and continued northward until the armistice on October 31. *Mesopotamia*—Concurrently with the drive in Palestine, the British advanced from their base at Baghdad, forced the surrender of the Turks on their front in the Battle of Sharqat, and entered Mosul on November 3 (the last Turks left the city on November 10).

entered Nazareth and just missed capturing Liman von Sanders. Lawrence and his Arabs took Der'a at the junction of the Palestinian railways and the Hejaz line, and the Australians and New Zealanders captured Amman and blocked the Turkish Fourth Army, taking 10,000 prisoners.

Damascas was reached by the Desert Mounted Corps on October 1, and Homs by the 5th Cavalry Division on October 16. The latter then went on alone because the 4th Cavalry Division was prostrated by malaria and influenza, and a last action was fought at Haritan on October 26 before news arrived that an armistice had been concluded with Turkey. The 5th Cavalry Division had marched 550 miles in 38 days. Allenby took 75,000 prisoners, while

British losses amounted to a little more than 5,600. A plan of genius involving great risks for the cavalry, which had to live on a denuded countryside, had ended with one of the most crushing victories of modern times.

Advance to Mosul

General (later Field Marshal) Sir Henry Wilson, who had succeeded Robertson as chief of staff in February, 1918, was inclined to subordinate military considerations to political ends. These included saving Georgia, Russian Armenia, and Russian Azerbaidzhan from the Turks and the Germans, and securing the oilfields of Mosul. General Marshall, having lost two divisions to Allenby, had a difficult problem to face when he was ordered by Wilson to begin his advance up the Tigris. He allotted to the operation a corps under the command of Lieutenant General Sir Alexander Stanhope Cobbe. At first there seemed to be no great necessity for haste, but in mid-October the Turks secured the good offices of Spain in approaching President Woodrow Wilson in their quest for peace. The fact that they were seeking an armistice made Mosul more attractive than ever and spurred Henry Wilson and his political masters to establish a *fait accompli* in the eyes of the world. In the Balkans, after General Louis Franchet d'Esperey's crushing victory in Macedonia in September and his advance to the Danube, the British commander, General Sir George Francis Milne, had wheeled right to the Turkish frontier on the Maritsa River, but there had been no further fighting. Turkish plenipotentiaries reached Mytilene, Lesbos, on October 20, and from then on Marshall advanced as fast as he could, starting on October 23. Ismail Hakki, commanding the Turkish Tigris Group, withdrew to the Little Zab River, a tributary of the Tigris 50 miles to the north.

Marshall pursued the Turks at great speed, and his leading cavalry brigade, covering 77 miles in 39 hours, forded the Little Zab. Ismail Hakki maneuvered neatly to face the threat to his flank, withdrawing all troops on the left bank to the right and dismantling his pontoon bridge, but he was given no respite. On October 26, the British brigade discovered another ford over the Tigris 30 miles farther north and came down in the enemy's rear; the next day, Hakki retired to a position 5 miles north of Sharqat (Qal'a Sharqat). While the British main body was closing on him, the cavalry brigade found itself in a perilous situation, but, having been reinforced by the remainder of its division and some infantry, held its own in heavy fighting.

The Battle of Sharqat was fought on October 29, and though the infantry failed to break through, the Turkish commander realized that he was in a hopeless situation and surrendered early the next morning, having lost 11,300 prisoners and 51 guns, whereas the British loss was only 1,886. The armistice signed in the *Agamemnon* in the harbor of Mudros (now Moudros), Lemnos, on October 30, came into operation the following day.

The Indian cavalry division was ordered to take Mosul as soon as possible, relying on local resources for food and fodder, and it reached a position 12 miles south of the city on the evening of November 1. After much haggling, the Turkish government was told that if it would withdraw without making further difficulties, the British government would refrain from demanding its surrender under a clause in the armistice that stipulated that all garrisons in Mesopotamia must lay down their arms. Halil Pasha, commanding the Sixth Army, protested that the remnant of the army was not a garrison but a field force, but he gave way in the end. The British entered Mosul and installed themselves firmly on the Caspian Sea, reoccupying Baku, which they had formerly held with a token force in aid of the Russian garrison, but from which they had been compelled to withdraw because their allies fled whenever the Turks attacked.

The campaigns in Mesopotamia cost Britain and India 92,500 men, of whom 18,620 were killed or died of disease. It would seem that the oil wells and pipelines might have been more economically safeguarded. From another aspect, Mesopotamia does credit to the United Kingdom and India. Except for the Russian operations in the Caucasus, they bore the weight of the war with Turkey, a stupendous burden in view of the British effort on the Western Front, at sea, and in the air.

12. Balkan Campaigns

BY *BRIGADIER GENERAL VINCENT J. ESPOSITO,*
U.S.A. (RET.)

Major European powers had direct interests in the Balkan states in the period before World War I. Austria-Hungary, having absorbed the former Turkish provinces of Bosnia and Hercegovina in 1908, had visions of further expansion to the south. Russia, self-appointed guardian of "her little Slavic sisters," feared an Austrian advance to the Dardanelles. Germany needed access to the sections of the Baghdad Railway running through Serbia and Bulgaria to join forces with her Turkish ally. In the Balkan states themselves feelings of nationalism were strong, and the desire to merge similar ethnic groups and the claims to adjacent provinces bred bitter hatreds. It was inevitable that, when Austria-Hungary set out to punish her troublesome little neighbor Serbia, all of the Balkan states would become embroiled.

In summary, three Austrian offensives against Serbia in 1914 were thrown back by the brave Serbs, but no further action of importance took place there until October, 1915. Then, as the German need for the Baghdad Railway became acute and Serbia stubbornly denied passage through her territory, German, Austrian, and Bulgarian troops in superior numbers overran Serbia and her stanch ally Montenegro. (Bulgaria, finding the offers of the Central Powers more attractive than those of the Allies, had joined the former on October 14.) In an attempt to help Serbia, the Allies established a front in Greece based on Salonika, but it had not grown sufficiently in time to render material aid. The Greek government wavered between a pro-Ally and a pro-German attitude according to whether Premier Eleutherios Venizelos or King Constantine I wielded power. Finally, in June, 1917, the pro-German King was forced to abdicate, and Greece joined the Allies. Romania weighed the offers of both sides and waited for a propitious time to join the winning side. Although she chose the eventual winner, she timed her entrance poorly. Entering the war in August, 1916, she was promptly crushed by an avalanche of German, Austrian, Bulgarian, and Turkish troops before the Allies could help her. Finally, in September, 1918, when the Germans' efforts were concentrated on their collapsing Western Front and Austria was fully occupied in Italy, the greatly enlarged Allied Salonika armies came to life and moved against isolated Bulgaria, forcing her to seek an armistice.

AUSTRIAN INVASIONS OF SERBIA, 1914

With a neutral Bulgaria on Serbia's eastern border, the Austrians could attack Serbia only from the north and west in 1914. There they were confronted by the Danube, Sava, and Drina rivers, which were wide and unfordable. Behind the rivers, mountain ranges presented formidable obstacles to offensive military operations. Austria-Hungary possessed an overwhelming superiority in manpower, and the Serbs realized that they would have to fight a defensive war until the Allies could come to their aid. General Radomir Putnik, the Serbian military commander, therefore planned to hold the river lines at the border with outposts while he concentrated his main forces in a central position just east of Valjevo. When the direction of the main Austrian attacks became known, he could meet them with most of his strength. Although his troops were woefully weak in automatic weapons, artillery, and transport, most of them were veterans of the Balkan Wars of 1912-13 and were hardy and determined individuals.

On August 12, three Austrian armies, totaling 19 divisions, began their invasion—the Second Army from the north, and the Fifth and Sixth armies from the west. To meet them, Putnik had 12.5 divisions organized into three small armies and totaling about 200,000 men. One corps of the Austrian Second Army quickly captured Sabac (Shabats), and by August 15 the Fifth Army had pushed its way against stubborn resistance to the Jadar River. The next day, Putnik launched a strong counterattack that drove the Austrians back across the border. The Austrians contributed substantially to their own defeat: General Oskar von Potiorek failed to coordinate and direct the operations properly, and the brunt of the invasion was borne by only 8 of the available 19 divisions. Moreover, the Austrians underestimated the speed of the Russian advance in Galicia and were forced to draw first half and then all of the Second Army from the Serbian front to counter the Russians.

On September 8, Potiorek launched a second invasion across the Drina and the Sava. Initial gains were made, but on September 16 a strong Serbian counterattack brought the invasion to a halt. The Austrians were not completely expelled from Serbia, however, and

Map 46. AUSTRIAN INVASIONS OF SERBIA, 1914. At the outbreak of war, Austria proceeded immediately to punish Serbia. Three invasions were launched in rapid succession. In the first, the Jadar River was reached, but the offensive was mismanaged and the Austrians were driven back across the border. The second invasion was promptly halted by a strong Serbian counterattack; the Austrians, however, retained a foothold in Serbia. The Serbs then withdrew to better terrain and braced themselves for the third offensive. They were forced to give ground, but eventually counterattacked with determination and again expelled the Austrians from Serbia. Threatened by the Russians in Galicia, the Austrians suspended operations against the Serbs.

retained bridgeheads on both rivers. With his forces extended and short of artillery and munitions, Putnik withdrew to higher ground on a line running north and south through Valjevo.

On November 5, Potiorek began his third invasion. By November 15, Valjevo had been captured; by November 29, Belgrade had been evacuated, and the Serbian armies pushed 20 miles east of Valjevo. Inspired by an appeal from old King Peter I, who appeared at the front with his rifle and bandoleer of ammunition, the three Serbian armies counterattacked fiercely on December 3. By December 9, the Austrians were so hard pressed that Potiorek ordered a retreat. The last of the invaders withdrew across the border on December 15. Nurtured by hatred, the fighting on both sides had been barbaric. General Putnik, sixty-seven years old and confined to his room by infirmity, had conducted from maps a brilliant series of operations through his remarkable comprehension of the influence of topography on military campaigns.

Because of their preoccupation with the Russians in Galicia, the Austrians suspended operations against Serbia, but they left a terrible legacy. An epidemic of typhus that had struck their army was inherited by the Serbs in its full virulence. By April, 1915, when the scourge was overcome, more than 70,000 Serbian troops and many civilians had died.

BULGARIA'S ENTRY INTO THE WAR

The Serbs had not been misled by Bulgarian neutrality during the Austrian invasions. They knew that the Second Balkan War of 1913 had made the Bulgarians their mortal enemies, and that the latter were merely biding their time. In the spring of 1915 the Germans forced the issue. The Allies were at the Dardanelles, and it was imperative that the Baghdad Railway be opened through Serbia and Bulgaria to permit the movement of troops and supplies to Turkey. The German plan was to have Bulgaria enter the war and to crush Serbia with a combined German, Austrian, and Bulgarian invasion. Both sides had made attractive offers of territorial gains to Bulgaria. The offers of the Central Powers, combined with pro-German sentiment, caused Bulgaria to favor them, but from a military point of view she could not declare war while the British-Turkish issue on the Gallipoli Peninsula was in doubt. When it became apparent that the British Dardanelles operation was a failure, however, Bulgaria decided to cast her lot with the Central Powers. On September 6, Germany, Austria-Hungary, and Bulgaria signed a convention agreeing to joint action against Serbia in the following month.

COLLAPSE OF SERBIA

Alarmed by the Bulgarian mobilization, the Serbs pressed the Allies for permission to attack, but the latter, still hopeful of bringing all the Balkan states into the war on their side, refused. A Serbian attack at that time would have made little difference, however, for the overwhelming forces of the Central Powers arrayed against Serbia presaged her ultimate defeat. Four armies totaling 300,000 men were massed on the Serbian border: in the north, the German Eleventh and Austrian Third armies, which were concentrated east and west of Belgrade, respectively; and in the east, the Bulgarian First and Second armies, in position from north to south,

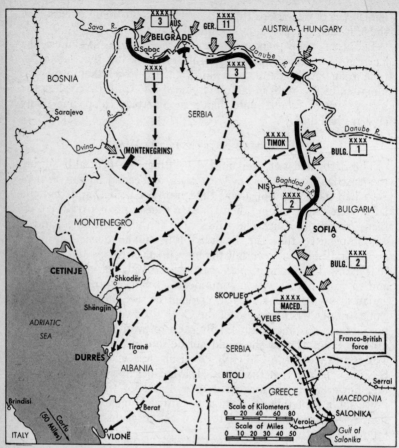

Map 47. CONQUEST OF SERBIA, 1915. In October, 1915, a combined German-Austrian-Bulgarian offensive was launched against Serbia to open the vital Baghdad Railway. The Serbs, greatly outnumbered and forced to defend themselves on a vast front, were soon overwhelmed. A small Franco-British force advanced from Salonika to help the Serbs, but was turned back by superior Bulgarian forces. In one of the most harrowing retreats in history, 150,000 Serbs finally reached the Adriatic Sea, from where they were transported to the island of Corfu. They were moved to the Salonikan front in 1916, and played a key role in defeating the Bulgarians and regaining their homeland.

respectively. Additional troops were available in the rear areas. German Field Marshal August von Mackensen commanded all except the Bulgarian Second Army; this army, operating under the Bulgarian General Staff, was to isolate the Serbs by cutting the railroad from Salonika.

To meet this onslaught the Serbs had only 200,000 men divided among five armies: the First and Third armies along the northern frontier; and the Timok, Second, and Macedonian armies facing Bulgaria. Outnumbered and threatened from two directions, Serbia had chosen a vulnerable extended linear type of defense. After a heavy bombardment that began on October 6, the German and Austrian armies commenced their passage of the Sava and the Danube the next day. Belgrade fell on October 9. The Serbian First and Third armies counterattacked fiercely but unsuccessfully, and to the east the Bulgarian First Army crossed the border on October 11. By October 18, Mackensen had all of his troops across the rivers and began a full-scale attack. The Serbs on his front were forced back progressively but withdrew in good order to the south and the southeast. As they fell back, they blew up stores and depots, and all able-bodied Serbian men left fields and factories to join the re-treating armies. To the south the Bulgarian Second Army overcame the opposition of the weak Macedonian Army and, on October 23, captured Veles (now Titov Veles), thus preventing an Anglo-French force of two divisions that was advancing from Salonika from joining the Serbs. These troops, which were all that the Allies could muster to aid Serbia, had arrived too late and in too few num-bers to influence the campaign, and by mid-November the Serbs had only the alternatives of surrender or of retreat over the rough mountains. They chose the latter course, and there followed one of the most dramatic and difficult retreats in history. Hard pressed and plagued by hunger and cold, 150,000 men finally reached the Adri-atic Sea, whence Allied ships transferred them to Corfu; later they were to join the Allied forces on the Salonikan front. More than 100,000 Serbs had been killed or wounded in the campaign, and 160,000 had been taken prisoner.

The pursuit by the armies of the Central Powers was halted at the Albanian and Greek borders from political rather than from military considerations. Bulgaria wanted to follow the Serbs into Albania, but she was stopped by both Germany and Austria, which did not want her to possess a port on the Adriatic. Similarly, to pre-vent Austria and Bulgaria from gaining a port on the Aegean Sea, the Germans precluded their advance to Salonika to clear the Allies from Greece.

ROMANIAN INTERVENTION

Romania's resources of grain and petroleum placed her in the enviable position of being wooed by two suitors. Allied and German competitive buying increased her wealth, but as time went by, it became more and more difficult for her to remain neutral. Ambitious to expand her territory, she eyed the tempting bait of Bucovina, the Banat of Temesvár (Timişoara), Maramures, Crişana, and Transylvania, which the Allies offered for her active participation in the war. Germany was at a disadvantage in bartering, for the areas desired by Romania belonged to her own allies. In mid-1916 the situation seemed favorable to the Romanians: Germany was faltering at Verdun, and the Allies were advancing on the Somme; Austria was bogged down in her Italian venture; General Aleksei Brusilov's offensive on the southern Russian front was forcing the Germans back; and the Allied Salonika armies were preparing to invade Bulgaria from Greece. If Romania now struck south in conjunction with the northward drive of the Salonika forces, the chances of crippling Bulgaria and of cutting the Baghdad Railway to Turkey were excellent. Instead, for two months she bargained with the Allies for further concessions and finally entered the war on August 27, 1916. By then the situation had changed, and the Central Powers had ample troops available to send against Romania. The latter's political maneuvers had been observed closely by the Germans, who anticipated her entry into the war and had prepared suitable countermeasures. Mackensen, in command on the Bulgarian front, was ordered to organize an army from the available German, Bulgarian, and Turkish forces. The German Ninth and Austrian First armies were directed to concentrate their forces on the Transylvanian frontier, while to the north the Austrian Seventh Army faced the Russian Ninth Army across the border. The concentration of the armies in Transylvania was to be completed by September 30, the earliest date on which it was anticipated that Romania would declare war.

Despite Allied pressure to join in operations with the Salonika forces to isolate Turkey, the Romanians decided to realize their dream of regaining Transylvania, a venture that would have little effect on the final outcome of the war. They had mobilized 560,-000 men and organized them into four armies and a small reserve. The First, Second, and Fourth armies were to advance across the mountains into Transylvania, while the Third Army protected the border against Bulgaria. The greatest weakness of the Romanian Army was its shortage of matériel. There was a dearth of rifles, machine guns, artillery, and signal equipment. Moreover, with

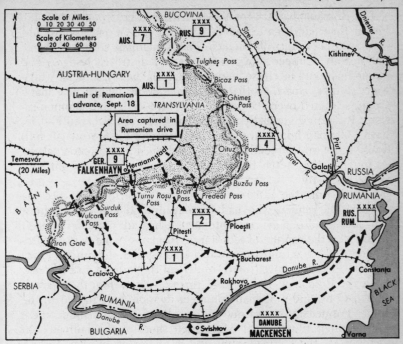

Map 48. FALL OF ROMANIA, 1916. Romania entered the war in August, 1916, at a time when the Central Powers were not pressed elsewhere and could concentrate their forces against her. The Romanians advanced to regain their treasured Transylvania—a venture which would have no effect on the outcome of the war—and made some progress. Soon Austro-German resistance stiffened and brought the advance to a halt. Then coordinated offensives by Field Marshal August von Mackensen's Army of the Danube (Germans, Bulgarians, and Turks) from the south and General Erich von Falkenhayn's German Ninth Army from the northwest overwhelmed the Romanians and the Russians assisting them, and drove them into northeastern Romania with a loss of 400,000 men. For all practical purposes, Romania was eliminated from the war.

neither combat planes nor antiaircraft artillery, Romania was at the mercy of the Central Powers in the air. Lacking factories to manufacture military supplies and unable to import them from the belligerent countries, she went to war with a scant six-week supply of munitions, relying on her allies' promise of shipments of 300 tons daily through Russia and the Black Sea. Additional Allied aid was promised: energetic Russian action against the Austrians, particularly by the Ninth Army; reinforcement by three Russian divisions on the day war was declared; and an Allied drive northward from Salonika to divert Bulgarian attention.

The Romanian attack toward Transylvania began on August 28. Earlier than had been expected, it caught the German Ninth and Austrian First armies off balance. The Romanians advanced slowly but steadily, hampered by poor roads and destroyed bridges. The mountains could be crossed only through the passes, some of which were 40 miles apart, so that the armies were divided into many groups scattered over a 200-mile front without lateral communications. Resistance gradually increased as General Erich von Falkenhayn's German Ninth Army and the Austrian First Army got into position. By mid-September, after an advance that extended about 40 miles in the center, the Romanian offensive was brought to a virtual standstill.

At this time the situation on the southern front had become critical. Mackensen, who had been ready and had crossed from Bulgaria into Romania on September 1, had advanced far enough to threaten the capture of Constanţa, Romania's sole port of entry on the Black Sea, and the railroad leading inland from it. Three Russian divisions moved south to defend the railroad and the city, while the Romanian Third Army, three divisions from the Transylvanian front, and a Serbian volunteer division were rushed to the scene. Formed into an army under a Russian commander, these units temporarily stopped Mackensen short of the railroad. On October 20, the German commander, reinforced by two Turkish divisions and with his entire army well equipped, resumed the offensive. Low on ammunition and plagued with supply difficulties, the Russo-Romanian army was forced back. On October 23, Mackensen captured Constanţa and the railroad. Leaving part of his force in a strong position north of the railroad, he moved the rest to Svishtov, where it would be in a position to cooperate with Falkenhayn's drive into Romania.

Meanwhile, Falkenhayn had pushed the Romanians back through the mountain passes and was preparing a major offensive. He had no time to lose, for the approaching winter would seriously interfere with the movement of heavy guns and supplies through the mountain passes and would immobilize his army. Therefore, he struck on November 10. The Romanians fought stubbornly and well, but their leaders were inexperienced, and supplies and munitions were low. (Of the 300 tons of ammunition scheduled to be delivered daily by the Allies, only 30 tons actually arrived.) On November 23, Mackensen launched an attack from the south to join Falkenhayn. Relentlessly, the two German leaders forced the

Romanians back. The latter attempted two attacks across the Danube against Mackensen to prevent his juncture with Falkenhayn. The first, in early October, was disrupted by a sudden flood; the second, in early December, was initially successful and resulted in the capture of 3,000 prisoners, but Falkenhayn sent troops to attack the Romanian flank and rear, and the Romanians fell back in panic. By early January, the Romanian Army, now numbering only 150,000 men, had been driven behind the Siret River in eastern Romania, where it was saved only by bad roads and torrential rains, which forced the Germans to end their pursuit. Romania had lost 400,000 fighting men and had been eliminated as an effective ally. Her vital granaries and oilfields, damaged but not destroyed, were now in the hands of the Central Powers.

Greece and the Salonikan Front

Greece was obligated by a 1913 treaty to come to the aid of Serbia if the latter were attacked by Bulgaria. By the terms of the treaty, Serbia was to provide 150,000 men for the Bulgarian front, but she could not do so because of the German and Austrian concentrations on her northern frontier. Although the Greeks consequently refused to enter the war, Premier Venizelos' suggestion that the Allies provide the 150,000 men was agreed to, and Allied troops began to land at Salonika on October 3, 1915. The Central Powers commenced their advance into Serbia on October 7. The Allied Salonika force under French General Maurice P. E. Sarrail which was called the Armée d'Orient started north on October 12. It comprised only 40,000 British and French troops and, as we have seen, was soon cut off from the Serbs by the Bulgarians and pushed back to the Greek border. Had the Bulgarians not been ordered by the Germans to stop at the frontier, they probably would have destroyed the Allied force and its base at Salonika. On the other hand, had the Greek Army of 350,000 men joined the Allies, Serbia might have been saved.

Greek political affairs now troubled Sarrail. Pro-German King Constantine I (his wife was the Kaiser's sister) had denounced Venizelos' agreement, forced him to resign on October 5, and repudiated the treaty with Serbia. Sarrail had intended to retain his position on the Greek border, but two Greek corps stood between him and his base at Salonika, and in view of the King's attitude he withdrew to that port. The base was now greatly expanded and strongly fortified, and eventually became known as the

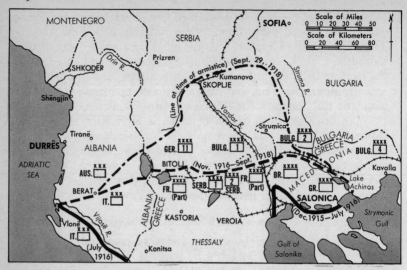

Map 49. SALONIKAN FRONT, 1915–18. The Salonikan front was established in 1915 to help the Serbs, but Allied troops arrived too late and in too little strength to prevent the fall of Serbia. The Allied forces were built up steadily and engaged in limited offensives during 1916 and 1917, without gains of consequence. In September, 1918, under energetic leadership and aided by the exhaustion of the Central Powers, a successful offensive was launched which broke the Bulgarians and forced them to seek an armistice. The Serbian Army, transferred from Corfu, played a major role in the successful operations on the Salonikan front.

"Bird Cage." Allied troops trickled in steadily, and by July, 1916, Sarrail had about 250,000 men, including the re-formed Serbian Army, which had arrived from Corfu.

Not only was Sarrail's political situation obscure, but his command relationships were fraught with friction. The various governments persisted in sending instructions directly to their contingents; there were five of these, and Sarrail experienced much difficulty in exercising authority and control. In addition, each arrival or movement of troops was reported by Athens to Berlin, so that the Central Powers were apprised of every detail of the Armée d'Orient. When Romania entered the war in August, 1916, Sarrail moved to protect the Romanian mobilization by pinning down the Bulgarians. He attacked with his left wing (mostly Serbs) on September 10, while his right wing remained on the defensive. His total force, now called the Armées Alliées en Orient, numbered 350,000. The left wing gained spectacular successes and drove the Bulgarians from Bitolj (Monastir), but the right wing was forced back by the Bulgarians. Bickering between Sarrail and his subordinates and poor support of the Serbs by the other allies had made an important victory impossible.

Meanwhile, a smoldering revolutionary movement among the Greeks of Macedonia erupted against their pro-German King and his ministers. The spark was provided by arrangements made by Athens to allow the Bulgarians to take over fortifications at the border from Greek troops. Salonika had a real revolution, and Greek soldiers and civilians renounced their allegiance and subdued the royalist minority. Venizelos and the commander of the Greek Navy established a revolutionary government in Crete, and as the revolution spread, soldiers and police joined the Allies. The city of Salonika was virtually under Sarrail's control; the Allies took charge of the Greek Fleet, the railroads, and the port of Piraeus; and marines landed in Athens and censored its newspapers.

In May, 1917, Sarrail attempted another offensive, but the Serbs, still angry because they had not been properly supported in the 1916 attack and torn by dissension, caused the operation to falter before any appreciable success had been gained. In June, the ineffective negotiations between the Allies and Greece came to a head. Célestin Jonnart arrived in Greece as Allied high commissioner, and French troops landed on the Isthmus of Corinth. Jonnart demanded the abdication of Constantine, who yielded the throne to his second son, Alexander, and sailed on a French vessel for Germany. Venizelos was recalled to power, and on July 2 the new government declared war on Germany and Bulgaria. The addition of the Greek Army permitted the transfer of British divisions needed in Palestine. In December, the incompetent Sarrail was succeeded by an energetic commander, General Marie Louis Adolph Guillaumat. When Guillaumat was recalled to the Western Front in July, 1918, he was replaced in turn by General Louis Franchet d'Esperey, an excellent soldier.

FALL OF BULGARIA

When the German drives of early 1918 on the Western Front failed and the Allies took the offensive, the Germans bled all their other fronts of men and equipment to bolster their defense. Only the staff and a few small units were left with their Eleventh Army, and the Bulgarians had to supply divisions to fill it out. Since Austria needed all her strength for the Italian front, Bulgaria was

Map 50. MAXIMUM EXPANSION OF CENTRAL POWERS, JULY, 1918. The Central Powers controlled the greatest expanse of territory in July, 1918. The Treaty of Brest-Litovsk had permitted the occupation of vast areas of the Russian Empire. Except for Greece and the southern part of Albania, all of the Balkans were under the Central Powers' control. On the Western Front the Germans were on the Marne River, and occupied rich northern France and all but the northwest corner of Belgium. In Italy the Austrians and Germans occupied the rich northeastern plain down to the Piave River.

virtually alone and ripe for collapse. Franchet d'Esperey had 350,-000 combat troops, who were well equipped and high in morale. They were opposed by 310,000 men, predominantly Bulgarians, who were short of food, clothing, and munitions and were low in morale.

The Allied High Command decided to launch an attack in the Balkans in conjunction with their final drive against the Germans on the Western Front. On September 14, 1918, a heavy bombardment on the Bulgarian lines began, and an initial striking force of six Serbian and two French divisions attacked. A general assault was delivered on September 15 and 16 by British, Serbian, French, Greek, and Italian troops. The offensive was an amazing success from the start. By September 17, the Allies had advanced 20 miles, the Serbs especially distinguishing themselves in furious charges. By September 27, the road to Sofia lay open as the remnants of the Bulgarian armies, split and demoralized, straggled homeward. The Eleventh Army was cut off and forced to surrender.

It was useless for the Germans to urge the Bulgarians to rally. These sturdy peasants were finished with war and were intent on returning home for the harvest. On September 26, Bulgarian emissaries arrived under a flag of truce to request an armistice. Granted on September 29, it provided for demobilization of the Bulgarian Army, evacuation of all occupied territories, surrender of means of transportation, and permission for the Allies to use Bulgarian territory for further operations. No such operations were necessary since both Germany and Austria were in their death throes, and the war ended on November 11.

The Allied Salonika venture remains a controversial subject. Some mark it as a waste of men and resources, while others believe that it had great strategic significance. When its accomplishments are considered, however, the former view appears to be the more logical. The campaign failed to achieve its principal objective—the severance of German-Turkish communications—in time to have any effect on the war, and it did not pin down enough German and Austrian troops to affect adversely their operations in other theaters. Its sole achievement was to defeat the Bulgarians, who in any event would have fallen with the Germans and Austrians a month later. It did protect Greece, but the Greeks themselves were capable of holding their own against the Bulgarians.

For three years, hundreds of thousands of Allied troops suffered in the malaria-infested Salonikan area. British official records list during the campaign 481,262 hospital cases, of which only 18,187 were wounded; French official records in the brief period June–August, 1916, show 35,122 hospital cases, of which 672 were wounded.

13. The War at Sea

BY REAR ADMIRAL JOHN D. HAYES, U.S.N. (RET.)

From the naval point of view, World War I was essentially a struggle between a group of powers that had to obtain their means of waging modern war from within the heart of the European continent and a group that was able to obtain these means overseas. For a time, the second group did include Russia, but that nation collapsed when the maritime powers, Great Britain and France, were unable to overcome geography and reach her with waterborne resources.

Great Britain lies like a breakwater across the sea communications of Germany, whose access to the maritime world is through the North Sea, the Strait of Dover, and the English Channel, waters dominated for centuries by the British Navy. British trade routes, on the other hand, were free from direct German naval threat with the exception of those to Scandinavia. Nevertheless, the geography of the peninsula of Europe enabled Germany to keep the main water routes to Russia closed despite British sea power.

The war at sea in World War I became primarily a contest between the navies of Great Britain and Germany. The former received assistance from the French and United States navies, but the navies of Italy and Austria did little more than counter each other in the Adriatic Sea. The Russian Navy, weak in morale, was locked in the Baltic and Black seas, while the navy of Turkey consisted mostly of two ships of the former German Mediterranean Squadron and their crews. The navy of Great Britain had been its first line of defense for centuries, but the German Navy was a relatively new creation, a product of German nationalism and overseas aspirations. It was essentially a surface navy, designed to challenge the sea power of Britain in the narrow waters of the North Sea. In the end, it contested this power on the oceans with the submarine and came close to winning the war.

Prussia began laying the foundations of German naval power in 1853–54, when it purchased from Oldenburg a small piece of territory on shallow Jade Bay in the southeastern corner of the North Sea. A port, Wilhelmshaven, was constructed there at great expense and completed in 1869. By annexing Holstein in 1864 after the war with Denmark, Prussia also obtained the excellent port of Kiel. A canal between Kiel and the Elbe River estuary connecting the Baltic and North seas was completed in 1895. By 1914 this canal had been deepened and widened so that the largest ships of the German Navy could transit it.

The growth of the German Navy was stimulated by trade competition with Great Britain and by a growing antagonism toward that strong maritime power. Bills for increased naval construction were enacted in 1898, 1900, and 1905, the last calling for a fleet built around 40 battleships to be completed by 1917. A navy that could challenge Great Britain was thus created over opposition of the Imperial General Staff and of liberal elements in the Reichstag. It was primarily the work of Admiral Alfred von Tirpitz, who was the first trained seaman to serve as Secretary of State for Naval Affairs, and who had the support of Emperor William II.

This expansion of the German Navy could not help affecting Great Britain. While the modern British Fleet had been building since 1889 as an answer to the current naval ambitions of France and Russia, these two countries no longer presented a threat to Britain after 1904. Instead, the rising German Navy forced the British into an alliance with them. The development of the Triple Entente permitted the area of activity of the British Fleet to be transferred from the Mediterranean Sea and the English Channel to the North Sea, and a major naval shipbuilding program was inaugurated to maintain a 60 per cent superiority over the Germans. The armament and the speed of warships were improved, and oil was adopted as fuel. This progress culminated in the design of the five powerful battleships of the *Queen Elizabeth* class, which were armed with 15-inch guns and could make 27 knots.

In both Britain and Germany the capital ship monopolized naval planning to the exclusion of more modern types, such as the destroyer, the submarine, and the airplane. The British Navy stressed speed and the largest possible caliber of guns in order to retain initiative and the offensive, while the Germans emphasized hitting power and strong construction at the expense of speed and radius of action, which they considered secondary for a navy built primarily for attrition operations in the North Sea.

The skill of their naval designers and the competence of their officer corps made the German Navy, ship for ship, a formidable rival to that of Great Britain. In many technical features of gunnery and damage control, the Germans were superior. War planning in both countries, however, left much to be desired. Navies had gone through a long period of technological changes but had experienced little combat to test the strategic and tactical effects of these changes.

In Germany, Admiral von Tirpitz, in his efforts to keep the navy independent, had allowed the General Staff to ignore his service in their war plans. No provisions were made for such joint operations as seizing the Continental side of the English Channel or stopping the flow of troops and supplies from England to France. At the same time, the German Navy, in its concentration on the capital ship, failed to develop the full potentiality of the torpedo, the mine, and the submarine, obvious weapons of a lesser naval power.

In Great Britain the two services also made their war plans separately. The admirals expected to conduct a close blockade of Germany and to employ ground forces in amphibious operations on the German coast, ignoring the development of steam navies and high-powered ordnance, which would make such plans difficult to carry out. They also ignored the fact that British military leaders were thinking about something entirely different. The latter, despite their country's control of the seas, were worried about invasion, and they made plans for employing their forces offensively, not in exploiting the mobility and freedom of action of sea power but rather in reinforcing the French Army on the Continent. This revolutionary change in British strategy stemmed from staff conversations with the French that began in 1906. Although these conversations never reached the form of agreements or plans, they committed the small British regular army of seven divisions to employment in France in the event of war with Germany. When war finally came, these seven divisions were followed by millions of men.

EARLY ACTIONS

The opening of the war found Winston Churchill as first lord and Prince Louis of Battenberg as first sea lord, the highest civilian and naval positions in the Admiralty. Admiral Sir John Jellicoe (later 1st Earl Jellicoe) had command of the British Grand Fleet. This fleet was at its war base in Scapa Flow in the Orkney Islands, while the German High Seas Fleet cut short its cruise to Norway to return to the Jade. Since both fleets were built around battleships and battle cruisers, it is necessary only to compare figures in these types to get an idea of comparative naval strengths. The

Grand Fleet had 19 dreadnoughts, 8 predreadnoughts, and 4 battle cruisers; while the High Seas Fleet had 13 dreadnoughts, 8 predreadnoughts, and 4 battle cruisers. In the Mediterranean the British had 3 battle cruisers, and the Germans 1. A total of 8 cruisers and 96 torpedo craft guarded British coastal areas, especially the Strait of Dover. The British had 24 new and 31 old submarines, while the Germans had 10 new and 18 old ones.

The first naval operation of the war, which took place in the Mediterranean, was a decided victory for the Germans. This was the escape of the battle cruiser *Goeben* and the light cruiser *Breslau* to Constantinople. Vice Admiral Wilhelm A. T. Souchon boldly took action on his own initiative while the British commanders were receiving conflicting instructions from the Admiralty. The two ships were added to the Turkish Navy, a step that had a decided effect in bringing Turkey into the war on the German side.

The British took the initiative in the first surface action in the North Sea. On August 28, 1914, a sweep by five battle cruisers toward Helgoland resulted in a light-force action that cost the Germans three cruisers. This action set the pattern of ambush and hit-and-run raids that characterized North Sea fighting throughout the war.

A few weeks later, on September 22, the German submarine *U-9* sank three British cruisers, the *Cressy*, *Hogue*, and *Aboukir*, off the coast of the Netherlands. This action made a deep impression on both naval commands. It caused the withdrawal of the Grand Fleet to the north of Ireland, while bomb and net defenses were installed at Scapa Flow. The fleet was therefore 300 miles away from the North Sea when the German Army captured Antwerp and almost took the Channel ports. This series of setbacks, combined with a lack of the action that the British public had expected from its fleet, caused the resignation of Prince Louis of Battenberg and the reappointment of the 1st Baron Fisher, who had been first sea lord from 1904 to 1910. On November 2, 1914, the North Sea was declared a war zone and mined, and neutral shipping was instructed to proceed by certain channels or accept the risk involved. This step gave the Germans a precedent for justifying the war zone which they declared around Great Britain in February, 1915, in their all-out submarine campaigns.

A major task of the British Fleet, second only to the security of the British Isles themselves, was the protection of overseas trade and of troop movements against the German cruisers that were on foreign stations when the war commenced. The *Emden*, which had been detached from the German Far East Squadron to raid in the Indian Ocean, sank 15 ships before she was finally run ashore by the Australian cruiser *Sydney*, and the *Karlsruhe* in the West Indies destroyed 17 ships before she was destroyed by an internal explosion. Meanwhile, other raiding cruisers destroyed a few more British ships.

The German Far East Squadron, under Vice Admiral Maximilian von Spee, posed the principal threat to British shipping and convoys in the Indian and Pacific oceans. This squadron, consisting of the armored cruisers *Scharnhorst* and *Gneisenau* and the light cruiser *Nürnberg*, crossed the Pacific and was joined by two more light cruisers, the *Leipzig* and the *Dresden*. Off Coronel, Chile, on November 1, 1914, it met an inferior British squadron, consisting of the armored cruisers *Good Hope* and *Monmouth*, the light cruiser *Glasgow*, and the auxiliary cruiser *Otranto*, under Rear Admiral Sir Christopher Cradock. The Germans sank the two armored cruisers in a short action, and the other British ships made their escape.

This disaster brought a quick reaction from Lord Fisher. The battle cruisers *Inflexible* and *Invincible* were sent to the South Atlantic, where they were joined by four other cruisers. In the meantime, the German squadron had entered this area on its way home. The British ships were coaling at the Falkland Islands on December 8, when Admiral von Spee, unaware of their presence, decided to raid the British station. The result was that the Germans were caught in a running fight with a superior force. Only the *Dresden* escaped, and she was found and destroyed three months later off the Juan Fernández Islands.

By December, 1914, therefore, the German surface-raider threat was ended. Conditions had changed since the days of the *Alabama* in the American Civil War. Dependence on coal plagued the German cruisers, and radio telegraphy made it relatively easy to track them. The submarine would be the commerce raider of the future.

In the North Sea the German battle cruisers had made a sweep in November, 1914, and on December 16, they bombarded Scarborough, Hartlepool, and Whitby on the English coast. These operations were undertaken for the purpose of drawing out and engaging detached British forces. On January 24, 1915, these ships made a sweep to Dogger Bank, two-thirds of the way across the North Sea, hoping to catch British light forces patrolling in the area. A short time before, however, the British had obtained a code book that had been jettisoned from a German cruiser grounded in the Baltic and recovered by a Russian diver. Since the Germans never radically changed their codes, the British thereafter were able to secure advance information on their operations.

Rear Admiral David Beatty with five battle cruisers, the *Lion*, *Tiger*, *Princess Royal*, *New Zealand*, and *Indomitable*, and a light cruiser squadron, thus could leave the base at Rosyth in the Firth of Forth just a few minutes after Rear Admiral Franz von Hipper, with three battle cruisers, the *Derfflinger*, *Moltke*, and *Seydlitz*, and the armored cruiser *Blücher*, cleared the Jade. When the Germans reached a point about 30 miles north of Dogger Bank and 180 miles west of Helgoland at 7 A.M., they found the British waiting for them. Hipper immediately reversed course and sped for his base with the British in pursuit. Shortly before 9 A.M., the British ships began to come within range and opened fire on the *Blücher*, the last ship in the German column. Fire was later shifted to other German ships, and the *Seydlitz* was seriously damaged. The Germans concentrated on the *Lion*, the leading British ship, which was struck several times, causing her to fall out of line. Poor fire distribution and faulty communications on the part of the British allowed the three battle cruisers to escape. The *Blücher* was sunk, but not before a British photographer obtained one of the best naval photographs of the war. The Germans profited from this defeat, for they strengthened the side plating and turret tops of their battle cruisers and improved the protection of the magazines and ammunition supply. These changes were to pay large dividends a year and a half later at Jutland.

DARDANELLES CAMPAIGN, 1915

By 1915 the war on the Western Front had stabilized into one of grinding attrition that was to absorb millions of men and such vast quantities of ammunition that the economies of all countries almost collapsed under the strain. Since Britain was then the only Allied power that held the initiative, some British leaders looked for means of outflanking the German position and establishing communications with Russia. Lord Fisher wanted a combined naval and military attack in the Baltic and started a building program for such a great amphibious undertaking. This plan, however, was not considered seriously by anyone else. It could succeed only at enormous cost, for the Germans feared such an attack and would have resisted it furiously.

An alternative was opening the Dardanelles. Churchill, who at first espoused the Baltic plan, now shifted his interest to what appeared to be a less costly project. French military leaders and some British opposed the operation, which they feared would withdraw or withhold troops from France. The 1st Earl Kitchener, who was the Secretary of State for War, wanted to strengthen Russia but refused at this time to make any troops available. Churchill accordingly agreed to a primarily naval attack.

Fisher would agree to the Dardanelles operation only if certain conditions, including the use of troops, were fulfilled. Churchill solved his dilemma by going over Fisher's head to the naval commander in the area, Vice Admiral Sackville H. Carden, who provided a plan that combined reduction of the Dardanelles forts by naval gunfire with minesweeping. Obsolete French and British battleships, whose loss would not affect the balance of sea power, were to be used. The new battleship *Queen Elizabeth* was added, and an enthusiastic Churchill could see the Dardanelles forts falling successively before her 15-inch guns.

Carden's plan had made no provision for dealing with mobile artillery, and Churchill assumed that the British intelligence reports were correct. These, however, gave information only on the forts and none on the action of General Otto Liman von Sanders, head of the German military mission to Turkey. Liman von Sanders realized that, in addition to the forts, the minefields would have to be covered by mobile artillery. He bypassed Constantinople in the movement of this artillery and, by keeping its movement secret even from the German commander of the Dardanelles defenses, prevented British intelligence from learning of its existence.

After the combined naval attack was agreed on, British leaders hurried the project and failed to make proper preparations, especially for minesweeping. The first attack of the Franco-British squadrons on the outer forts was made on February 19, 1915, and a second attack followed on February 25. The outer forts were reduced, but after the initial bombardments it became evident to Carden that amphibious troops were needed. Churchill ignored his requests, insisting that he go on with the original plan. Operations were renewed on March 4, and were continued for two weeks, with the big ships bombing by day and the minesweepers attempting to sweep at night. The latter could make little progress against the current, however, and suffered heavily from the field guns.

Carden's health finally broke down, and he was relieved by Rear

Admiral Sir John de Robeck, who decided on an all-out daylight bombardment with minesweeping operations under its cover. This attack was made on March 18. Things went well until early afternoon. The forts appeared to have been silenced, but when the minesweepers proceeded to their work, the field guns drove them back with heavy losses. A French battleship, *Bouvet*, had already been sunk by an unswept mine. De Robeck recalled his heavy ships, and in the retirement another battleship and a battle cruiser were destroyed by mines, while a second cruiser was damaged. Two other ships were put out of action by gunfire. De Robeck ordered a general withdrawal.

The whole problem was then reappraised, and a purely naval attack was abandoned. The campaign against Constantinople was to go on, however, with the army now given the main task and the navy assisting it. An army force under General Sir Ian Hamilton, consisting of a regular division from England, the Australian and New Zealand troops, a naval infantry division, and a few French, had been assembled in Egypt. This force was not prepared for assault amphibious operations, however, and a month was lost in reloading. Liman von Sanders thus had the time he needed to get ready for the attack, which was made on the Gallipoli Peninsula on April 25, 1916. The whole campaign eventually failed, the Allies suffering their most costly setback of the war. The result was a shake-up in the British cabinet that included the removal of Churchill.

BATTLE OF JUTLAND, 1916

The next major naval action, the Battle of Jutland (or Skagerrak, as it was called by the Germans), took place on May 31–June 1, 1916. The war had been in progress for almost two years before this main fleet action, toward which the building and training of navies had been directed for a generation, finally took place. The two fleets had been acting on the defensive, but events in early 1916 brought a change in their attitude. Russia, blockaded by Germany, was suffering more than Germany, blockaded by Britain. To break this blockade the Allies would have to gain control of the Baltic, and before this could be done the High Seas Fleet had to be destroyed. The Grand Fleet now had suitable bases along the east coast of Britain closer to Germany and was in a better position to press for the necessary decisive action. On the German side, command of the High Seas Fleet had been taken over by a new man,

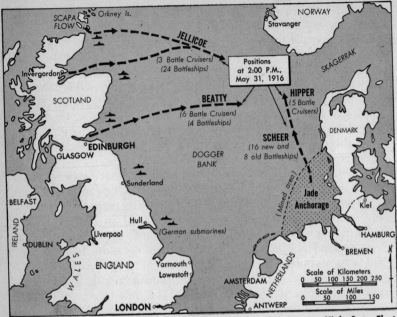

Map 51. BATTLE OF JUTLAND, 1916: OPENING PHASE. The German High Seas Fleet
sortied from its base in the Jade Bay anchorage to raid Allied shipping off Norway and
attack the British blockading force. The British, by decoding German radio messages,
learned of this move, and their Grand Fleet put to sea to intercept it. By 2 P.M. on May
31, the two fleets were in the positions shown. At this time, neither Adm. Sir John
Jellicoe nor Adm. Reinhard Scheer knew that he was confronting his opponent's main
fleet.

Reinhard Scheer, a choice of Tirpitz and an advocate of offensive
action. Scheer planned a series of raids in which all forces, including submarines and zeppelin airships, would be used. The purpose
of these raids was to draw out detachments of the British fleets,
which would be attacked by submarines and surface forces.

The first German raid was made by a force of battle cruisers,
which on April 25, 1916, bombarded Lowestoft and Yarmouth.
Scheer next planned a bombardment of Sunderland, but bad
weather caused him to make instead a sweep to the north to raid
Allied shipping off Scandinavia and possibly attack the British
blockading force, the 10th Cruiser Squadron. If necessary, he could
withdraw via the Skagerrak.

The High Seas Fleet, with 16 modern and 8 old battleships
under Scheer and 5 battle cruisers under Hipper, sortied from the

Jade for this operation in the early hours of May 31, and headed north with Hipper about 50 miles ahead of Scheer. Since the British were still reading coded German radio dispatches, the Grand Fleet got to sea even before the Germans. The main body under Jellicoe, which consisted of 24 dreadnoughts and 3 battle cruisers with attached light forces, left Scapa Flow and Invergordon at about 10 P.M. on May 30. At the same time, the scouting force under Admiral Beatty, consisting of six battle cruisers and four modern battleships of the *Queen Elizabeth* class, left Rosyth. Both groups proceeded eastward separately. At 2 P.M. on May 31, Beatty was to be 70 miles south of Jellicoe, and if at this time he had not sighted the Germans, he was to turn north and join the commander in chief. Neither Jellicoe nor Scheer knew that the main body of the other's fleet was at sea, for Scheer had taken the precaution of having the radio guard ship in port acknowledge all messages addressed to him.

Shortly before Beatty was to turn north, one of his cruisers sighted smoke to the east, which was found to come from a Danish freighter that had been stopped by two German destroyers. This contact brought on the battle, for at 2:20 P.M. Beatty turned southeast and increased speed, hoping to get between the enemy and his base. Meanwhile, Hipper, on learning of the contact, turned to a northwesterly course to develop it. The light forces screening Beatty and Hipper had by this time been drawn off to the north, so that at 3:25 P.M. the battle cruiser squadrons sighted each other without previous warning. Beatty's four battleships were several miles astern of him.

To prevent the British from getting between him and Scheer, Hipper reversed course. With both forces on parallel courses, fire was then opened at about 17,000 yards and continued for an hour. The German fire was more effective, sinking the battle cruiser *Indefatigable* at 4:06 P.M. and the *Queen Mary* at 4:26 P.M. Beatty's flagship, the *Lion*, lost a turret, as did the German *Seydlitz*. Other ships on both sides also received hits. The Germans at this time were leading the British battle cruisers toward the main body. The German battleships were sighted at 4:33 P.M. by the 2d Light Cruiser Squadron under Commodore William E. Goodenough, who in Beatty's van was alone properly performing the duties of a light force. Beatty held his course until 4:40 P.M., when, with the High Seas Fleet in sight, he turned north to come close to Jellicoe. His four heavy battleships, which by this time had

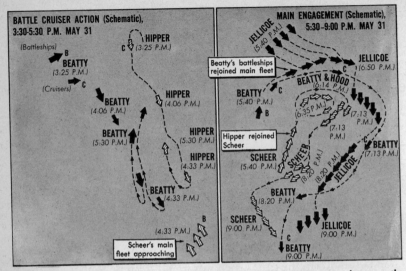

Map 52. BATTLE OF JUTLAND, 1916: FINAL PHASE. The first action was between the scouting forces of Rear Adm. David Beatty and Rear Adm. Franz von Hipper. Hipper sought to lure Beatty south to the main German force under Scheer. Beatty spotted Scheer in time and reversed his course, attempting in turn to lure Scheer to Jellicoe's battleships. The two main fleets met at about 6 P.M. and engaged each other until dark; Jellicoe, meanwhile, succeeded in getting between Scheer and his base. During darkness the Germans broke through the British formation and escaped to the Jade anchorage. Both sides suffered serious but not crippling losses. The German High Seas Fleet made no major sorties thereafter.

taken the German battle cruisers under fire, continued on a southerly course until 4:57 P.M., passing Beatty and covering his rear. The pursuit north lasted until 6 P.M., during which time Goodenough, under fire of the German battleships, nevertheless maintained contact and sent accurate reports.

The battleship squadrons of the Grand Fleet in the meantime were approaching on a southeasterly course, while the battle cruisers, under Rear Admiral Sir Horace Hood, were considerably to the east. The choice of deployment of the battleships from a cruising formation of line of divisions into a long line ahead had to be made on either the right-hand or the left-hand division. Since this decision depended on the location of the German battle lines, Jellicoe delayed his deployment signal until 6:14 P.M., when he finally obtained the correct position of the German main body from Beatty. He deployed his squadrons to the left and took an easterly course to get between the German Fleet and the coast. This maneuver took about 20 minutes, during which time Beatty's cruisers crossed the line of deploying battleships and took up stations in their van. Hood took position ahead of Beatty, while Beatty's four battleships took position in the rear of the battleship squadrons of the Grand Fleet.

The German main body, led by Hipper, was then on a northeasterly course. Hood's battle cruisers first came into contact with the Germans and took them under a heavy fire, which put the *Lützow*, Hipper's flagship, out of action at 6:33 P.M. Hood's flagship, the *Invincible*, was herself sunk by fire from the German battle cruisers and the leading battleships.

The battleships on both sides were now beginning to engage, with the Germans in a bad position, the whole British fleet crossing their van. By 6:26 P.M. the German battle cruisers in the lead were forced to turn away to prevent being caught in a trap. At 6:35 P.M., Scheer ordered his famous *Gefechtskehrtwendung* (emergency retirement by ripple movement from the rear), a maneuver that his ships had often practiced, and which was successfully accomplished despite an elbow in the line.

In the poor visibility, Jellicoe did not see this turnaway and lost contact with the enemy. Keeping to his purpose of getting between the Germans and their base, however, he changed from an easterly to a southeasterly course. Scheer, having successfully extricated himself, for some unknown reason once more reversed course and returned to the battle on an easterly heading, almost at right angles to the British battle line, which in the meantime had changed to the south.

The German Fleet was no sooner turned on an easterly course again than it was reported at 7:00 P.M. by the ever-watchful Goodenough. A few minutes later, at 7:05 P.M., the British battle cruisers commenced firing, and some of the battleships shortly followed suit. The range was down to 7,500 yards, and visibility conditions were now most favorable to the British. At 7:13 P.M., Scheer again extricated his battleships from a bad position by an emergency retirement behind the continued engagement of his battered battle cruisers and a destroyer torpedo attack. The torpedo attack was successful, for at 7:21 P.M. Jellicoe ordered a turnaway of 45° from south to southeast. The British battleship divisions remained on this course for 14 minutes, until the German torpedoes passed their line, whereupon Jellicoe again returned to a southwesterly course. The turnaway maneuver lost Jellicoe his chance to destroy the German Fleet.

After breaking contact, the Germans changed to a southerly course. From 8 to 9 P.M., the British were generally on southwesterly courses, and the battle cruisers in the van again made contact and scored some hits before the Germans turned away to the west. In the closing daylight, Jellicoe now decided not to endeavor to regain contact, and at 9 P.M., realizing that he was between the Germans and their bases and in a favorable position for action the following morning, he put the fleet on a night course of south. A light cruiser squadron was placed in the van, while destroyers covered the rear. At 9:30 P.M., the British battleship squadrons were approximately ten miles east of the German High Seas Fleet, while the British battle cruisers were approximately five miles ahead of it.

Scheer, who knew only that the British were east of him, was determined to break through and return to his base. Putting his heaviest ships in the van, he set his course to the southeast with orders to hold it regardless of cost. The result was a series of confused but deadly night encounters from 10 P.M. to 2 A.M., as the Germans forced their way through the British light forces, leaving a trail of burning vessels to mark their course as surely as the compass in Scheer's flagship. Two British battleships saw this night action but did not report it, and Jellicoe himself failed to realize the significance of the gunfire astern. It was not until 5:40 A.M. that he knew the German Fleet had evaded him. Scheer anchored in the Jade about noon on June 1, and, with all chance of further action gone, the Grand Fleet headed back for its bases.

The Battle of Jutland, involving over 250 ships, was and probably will remain the greatest battle in naval history. It was also one of the most indecisive and subsequently the most studied. Records were kept in every ship, even in the height of action, of almost every happening pertaining to navigation, ordnance, propelling machinery, and casualties. Approximately 10,000 messages were sent during the battle, and 300 action reports were prepared after it. Sufficient data was available to locate 65 per cent of the major-caliber hits. The wealth of material resulted in the battle's receiving an emphasis in naval circles far greater than it deserved. The myth of the battle-line engagement was preserved for another 25 years, after the airplane and the submarine had changed the whole nature of naval warfare. The indecisive result should have revealed that technological advances had outdistanced the commander's means of controlling his forces, and that the tactical doctrine of steam navies had not yet reached full development.

Both sides showed inability to use light forces properly for reconnaissance and security. The Germans were superior in gunnery and ship handling. By holding to the principle of the offensive, Scheer extricated his fleet from some dangerous situations. Jellicoe, obsessed with the safety of his battleships, missed his one chance to obtain a decisive action. The result was that the German Fleet remained to be a bulwark for its submarines. The British were forced to keep a mass of light craft locked up with the Grand Fleet when they were urgently needed for the struggle against the submarine. Far more important perhaps, the High Seas Fleet, by still barring the Baltic, hastened the destruction of Russia and the consequent rise of Communism.

ALLIED BLOCKADE OF GERMANY

After Jutland, surface action almost ceased, and the war at sea became a war against trade that was as much a form of economic as of naval warfare. A history of World War I must therefore include not only the struggles on land and at sea but also the warfare against trade, primarily the overseas trade that was so important in the economic life and war potential of both Great Britain and Germany. This war against seaborne trade can be divided into (1) the blockade of Germany by the Allies, including the regulation of trade with neutrals bordering on that country, and (2) the German submarine campaign and the Allied defense against it. The Allied blockade of Germany falls into two distinct periods. The first spans the two and a half years during which the United States was a neutral. During this time international law still had some force, but when the United States became a belligerent on the Allied side, legal aspects were set aside. In the Allied view, this course was justified by Germany's unrestricted submarine warfare.

The oceans of the world have been described by the naval philosopher Alfred Thayer Mahan as a great common, used in war by both belligerents and neutrals. Because of this, there has grown up a body of custom, generally called international law, for the conduct of sea trade in wartime. This law gives a belligerent the right to capture an enemy's merchant vessels, to stop trade into and from enemy ports, and to confiscate those goods found at sea which are to be used by the enemy for war purposes. To accomplish these objects, a belligerent war vessel has the right of visit and search—that is, the right to stop all vessels to determine their nationality and to learn whether or not they are breaking a blockade or carrying contraband. Private goods at sea are not subject to outright confiscation, however, but must be condemned in an admiralty court, generally known as a prize court.

In the nineteenth and early twentieth centuries efforts were made to codify this international law by agreements between the maritime nations. The Declaration of Paris in 1856 abolished privateering, declared that a blockade to be binding must be effective, and gave protection to all neutral goods except contraband. The Declaration of London in 1909 attempted to define and specify contraband. Absolute contraband was to comprise military goods and conditional contraband goods that could be put to war purposes, while free goods, including such items as raw cotton, fertilizers, and metallic ores, could not be declared contraband.

Neither the Declaration of Paris nor that of London took into account the changes taking place in modern war. Naval weapons such as the submarine, the torpedo, and the mine had made the old type of close blockade as well as visit and search at sea impossible. Under the modern concept of total war, all commodities were considered to have military value. Finally, Germany had on her land borders several Continental neutrals whose trade with her a naval force could not interdict.

New methods therefore had to be adopted by the major maritime power, Great Britain, to cut off the seaborne trade of the Central Powers, especially Germany, and to prevent the means of war in the form of goods from reaching these countries from overseas. This was finally done by a system of trade controls that was to give new meaning to the term "blockade." In this new form, economic pressure was brought to bear not so much by naval ships directly as by a system of trade restrictions that control of the sea made possible. In 1915 and 1916 these restrictions or blockade in its new form gradually evolved within the five following categories:

(1) Inspections in port replaced the visit and search of former days. The dangers of modern weapons and the size and variety of cargoes carried made the old method of inspection at sea impossible. Instead, British cruisers directed suspected neutral vessels into ports for examination. These ports were the Downs, for trade through the English Channel; and Kirkwall in the Orkney Islands, for the northern route, where a cruiser squadron was stationed to enforce the new system.

(2) Rationing was a method by which the Continental neutrals bordering on Germany were allowed supplies sufficient only for

their own use. Based on an elaborate statistical system, it was given legal sanction after a British prize court condemned the steamer *Kim* for carrying an amount of lard to Denmark far in excess of that country's normal imports.

(3) Written clearances in the form of letters of assurance, or navicerts, were given to neutral ships sailing to Europe from the United States or other neutral nations. A navicert certified the contents of the cargo, thereby speeding a ship's examination. Most neutral shipping companies except those of Sweden, which were forbidden to do so by their government, cooperated with the Allies in both rationing and inspection and accepted navicerts. Sweden was still linked economically to Germany, and the Allies could not forget that it lay athwart their own lines of communication to Russia.

(4) Blacklists were publications of names of firms that were known, either through Allied intelligence or by postal and telegraphic censorship, to be trading with the Central Powers. Neutral ships were forbidden to transport their goods.

(5) Bunker control, or the issue of British coal to neutral vessels, was the club that made the other controls possible. Great Britain not only supplied coal to European countries for industrial and commercial use but also controlled most coaling stations. (At this time, American coal offered little competition to the British product.)

By the beginning of 1916 the blockade in its new form was becoming effective. What had begun as an excellent code without machinery had become under the Ministry of Blockade an excellent machinery without a code. Shortages of fibers, oils, fats, lubricants, and fertilizers began to be felt in the Central Powers. Combined with the crop failure of 1916, they caused considerable suffering among the civilian populations, although the armed forces of these nations never experienced shortages in armaments or supplies.

When the United States entered the war in April, 1917, it placed restrictions on trade that the Allies would never have attempted while it was still a neutral. Controls could now be effected at the source, and most of the machinery of the blockade could be abandoned. By the autumn of 1917 the Central Powers were deprived of all foreign supplies.

Like the blockade of the Confederacy in the American Civil War, the contribution of the Allied blockade of Germany to the final victory is difficult to assess. Victory certainly could never have been secured solely by economic encirclement, but when the armies of the Central Powers began to be defeated, the collapse came with the crumbling of civilian morale brought on by deprivations. In expanding her industrial economy before the war, Germany had come to depend too heavily on overseas trade for food and raw materials. The lesson of World War I was that she must draw these necessities from the Eurasian continent.

The blockade of Germany was essentially a form of economic warfare, but it was based on control that the British Navy had maintained for a century and more. Where the arms of British sea power could not reach, however, economic warfare broke down, as it did with Sweden in the Baltic and Romania on the Black Sea.

German Submarine Campaign

Germany's answer to the Allied blockade was its submarine campaign against merchant shipping. In order to view this submarine warfare properly as a form of blockade of Great Britain, certain facts must be kept in mind:

(1) Four-fifths of Britain's food, all of her raw materials except coal, and half of her iron had to be imported.

(2) British war plans had assumed that the Grand Fleet, by containing the High Seas Fleet, would maintain control of the seas and thus preserve the overseas lifeline. The Allies could therefore proceed with the blockade of Germany without fear of retaliation.

(3) Command of the sea enabled the Allies to draw on the resources of the United States and to deny these resources to Germany. The United States therefore became the major and even the predominating force in the struggle.

(4) Despite the size and efficiency of the High Seas Fleet, the Germans were unable to change the prewar naval situation by surface forces alone.

(5) The submarine was singularly fitted for attacking the large concentrations of shipping in the approaches to the British Isles.

The success of the U-9 in sinking three cruisers in a matter of minutes in September, 1914, opened the eyes of German naval officers to the potentiality of the submarine, and as early as November of that year German naval authorities recommended its use against British sea trade. The German political point of view, however, was that, while there were no legal obstacles to a U-boat campaign, a decision to embark on this new type of warfare would be made only when the military position on the Continent was so secure that there could be no doubt of the eventual outcome.

By February, 1915, the campaign on the Western Front had been stalemated, and it was apparent that the war was not to be the short one that the General Staff had planned. In November, 1914, Great Britain had declared the sea approaches to Germany a war zone forbidden to merchantmen. In addition, the list of contraband had been extended to include even grain. The Germans knew that such economic pressure would increase, with their country becoming a fortress beset, and it was this knowledge that led them to decide to use submarines in the war against Allied seaborne trade. On February 4, 1915, the waters around the British Isles were declared a war zone where (effective February 18) submarines would destroy enemy ships and neutral merchantmen would travel at their own risk.

The submarine was unable to comply with the rules of international law adopted for a war against trade by cruisers, for it could ensure its own safety only by sinking ships without warning. The German leaders failed to take into account the reaction of world opinion, especially opinion in the United States, to the changes in the rules of warfare, which they were unilaterally adopting to suit the new weapon. They tried to justify their stand on the ground that Great Britain had been the first to violate international law, but they failed to recognize that British policy offered neutrals an alternative, while their own presented only an ultimatum: cease trade with the Allies or risk destruction of life and property.

The one nation strong enough to dispute the new German attitude toward international law had only a small merchant marine, but American public opinion was shocked at the loss of life that this new warfare would evidently cause, and the United States government refused to compromise on the rights of its citizens to travel under the protection of international law.

After the sinking of the *Lusitania* on May 7, 1915, with the loss of 128 American lives, three notes were required to convince the German government that it had to take cognizance of American public opinion. The first indication of a tendency to yield appeared when Berlin made apologies and offers of reparations for the destruction of two United States freighters, which the Germans claimed had been sunk by mistake. On August 19 the British liner *Arabic* was sunk under conditions similar to those of the *Lusitania*, but before any action could be taken by the United States, Germany requested President Woodrow Wilson to await official investigation. On September 1 the German government submitted the information that the *Arabic* had been destroyed in error after the German commanders had been instructed not to sink liners without warning and without providing for the safety of the passengers. On March 24, 1916, however, the British Channel steamer *Sussex* was torpedoed with the loss of several American lives. After a brief correspondence, on April 18, the United States government demanded assurances that ships would no longer be sunk without warning and without regard for the safety of persons on board, and threatened to sever diplomatic relations if such assurances were not given. Faced with an ultimatum, the German government yielded, but in its reply of May 4 included a statement that it expected the United States to induce Great Britain also to observe the rules of international law. The United States refused to admit that the rights of its citizens could be held conditionally, and there the matter rested until January, 1917.

Behind these events lay a controversy within the German government. The naval administration headed by Admiral von Tirpitz held that the more vigorously the war was prosecuted, the sooner it would come to an end, and that, since the economic life of Great Britain was entirely dependent on shipping, it was the duty of the German Navy to strike her in this area. Chancellor Theobald von Bethmann-Hollweg held that it was his duty to make diplomacy succeed, and this view, which had the support of the Emperor, prevailed for a time. On March 16, 1916, Tirpitz resigned. Admiral Scheer refused to use submarines against merchantmen in the approaches to Great Britain under the restricted conditions required by international law and withdrew them for use against military targets. In the Mediterranean and in the White Sea off Arkhangelsk the submarine war against shipping continued with considerable success under the restricted conditions.

The submarine policy of the navy was approved by the German people, who wanted to strike at Britain in any way possible. By the end of 1916 it was evident that Germany was not winning the war. After a German offer of peace negotiations had been rejected by the Allies, the naval party received the powerful support of Field Marshal Paul von Hindenburg and General Erich F. W. Ludendorff. The Chancellor acquiesced, and on January 31, 1917, the German government announced the resumption of unrestricted warfare after February 1. The United States was left with no choice but to break off diplomatic relations on February 3, and, after several attacks on American ships, to declare war on Germany on April 6, 1917.

The German decision to adopt unrestricted submarine warfare was made on the assumptions that (1) six months of such a campaign would force the British to sue for peace, (2) the United States would probably not become a serious military factor within this time, and (3), if it did, German submarines would prevent American troops from reaching France. None of these assumptions proved valid, but the British people did not know how close they came to defeat until after the war. In the spring of 1917 one ship in four that left Britain did not return, and Admiral Jellicoe, then first sea lord, admitted that the war could be lost by November.

Britain was saved by the convoy system and by German overconfidence. The adoption of a policy of convoying ships rather than patrolling areas had been advocated for some time by a group of younger officers in the Royal Navy, but they could not overcome the opposition of their seniors until they obtained the sponsorship of Rear Admiral William S. Sims, commander of the United States forces in European waters. The Germans put their faith in an all-out effort that would produce very heavy losses in shipping in a few months rather than in a sustained effort over a longer period. All available submarines were sent to sea, maintenance was curtailed, and submarine building was cut back. By the autumn of 1917, however, this gamble had been lost, and resumption of building in 1918 was too late to affect the issue.

Meanwhile, for every submarine unit the Germans put into the attack, the Allies had to muster 20 units to counter it. Reports of submarine losses indicate that 39 per cent were destroyed by patrols, 30 per cent by mines, and 8 per cent by submarines, with aircraft a poor fourth. Casualties in the German submarine service ran as high as 50 per cent. Nevertheless, submarine crews played no part in the mutinies within the fleet that in large measure brought on the surrender of Germany. They remained loyal to the end.

Proper allocation of shipping was almost as important to the salvation of Great Britain as the convoy system, the antisubmarine weapons, and German overconfidence. In addition to the losses by submarines, a large amount of British shipping had to be withdrawn from trade for military uses. Building programs in the early days of the war were devoted primarily to naval vessels, and until 1918 merchant shipbuilding was never able to compensate for the losses. In the beginning of the war it was impossible to obtain any form of allocation of shipping, and different interests often bid against each other. By 1917, however, most commodities were under government control, and it was possible to set up an agency for the control of shipping with representatives from such users as the War Office, Board of Trade, Ministry of Munitions, and Ministry of Food. War risk insurance was provided to induce neutral merchant vessels to continue trading with the Allies. By 1917 all maritime countries except the Netherlands allowed their ships to be used, and the Dutch ships were taken over by right of angary. German ships interned in American ports were put into the shipping pool after the United States became a belligerent.

The American role in the war at sea was not dramatic. Naval units served as parts of British naval task forces. American destroyers operated out of Queenstown (now Cobh), Ireland, and patrol craft of other types operated elsewhere. United States transports carried a large proportion of American troops to Europe but, despite the demands on Allied shipping, not the major portion. A division of battleships reinforced the Grand Fleet, and another was stationed in Bantry Bay, Ireland, to cover the disembarkation ports of Brest and Saint-Nazaire.

In summary, Germany's unrestricted submarine warfare, while threatening the Allies with defeat, brought the United States in on their side. The defeat of the U-boat by the convoy system made possible the transportation of 2 million American soldiers to France, or enough to offset the collapse of the Russian Army and to assure Allied victory.

14. The War in the Air

BY LIEUTENANT GENERAL IRA C. EAKER,
U.S.A.F. (RET.)

The principal national contenders in the air fighting of World
War I were Germany, France, and the British Empire. Italy, Austria-Hungary, the United States, and Russia played minor though
not inconsequential roles. Of these powers, Germany was the best
prepared for the new warfare in the skies, as she was for the traditional battles on the ground. The Germans had prepared methodi-
cally and diligently for every foreseeable aspect of war, while
Britain slept, and French generals preached that victory was to be
achieved by determination and bayonets. Moreover, Germany was
a highly industrialized nation, possessing the seed corn needed for
air armadas: aircraft factories, skilled artisans, and better aircraft
and engine designs than those of her rivals.

France stood next in capacity for air warfare. Her people had
shown tremendous interest in the first European flights of the
Wright brothers near Paris, had reacted enthusiastically to the exploits of the Brazilian Alberto Santos-Dumont, and had taken
great pride in their own air pioneers, such as Louis Blériot and
Henri Farman. Moreover, France was not far behind Germany in
number of aircraft and in size and number of aircraft factories.

Great Britain had had fewer outstanding early pilots and engine
builders. Her air industry was so underdeveloped that her first five
air squadrons sent to France in August, 1914 (all she had at the
time), were equipped largely with planes and engines of French
design. At the same time, she was a highly industrialized nation
with large numbers of skilled workers.

The Austrian and Italian air forces were of less importance (note
that Italy did not become a belligerent until May, 1915), though
the Italians were the first to employ airplanes in warfare, having
used them to drop a few crude bombs on Arab tribesmen during
their conquest of Libya in 1912. The Russians had experimented
with unusually big airplanes but without much success, and their
small air force consisted of French planes.

Although it had been two American citizens, Wilbur and Orville
Wright, who had made the first successful heavier-than-air (air-

plane) flight, the United States remained surprisingly apathetic toward aviation in general and the 1914–16 air operations in Europe in particular. Even the glaring deficiencies shown by the 1st Aero Squadron, which (equipped with 16 training planes) had accompanied Brigadier General John J. Pershing's expeditionary force into Mexico in 1916, failed to rouse either military or industrial leaders to corrective action. Consequently, when the United States finally declared war on Germany in April, 1917, it did not have a single combat airplane. American aviators had to be trained in French and British schools and fly French and British aircraft.

While the major air operations of World War I took place over the battlefields of France, military aviation also played a valuable part in the operations in northern Italy. The Germans used aircraft effectively in their defeats of the Russians along the Eastern Front, and the employment of airpower by General Sir Edmund Allenby against the Turks in Palestine remains a classic example of the proper use of aircraft in mobile warfare.

The air phase of World War I can be best understood by a consideration of the basic elements of air fighting: men, machines, organization, and tactics.

THE MEN

Man has always been the prime element in war; he initiates it, directs it, fights its battles, and designs and builds its weapons. In any military operation the leader is likewise all important, but World War I found its fledgling air forces practically leaderless. Military aviation was less than 10 years old. Military history and doctrine were replete with examples of great generals and famous admirals, but in all the annals of warfare there was not a single page on the planning and conduct of air operations. Officers and men were as little tested as their equipment. Leadership had to be established by competence and survival in action.

From the first this challenge attracted men of daring and energy from other branches of the armed forces and from civil life. The aviators of the opposing armies were volunteers, picked for physical fitness and eager to match themselves against the risks of this new sort of war. They rode frail, underpowered craft into a strangely different field of battle, where the impersonal forces of wind, weather, and lack of oxygen could be more deadly than the human enemy. There were no trenches for protection but only a chance cloud or the sun's glare for momentary concealment—no safe place to hide—in the empty reaches of the sky. The aviator often fought and died alone. Even his training was full of hazards: more fliers lost their lives in training than in combat. Typical of the breed of fighting men that air warfare attracted was the Lafayette Escadrille, composed of American adventurers and idealists who volunteered for service with the French early in the war and established an excellent combat record.

The air force commanders who came up through this stern testing were mostly young, enthusiastic, and aggressive. The outstanding personality among them undoubtedly was Major General (later Air Chief Marshal) Sir Hugh Trenchard of Great Britain, now generally recognized as the founding father of modern airpower. A commander of intelligence, vision, and method, able in presenting his views, he built the Royal Air Force into the most efficient air service in Europe. Brigadier General Maurice Duval of France, the expert Lieutenant General Ernst von Hoeppner of Germany, and Colonel (later Major General) Giulio Douhet of Italy all achieved distinction as skilled air force commanders and prophets of the coming greatness of air power. Brigadier General William Mitchell showed considerable talent in directing the operations of the American air units in France; a convinced disciple of Trenchard, he later devoted his life to championing the airplane as the decisive weapon of future wars.

Initially, air fighting was a thoroughly individualistic affair. Fliers kept scores of their kills, those in the Allied air forces with five or more to their credit being termed "aces." Some became legendary figures—William Avery Bishop, the Canadian; Georges Marie Guynemer, the French ace who scorned maneuvering, always attacking with headlong fury; Manfred von Richthofen, the "Red Knight" of Germany; Albert Ball, the deadly Englishman; the Americans Raoul G. V. Lufbery and Edward V. Rickenbacker—and Edward Mannock, Oswald Boelcke, Max Immelmann, René Fonck, Frank Luke, Jr., and many others.

Less publicized and therefore seldom known to fame were the pilots and observers who performed the humdrum but vital tasks of adjusting artillery fire, photographing enemy positions, and scouting far behind enemy lines, their slow, lumbering planes often easy victims for enemy fighter pilots. The bomber crews, harried by enemy fighters and antiaircraft guns by day and risking weather and navigational errors (their instruments being few and crude) by night, also served largely unnoticed. Possibly the most risky of the airmen's missions was that of the crews of the observation balloons, hung defenseless between earth and sky as they watched for telltale enemy activity and directed artillery fire.

Through all this dangerous duty, above the bloody grapplings in the mud below, ran a thin gleam of the chivalry of older wars. An opponent whose guns had jammed in an aerial dogfight might be (if rarely) spared. Messages might be dropped over an enemy airdrome, telling of the fate of a pilot missing from it. The average aviator might occasionally be charged with indiscipline, but he normally was nevertheless a ready, self-reliant fighting man.

The Machines

Most of the World War I air operations were carried out by heavier-than-air machines. All armies made extensive use of lighter-than-air observation balloons, however, and most of them had experimented with various types of dirigibles. The Germans had done the most outstanding work in this last-named field and had developed a fleet of large, rigid-type dirigibles. Excellent weight lifters capable of cruising long distances (one of them made a successful 96-hour, 4,225-mile, nonstop flight between Bulgaria and northeastern Africa in November, 1917), these impressive aircraft initially scored considerable success. However, their size and relatively slow speed made them increasingly vulnerable to the Allies' constantly improving fighter airplanes and antiaircraft artillery, and they lacked the structural strength to withstand severe storms. These weaknesses resulted in their being gradually driven from the skies.

The typical military airplane at the beginning of World War I was unarmed, slow, fragile, and mechanically unreliable—hardly beyond the experimental stage and capable of carrying only enough fuel for a short flight. Exact figures are not available, but it is probable that all the original belligerents together could put fewer than 2,000 serviceable machines into action. In addition, most of the so-called aircraft factories operating in 1914 (Germany was credited with about 12, France with 8, and Britain with 6) were merely small shops, employing a few hundred skilled artisans. Airplanes were built largely by hand on a cut-and-try basis. There was nothing comparable to the tremendous shipbuilding and armament industrial complexes that provided weapons for the sea and land forces of the period. Aircraft engines were inefficient and heavy for the power they delivered, averaging six to eight pounds of weight per horsepower.

From this primitive stage the brutal necessities of war and the increasing appreciation of the potential importance of air operations soon led to dramatic improvements in airplane design and production. The nondescript general-purpose plane of 1914 began to evolve into several new types designed for specific functions. Swift fighter planes, generally single-seaters (though some of the most effective British fighters were two-seater models), were employed to hunt down other aircraft. These fighter aircraft—such as the French Nieuport and Spad, the British Camel, and the German Fokker—shared the fame of the aces who flew them and are probably the best-remembered aircraft of the war. The two-seater observation planes were slower but usually had a longer range; by 1918, German observation planes could operate at higher altitudes than could most Allied fighters. Frequently they carried special cameras for aerial photography of enemy positions or primitive radio equipment for the direction of artillery fire.

The resulting race for air supremacy over the Western Front produced series of improved planes on both sides. Speeds became greater, ceilings (the maximum height at which a plane could operate) were pushed upward, and the rate of climb increased. Air battles demonstrated that airplane quality and performance were even more important than total numbers. Air superiority shifted back and forth between the two sides as new types of aircraft were introduced and tactics developed to exploit their particular capabilities. In 1916, for example, the British ruled the skies over the Somme battlefield; nine months later, in the spring of 1917, Hoeppner had wrested it from them. On the whole, the planes of both sides were fairly evenly matched, neither being able to maintain any distinct superiority in plane and engine construction, though the Germans might be credited with slightly greater technological aptitude.

In 1915 the machine gun became the standard weapon for airplanes, though the problem of how to mount these weapons so as to obtain the most effective use of their firepower took considerable time to solve. Some fighter aircraft carried a light machine gun (such as the British Lewis gun) mounted in the center of their top wing in order to give fire forward above the propeller. A French flier obtained greater accuracy by mounting a machine gun just in front of his cockpit, so that it could fire directly through the rotating blades of his plane's propeller. This enabled him to aim his gun simply by pointing his plane at his opponent; light armor on the inner surface of the propeller gave that vital part rough-and-ready protection from such bullets as struck it. German technical skill made this concept obsolete by developing a system of mechanical linkages that synchronized the revolutions of the propeller and the rate of fire of the machine gun. This system was soon copied by the Allies and became standard equipment on fighter planes, though some still retained the machine gun on the top wing. Observation planes and two-seater fighters were variously armed; usually the pilot had one or two fixed guns mounted like those on the fighter aircraft, and his passenger had one or more movable guns. Since increasing attention was being given to all-round protection, one of these might be mounted so as to fire through the floor of the rear cockpit. A few special fighters carried heavy machine guns or even light cannon; airplane armor made its first tentative appearance.

By 1917 the aircraft industry began to develop the skills necessary to turn out larger aircraft designed primarily for bombing. Previously, some observation planes had been modified so as to carry light bombs slung under their wings. Smaller bombs had been carried in the cockpit and dropped hopefully over the side by hand; the French had tried but abandoned the idea of scattering showers of steel darts called fléchettes. Some of the new bombers, such as the British DH series, were still modified observation craft. Others were big, slow biplanes like the British Handley Page bomber, the Italian Caproni, and the German Gotha. The Handley Page, which came too late to take a serious part in the air war, was capable of carrying sixteen 112-pound bombs and fuel for an eight-hour flight. These bombers, in turn, were subdivided into day- and night-bombing planes; generally speaking, the former were lighter and faster, the latter slow but capable of carrying a much greater bomb load.

Naturally, this increase in airplane numbers, types, and capabilities could be brought about only through an unparalleled development of the aircraft industry. That of France and Britain grew steadily, and the French effort especially (though plagued by a multiplicity of plane and engine types) was so well directed that France was able both to supply her own needs and to furnish large numbers of excellent aircraft to her allies. Germany, thanks to an early start and a broad industrial base, could outproduce either France or Britain until early in 1918. Thereafter, diminishing raw materials and heavy demands for munitions for the German Army prevented her efficient aircraft industry from keeping pace with her losses in combat.

The United States aircraft industry was of necessity hastily built from the ground up after the American entry into the war. By agreement with its allies, the United States furnished their aircraft industries with needed raw materials (sprucewood, linen, chemicals, fuels, and lubricants); in exchange, Britain and France trained American fliers and mechanics, and France provided planes for the first United States air squadrons. Since fighter aircraft were evolving so rapidly that any selected type would be obsolescent before it could be put into production in the United States, it was further agreed that the United States would produce the DH-4 (a sturdy, British-designed plane used as an observation plane and as a light bomber) for all of the Allies, and would in addition develop and produce a new type of engine (dubbed the Liberty engine) in ample quantity to satisfy its own DH-4 production and French and British requirements. American production got under way too late to be of importance, but it could have been a considerable factor had the war continued into 1919.

By the war's end, approximately 8,000 Allied planes were arrayed against 3,300 enemy aircraft. Back of the men who flew these aircraft were the much larger forces of mechanics, armorers, and supply personnel in the service parks and repair depots behind the lines. The importance of their work can be understood when it is realized that an airplane of this period lasted only a few weeks in combat. Thereafter, even if not destroyed, it normally required extensive repairs. A significant figure is available to illustrate this fact: The British had 1,300 planes operating in support of their armies at the beginning of the Second Battle of the Somme. When the fighting ended a few weeks later, 1,100 of the original 1,300 planes had been destroyed or damaged and had to be replaced.

It should be noted that though the major emphasis in World War I was on air operations in support of the armies, the contending navies steadily developed their own air elements for overwater scouting, fire direction, and bombing attacks on submarines and surface ships. Originally, the aircraft used were seaplanes, which operated from established naval bases. Later, battleships and cruisers began to carry one or more light planes, and fast merchant vessels were converted into seaplane carriers which could accompany the fleets on extended operations. Since seaplanes lacked the speed and maneuverability of land-based planes, the British eventually developed the first modern aircraft carrier (commissioned into the Royal Navy in October, 1918), capable of both launching and recovering the latter type. Probably naval aviation's most valuable mission during the war was its antisubmarine work, a task for which dirigibles proved very satisfactory.

ORGANIZATION

In 1914 the airplane was still a new and unproved auxiliary to the armies and fleets. Its intended missions were observation, reconnaissance, and courier duty—functions generally viewed as extensions of the conventional military signal communications systems for lack of a more definite classification to assign them. Consequently, the Germans grouped their air service with railway troops and signal units as communications troops, and the French Army and Navy administered their respective aviation elements as subdivisions of their communications services. In the United States, military aviation was a responsibility of the Signal Corps from 1907 to 1918, when the Air Service was organized. (In June, 1917, General Pershing had already detached the aviation units serving in France from the Signal Corps, reorganizing them as the Air Service, American Expeditionary Force.) Britain had followed a far different course, combining all of its aviation units into a Royal Flying Corps, but on July 1, 1914, just before the outbreak of the war, this force was broken up. The Royal Navy set up its own air force under the title of the Royal Naval Air Service, while the Royal Flying Corps became merely the air arm of the British Army, where it had equal status with the cavalry, infantry, and other combat arms.

As the war progressed and the importance of military aviation became more firmly established and more generally recognized, its management gradually moved to higher levels. Britain again led the way. By 1918, largely as a result of German air raids (first by zeppelins and later by Gotha bombers) on London, popular dissatisfaction with Britain's air defenses had led to protests in Parliament. Cooperation between the Royal Flying Corps and the Royal Navy Air Service had been limited; moreover, the two groups were struggling bitterly over the limited supplies of planes, engines, and personnel available. On the advice of a board headed by Lieutenant General Jan Christiaan Smuts (who was strongly supported by his fellow member, Winston Churchill), a separate Air Ministry was set up in the British government in December, 1917. This placed its head, the air minister, in the War Cabinet as an equal partner (at least in theory) of the secretary of state for war and the first lord of the admiralty. Furthermore, in April, 1918, the Royal Flying Corps and the Royal Naval Air Service were recombined into the Royal Air Force, which was given equal status with the Royal Navy and the British Army.

Both France and Germany continued to retain their air services as organic parts of their armies and navies, but both established subcabinet posts (assistant secretaries or undersecretaries) to coordinate the administration of such matters as engine and aircraft construction, allocation of personnel, and formulation of military aviation budgets.

In the United States a series of tentative reorganizations in May, 1918, had at last converted the Signal Corps' Aviation Section into the independent Air Service, but had divided the necessary authority between a director of military aeronautics and a Bureau of Aircraft Production. Within three months, aircraft production was in such chaos that the post of second assistant secretary of war was created to provide an official with sufficient authority to untangle it. At the same time, this secretary functioned as director of the Air Service and so was able to deal with military aviation problems as a whole.

On the fighting fronts the organization of the various air forces was very similar. Each national commander had a senior air force officer as his adviser on all matters relating to military aviation. Thus in the American Expeditionary Force (organized according to French and British experience), General Pershing's Air Service was commanded by Major General Mason M. Patrick; General Patrick, in turn, had General Mitchell as his assistant for operations and Brigadier General Benjamin D. Foulois as an assistant for training and supply. At the next lower level of command, each army commander had an aviation officer as a member of his staff. These officers coordinated air operations for their respective commanders, prescribed tactics, negotiated for flying fields, and allocated supplies and replacements.

The basic air force tactical organization was the squadron, usually composed of aircraft of one type only, and so designated as a fighter, observation, bomber, or service squadron. Fighter squadrons were equipped with approximately 18 planes, observation and bombing squadrons with 12. A fighter squadron would have from 20 to 25 aviators, and observation and bombing squadrons as many as 50, including observers and bombardiers. In addition, each squadron had 100 to 150 ground crew personnel. The service squadrons were responsible for the logistical support of the combat squadrons.

It was usual for squadrons to be assigned to the direct support and operational control of armies, where (as noted above) their operations would be coordinated by the aviation staff officers concerned. As the war progressed, the need for larger and more flexible air commands developed, and squadrons would accordingly be formed into groups, and these groups on occasion were assembled into wings. As a climax, in 1918 the French organized most of the planes that could be spared from their hard-pressed armies into an aviation division of 432 fighters and 193 day bombers, thus establishing a strong, mobile force that could be readily shifted to any part of the Western Front to meet an emergency or exploit an opportunity.

Also in 1918, General Trenchard established his famous Independent Air Force (average strength, approximately 75 day bombers, 49 heavy night bombers, and 16 fighters) with the mission of bombing rail and industrial centers behind the German front. This was the first strategic air force to be established. Hindered in its avowed primary mission by bad weather and heavy losses, it still furnished a powerful air reserve. (It should be noted that this force did not utilize mass air attacks, such as became common in World War II.)

In October, 1918, Trenchard was organizing an Inter-Allied Independent Air Force, made up of contingents from all of the Allied air forces, to support the projected 1919 campaign by air strikes deep into Germany. As the commander of this force, Trenchard was to operate under the direct control of Marshal Ferdinand Foch, the Allied commander in chief. The armistice of November 11, 1918, scuttled his hope of leading it on raids against Berlin.

TACTICS

In the early months of World War I airplanes were commonly employed as scouts, with varying success. As they sought out the enemy's forces, they often passed enemy planes bound on similar missions. At first, pilots and observers might wave to opposing crews as they met, if not as a greeting, at least in recognition. It was soon realized, however, that these missions were important to the enemy's operations and should be opposed. Aviators began to arm themselves with odd collections of rifles, shotguns, and pistols and to make clumsy efforts to intercept and destroy enemy aircraft. Improvement of airplanes and weapons made these clashes increasingly deadly, and fighter aircraft tactics rapidly became the largest phase of air operations.

As fighter planes took an increasing toll of the slower observation planes, the latter were sent out under the escort of friendly fighters. In early 1916, however, the French discovered that their fighters could be more effectively employed on offensive patrols over the enemy's lines to search out, surprise, and shoot down the enemy fighters—and even, if possible, to attack German forward airdromes. By thus gaining local air superiority and keeping the enemy on the defensive, the French fighters enabled their observation planes to operate freely without escorts. During the Battle of the Somme that same year the British employed this technique aggressively and systematically and achieved outstanding success.

The actual tactics of these air battles were quite simple. Underpowered and fragile, the planes of the period had an inconvenient tendency to come apart if subjected to violent maneuvering. Successful pilots usually sought to gain altitude, diving from out of the sun on enemy aircraft passing below them and trusting to speed and surprise. Planes patrolled singly or in small groups, attacking any enemy aircraft encountered in their assigned area.

The size of the tactical units involved in these operations grew steadily, if slowly. In this, as in so many other aspects of air warfare, the methodical Germans seem to have set the pace, employing strong units of picked fighter pilots—such as Richthofen's famous, gaudily painted circus—at critical points. By 1918, formations of 50 fighters were not uncommon. A clash between two such groups could lead to a wild, scrambling dogfight—a mass of confused individual engagements in which each fighter sought to get "on the tail of" (behind) his opponent.

Initially, as previously mentioned, squadrons were assigned to armies and so were tied to their areas of operations. During the later stages commanders on both sides began to realize that the inherent mobility of aircraft permitted their concentration at the decisive point of the battle, and accordingly would assemble all available air strength to support the divisions spearheading the attack. As an example, the American Saint-Mihiel offensive was supported by both the British Independent Air Force and the French Aviation Division, as well as by American, Italian, and Portuguese aircraft. Once the operation had been successfully concluded, most of these planes were shifted to other sectors of the front to support other operations.

The observation planes naturally worked more closely with the ground forces than did the fighter planes. The development of effective aerial cameras enabled army commanders to keep constantly abreast of changes in the enemy's defenses and dispositions. Eventually, thousands of aerial photographs were distributed to infantry divisions to replace outdated maps. Likewise the development of radio equipment greatly improved air-ground communications and made it possible for air observers to direct artillery fire effectively. Since artillery fire was the backbone of both offensive and defensive operations during this period, the importance of this service can easily be appreciated. In this mission the airplane was effectively supplemented by the captive observation balloon. Though unable to attain the height to which observation planes could climb or to fly over enemy-held territory, the balloon had the advantages of a fixed position (which enabled its observer to orient himself more exactly) and direct telephonic communication with the artillery units it served. The natural vulnerability of its big bag of inflammable hydrogen gas was at least partially compensated for by emplacing it in a ring of antiaircraft weapons.

During 1917–18 a new aerial technique, commonly known as the attack mission, appeared. Besides gaining air superiority in the skies above the battlefield, fighter aircraft were made responsible for attacks with machine-gun fire and light bombs against enemy ground forces. Attack aviation was frequently employed against the enemy trench system in support of assaults by friendly infantry. It was very effective against troops and vehicles caught in railroad yards or on the march. If the enemy were retreating through rough country where frequent defiles made it difficult for his troops to deploy off the road, the results could be devastating. In 1918, Italian and British aircraft mauled the Austro-Hungarian forces retreating after their defeat at Vittorio Veneto. French fliers pounded the retreating Bulgarians in the Balkans, and Allenby's air force broke up large elements of the Turkish troops retreating before him in Palestine. Possibly, however, the greatest success of attack aviation occurred in March, 1918, when all possible Allied aviation was committed (as the only mobile reserve available) to check the victorious German columns following up the retreating British Fifth Army. Employed energetically, Allied airmen gained time for Allied ground forces to patch their broken front.

Though some military leaders had for years visualized the possible use of aircraft as bombers, World War I bombing operations were of relatively little importance. Neither satisfactory planes, bombs, navigational instruments, nor bombsights were available. The bombing planes employed were too slow and usually lacked sufficient range to reach vital enemy targets. Despite the courage of the bomber crews, neither day nor night raids met with outstanding success. The German raids against the London area did force the withdrawal of some of the best British fighter units from France for home defense, but the Germans found their losses dishearteningly heavy. Bombing operations proved most useful when directed at enemy communications close behind the front during major ground offensives.

There were occasional instances of the air supply of ground troops, both in dropping food and ammunition to cut-off units and in the use of zeppelins or heavy bombers to move supplies to hard-to-reach areas of Africa or Asia Minor.

In general, both sides learned that air superiority was hard to win and was seldom complete. In 1917 and 1918, by securing strong air support, Allenby was able to destroy the Turkish-German air units opposing him in Palestine and so to blind the Turkish ground forces. This enemy aviation was weak numerically and qualitatively, however, and was isolated beyond the hope of effective reinforcement. In contrast, on the Western Front the Germans remained able even in 1918 to secure local air superiority by hurriedly concentrating their remaining picked fighter units.

In the air, as on the ground, retention of the initiative proved decisive. Though ground commanders might protest, it was repeatedly proved that better results could be obtained by concentrating friendly aircraft for offensive action against enemy aircraft and air bases than by parceling them out for the defense of assigned sectors of the front.

Significance of Air Warfare

A new dimension had come to warfare; as Napoleon had predicted, "He who holds the high ground will win." The true lessons of World War I air warfare, however, were blurred by the fact that the aircraft employed, despite amazing improvement during the four years of combat, never achieved the desired level of technological development. Like the tank, they remained short-ranged, relatively slow, and mechanically unreliable weapons, seldom capable of independent action, and therefore only auxiliaries (if important ones) of the infantryman and the gunner. Only a few military leaders had the vision to see the future possibilities of either of these emerging weapons, although 21 years later, the air-armor team swept across Europe, and air superiority became the key to victory.

World War I trained the air force commanders of World War II: Hermann Göring, Sir Charles Portal, Arthur Travers Harris, Henry H. Arnold, Carl Spaatz, and many others. It taught hard lessons for those willing to learn: the need for a strong industrial base, ready for quick conversion from peacetime manufacturing to the production of air armaments; the importance of keeping planes and engine types to a minimum, both to speed up aircraft production and to simplify problems of maintenance and supply; and the value of vision and imaginative leadership. Above all it demonstrated that, in Trenchard's words, "the airplane is an offensive weapon."

15. Diplomatic History of the War: Negotiations During the War

BY ERNEST R. MAY

At the outbreak of war in 1914 the German and Austro-Hungarian empires were united by an alliance that dated back to 1879. Though each of the two governments declared war separately on the common enemies and neither invoked the formal alliance, both emperors declared that the two states would fight together to the end, neither making peace without the other.

Of the nations on the opposing side, only two, France and Russia, were formally allied. The British government had understandings with both, but was not committed to join them in war, and in fact the London cabinet debated for several days before deciding on its course. Then, on August 4, Britain declared war against Germany not because France and Russia had done so, but because Germany had invaded Belgium, and Belgian neutrality was guaranteed by an 1839 treaty of which Britain was one of the signatories. On September 5, 1914, however, the British, French, and Russian governments signed the Pact of London, pledging themselves to make no separate peace. The three powers which before the war had formed the Triple Entente thus became allies. In addition, each entered into comparable engagements with other states fighting the Central Powers: Serbia, which had been the first belligerent; Montenegro, which was Serbia's ally; Luxembourg, which the Germans invaded on August 2, 1914; and Belgium. Portugal affirmed her long-standing alliance with Britain, even though the Central Powers did not formally declare war on her until 1916.

JAPANESE INTERVENTION

Within a month after the declarations of war in Europe, Japan joined the Allies. Though the British government advised Tokyo that it did not interpret the Anglo-Japanese alliance of 1902 as requiring Japan to enter the European war, hostilities at sea were soon extended to the Pacific, and the British Dominion governments in Australia and New Zealand made it clear that they meant to seize Germany's possessions there. The Japanese government volunteered to enter the war. The British Foreign Office then suggested that the Japanese might confine their operations to the Pacific and not attack the German leasehold of Kiaochow in China, but Japan was not receptive to this proposal. On August 15, it dispatched an ultimatum to Berlin, demanding the withdrawal of German naval craft from Japanese and Chinese waters and the unconditional surrender of the leasehold, "with a view to eventual restoration of the same to China." The seven-day time limit expired without Germany's replying; on August 23, the Japanese government formally declared war; and in October it announced its adhesion to the Pact of London, thus becoming one of the great Allies and pledging itself to negotiate no separate peace.

Turkish Intervention

The adherence of Japan to the Allies was soon offset by Turkey's intervention on the side of the Central Powers. Though Britain had traditionally been a supporter of the Ottoman Empire, and British and French firms had large investments in Turkey, German influence had been rising steadily. The Young Turks who had seized power in 1908 regarded the existence of British and French spheres of influence in the Levant as inimical to their pan-Turkish aspirations; they also considered Russia their chief enemy in the east, the Black Sea, and the Balkans. Their leaders, War Minister Enver Pasha, Interior Minister Mehmet Talaat Pasha, and Navy Minister Ahmed Djemal Pasha, were admirers of Germany, and in 1913 the Turkish government had agreed to have its army reorganized by a German general, Otto Liman von Sanders. In July, 1914, Enver went to Berlin and there negotiated a secret treaty of alliance (signed August 2), by the terms of which Turkey was to become a belligerent, receiving in compensation portions of conquered Russian territory and, if Greece and Bulgaria entered the war on the opposing side, parts of their lands as well. Turkey was to remain neutral, however, until she had had an opportunity to ready her defenses.

After the outbreak of hostilities the Allies made some effort to induce Turkey to perpetuate her neutrality. The British government commandeered two warships that were being built in England for the Turkish government, but at the same time allowed two German warships, the *Goeben* and the *Breslau*, to slip through the Dardanelles and be transferred by Germany to the Turkish government. The British Prime Minister, Herbert Henry Asquith, remarked privately that international law would require the Turks to man the vessels with their own men, and "Turkish sailors cannot navigate . . . except on to rocks or mines." Meanwhile, British, French, and Russian diplomats suggested to the Ottoman government that agreements might be worked out under which Turkey would receive concessions in return for her neutrality.

But the Young Turks soon dispelled any doubts about their ultimate intentions. They retained German crewmen on the *Goeben* and *Breslau*, merely putting them into Turkish uniforms. When the Allied governments protested, the Porte ordered all British seamen dismissed from the Turkish Navy and appointed a German as commander in chief of the Turkish Fleet. At the instigation of Enver the Turkish press opened a violent campaign against the Allies and in favor of the Central Powers. On October 29, 1914, a Turkish fleet bombarded the Russian coastal cities of Odessa, Sevastopol, Feodosiya, and Novorossisk. The Allied governments demanded that the Turks make reparations and dismiss all Germans from their forces. After the Turks had refused to do so, the major Allies recognized a state of war (Russia on November 1, and Britain and France on November 5), and Turkey became a cobelligerent with Germany and Austria-Hungary.

ITALY'S ENTRY INTO THE WAR

The great prize among European neutrals was Italy. With Germany and Austria-Hungary, it had been a partner in the Triple Alliance, but for some time it had been drifting away from this tie. When the war opened and the German and Austrian governments asked Italy to join them, the Italian cabinet refused on the technical ground that Article 7 of the alliance treaty required consultation and agreement concerning any territorial change in the Balkan area, and that Vienna had not consulted Rome before making demands on Serbia. On August 3, the Italian government issued a proclamation of neutrality. From the outset, however, it was evident that Italy would probably at some point abandon this status and join one side or the other. Conservative and colonialist groups in the country favored the Central Powers, reasoning that an Allied victory would strengthen liberalism in Italy; give Britain total control of the Mediterranean Sea, thus checking future growth of the nation's African empire; and place Russia in such a commanding position in the southern Balkans as to halt Italian expansion there. Liberal, commercial, and nationalist groups leaned toward the Allies, fearing that conflict with Britain would strangle Italian trade and believing that Italy's wisest policy was to seek the annexation of Austro-Hungarian territories populated by Italians.

The Prime Minister, Antonio Salandra, was of the latter view. As early as September 30, 1914, he reported to King Victor Emmanuel III that Italy's only real choice was to remain neutral or to join the Allies, and that war against Germany and Austria-Hungary would be the most profitable course, but that hostilities should not be opened until spring, when the army would have had time to prepare for an offensive. Salandra did not, however, have the full support of the Italian people or even of a majority of the Chamber of Deputies. Three-fourths of the deputies were supporters of his predecessor, Giovanni Giolitti, who for obscure reasons had resigned his office in March, and Giolitti was not committed to the Allied cause. In public, therefore, Salandra confined himself to declaring on October 18 that the government would be "uninfluenced by any sentiment but that of an exclusive, unlimited devotion to our country, a sacred egoism [*sacro egoismo*] for Italy," and on December 3 that it would maintain "an alert and armed neutrality." For his part, Giolitti adopted a quasi-neutralist position, asserting in January, 1915, that "much [*parecchio*] may be obtained without going to war." These rival slogans, *"sacro egoismo"* and *"parecchio,"* ornamented Italian partisan debate throughout the winter of 1914–15.

Both the Allies and the Central Powers assumed that Italian favors were up for auction. The German General Staff, already alarmed by Austria's inability to make headway against the Russians on the Carpathian front, feared that Italian intervention would be followed by intervention on the part of Romania, Bulgaria, and Greece and that, at the very least, this would require a substantial diversion of German troops from the French and Russian theaters. German military and civilian authorities consequently bent every effort to persuade the Austrians to offer concessions to Italy. They encountered strong resistance in Vienna. When Austrian Foreign Minister Count Leopold von Berchtold agreed to contemplate such a policy, he was ousted by intransigents in the imperial government and replaced in January, 1915, by one of their own number, Count Stefan Burián von Rajecz. But even Burián was compelled eventually to yield ground. The German government dispatched former Chancellor Prince Bernhard von Bülow as a special ambassador to Rome, and he was presently authorized to offer the Italians territory from the Austrian borderlands as well as promises of economic concessions and future grants from the British and French empires. He also encouraged neutralist journalists and entered into secret conversations with Giolitti. Another special German envoy, Roman Catholic Center Party leader Matthias Erzberger, meanwhile appealed to Pope Benedict XV and to Italian Roman Catholics to help keep Italy out of the war.

The Allies were no less active. They subsidized journalists who advocated intervention on their side; one was the editor of the Socialist *Avanti*, Benito Mussolini. Their diplomats warned the Italian government that the Central Powers were not to be trusted and hinted that intervention on the Allied side would bring Italy large pieces of Austrian territory and a dominant position in the Adriatic Sea. The British and the French were compelled at first to be vague in their promises, for the Russian government backed Serbia's ambition for a great Yugoslavia and insisted that Serbia had first claim on the Allies. Planning for their attack on the Dardanelles early in 1915, however, the British became more and more convinced that Italian intervention was urgent; they threatened the Russians with possible curtailment of financial and other aid. Czar Nicholas II's ministers gave in. As a result, the three Allies were able to sign with Italy on April 26, 1915, the secret Treaty of London. By its terms, Italy was to enter the war on the Allied side and be rewarded subsequently with the Trentino; the Tirol to the Brenner Pass; Trieste; Görz (Gorizia); Gradisca; the Istrian Peninsula and adjoining islands; Dalmatia; such ports on the Adriatic coast as were not already assigned to Montenegro or Serbia; control over the foreign relations of Albania; recognized sovereignty over the Dodecanese, which Italy had occupied since 1912; the province of Antalya (Adalia) in Turkey, when and if Turkey were partitioned; and shares in the indemnity imposed on the Central Powers and in any African colonial spoils.

Salandra had decided in February to negotiate such a treaty. Nevertheless, he had continued through March and April to discuss possible terms with the Central Powers, constantly increasing his demands as the Germans and the Austrians appeared to yield. Then, on May 3, 1915, he showed his hand. He formally denounced the Triple Alliance and notified Berlin and Vienna that Italy was regaining her freedom of action. On May 13, having failed to obtain unanimous support from his cabinet for intervention, he resigned. Giolitti refused to take power, however, and chauvinists led by the poet Gabriele d'Annunzio clamored for war. On May 16, the King advised Salandra that he could not accept the resignation; Salandra resumed office; and on May 23, the Italian government formally declared war on Austria-Hungary. Subsequently, on November 30, it proclaimed its adhesion to the Pact of London. Italy had joined Britain, France, Russia, and Japan as one of the great Allies.

THE BALKANS

Bulgaria

On the very day of Italy's declaration of war, the Central Powers made a formal bid for Bulgaria's friendly neutrality. Though reduced in territory as a result of the Balkan Wars of 1912–13, that nation still commanded the principal communication lines between Austria-Hungary and Turkey; its intervention on the Allied side would require Austria to divert substantial resources from the Russian front and the Italian frontier and would make it much more difficult for Turkey to resist the British in the Dardanelles. Consequently, the Central Powers dangled before the Bulgarian government the promise of a heavy loan, the prompt cession of Serbian Macedonia, and the transfer to Bulgaria of the lands she had lost to Greece and Romania if those states should intervene on the Allied side.

The Bulgarian government already leaned toward the Central Powers. The Bulgarian King, Ferdinand I, was a German prince who had favored joining Germany and Austria-Hungary from the outset of the war. The Premier, Vasil Radoslavov, had merely insisted on waiting until a favorable opportunity presented itself. With the offer of the Central Powers in hand, Radoslavov became less cautious. On May 29, he received a counterproposal from the Allies, offering Bulgaria part of Serbian Macedonia, Thrace to the Enez–Midye line, and Kaválla, and promising in addition to "regulate" the long-standing Bulgarian-Romanian conflict over Dobruja. Attractive though these terms might have been, they were all contingent on the agreement of Serbia, Greece, and Romania and on the ability of the Allies to compensate those states elsewhere. Ferdinand and Radoslavov realized that the Central Powers, if victorious, would be in a better position to reward Bulgaria, and they continued negotiations with Berlin, Vienna, and Constantinople. In July, they secured from Turkey a concession forced in their behalf by the Germans and Austrians. Turkey ceded to Bulgaria, in a

treaty ratified on September 22, the land west of the Maritsa and
both banks of that river, except for the city of Edirne (Adriano-
ple). Meanwhile, on September 6, the Bulgarian government agreed
to a secret alliance with Germany and Austria-Hungary. By its
terms, Bulgaria was to join in operations against Serbia and was in
compensation to receive after the war all of Serbian Macedonia
and most of northeastern Serbia as far as the Morava River; if
Greece and Romania entered the war, Bulgaria was also to receive
the lands lost earlier to them.

As German and Austrian forces mobilized for a southward offensive, the Serbs yielded to urgent pressure from the British and the
French and offered Bulgaria immediate concessions in Macedonia,
but the Bulgarian government was not deterred from its course. In
October, 1915, when the forces of the Central Powers struck the
Serbian lines, Bulgarian troops joined them. Bulgaria declared war
on Serbia on October 14, and within a few days Serbia and the
other Allies declared war on her.

Romania

At the time of Italy's intervention in the war, Romania had almost thrown in her lot with the Allies. The pro-German King,
Carol I, a cousin of the German Emperor, had died in October,
1914, and had been replaced by his ineffectual nephew, Ferdinand I.
A number of leading Romanian statesmen, including most of
the Liberal Party leaders and Take Ionescu and Nicholas Filipescu
of the Conservative Party, advocated joining the Allies, but the
Premier, Ion Brătianu, insisted on opportunistic caution and succeeded in resisting demands that Romania act in concert with
Italy. Throughout the first two years of the war, Brătianu held his
ground. Ever more tempting blandishments were laid before him
by the representatives of the Central Powers and the Allies, but not
until the summer of 1916 did he weaken. By that time the Allies
were offering to double the territory of prewar Romania by ceding
to her Bucovina, Transylvania, the Banat of Temesvár, Maramureş,
and Crişana. Moreover, the Austrians had denuded the Hungarian
frontier in order to mount an offensive against Italy, and this constituted an open invitation, as an Austrian statesman later wrote,
for "a Romanian military promenade." Brătianu gave in and on
August 17, 1916, signed with the Allies the Treaty of Bucharest,
under which Romania was to receive all that they had previously
offered in return for a prompt attack on Austria-Hungary. Despite

a divided vote in his cabinet, Brătianu kept this pledge and, on August 27, declared war.

Greece

The Greek government also came close to joining the Allies in 1915, not because of the Italian intervention, but because of the Turkish concessions to Bulgaria. The most popular public figure in the country, Eleutherios Venizelos, had been in favor of Greece's entering the war in 1914, but the King, Constantine I, and the royalist party had insisted successfully on a policy of neutrality. With evidence that Bulgaria was about to enter the war, however, Venizelos renewed his appeals, arguing that Greece should fulfill her 1913 treaty with Serbia, by the terms of which she was to send 150,000 troops to Serbia's aid if that nation were attacked by Bulgaria. In August, 1915, the King reluctantly recalled Venizelos to the premiership and even more reluctantly accepted Venizelos' decision that, since Greece did not have the requisite 150,000 men, the Greek government should invite the Allies to send such a force through Greece to the aid of Serbia. The Premier issued the invitation, and in October an Allied force landed at Salonika. But when Venizelos stirred the National Assembly to a vote in favor of war with Bulgaria and Turkey, the King balked. He forced Venizelos to resign on October 5, and brought in first Alexandros Zaïmes and then Stephanos Skoulodes as premiers who would preserve Greek neutrality.

Both the Central Powers and the Allies exerted continual and mounting pressure on the Greek government. Bulgaria seized a fortress on the Greek frontier. The French commander at Salonika, General Maurice Sarrail, fomented antiroyalist agitation; and the French government eventually made a formal demand that the king hold new elections, presumably so that Venizelos' popularity could be proved. Then, after Romania joined the Allies, Venizelos proclaimed an open revolt, set up a provisional government at Salonika, and on November 25, 1916, issued a declaration of war against Germany and Bulgaria. Aided by French and British funds and naval support, he succeeded in establishing his sway over roughly half the country. In June, 1917, Constantine agreed to abdicate and allow his young son, Alexander, to become King and Venizelos to resume office as Premier. Venizelos immediately sent Greek troops into battle alongside the Allies, and the governments of the Central Powers soon formally recognized a state of war with Greece.

PLANS FOR PARTITION OF THE OTTOMAN EMPIRE

Constantinople Agreement

During all this time the major Allies had been negotiating among themselves about the postwar distribution of the Ottoman dominions. The so-called "Eastern question" had occupied much of the attention of European diplomats for most of a century and a half, and contrivance had been piled on contrivance to keep the sultanate more or less intact. However, with Turkey's entry into the war on the German and Austrian side, statesmen in the Allied capitals concluded that the demolition of that empire was inevitable. The Russian government had traditionally sought free egress for Russian shipping from the Black Sea, and early in 1915 the Czarist foreign minister, Sergei Sazonov, asked the British and the French to agree in principle that after the war Russia should have control over the Turkish Straits. Though British governments in the past had held to the conviction that Russia should be barred from the eastern Mediterranean, the London cabinet quickly agreed that this position would not be tenable after the war. Foreign Secretary Sir Edward Grey issued cautious statements to prepare public opinion for a reversal of the policy; then on March 12, 1915, he signed a secret convention with the Russian ambassador in London, according Russia the right to control Constantinople and the Turkish Straits after the war, provided that "the aspirations of Great Britain and France in the Ottoman Empire as well as in other regions are realized." On April 12, the French foreign minister, Théophile Delcassé, signed a similar convention with the Russian ambassador in Paris. As we have seen, the secret Treaty of London, concluded in the same month, provided that Italy should have Antalya if the Ottoman dominions were divided among the Allies.

Egypt

For the British and French, the chief problem was to draw up arrangements for the areas south of Turkey proper that were nominally under Ottoman control—the Levant, Mesopotamia, and the Arabian Peninsula. After Turkey's entry into the war, the Allies had been alarmed over the possibility of the Sultan's arousing the Moslem world in a crusade against Christians. In part to prepare for such a contingency, in part to counter an expected Turkish offensive against the Suez Canal, the British government decided in November, 1914, to end the fiction that their high commissioner in Cairo was merely an adviser to the Egyptian government, to proclaim a protectorate over Egypt, and to proceed to formal annexation of that land. Getting wind of this plan, the French protested that they should be entitled to do likewise in Morocco but that Moslem unrest in that area made it impossible to do so, and that both allies should thus refrain from any immediate steps toward enlarging their empires. The British did go on to proclaim a protectorate over Egypt on December 18, 1914, and to depose the pro-Turkish Khedive, Abbas II Hilmi, but desisted from annexation.

Nejd Treaty and McMahon Letters

Meanwhile, in the Ottoman dominions themselves, British agents entered into separate and uncoordinated negotiations with Moslem leaders, endeavoring to detach them from the leadership of Sultan Mohammed V. The government of India sent first Captain W. H. I. Shakespear, the consul at Kuwait, and then Sir Percy Cox, the resident in the Persian Gulf, to negotiate a treaty with Sheikh ibn-Saud. Signed on December 26, 1915, this treaty recognized ibn-Saud as independent ruler of the Nejd and its dependencies, promised him defense, and granted him a subsidy in return for his friendly neutrality. The government of Egypt at the same time entered into correspondence with Husein, the Sherif of Mecca. In a series of letters exchanged in 1915 and 1916, Sir Arthur Henry McMahon, the high commissioner in Cairo, promised Husein "the independence of the Arabs" from the 37th parallel south, except for the coastal region "lying to the west of the districts of Damascus, Homs, Hama and Aleppo." In return, the Sherif agreed to be advised exclusively by representatives of the British government and to give Britain administrative privileges in the vicinity of Baghdad and Basra. Vague though their language was, these letters obviously contradicted the assurance given to Husein's rival, ibn-Saud, and when Husein on June 5, 1916, proclaimed an Arab revolt against the Turks and on October 29, 1916, declared himself King of the Arabs, the British cabinet had to announce with some embarrassment that it could only recognize him as King of the Hejaz.

Sykes-Picot Agreement

By that time, furthermore, the whole situation had been complicated even further by an Anglo-French agreement that was consistent neither with the Nejd treaty nor with the McMahon-Husein letters. After signing the straits agreements with Russia in March and April, 1915, the two western European allies had commenced negotiations to define their "aspirations . . . in the Ottoman Empire." Sir Mark Sykes acted for Britain; Georges Picot, for France. By the spring of 1916 the two negotiators had arrived at an understanding, the Russian government had given its approval, and a formal Sykes-Picot agreement was signed on May 16. It provided that Russia should receive, in addition to the straits, the Armenian provinces of Turkey—Erzurum, Trebizond (Trabzon), Van, and Bitlis—and northern Kurdistan along the line Muş–Siirt–'Amadiya to the Persian border. France was to have Cilicia—that is, the area west of the Armenian provinces and south of the line Ala Dağ–Kayseri–Ak Dağ–Yildiz Dağ–Egin (now Kemaliya)–Kharput—and the Syrian coast inland to Damascus, Homs, Hama, and Aleppo and south to the area of Haifa. Britain was to have Haifa and Acre on the coast and all of southern Mesopotamia, including Baghdad, while the area between the British and French holdings was to be divided into a zone of French influence covering the Syrian hinterland to Mosul and a British zone from there southward. Alexandretta (now İskenderun) was to become a free port, and Palestine was to be internationalized. Though the agreement made provision for one or more independent Arab states in the zones of influence, the terms did not accord with the pledges made either to Husein or to ibn-Saud. Partly for this reason, the British and the French endeavored to keep its provisions secret.

Saint-Jean-de-Maurienne Agreement

Italy nevertheless acquired a general knowledge of the Sykes-Picot understanding, and early in 1917 she asked for a supplementary accord with the other Allies in order to make more precise the vague clause about Turkish territory in the Treaty of London of 1915. On April 17, 1917, the Premiers of Britain, France, and Italy signed an agreement providing that Italy should have the right to annex most of the Vilayet of Konya, the sanjaks of Mentese (now Muğla), Antalya and İçel, and the vilayet and city of Smyrna (now İzmir), and to have a sphere of influence north of Smyrna. But this agreement stipulated that the concurrence of Russia was required. Because of the revolution in Russia, that concurrence was never obtained, and the agreement remained inoperative. Aside from an informal understanding, reached by the British and French premiers in December, 1918, that Britain should have Mosul in return for giving France a share in northern Mesopotamian oil, this Saint-Jean-de-Maurienne agreement was the last inter-Allied compact to touch on the future of the Ottoman Empire.

THE NEUTRAL NATIONS OF EUROPE

At the outset of the war, international law affecting belligerent-neutral relations was vague. The London Naval Conference of 1908–9 had produced the Declaration of London, codifying rules for the protection of neutral commerce, but by 1914 it had not been ratified by any of the major belligerent states. The United States formally asked that all the warring nations abide by the declaration, and the British, French, Russians, Germans, and Austrians agreed to do so but reserved the right to modify its terms as conditions changed. The declaration included lists of items that were to be treated as contraband, absolute contraband, and noncontraband. When it accepted the declaration, the British government added a few new items to the contraband list, and nearly every month brought forth a new order in council extending the list still further. In February, 1915, after the German government had confiscated stocks of food in Germany, food was in practice treated as absolute contraband; on August 21, 1915, cotton was taken from the noncontraband category and added to the contraband list; and on July 7, 1916, the government announced that it was abandoning the declaration altogether. In nearly every instance the French and the Italians followed suit.

Meanwhile, the Allies were jointly exerting other pressures on neutrals that might trade with their enemies. They urged neutral governments to establish embargoes on commodities that might be militarily useful to the Central Powers; they rationed shipments to nations bordering Germany and Austria-Hungary so that those nations were able to import no more than they had before the war; they published blacklists of neutral firms that traded with the Central Powers, forbidding their own subjects to have dealings with such firms; and they denied to neutral shippers the right to buy coal in Allied ports except on the condition of signing bunkering agreements, or pledges not to trade with or carry goods for the enemy. In addition, beginning in March, 1915, they established an undeclared blockade. Though for technical reasons avoiding use of the term "blockade," the British government on March 1 announced that it would endeavor to seize all "ships carrying goods of presumed enemy destination, ownership, or origin," and the French and Italian governments soon did likewise. The Allies thus made every effort to stop all flow of goods into and out of the territory of the Central Powers.

Owing to their geographical situation and their relatively limited naval capabilities, the Central Powers could not retaliate in kind. They pressed Continental neutrals to curtail trade with the Allies, but they were able to strike at the seaborne commerce of Britain, France, Italy, and Russia only by employing novel devices and methods. In November, 1914, the Allies had sown mines in the North Sea in order to prevent the German High Seas Fleet from sallying forth, and they had given notice that neutral vessels would enter this "mine war zone" at their peril. In the meantime, the Germans had discovered that submarines could elude the Allied naval patrols and operate even off the mouth of the Thames River. Exploiting the precedent set by the mine war-zone decrees, therefore, the German government announced on February 4, 1915, that, effective February 18, it would consider all the waters around Great Britain and Ireland as constituting a "war zone," that in this zone its submarines would endeavor to sink all Allied shipping, and that submarine commanders could not guarantee the safety of neutral vessels. Subsequently, the German government gave assurances that it would do its best to prevent injury to neutral interests, and in practice submarines generally refrained from attacks even on Allied vessels if they seemed likely to be carrying neutral passengers. Not until January 31, 1917, did the German authorities proclaim unrestricted submarine warfare. Thereafter, however, submarines sank Allied and neutral ships indiscriminately.

Netherlands

At the outbreak of the war the Dutch mobilized to defend their frontiers but also issued proclamations of neutrality. Though public opinion veered sharply toward the Allies as a result of the German invasion of Belgium and the alleged atrocities committed by German forces there, the government held to its course. After a time it became clear that the nation probably did not have to fear attack by the Germans, for Amsterdam was proving useful to them as a port of entry for goods from overseas. By the spring of 1916, the Dutch were more anxious over rumors that the Allies might invade their country in order to attack the rear of the German armies in France. To fend off threats from either side, the government kept the armed forces in a continual state of partial mobilization.

Meanwhile, both the Allied economic war and the German submarine campaign weighed heavily on the Dutch economy. To satisfy the demands of the Allies, the government formed on November 23, 1914, the Netherlands Overseas Trust Company, an organization of Dutch importers who were allowed by the Allies to receive goods on their guarantee not to re-export them to Germany or use them to replace Dutch goods so exported. Even this trust found itself severely rationed, however, and throughout the war the nation's vital export-import trade was much curtailed. The government protested to London and Paris about rationing, blacklists, and bunkering agreements. It also protested against British interference with the mails, the mine war-zone decrees, and specific violations of Dutch territorial neutrality by Allied warships and aircraft. At the same time, it protested against similar violations of Dutch neutrality by the Germans and against the submarine campaign. The government complained in particular of the sinking of the *Katwyk* in April, 1915, of the *Tubantia* and the *Palembang* in March, 1916, and of four grain ships in February, 1917. In some cases, Germany apologized and offered reparations, while in others it disclaimed responsibility or justified the sinkings. Finally the Netherlands government, with Germany's assent, took over German shipping in the Netherlands East Indies to replace some of the lost tonnage. In March, 1918, when the government acquiesced under protest to the seizure of all Dutch ships in American and Allied ports and accepted compensation for them, Germany declared this action unneutral and brought on a crisis by demanding the right to ship supplies through the Netherlands to Belgium. The Dutch achieved a compromise agreement with the Germans and thus managed to maintain their neutrality to the end of the war.

Switzerland

Though the neutrality of Switzerland was guaranteed by international agreement, the Swiss government took care after the outbreak of the war to keep its armed forces at maximum strength. The German-speaking majority of the population was pro-German, while the French-speaking and Italian-speaking population was generally pro-Ally, but the government was determined to maintain neutrality at any cost. It established a press censorship intended to hold down partisanship, and when there occurred public demonstrations, such as an anti-German riot that took place at Lausanne early in 1916, it apologized immediately to the potentially offended nation. Though both sets of belligerents carried on espionage and similar activities from headquarters within the country, the government attempted to suppress them only when they involved Swiss citizens and thus jeopardized the nation's neutrality.

The official policy did not, of course, spare Switzerland the penalties imposed by the belligerents' economic warfare. Like the

Dutch, the Swiss protested the undeclared Allied blockade and the German submarine campaign. Dependent on imports of coal from central Europe and imports of food from overseas, however, they had to make concessions to both sides. On October 11, 1915, they created the Swiss Economic Surveillance Society, a foreign trade corporation similar to the Netherlands Overseas Trust Company, whose members promised the Allies that imported goods would not be passed on in any form to the Central Powers. In September, 1916, the government negotiated an agreement with Germany by which cattle, cheese, and aluminum were to be exchanged for coal, iron, and steel; and in May, 1918, it arranged with the Allies to receive food in exchange for timber. London, Paris, and Rome protested the Swiss-German compacts, while Berlin and Vienna protested any agreements between the Swiss and the Allies. As a result, imports into Switzerland became increasingly meager, and by the time the war ended the population was on very short rations. But the majority of the people remained firm to the end in adherence to their traditional neutrality.

Denmark

In Denmark, public opinion was anti-German. Nevertheless, the government proclaimed its neutrality and simply mobilized part of the army and strengthened frontier defenses. It formed two merchant guilds, which the Allies allowed to receive imports on a guarantee against re-export to Germany. In 1915, it agreed to dispose of meat in the prewar ratio, with half going to Great Britain, 14 per cent to Germany, and the rest for home use; to divide butter evenly; and to give Britain five-eighths and Germany three-eighths of its fish.

Norway

Norway was pro-British from the outset, and though the Allied blockade sometimes aroused resentment, public anger rose most often against Germany on account of the losses of shipping and life caused by submarines. Some of the earlier losses were apologized and paid for. By 1916, Norwegian merchants were signing contracts against re-exporting articles allowed to pass by the Allies, and in October of that year the government forbade all submarines to enter Norwegian waters. By the summer of 1918, nevertheless, 769 ships had been sunk, with a loss of 1,008 lives, and 53 were missing with 704 on board. These statistics were partly offset by the fact that, in 1917, Britain cut off Norway's supply of coal because of her export of pyrites to Germany, and only furnished it again on condition that Norwegian ships make trips to France as well as to Norway. In August, 1916, the British government contracted for 85 per cent of the Norwegian fish catch. (This contract was taken over by the Norwegian government in 1918.)

With less than 4 per cent of its area under cultivation, Norway imported a large part of its necessary cereals. Government control of food and, ultimately, strict rationing were found necessary. In addition, whale oil was refined and used to make oleomargarine. A treaty with the United States of May 3, 1918, allowed Norway to import foodstuffs, coal, and farm machinery for home consumption only. In return, timber, wood pulp, fish, metals for munitions, and nitrates were to be shipped to France. While the bulk of Norwegian exports during the war went to the Allies, some were permitted to go to Germany.

Sweden

Of all the Scandinavian countries, Sweden had shown the strongest German ties. Most members of the court, of army and business circles, of the universities, and of the Conservative Party were sympathetic to the Central Powers. For years, fear of a Russian advance across Sweden and Norway to warm water, and apprehension of Russian aggression in the Baltic, had made Sweden look to Germany for protection. This attitude was carefully stimulated by Germany. A small but aggressive group known as Activists advocated intervention on the side of the seemingly victorious Central Powers, with the hope of securing the Åland Islands and Finland from Russia. The Socialists and Liberals were strongly for peace. The government, however, decided for neutrality, mobilized part of the army, and made common cause with Norway and Denmark in defending neutral rights. In January, 1915, export of munitions was prohibited, and, in November, belligerent submarines were forbidden to enter Swedish waters except in cases of emergency. Apologies were secured for several violations of neutrality, as in 1915, when Russian ships destroyed a German warship inside the three-mile limit, and in 1916, when a German cruiser fired on a Swedish submarine. In July, 1916, Sweden closed the exit from the Baltic through Swedish waters, but reopened it after a strong British protest. Perhaps by way of compensation, 10,000 horses were sold to Germany.

Swedish-Russian relations improved somewhat in the course of the war. Trade was brisk, and railroad connections, long delayed for strategic reasons, were made. Thousands of German and Russian invalided prisoners were exchanged through Sweden, and much relief work was done. A crisis was caused in 1916 when Russia fortified the Åland Islands, but it passed when Russia and Britain guaranteed that the fortifications would be removed after the war. The collapse of Russia removed the fear of that power. Sweden was particularly interested in Finland, where an important minority is Swedish. Beyond assisting refugees to escape, however, it did not intervene. To preserve order, the Åland Islands were occupied on February 19, 1918, but the Swedish forces were displaced by the Germans on March 2.

Sweden objected to British interference with imports and the mails, and by stopping British mail for Russia in January, 1916, she became involved in a serious controversy. An arrangement was finally made that reserved Sweden's right to claim damages. Until 1916 the Swedish government refused to permit merchants to make the usual contracts with the Allies concerning re-exports, and it finally agreed to do so only on condition that it supervise the working of the plan in Sweden. Both Britain and Germany wanted Swedish iron ore. By treaty, Sweden was bound to furnish a certain amount of ore to Germany, and the government refused to halt this export, but Britain acquired an increasing share of the Swedish output. Sweden continued to export timber for mine props to Britain despite the fact that Germany declared this material contraband and seized it whenever possible.

Spain

Spain was more fortunate than the northern neutrals in being farther removed from actual fighting. Nevertheless, there was some danger of her being drawn into the war, particularly through the German submarine campaign. Spain had interests and sympathies with both sides of the conflict. In 1916 she gave assurances to France concerning the Pyrénées boundary and Morocco, and she withdrew some garrisons from the boundary of Portugal, then fighting as Britain's ally. On the other hand, trade with Germany increased, and a number of newspapers were suspected of receiving German money. The mass of the people seemed strongly in favor of neutrality. Liberals, Republicans, and Socialists, through their sympathies with radical and anticlerical France, were pro-Ally.

Partly through dislike of French anticlericalism, church leaders, clericals, and Conservatives, together with most army officers, were pro-German. King Alfonso XIII appeared personally to favor the Allies, but he maintained a correctly neutral attitude, and his successive cabinets endeavored to curb violent outbreaks of sympathy for either side.

It was repeatedly charged that German submarines were obtaining supplies at unfrequented places along the coast, and though several damaged submarines were interned in Spain, some escaped, apparently with the connivance of local officials. Nevertheless, the German submarine campaign, especially after February, 1917, inflicted heavy damage on Spain. By August, 1918, one-fifth of the Spanish tonnage had been sunk, much of it outside the area covered by German decrees and some of it even in Spanish home waters, with considerable loss of life. The Spanish Cabinet finally announced that future losses would be made good temporarily by using equivalent German tonnage interned in Spanish ports. Germany would not at first agree to this plan. In October, however, preliminary steps were taken to put it into effect, but hostilities ended before much had been done.

THE UNITED STATES

Neutrality

From the outset of the war the United States faced formidable problems. As the world's greatest producer of foodstuffs, raw textiles, iron, steel, and petroleum, it carried on a large trade in peacetime with both the Entente and the Central Powers, and its economic interests were certain to be affected by prolonged hostilities. Moreover, it had a large immigrant population with ties to the warring nations; there was an upsurge of pro-Ally feeling in the country from the moment that Germany invaded Belgium and Britain declared war; there was also an early surge of sympathy for the Central Powers among the large numbers of citizens of German and Austro-Hungarian descent and among Irish Americans, who were traditionally anti-British. On the other hand, President Woodrow Wilson and Secretary of State William Jennings Bryan were eager not only that the United States remain neutral but that it set an example for other neutral states. In addition to proclaiming formal neutrality, therefore, the President called on the public to be "impartial in thought as well as in action."

Friction with the Allies

Despite these efforts the government soon found itself drawn into controversies with the belligerents. The State Department asked all the warring states to abide by the unratified Declaration of London. The Central Powers agreed, but the Allies introduced modifications and additions, and the President and Secretary of State became concerned lest the Allies not only interfere with American commerce but also precipitate disputes over neutral rights, such as those which had led to Anglo-American war in 1812. The United States government made a determined effort to persuade the British to accept the Declaration of London *in toto.* When this effort failed, it fell back on a policy of simply protesting specific infringements of neutral rights as defined in traditional international law. Because of the amount of American trade with Europe, the result was a long series of protest notes, some of which attacked in vigorous terms British practices of visit and search, rationing, and additions to the contraband list.

Submarine Issue

Controversy with Great Britain might have grown more acute had the Germans not issued their submarine war-zone decree in 1915. Wilson and his advisers found the German announcement shocking, for it seemed wholly to disregard the legal right of neutrals to trade with belligerents, and it threatened not only the property but also the lives of neutrals. Furthermore, as a practical matter, it put in jeopardy America's growing ocean commerce and the nation's recovery from the recession of 1914–15. On February 10, 1915, therefore, the secretary of state directed to Berlin a very strong note protesting the decree and warning "that the Government of the United States would be constrained to hold the Imperial German Government to a strict accountability . . . and to take any steps it might be necessary to take to safeguard American lives and property and to secure to American citizens the full enjoyment of their acknowledged rights on the high seas."

Although Germany modified its original threat and offered vague assurances for the safety of neutrals, Wilson remained wary. When the Allies proclaimed their *de facto* blockade in March, 1915, Secretary Bryan wished to protest, but Wilson insisted on waiting until the issues raised by Germany were settled. When an American citizen was killed in the torpedoing of the British vessel *Falaba* (March 28), and when an American tanker, the *Gulflight,* was attacked (May 1), the President considered renewing his protest but decided to be patient.

Lusitania *Incident*

On May 7, 1915, however, the giant British liner *Lusitania* was torpedoed in the Irish Sea; 1,198 passengers went down with the ship, and, of these, 128 were Americans. The American press denounced the action of the German submarine commander as an atrocity, and several leaders of American opinion saw the incident as a justification for war. Even Secretary Bryan, who was almost a pacifist, agreed that some new representations were necessary, and on May 13 a note was dispatched to Berlin calling on the German government to disavow the submarine commander, make reparation for the lives lost, and pledge that in future submarines would not be used against any passenger liners or merchantmen. When the German response proved unsatisfactory, the President ordered that a second note be sent. Bryan could not bring himself to approve it, even though it merely restated the demands in the first note. He resigned on June 8, the day before the note was dispatched, and was replaced by Robert Lansing. When the new German response, dispatched on July 8, proved unsatisfactory, a third *Lusitania* note went to Berlin on July 21. By that time, however, the President was satisfied that the Germans had in fact ceased submarine operations against passenger-carrying vessels and neutral merchantmen, and he elected to let the exchange of notes drag on inconclusively rather than be excessively punctilious and insist on formal compliance with his demands.

Increasing Friction with the Central Powers

On August 19, 1915, the British liner *Arabic* was sunk with American passengers on board. Though Lansing and others advised taking a strong stand and perhaps severing relations, Wilson chose to delay action in the hope that the German government would voluntarily apologize. Johann Heinrich von Bernstorff, the German ambassador in Washington, did in fact offer an apology, revealing at the same time that German submarine commanders had had orders ever since the *Lusitania* incident to avoid attacks on vessels that might be carrying passengers. Some correspondence ensued before October 5, 1915, when the German government disavowed the act, offered an indemnity, and promised that submarine commanders would, at least for the time being, have orders to follow the traditional rules of international law. Though the submarine issue was less pressing as a result, German-American relations did not become much easier, for the year 1915 and the winter of 1915–16 brought to light much evidence of espionage and sabotage committed by or financed by German and Austrian agents. This evidence caused the President to ask the recall of the German military and naval attachés, Captain Franz von Papen and Captain Carl von Boy-Ed; the Austrian ambassador and consul general in New York, Constantin Dumba and Franz von Nuber; and a German financial agent, Dr. Heinrich Albert, as well as to indict and bring to trial alleged German and Austrian agents.

Wilson's Early Peace Moves

Despite the *Arabic* settlement, therefore, President Wilson grew increasingly uneasy about the prospects for avoiding conflict with the Central Powers. Though having been in the past an opponent of military preparedness, he changed his mind and in the winter of 1915–16 became an advocate of limited measures to strengthen the army and navy. At the same time, he gave serious thought to promoting a negotiated peace in Europe and thus ending the danger to America's peace. At the very beginning of the war he had tendered his good offices to the belligerents, and he had subsequently explored the possibilities of mediation. By the end of 1915, however, he had come to consider the restoration of peace as not only morally desirable but important for the interests of his country. Consequently, he approved an extraordinary proposal made to him by his closest friend and unofficial adviser, Colonel Edward M. House, and sent House to Europe early in 1916 to seek a secret agreement with the Allies. House was to reach a general accord with the Allies about terms for peace. Then, when the Allied governments gave the signal, the President would issue an open appeal for peace negotiations. The Allies would accept this appeal. If the Central Powers refused to negotiate or entered into negotiations and refused to accept the terms previously agreed upon by the United States and the Allies, the United States government would join the Allies in the war. House actually arranged a pact along these lines; he and Foreign Secretary Grey initialed a memorandum of agreement on February 22, 1916. Wilson approved it, adding only the word "probably" before "leave the Conference as a belligerent on the side of the Allies, if Germany was unreasonable." But the Allies, perhaps because they interpreted this amendment as meaning that the United States would not carry out its part of the bargain, failed to invite Wilson to issue his appeal, and the agreement came to nothing.

Gore-McLemore Resolutions and the Sussex Crisis

Meanwhile, the President had to weather a domestic crisis. In the correspondence over the submarine issue, the German government had made the point that its undersea craft were at a disadvantage in adhering to the traditional rules of visit and search, for the Allies had fitted a number of merchantmen with large-caliber guns and had given merchant captains instructions to shoot on sight any German or Austrian submarine. Recognizing the force of this contention, Wilson and Lansing asked the Allies if they would not agree to a *modus vivendi:* They would agree to strip the armament from merchant vessels, and the Germans in return would promise that no ship would be sunk without inspection of cargo and provision for the safety of passengers and crew. When the Allies flatly refused, the Americans felt they had no choice but to revert to the position they had taken earlier and to insist that, despite the armament on some Allied vessels, German submarines should be bound by traditional law. News of the proposed *modus vivendi* had, however, leaked into the press, and a number of members of Congress took the view that its rejection entitled the United States to retreat from its position as a defender of neutral rights. Senator Thomas P. Gore of Oklahoma and Representative Jeff McLemore of Texas, among others, introduced in the Senate and the House resolutions that would have forbidden American citizens to take passage on belligerent vessels. The President opposed these resolutions. On February 24, 1916, in an open letter to William J. Stone, chairman of the Senate Foreign Relations Committee, he declared:

> For my own part, I cannot consent to any abridgment of the rights of American citizens in any respect. The honor or self-respect of the nation is involved. . . . To forbid our people to exercise their rights for fear we might be called upon to vindicate them would be a deep humiliation indeed. . . . It would be a deliberate abdication of our hitherto proud position as spokesmen even amidst the turmoil of war for the law and the right. . . . What we are contending for in this matter is of the very essence of the things that have made America a sovereign nation. She cannot yield them without conceding her own impotency as a nation, and making virtual surrender of her independent position among the nations of the world.

With this eloquent appeal and by means of various maneuvers, Wilson rallied a bipartisan coalition that decisively defeated the Gore-McLemore resolutions, but the episode had demonstrated that a substantial minority of public opinion was out of sympathy with the Administration's policy on the submarine issue.

Scarcely had this demonstration been made than a new international crisis broke out. On March 24, 1916, the British Channel steamer *Sussex* was torpedoed, reportedly with casualties among Americans on board. Though Secretary Lansing and Colonel House urged the President to act immediately and forcefully, he chose to wait. Then, on April 18, he addressed to Berlin a note declaring, "Unless the Imperial Government should now immediately declare and effect an abandonment of its present methods of submarine warfare against passenger and freight-carrying vessels, the Government of the United States can have no choice but to sever diplomatic relations with the German Empire altogether." On May 4 the German government replied that it was ordering submarine commanders for the time being to suspend all operations against merchant shipping. The United States had thus succeeded once again in achieving a diplomatic victory.

Renewed Friction with the Allies

While negotiating with the Germans about submarine warfare, Wilson endeavored to avoid controversy with the Allies. He had rejected Bryan's pleas for a protest against the *de facto* blockade of March, 1915, and despite outcries from injured growers and exporters he also declined to protest the British order in council of August, 1915, adding cotton to the contraband list. Instead, he allowed House to negotiate an agreement under which the British government purchased cotton to stabilize its price. Only on October 21, 1915, after the settlement of the *Arabic* case, did the Department of State file in London a note complaining that the undeclared blockade constituted a departure from traditional international law, and partly because of the continuing uneasiness in German-American relations, this note was relatively mild. After the *Sussex* settlement, however, the President displayed more concern about Allied infringements of neutral rights. Irritated by the failure of the British and the French to act upon the House-Grey memorandum of February, he had begun to doubt his original conviction that their attitudes and aims were morally superior to those of the Germans. At his direction, consequently, the Department of State dispatched to London a series of increasingly sharp notes protesting the blacklist, bunkering agreements, and other measures of economic warfare. On September 7, 1916, the President obtained from Congress legislation permitting him to ban imports and deny clearance to ships, and he let the British government know that he might make use of these powers to retaliate against the Allies if they did not modify their course.

Wilson's Final Peace Efforts

By the closing months of 1916, the position of the United States government was difficult. The Allies showed no sign of making concessions to the American demands, and there was danger that friction with them would become increasingly acute. There was even greater danger of a new crisis with Germany, for reports from Berlin told of mounting demands in military and naval circles and in the Reichstag for unrestricted submarine warfare. But the Presidential election campaign of 1916, in which Wilson had succeeded in achieving re-election, had shown beyond doubt that much of the public wanted the nation to remain uninvolved in the European conflict. Many observers believed, indeed, that Wilson had won because his supporters used the slogan "He Kept Us Out of War." There was thus a real possibility that the President might be forced to retreat from the positions he had taken in defense of international law and neutral rights and to yield the very things that in his letter to Chairman Stone he had said America could not yield "without conceding her own impotency as a nation, and making virtual surrender of her independent position among the nations of the world."

In these circumstances, Wilson turned again to the hope that negotiations might restore peace in Europe before a crisis occurred in United States relations with either the Allies or the Central Powers. With the help of his advisers, he drafted a note to the belligerent governments, asking them to inform him confidentially of the terms of peace that they would accept so that he might investigate possibilities for a settlement of the war. Before the President had decided to dispatch this note, Chancellor von Bethmann-Hollweg called publicly on December 12, 1916, for peace negotiations, perhaps believing that the restoration of peace was the only means of avoiding a decision for unrestricted submarine warfare, perhaps hoping thereby to make such a decision less unacceptable in American eyes, or perhaps simply concerned that Austro-Hungarian morale was crumbling and that the new Austrian Emperor,

Charles I, might seek a separate peace. Though the Allies declined this German invitation, Wilson nevertheless elected on December 18 to send his peace note to all the warring governments. As it turned out, the Central Powers replied brusquely on December 26 that any discussion of terms should be among the belligerents and that they would reserve any statement until such discussions began; the Allies responded on January 10, 1917, with a statement of relatively mild terms. Hoping to induce the Germans and Austrians to change their minds, the President on January 22, 1917, delivered an address to the Senate calling on both sides to accept "a peace without victory."

End of American Neutrality

The German government gave an unencouraging answer to Wilson's appeal. On January 31, moreover, it suddenly announced that, beginning the next day, submarines would attack any and all vessels in the earlier-defined war zone. The decision in favor of this decree had been made by the German government in a crown council held at Schloss Pless on January 7, 1917; the military and naval authorities had united in demanding it; and the Reichstag, in a resolution of October 11, 1916, had declared that it would abide by the decision of Field Marshal Paul von Hindenburg and General Erich F. W. Ludendorff, and these two officers advocated it. The Chancellor and his civilian supporters had been unable to hold out, even though they felt certain that the decision was tantamount to a declaration of war against the United States. Wilson, in view of his earlier pronouncements, had no choice except to sever diplomatic relations, and he did so on February 3, 1917.

In succeeding weeks the President waited in hope that the German government would back down, as it had in the past, but he was disappointed. The British liner *Laconia*, with Americans on board, was torpedoed on February 25, and several American vessels also were sunk. In addition, the British government communicated a copy of an intercepted message of January 19 from the German foreign minister, Arthur Zimmermann, to the German minister in Mexico, proposing a German-Mexican-Japanese alliance against the United States. The sinkings and the Zimmermann telegram, which was made public on March 1, aroused violent feelings among the American public, and the pacifist element, led by former Secretary of State Bryan, appeared a shrinking minority. In late February, when the President asked Congress for authority to arm

American merchantmen, action was blocked by a small minority, whom Wilson assailed as "a little group of willful men, representing no opinion but their own," but large majorities in both Houses indicated that they would have approved if given the chance to vote. Within six to eight weeks after the publication of the German decree, the President had reluctantly concluded that the United States could not remain neutral and that it had no choice except to intervene in the war. Consequently, he went before Congress on April 2, 1917, and asked for a declaration of war, saying that the nation would fight "for the ultimate peace of the world and for the liberation of its peoples, the German peoples included: for the rights of nations great and small and the privilege of men everywhere to choose their way of life and of obedience. The world must be made safe for democracy." The Senate approved the declaration of war on April 4 by a vote of 82 to 6; the House, on April 6 by a vote of 373 to 50.

LATIN AMERICA

The vicissitudes of the American republics as neutrals resembled those of the United States. All Latin American governments issued proclamations of neutrality soon after the outbreak of the war, and all put in force much the same stringent rules as those adopted in Washington. Each state had to contend, however, with the violent partisanship of pro-Ally and pro-German elements in public opinion. Owing partly to economic and cultural ties with Britain and France, the pro-Ally factions were in most places predominant; only in Argentina and Chile did large numbers of intellectuals and army officers sympathize with Germany.

Each state encountered difficulty in maintaining its neutrality. Colombia, for example, became engaged in lengthy correspondence with the British government because of the operation of a German radio transmitter at Cartagena, and the issue was resolved only by the closing of the station in December, 1914. Chile felt itself obliged to protest to the German government because of violations of its neutrality by German commerce raiders operating in the southern Pacific, for a German squadron on two occasions in 1914 overstayed the lawful time limit and drew excessive quantities of coal and supplies from harbors in Chilean-owned islands. This dispute was not settled until the Berlin authorities finally apologized in July, 1916. Each state also found its relations with the belligerents irritated because of interference with neutral trade. Most Latin

American governments protested or complained of the Allied blacklists, bunkering agreements, and import restrictions. Though none joined the United States in protesting the German submarine decrees of 1915 and 1916, all those with merchant shipping warned the German government that they would not disregard injuries to their vessels or citizens.

The breach between the United States and the Central Powers required nearly all the Latin American republics to re-examine their policies. President Wilson suggested that all of them should imitate his action. In Cuba and Panama, where American influence was strong, the governments acquiesced promptly; both declared war on April 7, 1917. Bolivia endorsed the American position on the submarine issue and then, on April 13, 1917, severed relations with Germany on the ground that Bolivian citizens had been endangered by the sinking of the Dutch ship *Tubantia* in March, 1916. Guatemala took the same action on April 27, 1917, because of Germany's failure to reply to its note of protest against submarine warfare. Honduras on May 17, 1917, and Nicaragua on May 19, 1917, severed relations with Germany, and both followed eventually with declarations of war—the former on July 19, 1918, and the latter on May 8, 1918. Costa Rica, though its government was not recognized by that of the United States, offered the hospitality of its waters to the United States Navy; on September 21, 1917, broke relations with Germany; and on May 23, 1918, declared war. Uruguay at first declared itself neutral in the American-German war, but in June, 1917, it issued a decree invoking "the principle of American solidarity" and declaring that no American nation "which in defense of its own rights should find itself in a state of war with nations of other continents will be treated as a belligerent." The Uruguayan government then opened its ports to American warships. On October 7, 1917, it proceeded to break off relations with Germany, but despite submarine incidents involving Uruguayan citizens, it did not go on to a declaration of war.

Peru severed relations with Germany on October 6, 1917, and Ecuador followed suit on December 7, 1917, but both stopped short of declaring war. The Dominican Republic, occupied by the United States, had no legal existence at the time. Haiti, though also occupied, retained nominal sovereignty, and its National Assembly refused in May, 1917, to issue a declaration of war. Subsequently, however, the assembly was dissolved and replaced by a Council of State, and this body complied with the wishes of the occupying power by declaring war unanimously on July 12, 1918. Paraguay proclaimed its sympathy for the United States but did nothing more. The Venezuelan government, after first refusing to state even moral approval of the American stand, shifted ground and on May 3, 1917, issued a proclamation like the Paraguayan. The Mexican government, involved in an uneasy relationship with the United States, proposed in February, 1917, that the American republics take common action to bring the war to an end. When this appeal was rejected, it simply lapsed into a strict neutrality, which it maintained throughout the war. El Salvador and Chile likewise remained neutral. Of the American republics, eight joined the Allies—Cuba, Panama, Guatemala, Nicaragua, Honduras, Haiti, Costa Rica, and Brazil; four broke off relations with Germany— Bolivia, Uruguay, Ecuador, and Peru; and seven maintained their neutrality—Paraguay, Venezuela, Mexico, El Salvador, Colombia, Chile, and Argentina.

Brazil

Brazil, the greatest of the Latin American states, had the closest relations with the Allies. In addition to ties with Britain and France, it possessed historic links with Portugal, and it had a large Italian population, principally in São Paulo. Partly in consequence, its people reacted immediately to the outbreak of war; Brazil became the only neutral state to protest the German invasion of Belgium. Despite increasing irritation in relations with the Allies, due mainly to British interference with the coffee trade and with Brazil's substantial merchant marine, public sympathy for the Allied cause showed no marked diminution. In February, 1917, when the Brazilian government filed a protest against the 1916 sinking of the Rio Branco, there was public rejoicing. When the Paraná went down on April 4, 1917, with three Brazilian crewmen among the dead, mobs attacked German properties. After the Tijuca was sunk on May 20, the government responded by seizing interned German merchantmen, and on October 26, 1917, after the Macau also had gone down, the Senate voted unanimously, and the Chamber of Deputies by 149 to 1, in favor of a declaration of war. Because of its own grievances and quite independently of the United States, Brazil thus became one of the Allied and Associated Powers.

Argentina

The Argentine Republic, then second among the Latin American states, also followed an independent policy. Though its people appeared largely pro-Ally, it had a considerably larger pro-German faction than its Portuguese-speaking neighbor. At the outset of the war, its government endeavored to establish a neutrality even stricter than that of the United States. It forbade its ports to armed merchant vessels on August 17, 1914, and subsequently interned several vessels that disregarded this rule. On December 8, 1914, it forbade any Argentine vessel to send radio messages without prior official clearance. In addition, it made representations to the British and German governments about interference with trade and submarine warfare. On April 10, 1917, President Hipólito Irigoyen issued a cautious statement of sympathy with the United States, and on April 21 his Foreign Ministry filed a strong protest in Berlin about the torpedoing of the *Monte Protegido*. The German government promised an indemnity for this vessel, however, and subsequently offered compensation for two other Argentine ships that were sunk.

Nevertheless, public opinion became increasingly anti-German, and in 1917 there were widespread demands for the severance of relations or even for a declaration of war. The pretext was the publication by the United States in September of intercepted correspondence from the German minister in Buenos Aires, Karl von Luxburg, in which the Argentine foreign minister was described as "a notorious ass and Anglophile," and the German government was counseled either to spare Argentine vessels or to make sure that they were sunk without trace [*spurlos versenkt*]. Both houses of the Argentine Congress voted in favor of breaking relations, but President Irigoyen refused to ratify their action and succeeded on September 23 in winning from the German government an apology and a disavowal of the minister's words. He then kept Argentina neutral until the end of the war.

CHINA

At the outbreak of war, China was still in turmoil following the revolution of 1911 and the overthrow of the Manchu dynasty in 1912. The President of the Chinese Republic, General Yüan Shih-k'ai, envisioned a restoration of the monarchy with himself as the founder of a new dynasty, and in 1915 he approached the Allied governments with the suggestion that they grant recognition to such a monarchy in return for China's joining them in the war. The British, French, and Russian governments were not unreceptive, but the Japanese government vetoed the project. Then, with the death of Yüan in June, 1916, such national unity as had existed in China practically disappeared. The government and National Assembly in Peking ceased to exercise control much beyond the boundaries of the capital city, and actual rule lay with various war lords commanding separate districts and living in uneasy alliance with one another.

The officials in Peking hoped to restore central authority and saw intervention in the war as a means of doing so. When the United States severed relations with Germany in February, 1917, they approached the American minister with a proposal that China follow suit in return for a $10 million loan from the United States. The minister readily agreed, only to have his action disavowed by the Department of State, which had no wish to seem to be purchasing Chinese support. The Peking authorities then turned to the Allied governments, suggesting that China might join them if suitably compensated. The European cabinets were still interested, and by this time the Japanese government had not only reconciled itself to China's entering the war but had decided that Japan might reap positive benefits therefrom. The Foreign Office in Tokyo asked Britain, France, and Russia for assurances of support for postwar Japanese demands in Shantung and the North Pacific and, after receiving them, notified both the Allies and the Chinese of its willingness to have China as an ally.

On February 24, 1917, a French ship, the *Athos*, had been torpedoed in the Mediterranean, with 543 Chinese coolies among the dead, and the Peking authorities on March 14 gave this incident as their reason for breaking off relations with Germany. Great dissension then arose over the issue of proceeding to a declaration of war. The National Assembly, on May 11, refused to vote such a declaration. Within a month the entire central government had been dissolved. Troops of the northern war lords entered Peking and installed a new cabinet, and on August 14, 1917, this body declared war by proclamation. China thus became, at least in name, one of the Allies.

16. Diplomatic History of the War: Termination of the War

BY ERNEST R. MAY

FIRST SIGNS OF PEACE

From the onset of hostilities neutral governments, peace advocates in the neutral states, and pacifists in the belligerent nations had kept their eyes open for any opportunities to end the war. The United States Department of State had quietly explored such possibilities during Bryan's tenure as Secretary, and Colonel House had traveled to Europe in 1915 and 1916 as President Wilson's unofficial emissary, investigating the attitudes of the warring governments with regard to peace terms and peace negotiations. Similar unofficial missions had been sent out in 1915 by the kings of Denmark and Sweden. In December of that year, a wholly nongovernmental effort was undertaken by a group headed by the American motor car manufacturer Henry Ford. Responding to appeals from such peace advocates as Jane Addams and Rosika Schwimmer, Ford chartered a ship, the *Oscar II*, sailed for Europe with a large number of pacifists, and announced that the group would sponsor a peace conference for the belligerents; the ship's radio broadcast the message "Out of the trenches by Christmas." But as none of the Scandinavian states would serve as host for the proposed conference, Ford gave up and went home, and the sessions finally held at The Hague in January, 1916, proved inconsequential. The same fate attended international conferences of Socialists, including a much publicized one scheduled to be held at Stockholm in the summer of 1917.

Sixte Affair

By the end of 1916, more than one of the belligerent governments had begun to consider the possibility of suing for peace. The German Chancellor's public appeal of December 12 had been prompted not only by considerations rising from the submarine controversy with the United States but also by pressure from Austria-Hungary. The new head of the Dual Monarchy, Emperor

Charles I, was concerned about the possibility of internal collapse, and, in addition to urging the Germans to propose general negotiations, he suggested to his mother-in-law, Archduchess Maria Antonia of Bourbon Parma, that an approach to the French government be made through the Bourbon princes serving in the Belgian Army. Arrangements were made, and in February, 1917, Prince Sixte (Sixtus) of Bourbon met with a personal envoy of the Emperor at Neuchâtel, Switzerland, to receive a statement of Austrian conditions for peace. In effect, the Emperor proposed a restoration of the *status quo ante bellum.*

When Sixte reported verbally to the French government on the Austrian proposal, President Raymond Poincaré and Premier Aristide Briand proved receptive. In March, they sent Sixte back to Switzerland to meet again with the Austrian representative and suggest an armistice providing for immediate cessation of hostilities on the Austro-Hungarian fronts. The French asked only that Austria agree in principle that Alsace-Lorraine be returned to France by Germany, that Belgium be restored to independence and indemnified, that the kingdom of Serbia be restored and given an outlet to the Adriatic through Albania, and that Russia have Constantinople. Sixte not only presented these terms to the Austrian envoy but proceeded to Vienna and laid them before the Foreign Minister and the Emperor. The Austrian government agreed to take them under advisement and actually went on in later March and early April to discuss their substance with the German Chancellor and William II, though without disclosing the fact that negotiations with France were in progress.

While the Austrians studied the Poincaré-Briand proposals, Briand ceased to be Premier of France. His successor, Alexandre Ribot, was personally hostile to the Bourbon princes and had more confidence than Briand in the ultimate triumph of the Allies. Ribot insisted on discussing the Sixte negotiations with the British Prime Minister, David Lloyd George, and in conversations that took place at Folkestone on April 11, 1917, he pointed out a fact that Briand had elected to disregard. The territorial pledges given by the Allies to Italy and Romania in the secret treaties of London and Bucharest were inconsistent with the terms that had been outlined for the Austrians. Lloyd George agreed that the gist of the Franco-Austrian negotiations had to be disclosed at least to the Italians. This was done during the meeting of the British, French, and Italian premiers at Saint-Jean-de-Maurienne in April, 1917, and the Italian proved obdurate in insisting on literal fulfillment of the Treaty of London. Thus, though Sixte visited Vienna again in May, the project was for all practical purposes abandoned. Later talks in Switzerland between other Allied and Austrian representatives were similarly inconclusive.

Reichstag Peace Resolution

The German government was meanwhile put under pressure not only by its weakening ally but also by a growing body of domestic opinion favoring some negotiated settlement of the war. At the outset of hostilities the Social Democratic Party had only voted to support the government after considerable debate, and the majority of its leaders maintained the position that the nation should stop fighting whenever its enemies conceded that they could not triumph. They combated Pan-Germans and others, generally of the right-wing parties, who insisted that the country should annex Belgium, Poland, or other such territories; they were supported in this moderate stand by members of the Progressive Party and of the left wing of the Catholic Center Party; and these three groups together constituted a majority in the Reichstag. When Chancellor von Bethmann-Hollweg issued his peace appeal in December, 1916, this majority enthusiastically supported him.

When this act was followed by the rejection of Wilson's peace note, the declaration of unrestricted submarine warfare, and war with the United States, the majority's leaders became concerned that their government was not pursuing peace with sufficient energy. Consequently, despite objections from the Chancellor and the high command of the army, they brought before the Reichstag a resolution declaring: "Germay has taken up arms in defense of her freedom, her independence, and the integrity of her soil. The Reichstag strives for a peace of understanding and a lasting reconciliation among peoples. Violations of territory and political, economic, and financial persecutions are incompatible with such a peace." It was passed on July 19, 1917, by a vote of 212 to 126. But the new Chancellor, Georg Michaelis, accepted it in a speech that interpreted away much of its meaning, and shortly afterward one of the Center Party leaders justified the resolution to a party caucus by citing a secret memorandum on the faltering morale of Austria-Hungary. Thus, like the peace appeal of December, 1916, the Reichstag resolution came to seem a tactical expedient employed by a nation still bent on achieving victory.

Papal Peace Effort

The Center Party's leaders had been prompted to support the peace resolution in part because they had had intimations that the Vatican was about to urge peace negotiations. Pope Benedict XV, installed shortly after the outbreak of war, had previously refrained from any action that might be interpreted as interference with the belligerents, or that might occasion criticism among anticlerical parties in France, Italy, and Austria or the Protestant and Orthodox majorities in Germany and Russia. By mid-1917, however, he had decided that the time had come for an effort to bring the warring governments together, and in June he sent Monsignor Eugenio Pacelli (later Pope Pius XII) to Germany to sound out opinion there. Pacelli reported that the Chancellor held very moderate views, while the Kaiser and the generals commanding the armies were noncommittal but not intransigent. Other envoys evidently sent in comparable reports with regard to the other belligerent governments; the Reichstag passed its peace resolution; and on August 1, 1917, the Pope addressed a public appeal to all the belligerents to accept a peace of compromise, making mutual concessions with regard to territorial issues, otherwise restoring the *status quo ante bellum*, and establishing an international organization for arbitration.

Journalists and officials in the Allied countries generally viewed this papal note as having been inspired by Germany and, like the Reichstag resolution, as constituting either a trick or a sign of approaching collapse. None of the Allied governments except the American made a formal reply. President Wilson's answer of August 27 stressed the moral objections to negotiations with governments that had, in his view, initiated an aggressive war and pursued throughout a policy of aggrandizement and conquest. The British government did, however, return an informal and confidential reply suggesting that the Allies might be willing to enter into further discussions if they were assured that Germany would restore and indemnify Belgium and agree to terms that would make renewal of the war impossible.

The Vatican communicated this word to Berlin and waited hopefully for the response of the German government, but the leaders of the German Army and Navy, supported by the representatives of right-wing groups, remained insistent that the war leave Germany in complete or partial control of Belgium. After a conference on September 11, 1917, among a number of the Kaiser's highest officials, it was agreed that the reply to the Pope should be moderate in tone but make no promise with regard to Belgium. When this reply was received at the Vatican, Benedict asked the German government to reconsider the possibility of offering a guarantee on Belgium, but the authorities in Berlin responded by making their previous answer public. This ended for the time being all chance of further negotiations.

Collapse of the Eastern Front

Though Russia had been the first of the Allied powers to go to war, and the Russian government had agreed in the Pact of London to engage in no separate negotiations with the Central Powers, the possibility of Russia's making a separate peace had existed from the very beginning. A number of members of the Russian aristocracy remained pro-German, and at various times individuals from the Russian court circle had talked unofficially with representatives of the Central Powers about possible negotiations. Count Sergei Witte, who had often in the past been a spokesman for the nation's rising commercial and industrial groups, spoke in favor of Russian withdrawal from the war. So did leaders of the growing radical, socialist, and revolutionary parties.

The government that came into power after the Revolution of March, 1917, was committed to continuing the war. It backed away from the policy of the Czarist government only by proclaiming on April 9, 1917, that its aim was "not the forcible seizure of foreign territories, but the establishment of a stable peace on the basis of the self-determination of peoples." When the Bolsheviks seized power in November, 1917, however, they went further; on November 8, the Congress of Soviets passed a resolution calling on all the warring powers for "an immediate peace without annexations . . . and without indemnities"; on November 21, the new Commissar of Foreign Affairs, Leon Trotsky, formally asked the Allies to agree to negotiations on such a basis. The Allied governments refused even to receive the communication. Conferring later that month in Paris, the Allied leaders agreed that they would not release Russia from its commitment under the Pact of London; they declared simply that the Allies "would proceed to a revision of war aims together with Russia, so soon as there shall be a government aware of its duties to the country and defending the interests of the country and not of the enemy."

Peace of Brest-Litovsk

The Bolsheviks nevertheless sent representatives under flag of truce to propose to the German and Austrian military authorities an armistice and the prompt opening of negotiations for a general peace. Conversations opened on December 3, 1917, in the fortress of the Polish town of Brest-Litovsk (now Brest). Though the Russian delegates endeavored at first to discuss only terms for a general armistice, they eventually agreed to talk of an armistice for the Eastern Front alone. On December 15, agreement was reached on a 28-day cessation of hostilities (from December 17), during which time terms for a final settlement were to be negotiated. On December 22, delegations representing the Bolshevik government and the Central Powers gathered at the same place. The German government had meanwhile concluded that it would insist at least on Russian abandonment of the Baltic provinces. (Hindenburg had declared at a crown council at Kreuznach on December 19, "I need them for the maneuvering of my left wing in the next war.") The Bolsheviks, however, called for the application of the principle of self-determination; and on December 28, the conference was adjourned temporarily so that the Russians could receive fresh instructions and make one last appeal to the western Allies to join the negotiations.

After the conferees reassembled in January, 1918, the Ukrainian Rada proclaimed the independence of the Ukraine. A separate Ukrainian delegation appeared at Brest-Litovsk, and the Russians reluctantly agreed, in accordance with their own principles, that it could negotiate for the Ukraine. Consequently, on February 9, the Central Powers signed with the Ukrainian delegates a treaty reestablishing peace and providing that the Ukraine should immediately supply Austria-Hungary and Germany with grain. The Austrians, desperately in need of food, agreed to cede to the new state the district of Chełm, to guarantee certain civil rights to the Ruthenian population in the rest of Galicia, and to create a separate crown land for the Ukrainians of eastern Galicia and Bucovina.

Negotiations between the Central Powers and the Bolsheviks had continued in the meantime. The leaders of the German delegation insisted in effect that all territory under the control of the German Army be renounced by Russia. Trotsky, now leading the Russian delegation, tried to oppose this demand. He also opposed the Ukrainian treaty. Pointing out that Bolshevism was spreading in the Ukraine, he withdrew recognition from the Ukrainian government. The Germans refused either to accept his position or to retreat from their own. In consequence, on February 10, Trotsky resorted to the expedient of declaring that the Russian government, instead of signing an unjust treaty, would simply proclaim peace and demobilize its forces. Though at first taken aback by this extraordinary procedure, the German government on February 18 responded by terminating the armistice and dispatching troops toward Petrograd.

Disappointed in their hope that the Germans would be compelled to accept their action, the Bolshevik authorities appealed for a new armistice. The Germans demanded that they agree to withdraw all forces from the Baltic area and the Ukraine, halt all propaganda activity in central Europe, and immediately open commercial relations with the Central Powers. On February 24 the Russians agreed. Delegations met again at Brest-Litovsk, and on March 3, 1918, a treaty of peace was signed. Under its terms the Russians surrendered all claim to Courland (Kurland) and western Poland and to Kars, Ardahan, and Batum (now Batumi) on the Turkish frontier, and agreed to evacuate Finland, the Åland Islands, Estonia, and Livonia. The treaty was ratified by the Congress of Soviets on March 18 by a vote of 724 to 276 (with 204 abstentions). By a supplementary treaty signed at Berlin on August 27, the Russian government also renounced its claims to Estonia and Livonia. Though neither treaty provided for the actual annexation by Germany of the territories renounced by Russia, both were interpreted by Allied and neutral observers as providing proof of Germany's imperialistic war aims.

Allied Interventions in Russia

During the negotiations at Brest-Litovsk the Allied governments had continued to hope that Russia might somehow return to the war as an active cobelligerent. Many of the Allied representatives in Russia believed that an alliance with the Bolsheviks might be arranged. After the breakdown in negotiations and the resumption of hostilities by the Germans, the French, British, and United States governments offered sympathy and support to the Russians, but these offers were withdrawn when the armistice was renewed and the treaty signed. In the meantime the three governments had been debating what action might be taken to prevent stores of supplies in Russia from falling into German hands. In February, 1918, it was decided for this purpose to land a small combined force at Murmansk, and with the consent of the local Bolshevik organization this was done in March. After the Soviet Congress' ratification of the Treaty of Brest-Litovsk, the Allies proceeded to enlarge this force and to extend the area of its control. The Russian government protested on June 28, but on July 7 the Murman Regional Council proclaimed the area independent and invited the force to remain. The Allies willingly agreed. The British and the French were already contemplating support for counterrevolutionary movements that might overthrow the Bolsheviks, repudiate the treaty, and put Russia back in the war. On August 2, 1918, another combined force occupied Arkhangelsk, and when counterrevolutionaries proclaimed an independent republican government of the north, the Allied commanders at Murmansk and Arkhangelsk gave it quiet support.

Another proposal, which had been debated since early in 1918, called for a Japanese expedition to Siberia. The Japanese government indicated its willingness to take such action if requested by its allies, and military opinion in London and Paris was generally favorable, the British and French general staffs reasoning that an attack on Siberia would not only prevent the supplies stored in that region from being transferred to the enemy, but would also compel the Germans to retain a certain proportion of their forces on the Eastern Front. Before sanction could be given for a Japanese landing in Siberia, however, the consent of the United States had to be obtained, and President Wilson and his civil and military advisers were all opposed to the plan. In April, 1918, when the British and the Japanese put a small force ashore at Vladivostok in order to take possession of military supplies there, the United States government protested. The month of May, however, saw armed hostilities break out between the Bolsheviks and a Czechoslovak legion that had been fighting with the Russians and, by agreement with the French, was being moved across Siberia to Vladivostok in order to be transported to the Western Front. On June 28 the legion, in company with certain Russian counterrevolutionaries, seized control of Vladivostok, and on July 17 President Wilson gave up opposition to a Siberian expedition, consented to Japanese landings, and agreed to send in American troops. A counterrevolutionary government was formed in Siberia under Admiral Alexander Kolchak, but the American commander, Major General William S. Graves, refused to give it any support or encouragement.

THE ARMISTICES
Allied Declarations on Peace Terms

When the Bolsheviks came to power in Russia, they published the texts of the secret treaties that the Allies had concluded earlier in the war. Allied leaders felt it necessary to counteract any unfavorable impression and also to make public declarations that might reassure the Bolsheviks and encourage them to continue in the war. The first to speak out was the British Prime Minister. Addressing the Trades Union Congress at Caxton Hall on January 5, 1918, Lloyd George declared that the Allies were not fighting a war of aggression against the German people, that the first aim of Britain was "the complete restoration, political, territorial, and economic, of the independence of Belgium and such reparation as can be made for the devastation of its towns and provinces"; the second was "the restoration of Serbia, Montenegro and the occupied parts of France, Italy and Rumania"; the third, the restoration of Alsace and Lorraine to France; and the fourth, an independent Poland. He concluded:

> If, then, we are asked what we are fighting for, we reply, as we have often replied—we are fighting for a just and lasting peace—and we believe that, before permanent peace can be hoped for, three conditions must be fulfilled. First, the sanctity of treaties must be re-established; secondly, a territorial settlement must be securely based on the right of self-determination or the consent of the governed; and, lastly, we must seek by the creation of some international organization to limit the burden of armaments and diminish the probability of war.

Partly so that Lloyd George might not seem the spokesman for all the Allied and Associated Powers, partly because the United States was not a party to any of the secret engagements among the European Allies, and partly because he believed that his nation had a broader and more unselfish view of the needs of the future, President Wilson hastened to issue a statement of his own views. Addressing Congress on January 8, 1918, he outlined "the only possible program" for peace in 14 points:

(1) Open covenants of peace, openly arrived at. . . .
(2) Absolute freedom of navigation upon the seas, . . . alike in peace and war. . . .
(3) The removal, so far as possible, of all economic barriers and

the establishment of an equality of trade conditions among all . . . nations. . . .

(4) Adequate guarantees given and taken that national armaments will be reduced to the lowest point consistent with domestic safety.

(5) A free, open-minded, and absolutely impartial adjustment of all colonial claims, based upon a strict observance of the principle that in determining all such questions of sovereignty the interests of the populations concerned must have equal weight with the equitable claims of the government whose title is to be determined.

(6) The evacuation of all Russian territory and such a settlement of all questions affecting Russia as will secure the best and freest cooperation of the other nations of the world in obtaining for her an unhampered and unembarrassed opportunity for the independent determination of her own political development and national policy and assure her of a sincere welcome into the society of free nations under institutions of her own choosing. . . .

(7) Belgium . . . must be evacuated and restored, without any attempt to limit the sovereignty which she enjoys in common with all other free nations. . . .

(8) All French territory should be freed and the invaded portions restored, and the wrong done to France by Prussia in 1871 in the matter of Alsace-Lorraine . . . should be righted. . . .

(9) A readjustment of the frontiers of Italy should be effected along clearly recognizable lines of nationality.

(10) The peoples of Austria-Hungary, whose place among the nations we wish to see safeguarded and assured, should be accorded the freest opportunity of autonomous development.

(11) Romania, Serbia, and Montenegro should be evacuated; occupied territories restored; Serbia accorded free and secure access to the sea; and the relations of the several Balkan states to one another determined by friendly counsel along historically established lines of allegiance and nationality; and international guarantees of the political and economic independence and territorial integrity of the several Balkan states should be entered into.

(12) The Turkish portions of the present Ottoman Empire should be assured a secure sovereignty, but the other nationalities which are now under Turkish rule should be assured an undoubted security of life and an absolutely unmolested opportunity of autonomous development, and the Dardanelles should be permanently opened as a free passage to the ships and commerce of all nations under international guarantees.

(13) An independent Polish state should be erected which should include the territories inhabited by indisputably Polish populations, which should be assured a free and secure access to the sea, and

whose political and economic independence and territorial integrity should be guaranteed by international covenant.

(14) A general association of nations must be formed under specific covenants for the purpose of affording mutual guarantees of political independence and territorial integrity to great and small states alike.

Bulgarian Armistice

In June, 1918, Radoslavov resigned as Premier of Bulgaria and was replaced by Alexander Malinov, whose enthusiasm for war had always been lukewarm. Through its official press the Bulgarian government began at once to express an interest in negotiations for a separate peace. Meanwhile, morale in the Bulgarian Army was disintegrating, and resistance to continued fighting was evident in Sofia and in the countryside. Fearing revolution, King Ferdinand left for Austria, where he pleaded with his allies to give him reinforcements and to reaffirm their earlier promises with regard to the future enlargement of Bulgaria's frontiers. His appeals went unheeded, and, after long and anguished debate, a crown council in Sofia decided to send an armistice commission to treat with the advancing French force commanded by General Louis Franchet d'Esperey. On September 29, 1918, an armistice was signed at the general's headquarters (it was accepted the next day). By its terms, Bulgaria promised to evacuate all Allied territory; permit the occupation of portions of her own land by French, British, and Italian troops; grant the Allies free passage through Bulgarian territory; give them free control of the Danube River and of Bulgarian shipping on that waterway; demobilize the Bulgarian Army; and turn over to the Allies all rolling stock and other means of transportation.

Turkish Armistice

With Bulgaria's surrender, Turkey was isolated; the Allies were pressing northward from Syria and Mesopotamia; elements of the Turkish Army were throwing down their arms; and bands of deserters, aggregating perhaps half a million men, were terrorizing the countryside. Shortly after the Bulgarian armistice, therefore, the government of Enver Pasha resigned and gave way to a nonpartisan cabinet headed by Ahmet İzzet Pasha. On October 14, 1918, this new cabinet appealed for an armistice. Negotiators then met on the island of Lemnos, and on October 30 signed an armistice. Under its terms the Turks agreed to open the Dardanelles and facilitate the clearing of minefields from the straits; surrender officers and garrisons in Tripolitania, Cyrenaica, Arabia, Syria, and Mesopotamia; withdraw all forces from northern Persia and Transcaucasia; permit the occupation by the Allies of strategic points in Turkey and, if necessary to prevent disorder, of the Armenian vilayets; give the Allies free use of Turkish merchant shipping; demobilize most of the army; and surrender the fleet.

Austrian Collapse

Beginnings of Disintegration. Within the Austro-Hungarian Empire, conditions had steadily deteriorated since the beginning of the war. Even before the accession of Emperor Charles I on November 21, 1916, the government had begun urging Germany to seek peace, and in 1917 in the Sixte affair it had sought ineffectually to bring about negotiations with the Allies. Only the Bolshevik Revolution and the treaties with Russia and the Ukraine prevented starvation and probably internal collapse in the winter of 1917–18. When the summer of 1918 came and Ludendorff's desperate offensives in the west failed, the Austrian ruler and his ministers concluded that they would have to seek peace even if it meant acting independently of Germany. If they did not, they feared, the empire would simply disintegrate, for the various nationalities of which it was composed were already threatening to break away.

A Czech committee had issued a declaration of war against the empire on November 14, 1915; the Czechoslovak National Council, headed by Tomáš Garrigue Masaryk, had been formed in 1916; Czech units had deserted en masse to fight with the Allies; representatives of the Czechs and Slovaks had met in congress at Pittsburgh, Pennsylvania, in 1918 to proclaim the formation of a Czechoslovak state; this state had quickly been recognized by the Allies; and the Czech and Slovak delegates in the Austrian Reichsrat had practically demanded that independence be accorded them.

Nationalism had manifested itself ever more strongly since the outbreak of war. In November, 1916, the Austrian and German governments had sought to appease the Poles by declaring their support of a united, autonomous Poland and creating a 25-man Council of State to exercise some governing power within the region, but this council had dissolved itself in 1917 when confronted with the refusal of the two powers to allow the creation of an independent Polish Army. A Polish National Committee in Paris, led by Roman Dmowski, won recognition from the Allies, which, on June 3, 1918, made Polish independence a war aim. Poles in the Reichsrat indicated that they too might support this committee.

In the south, numerous local councils of Croats and Slovenes had endorsed a declaration issued at Corfu on July 20, 1917, in which representatives of these two groups had joined with Serbs in calling for creation of a united South Slav (Yugoslav) state. Separatist sentiment was growing in Hungary, and numbers of German Austrians were calling for the dissolution of the empire and the creation of a separate Austrian state.

Appeals for Peace. After having failed in renewed efforts to obtain German agreement for a joint peace effort, the Austrian government on September 14, 1918, dispatched a note through neutral capitals to all the belligerent governments, inviting them to send delegates for a meeting in some neutral state where there could be "a confidential and noncommittal exchange of views." This appeal was rejected almost instantly by the United States and soon afterward by Britain and France. The convening of the Reichsrat on October 1, 1918, showed the government that its condition was desperate. All the nationality groups, including the German, issued declarations in favor of independence. On October 4, therefore, the Austro-Hungarian government dispatched a note to the United States requesting an armistice and offering to make peace on the basis of the Fourteen Points and subsequent declarations by President Wilson, but the United States Department of State replied on October 18 that the President could no longer agree to mere autonomy for the nationalities within the empire.

Fragmentation of the Empire. While officials in Vienna awaited this response and then anxiously meditated their reply to it, the Austro-Hungarian Empire fell apart. At Agram (now Zagreb) on October 19, 1918, an assembly of Croats, Slovenes, and Serbs asserted its sovereignty over the South Slav portions of the Dual Monarchy, and most of the districts south of the Drava River accepted this decree. In Warsaw, on October 7, a three-man Regency Council, which had been installed late in 1917 as the successor to the disbanded Council of State, proclaimed Poland an independent state; on October 15, the Polish deputies in the Reichsrat declared themselves "subjects and citizens of the free and united Polish State"; and by October 31, the Austrian garrisons had been ousted from Polish Galicia. On October 16, Emperor Charles had made a last effort to regain the loyalty of these groups by offering to transform the monarchy into a federation of self-governing nations, but the Yugoslavs and the Poles rejected the proposal. From the United States, Masaryk proclaimed the independence of Czechoslovakia, and the Czechs in Prague held a bloodless revolution on

October 28 and removed all officials of the old empire. A Hungarian National Council, which had taken office in Budapest on October 25, appealed to the emperor to release them from their vows of fealty, and he regretfully did so on November 1. Meanwhile, the German Austrian members of the Reichsrat had resolved in favor of independence for German Austria, and assemblies in Bucovina had announced the secession of that region and its adhesion to Romania.

The Armistice. Confronted with these dismaying events, the emperor and his officials abandoned all hope of negotiating for peace. On October 27, they offered to accept an armistice on almost any terms, and on November 3, at the Villa Giusti near Padua, their delegates signed an armistice providing for the immediate cessation of hostilities; demobilization of all Austro-Hungarian forces; evacuation of the Tirol, the Dalmatian coast, and the territory claimed by the Yugoslavs; surrender of all railway equipment and most of the fleet; and a grant to the Allies of power to move freely through the empire, occupy any part of it, and requisition supplies for their troops.

German Armistice

In August, 1918, when the Allied armies assumed the offensive in the west, the German High Command concluded that all hope of victory had disappeared. The state of morale on the home front had been revealed by the Reichstag peace resolution of July, 1917, and, despite the termination of fighting in the east, by a wave of strikes in munitions plants in January, 1918. Under the pressure of the Allied advance, the morale of troops in the field began to crack. Consequently, in a conference held at Spa on September 29, General Ludendorff asked the civil officials of the government to arrange an armistice "without delay." By that time the Austrian government had issued its first appeal for peace, Bulgaria had sued for terms, and members of the Reichstag were calling for extensive changes in the German cabinet.

First Exchange of Notes. Chancellor Georg von Hertling, who had succeeded Michaelis on November 1, 1917, resigned almost as soon as the High Command made its demand. His successor, Prince Max of Baden, was ordered by the Kaiser to comply with the generals' wishes, and on October 4, 1918, he dispatched through neutral channels a message to President Wilson, asking him "to take in hand the restoration of peace," and declaring that the German government accepted "as a basis for the peace negotiations" the

Fourteen Points and others of Wilson's pronouncements. The American public, through its newspapers and spokesmen in Congress, greeted this message hostilely and called for "unconditional surrender," however, and the Allies advised Wilson that its aim was merely to divide Germany's enemies. Though Wilson decided not to dismiss it, as he had the Austrian appeal of September 14, he responded to it coolly, asking in a message of October 8 whether the German government would agree that his points and principles were to be the bases of peace so that negotiations would merely concern their application and, secondly, "whether the Imperial Chancellor is speaking merely for the constituted authorities of the Empire who have so far conducted the war."

Second Exchange of Notes. This answer surprised the new Chancellor. He was forming a cabinet representative of the majority parties in the Reichstag, and he had declared that it would be responsible to that body and not, as in the past, only to the Kaiser. After conferring with military leaders and finding them little changed in their views, he and his advisers agreed that Wilson's questions should be answered in the affirmative. On October 12, therefore, the German Foreign Office replied that Germany "accepted the terms laid down by President Wilson in his address of January 8 and in his subsequent addresses as the foundations of a permanent peace of justice," and that the Chancellor now spoke "in the name of the German Government and of the German people." This message, too, had a cold reception in the United States. Wilson, now under intense criticism both at home and abroad for entering into any negotiations at all, answered with four conditions: (1) the terms of the armistice were to be determined by the military advisers of the American and Allied governments; (2) no arrangement could be accepted "which does not provide absolutely satisfactory safeguards and guarantees of the maintenance of the present military supremacy of the armies of the United States and of the Allies in the field"; (3) submarine operations would have to cease immediately; and (4) the German government would have to show evidence that it had reformed its character.

Third Exchange of Notes. This second American note was puzzling. The Chancellor summoned a conference of the nation's principal civil and military officials to consider how it should be answered. He found to his astonishment that Ludendorff had changed his mind: The army could fight on, the general now said; an armistice on Wilson's terms was unnecessary and undesirable. The Admiralty opposed acquiescence to Wilson's third demand, but most of the civil ministers contended that the public desire for peace was so great and the state of civilian morale so low that the government could not break off negotiations. Endeavoring to effect a compromise among these wholly divergent opinions, Max drafted and dispatched to Washington on October 20 a note agreeing that "the conditions of an armistice should be left to the judgment of the military advisers, and that the actual standard of power on both sides in the field has to form the basis for arrangements safeguarding and guaranteeing this standard"; stating that submarine commanders had been ordered to stop attacking passenger vessels; and asserting that the German government was "free from arbitrary and irresponsible influence" and was "supported by the approval of the overwhelming majority of the German people."

Wilson replied on October 23 that, in view of the concessions made by the Germans, he could not decline to take up with the Allies the question of a possible armistice. But he went on to declare "that the only armistice he would feel justified in submitting for consideration would be one which should leave the United States and the powers associated with her in a position to enforce any arrangements that may be entered into and to make a renewal of hostilities on the part of Germany impossible." He also asserted harshly that he remained unconvinced that the German government represented the German people, and that if the United States "must deal with the military masters and the monarchical autocrats of Germany now, or if it is likely to have to deal with them later . . . , it must demand, not peace negotiations, but surrender."

German Collapse. On October 27, the German government replied with a simple reaffirmation that "far-reaching changes" had been made and were being made in the constitutional system, and that it awaited "proposals for an armistice which shall lead toward that peace of justice the President had outlined in his proclamations." In the meantime, however, the fabric of German society had begun to split. Reichstag leaders and newspaper editors called openly for the Kaiser's abdication, and Prince Max secured the dismissal of Ludendorff. On November 3, units of the fleet began to mutiny, winning support from dock workers in the port cities. By November 8, revolution had spread throughout the Rhineland. King Louis III of Bavaria abdicated, and workers, soldiers, and peasants moved to set up a Soviet-style government. Hamburg fell to left-wing Socialists, and agitators there endeavored to organize forces for a march on Berlin. In the capital itself, Social Democrats demanded the creation of a republic, and on November 9 the leaders of the army informed the Kaiser that they could no longer guarantee his safety. Striving to stay the mobs that were already parading the streets of Berlin, Prince Max announced that the Kaiser and his heirs renounced the throne. Though William never agreed to this act, he finally reconciled himself to the counsels of prudence and, on November 10, fled to the Netherlands.

Meanwhile, on November 5, the government had received Wilson's fourth and last note, stating that the United States and the Allies were prepared to receive a German delegation and communicate armistice terms to it. Max and his ministers selected Centrist leader Matthias Erzberger to head a four-man delegation, and it met on November 8 with Marshal Foch and other Allied officers in a railroad car on a siding at Compiègne. On November 9 the delegation accepted the terms offered them. Germany was to cease hostilities and evacuate France, Alsace-Lorraine, Belgium, and Luxembourg within 14 days from the signature of the armistice; the left bank of the Rhine and all territory on the right bank within a 30-kilometer radius of the principal crossings (Mainz, Koblenz, and Cologne) within 31 days; East Africa, within an unspecified period; and lands previously belonging to Russia "as soon as the Allies, taking into account the internal situation of these territories, shall decide the time for this has come." Germany was also to surrender to the Allies a specified number of guns, airplanes, railroad cars, locomotives, trucks, and warships and all submarines. It was to renounce the treaties of Bucharest and Brest-Litovsk and agreements supplementary to them. In addition, it was to grant the Allies free access to its eastern regions and give them permission to requisition supplies for their forces, and it was to understand that the blockade would continue in force. Though protested by Hindenburg, these terms were accepted in Berlin, and early on the morning of November 11 the armistice agreement was signed by the delegations at Compiègne. The war was over at 11 A.M.

17. Diplomatic History of the War: Peace Conferences and Peace Treaties

BY ERNEST R. MAY

ORGANIZATION AND PROCEEDINGS OF THE CONFERENCES

A conference among the victorious powers convened in Paris on January 18, 1919. Each of the major belligerents (Britain, France, Italy, the United States, and Japan) was represented by a five-man delegation, assisted by varying numbers of experts and secretaries. The lesser belligerents had smaller delegations. All of these met periodically in plenary sessions of the conference, but the real power of decision was soon vested in a Supreme Council (Council of Ten) consisting of two representatives from each of the five great states, and later in a Council of Four, consisting of President Wilson, Prime Minister Lloyd George, Premier Georges Clemenceau of France, and Premier Vittorio Orlando of Italy. Numerous commissions were created to study special subjects, and these commissions reported to the Supreme Council, which then approved recommendations to be put before the plenary sessions. The Council also called in representatives of other belligerents, of neutral states, and of states in process of formation when questions affecting their interests were under discussion.

First Phase: January 18–February 14, 1919

Through negotiations preceding the German armistice, President Wilson had won agreement from the Allies that the peace should be based on the points and principles he had enunciated, the only exceptions being that "freedom of the seas" was to be left for later definition and that Germany was to make compensation for the damage done to the civilian populations of the Allied states. His ideals had been hailed by spokesmen for public opinion in all the Allied nations. At the outset, at least, he was the dominant figure among the conferees, and he was able to insist that the first order of business should be the framing of a charter or Covenant for a

League of Nations and that this Covenant should be made an integral part of the treaties of peace. He himself took the chairmanship of the Commission on the League of Nations, which was to draft the Covenant and submit it to the conference, and he saw to it that no unrelated problem came to the point of decision before that work was finished.

Colonial Mandates. It proved impossible, however, to frame the document without reaching some decision on the disposition of former German colonies, since Wilson took the position that, while these colonies could not be returned to Germany, they should not be treated as spoils of war, and their governance should be of primary concern to the proposed League. Representatives of Japan and the British Dominions opposed the President on this issue, for Japan desired the German Pacific islands north of the equator and the former German leasehold of Kiaochow in China; Australia wished to annex outright German New Guinea and the German islands south of the equator; and the Union of South Africa wanted similarly to take possession of German Southwest Africa. No meeting of minds seemed possible until Lieutenant General Jan Christiaan Smuts of South Africa devised a compromise formula. He proposed that all the former German colonies be transferred to the League, but that the League assign a mandate for the governance of each one to some member state and that these mandated territories be divided into three classifications: (1) those capable of eventual independence, in which the mandatory power would merely render "administrative advice and assistance," (2) those, particularly in central Africa, where the mandatory power would have to take responsibility for administration, and (3) "territories, such as Southwest Africa and certain of the South Pacific islands, which, owing to the sparseness of their population, or their small size, or their remoteness from the centers of civilization, or their geographical contiguity to the territory of the Mandatory, and other circumstances, can best be administered under the laws of the Mandatory as integral portions of its territory." Though this last clause permitted virtual annexations by the Union of South Africa, Australia, and Japan, subject only to the requirement that they file an annual report with the League on conditions in the mandated territory, it proved acceptable to Wilson, who feared that the Dominions and Japan might otherwise refuse to endorse the Covenant. Smuts' solution was approved.

Covenant of the League. No other serious problem arose during the first stage of negotiations. The French delegation did urge strongly that the projected international organization be equipped with a general staff and given additional power with which to enforce its decrees, but Wilson insisted that an organization that appeared to be a permanent military alliance would be unacceptable to the American public. The other members of the commission yielded to the President and eventually accepted a Covenant that closely resembled a draft that Wilson had initially put forward. It provided for an Assembly in which each member state, including self-governing Dominions and colonies, should have one vote; and a council composed of representatives of the United States, Britain, France, Italy, and Japan, together with representatives of four other states, as chosen by the Assembly. The Council was to formulate plans for general disarmament and for the creation of a Permanent Court of International Justice; and, on reference from any member state, was to inquire into any situation threatening to cause a rupture between states, to report on the facts, and to make recommendations to the parties, the Assembly, or the member states. The agencies of the League, including a permanent Secretariat, were to register all treaties, and no treaty was to be binding unless it was so registered. They were also to exercise some control over traffic in arms and to endeavor to secure fair and humane conditions for labor.

The states joining the League were to promise that they would not resort to war with one another and that, if a dispute proved insoluble by ordinary methods, they would submit it for arbitration or for investigation and recommendation by the Council. Most important of all, they were to pledge themselves to regard the security of any member as a matter of concern for all. Articles 10, 11, and 16 of the Covenant provided:

(10) The Members of the League undertake to respect and preserve as against external aggression the territorial integrity and existing political independence of all Members of the League. In case of any such aggression or in case of any threat or danger of such aggression the Council shall advise upon the means by which this obligation shall be fulfilled.

(11) Any war or threat of war, whether immediately affecting any of the Members of the League or not, is hereby declared a matter of concern to the whole League. . . .

(16) Should any Member of the League resort to war in disregard of its covenants . . . it shall *ipso facto* be deemed to have committed an act of war against all other Members of the League. . . .

On February 14, 1919, President Wilson presented the completed draft to a plenary session of the conference, declaring proudly, "a living thing is born." That evening he left for a short visit to his homeland.

Second Phase: February 15–June 28, 1919

Amendments to the Covenant. In the United States, President Wilson discovered opposition to the Covenant already in flower. The opposition Republican Party had won control of both Houses of Congress in the mid-term elections of 1918, and its leaders were critical of Wilson for having gone in person to Paris, for having included no conspicuous Republican or member of the Senate in the American delegation, and for having agreed to a Covenant that might conceivably allow League interference with American tariff and immigration laws, abridge the Monroe Doctrine, or draw the United States into future European wars. On March 4, 1919, Senator Henry Cabot Lodge, the senior Republican on the Foreign Relations Committee, read into the *Congressional Record* a resolution declaring the Covenant "in the form now proposed" unacceptable. It was signed by 38 senators, or more than one-third plus one, which, under the United States Constitution, could prevent ratification of a treaty. By the time President Wilson returned to Paris on March 14, he and the other conferees knew that he would have to seek amendments to the original Covenant, and he quickly reconvened the Commission on the League of Nations and proposed new language that would specifically exclude tariff and immigration matters from the competence of the League, provide for a member state's voluntary withdrawal, and explicitly recognize the Monroe Doctrine.

In return for accepting these amendments, however, other delegations requested approval for other changes in the Covenant or asked for concessions by the President on economic or territorial issues. In the League of Nations Commission the French returned to their appeal for an international organization backed by permanent force. Although Wilson still could not yield to their view, he did give in to the extent of agreeing to sign with France and Britain a separate treaty of guaranty (June 28), under which the United States and Britain promised to come to France's aid if she suffered an unprovoked attack. (This treaty was never ratified in either Washington or London.) The Japanese asked that the President insert in the preamble to the Covenant phrases endorsing the principle of racial equality. Recognizing the difficulties that such phrases might cause in the British Dominions and in the United States, Wilson also had to refuse this demand. To mollify the Japanese and ensure that they accept the Covenant and join the League, however, he abandoned his opposition to their taking over the former German leasehold of Kiaochow as outright spoils of war, and contented himself with a promise that they would eventually return the territory to China. The French, the Japanese, and others then accepted his proposed amendments. The revised Covenant implicitly excluded tariff and immigration questions, provided that any state could withdraw from the League on two years' notice, and declared in a new Article 21: "Nothing in this Covenant shall be deemed to affect the validity of . . . regional understandings like the Monroe Doctrine. . . ."

Reparations Issue. While the League of Nations Commission resumed its sittings, the Council of Ten, succeeded by the Council of Four, turned to the framing of articles for the German peace treaty. One crucial issue that arose at once concerned the indemnities or reparations to be exacted from the vanquished. The French and British delegations obtained American acceptance of their view that the costs of the war should include such items as pensions to veterans and payments to the widows and children of the slain. The Commission on Reparations reported, however, that the resultant levies would far exceed anything that the defeated Germans could pay. The French took the position that the treaty should nevertheless contain such provisions. The British urged that the reparations be scaled down to a figure approximating expert calculations of the maximum that Germany could afford, while the Americans argued for reducing the figure still further in order to permit some degree of German recovery. Finally, the Council of Four agreed on a compromise. A Reparations Commission would subsequently fix the sums that Germany was to pay; the treaty of peace itself would merely compel the Germans to accept responsibility "for causing all the loss and damage to which the Allied and Associated Governments and their nationals have been subjected as a consequence of the war imposed upon them by the aggression of Germany and her allies." Included in the final treaty as Article 231, this was to become known as "the war-guilt clause," and to be the subject of many German polemics during the 1920's and 1930's.

German Frontiers. The French urged not only that heavy economic burdens be laid on Germany but also that she be weakened as much as possible by losses of territory. They advocated the creation in the east of a large and strong Poland—"*grande et forte, très forte*," in the words of the French foreign minister, Stéphen J. M. Pichon. The British and the Americans, though committed to the creation of an independent Poland, were fearful lest new frontiers in the east create irredentist movements that would be sources of trouble in the future. They argued, therefore, for boundary lines that would more or less follow discoverable lines of nationality. The compromises finally reached gave the province of Posen (Poznań) to Poland and created the Polish Corridor west of the Vistula River, giving the new nation access to the Gulf of Danzig. Danzig (Gdańsk) itself, largely German in population, was made a free city. Plebiscites were ordered for the districts of Marienwerder (Kwidzyń) and Allenstein (Olsztyn); held in 1920, they returned these areas to Germany. A plebiscite was also ordained for Upper Silesia. Held in 1921, it resulted in a partition; the eastern third went to Poland, while the less industrialized western parts reverted to Germany.

In the west the French wished to detach from Germany the left bank of the Rhine, creating an independent buffer state or a permanently occupied zone. The British and the Americans opposed these proposals, just as they opposed those that might cause irredentist movements in the east. After a prolonged dispute, during which Clemenceau once accused Wilson of being pro-German and Wilson summoned his official ship, threatening to break up the conference and go home, the Council of Four arrived at a set of compromises. France was given full title to Alsace-Lorraine and also to the coal mines of the Saar, which were expected to compensate her for wartime losses. The area itself was for a period of 15 years to be governed by the League of Nations and occupied by Allied forces. At the end of that time a plebiscite was to determine its final disposition. In addition, the southern part of the Rhine Province, Birkenfeld, the Rhenish (Bavarian) Palatinate, and Mainz and its environs were also to be occupied for 15 years. Another zone, including the central sector of the Rhine Province and Koblenz and its environs, was to be occupied for 10 years. The northern part of the province and the Cologne region were to be occupied for five years. On the right bank of the Rhine, Germany was forbidden to construct any fortifications or to maintain armed forces within 50 kilometers of the river, and the whole Rhineland was to be permanently demilitarized.

Fiume Issue. Premier Orlando of Italy insisted that, before the German treaty was concluded, the Big Four should reach agreement on certain questions not connected with that treaty but which were of concern to Italy. Specifically, he desired a promise from Wilson and the Allies that the provisions of the secret Treaty of London of 1915 would be executed, and that in addition Italy would be given the city of Fiume, which had a large Italian population but which was surrounded by Yugoslav territory and was expected to serve the new state of Yugoslavia as its primary Adriatic port. The British and French, who were parties to the London treaty, took the position that they would either stand by that document, which did not assign Fiume to Italy, or consider it null and void, examine the Italian claim to Fiume, and also re-examine the Italian treaty claims to the Tirol, the Trieste region, and the islands of the Adriatic coast.

Wilson, who had not signed the London treaty, took the position that all decisions should be based on considerations of nationality, with due regard to the economic and strategic interests of both the Italians and the Yugoslavs. After studying the issue, he concluded that Fiume should remain with Yugoslavia. He had already retreated from many of the principles he had announced during the war: he had acquiesced in punitive territorial and economic clauses for the German treaty, and he had yielded Kiaochow to the Japanese. On the Fiume issue, however, he proved immovable, and on April 24, 1919, Orlando and his colleagues angrily left Paris. The final provisions of the German treaty were therefore composed by a council of three—Wilson, Clemenceau, and Lloyd George.

THE PEACE TREATIES

Treaty of Versailles

The completed treaty, containing 440 articles and covering 200 pages of text, was approved by a plenary session of the conference on May 6, 1919. In addition to incorporating the Covenant of the League and the financial and territorial provisions that had resulted from the debates among the Council of Four, the final text also stipulated that after March 31, 1920, the German Army should not consist of more than 100,000 officers and men and that the Allies should have the right to try Germans guilty of violations of the laws of war and to arraign the Kaiser before a special international tribunal "for a supreme offense against international morality and the sanctity of treaties."

Wilson and the Allies had originally conceived of the Paris meetings as merely a preliminary conference, assuming that it would be followed by a full-scale conference with the Germans. Partly because of the time that the preliminary conference took, partly because of the increasing internal disorganization in Germany itself, this plan was at some point abandoned. The Paris conferees agreed instead simply to submit the draft to a German delegation and give the German government a period in which to return written observations on it. This was done on May 7; the German commentary was submitted on May 29; all changes proposed by the Germans were formally rejected; when the Germans still delayed signing, the Allies made preparations for renewed military action; and on June 23, the German authorities declared that they were compelled to yield before this threat of force. On June 28, in the Hall of Mirrors at Versailles, a German delegation finally endorsed the document.

Treaty of Saint-Germain-en-Laye

A treaty for Austria had meanwhile been drafted, and an Austrian delegation had been summoned to Paris to receive it. The same procedure was followed (as indeed it was with the other defeated states—Bulgaria, Hungary, and Turkey): written comments were received and answered by the Allied and Associated Powers. The only difference was that certain minor concessions resulted from these exchanges. The final treaty did not arraign the former Austrian Emperor as a criminal, although it did call on Austria to deliver war criminals for trial. It specified financial reparations and reparations in kind and required Austria to demobilize her forces and renounce compulsory military training. It also forbade Austria to unite with Germany, and it provided for the surrender by the Austrian government of all claim to territories that were to be transferred to Italy, Romania, and the new Yugoslav, Czechoslovak, and Polish states. Austria thus gave up all lands beyond the historic frontiers of Bohemia, Moravia, and Slovakia, all claim to Bucovina, and all lands south of the Karawanken (Karavanke) Mountains and the Mur River. The treaty did provide, however, for a new frontier with Hungary in which Burgenland remained with Austria, and it allowed for plebiscites in the regions of Klagenfurt and Teschen. (The former, held in October, 1920, gave the area to Austria; the latter was not held, but in July, 1920, the Conference of Ambassadors, successor to the Supreme Council, divided the region between Czechoslovakia and Poland.) The Austrian delegation signed the treaty at Saint-Germain-en-Laye on September 10, 1919.

Treaty of Neuilly

On September 19, 1919, the Allied and Associated Powers presented a Bulgarian delegation with a draft treaty. In its final form it contained war crimes, reparations, and military clauses much like those in the Austrian treaty. It provided for a frontier between Bulgaria and Yugoslavia that generally favored the latter, and it required Bulgaria to surrender both Eastern and Western Thrace. The treaty was signed by the Bulgarian delegation at Neuilly-sur-Seine on November 27, 1919.

Treaty of Trianon

The victors had planned to deal concurrently with the Austrians and with representatives of the newly independent Hungarian state, but revolutionary disturbances brought to power in Budapest a Communist regime headed by Béla Kun, and the conferees in Paris decided to wait before presenting a treaty to the Hungarians. On June 13, 1919, the Supreme Council simply sent a message to Béla Kun ordering him to withdraw Hungarian forces from the territories that by then had been assigned to Czechoslovakia and Romania. Hungary was thus required to abandon the Pressburg (Bratislava) region, the Great Schütt, and Slovakia to the one, and Transylvania, part of the Hungarian plain, and part of the Banat to the other. When a Hungarian delegation was invited to Paris in November, 1919, these new frontiers were formally provided for in the treaty presented to it, and it was asked to give up Burgenland to Austria, and Slavonia, northeastern Croatia, and the remainder of the Banat to Yugoslavia. The war crimes, reparations, and military clauses were similar to those in the Austrian and Bulgarian treaties. The Hungarian delegation finally signed the treaty at Trianon on June 4, 1920.

Treaty of Sèvres

Of all the treaties, the harshest was that imposed on Turkey and signed by a Turkish delegation at Sèvres on August 10, 1920. Its war crimes, reparations, and military clauses were similar to those in the Austrian, Bulgarian, and Hungarian treaties, but the Sèvres agreements also provided that inter-Allied commissions should remain in Turkey to ensure the fulfillment of these clauses, to devise a new judicial system for the nation, and to regulate navigation in the straits. The straits were to be open as if they were international water. Turkey was to renounce all claim to Egypt, the Sudan, and Cyprus; acknowledge the Hejaz, Syria, Mesopotamia, and Armenia as free and independent states; and cede Thrace, Crete, and most of the Aegean Islands to Greece and the Dodecanese and Kastellorizo to Italy. Smyrna and its environs were to receive autonomy under administrative control by Greece, and a local assembly was to have the right after five years to apply for incorporation in the kingdom of Greece. Similarly, Kurdistan was to have an autonomous regime arranged by an international commission, and it was to have the right to become independent upon application to the League of Nations. The Ottoman Empire was thus to be reduced to a fragment of Turkey proper. As it turned out, however, the Treaty of Sèvres was never put into force, and it was eventually replaced by the milder Treaty of Lausanne.

Treaty of Lausanne

Turkish nationalists led by Mustafa Kemal (later Kemal Atatürk) refused to accept the Treaty of Sèvres, and their forces drove the Greeks from Smyrna and threatened the Allied position in the Dardanelles. The Allies therefore agreed to convene a new conference with the Turks, and a treaty was signed at Lausanne on July 24, 1923. Under its terms, Turkey recovered full administrative control of its own territory and regained sovereignty over part of eastern Thrace, including the city of Edirne, and over Smyrna, Kurdistan, and Armenia. Turkish possession of the Kars and Ardahan districts had been recognized by the Soviet Union in 1921. In return, Turkey agreed to demilitarize zones around the Bosporus and the Dardanelles and an area on the Greek and Bulgarian borders in Thrace. A separate Straits Convention, signed at Lausanne on the same day, provided that the straits should remain open except in time of war, when Turkey could close them for her own defense or to enforce her neutrality.

RATIFICATION OF THE TREATIES

Nonratification by the United States

Despite the amendments that President Wilson had succeeded in introducing into the Covenant of the League of Nations, his Republican opponents were not assuaged. Republicans in the United States Senate were divided into three groups: one that opposed ratification of the German treaty in any form; one that wished the Senate to introduce serious amendments to the treaty or, in ratifying it, to state strong reservations about parts of it; and one that wished to enter less strong reservations. These factions were known respectively as "irreconcilables," "strong reservationists," and "mild reservationists," and each had a small number of allies among senators from the President's own Democratic Party. Since the Senate Foreign Relations Committee had been so constructed that "irreconcilables" and "strong reservationists" formed a majority, it was able to delay presentation of the treaty to the Senate, and meanwhile public sentiment against the document grew. The treaty came to be opposed by many German-Americans who felt that it was too harsh toward their fatherland, by Hungarian-Americans who resented the settlement in the Balkans, by Italo-Americans angered by the Fiume dispute, by Sinophiles who regarded the Kiaochow clause as shameful, by liberal idealists disappointed that Wilson had compromised with so many of his points and principles, and by conservatives who feared that membership in the League might involve the United States in future economic or political difficulties.

To counteract the public swing against the treaty and to stimulate renewed enthusiasm for it, the President set out on a speaking tour of the country, but he collapsed at Pueblo, Colorado, on September 25, 1919, and shortly after his return to Washington suffered an incapacitating stroke. Many of his advisers concluded that there was little hope of ratification unless the Democrats compromised with the "mild reservationists," but Wilson, directing the battle from his sickbed, rejected all such suggestions. Thus when the treaty came up for a vote in the Senate on November 19, 1919, Democrats insisted on ratification without reservations, and it failed of passage both when brought up in such form and when brought up with reservations attached. The same alignment holding, it failed a second time, on March 19, 1920.

The new Republican Administration of Warren G. Harding, which took office in March, 1921, negotiated a separate treaty of peace with Germany, signed at Berlin on August 25, 1921; one with Austria, signed at Vienna on August 24, 1921; and one with Hungary, signed at Budapest on August 29, 1921. (The United States had not been at war with Bulgaria and Turkey.)

Ratification by Other Powers

The treaties of Versailles, Saint Germain, Neuilly, and Trianon had meanwhile been ratified by other signatories. The German treaty went into force on January 10, 1920, and the League of Nations began functioning on January 16, 1920. The Great War, as it was long called, thus officially came to a close.

18. The Postwar World

BY ERNEST R. MAY

The armistices of 1918 and the treaties of 1919 and 1920 brought peace to only part of the world, for wars continued in eastern Europe, the Middle East, and Asia. In Russia, civil conflict raged through 1919, and the Bolsheviks did not succeed in reconquering the Caucasus, the Ukraine, and the territory between Petrograd (now Leningrad) and the Baltic Sea until early in 1920. In that year they negotiated treaties recognizing the independence of Estonia, Latvia, Lithuania, and Finland. Meanwhile, however, the Polish government had come to the aid of the defeated Ukrainians, and war between Russia and Poland continued through the spring and summer of 1920. After suffering initial reverses, the Bolsheviks rallied and drove almost to the outskirts of Warsaw. The Poles, reinforced by French officers and money, then pushed them back. Peace negotiations opened in September, 1920, and a treaty of peace delimiting the Soviet-Polish frontier was signed at Riga on March 18, 1921. In Hungary the Communist government of Béla Kun declared war on Romania on April 22, 1919, only to have the Romanians march toward Budapest, forcing Kun to flee the country on August 1. On March 1, 1920, a reactionary regency was established under Admiral Miklós (Nicholas) Horthy. In Albania a nationalist uprising early in 1920 compelled the Italians to withdraw their occupying forces and, on August 2, to recognize the nation's independence.

In Turkey, Mustafa Kemal battled from 1919 to 1922 to drive the Greeks from Smyrna (now İzmir) and to force the Allies to revise the Treaty of Sèvres. In Syria, nationalists rose against the French, who had been assigned a mandate over the area by the inter-Allied Conference of San Remo of April, 1920; much blood was shed before the French consolidated their control over Syria proper, and the Republic of Lebanon successfully proclaimed its independence (1926). In Iraq, which the Conference of San Remo had designated as a British mandate, there were uprisings in 1920. In Arabia there was fighting in 1919 between ibn-Saud and King Husein of the Hejaz, and it was not until 1925 that the former succeeded in consolidating his control over the entire peninsula. In

Iran, which a treaty of August 9, 1919, placed under British protection, a nationalist uprising was backed by the Soviet Union; it was only ended in February, 1921, with the triumph of the British-backed military chieftain Reza Khan Pahlavi. The British treaty was denounced, and both Russians and British left the country. In Afghanistan, Emir Amanullah Khan declared war against the British in 1919, and peace was not fully restored until they recognized the complete independence of the nation in November, 1921. In China, civil war continued without interruption.

Nor did peace in the full sense of the term come even to Western Europe. The new German Republic was tormented by insurrection in the Polish provinces in 1918 and 1919, by separatist movements in the Rhineland nurtured by the French occupying authorities, by an independent Communist republic established briefly in Bavaria in April, 1919, and by the violent agitation of both Communist and right-wing nationalist groups elsewhere in the country. All of these difficulties were increased by the Allied blockade, which, continuing throughout the period of treaty making, brought much of the population to the point of starvation.

The Allies themselves, despite their hard bargaining at Paris, proved unable afterward to agree on the measures to be applied to Germany. A conference held at Spa in July, 1920, determined the percentage of reparations that each of the victors should obtain from the defeated state. Other conferences at Paris (January, 1921) and London (February–March, April–May, 1921) altered these percentages and fixed the payments in money and in kind that the Germans were to make. The French became increasingly irritated by the failure of the Germans to meet these obligations. They suggested repeatedly that the Allies invoke the sanctions provided in the Treaty of Versailles and occupy the Ruhr. The British opposed this suggestion and at conferences at London (December, 1921) and Genoa (April, 1922) proposed as partial compensation a new treaty guaranteeing the French frontiers. Nothing came of this proposal nor of further conferences at London (August and December, 1922). Dissatisfied and alarmed by the fact that Germany and Russia had signed a treaty of commerce and friendship at Rapallo on April 16, 1922, the French defied the British and proceeded to occupy the Ruhr in January, 1923.

The conferences that exacerbated disagreements were not, of course, the only ones held. A large assemblage of delegates met in Washington in the winter of 1921–22 and framed a treaty of naval limitations that permitted cutbacks in capital ships by all the major maritime states; a nine-power pact providing for the maintenance of the open door for trade in China; and a four-power pact dissolving the 20-year-old Anglo-Japanese alliance and substituting for it an Anglo-American-Japanese-French compact providing for mutual consultation in the event of disturbances in the Pacific area. In 1922–23 delegations at Lausanne framed a new Turkish treaty. For all practical purposes, however, tranquillity was not restored to Europe until 1925, when the French evacuated the Ruhr, and representatives of the major European states concluded the Locarno treaties, which included guarantees of the Franco-German and Belgo-German frontiers against aggression.

Political Consequences of the War

The war and the peace treaties obviously wrought great changes in the political geography of Europe. Germany was reduced in size, while France and Italy were enlarged. There was a large independent Poland between Germany and Russia, and the Baltic states and Finland also became independent. Where the Austro-Hungarian Empire had been, there were Czechoslovakia, a tiny Austrian republic, an independent Hungary, a greater Romania, and a united Yugoslav state. Most of the frontier lines in the Balkans were new, and so were those on post-1920 maps of the Middle East. In general, the boundaries of states followed more closely than ever the distinguishable lines of language and nationality, though there were significant minorities of Germans in Czechoslovakia and Poland and of Magyars in Czechoslovakia and Romania.

In Europe, however, the geographical changes brought about by the war were probably less significant than the institutional changes. Where before the war there had been 19 monarchies and 3 republics, by 1922 there were 14 republics, 13 monarchies, and 2 regencies (Albania and Hungary). And, more important still, many of the postwar states, republics and monarchies alike, had adopted or were to adopt ideologies quite different from those that had animated either republics or monarchies before the war. The revolutionary Marxism of the Bolsheviks triumphed in Russia. Socialists governed the Austrian Republic and, for a time, Germany, and Socialist parties made electoral gains in both Britain (1923) and France (1924). In Bulgaria, in 1919, Alexander Stamboliski and his Agrarian Party took power and established a dictatorship that gave primacy to the interests of peasants. In Italy, in October, 1922,

Benito Mussolini and his black-shirted Fascists seized control of the government and set up a regime that boasted of suppressing civil liberties and of subordinating the individual to the interests of the state. Government, whether in representative forms, as in France and Britain, or in totalitarian forms, as in Russia, Bulgaria, and Italy (and later in Nazi Germany), sought to be of and for, if not necessarily by, the masses. Except in Poland and Hungary, where old-fashioned regimes held sway, every nation in Europe adopted programs for land redistribution and enacted some kind of social service legislation. This formed a dramatic contrast with the past, when all but a few European governments had been avowedly of, for, and by a small minority. Nor was this transformation confined to Europe, for similar movements emerged in Mexico, Peru, India, and China.

ECONOMIC CONSEQUENCES OF THE WAR

The fighting in Europe destroyed many of the communications lines and factories of the Continent, but most of this physical damage proved relatively easy to repair. By 1922 the production of materials like coal, iron, and steel, the output of manufactures, and railroad mileage were all higher than in 1912, and despite tariff barriers raised by the new states intra-European commerce had also staged an almost complete recovery. Many changes had, of course, taken place. Industries were turning to mass production and, where possible, were using machines in place of human labor. Partly as a result of this but even more as a result of political changes, the work day was growing shorter. The eight-hour day, which had once seemed an impossible dream, became a reality. But neither mass production nor changes in working conditions nor even changes in consumer interests, such as the general passion in western Europe and the United States for new houses and motor cars, can be attributed to the war. Insofar as economic changes are traceable to that conflict, they lie rather in the realm of finance, for the war had one clear result: It transferred the center of wealth from Europe to North America.

The European victors were left owing their former ally an aggregate of $10 billion; when the exchanges were freed in 1919, the British pound dropped by one-fifth in value as compared with the dollar, while the franc fell by 50 per cent. The effort made particularly by the French to wring reparations payments from Germany was due in part to a desire to recover lost ground. The Germans, when pressed, proved unable to pay. Inflation made the German mark worthless; it stood at 4.6 million to the dollar in August, 1923, and at 4.2 trillion to the dollar in November. An international committee, headed by Charles G. Dawes of the United States, recommended that a new financial system be adopted by the Germans and that reparations claimed by the Allies be scaled down, and this Dawes Plan was adopted in 1924. But the inflation wiped out savings, worked great hardship on the German middle classes, and helped to prepare the way for Adolf Hitler's seizure of power in 1933. And, to a lesser extent, financial disturbances worked hardships on the middle classes all over Europe and thus strengthened the tendency toward government of and for the masses.

Psychological Consequences of the War

If the war's economic consequences were narrower than contemporaries predicted, its psychological effects were profound and were quite different from what most people of the time foresaw. During the war, politicians and publicists spoke of the great days to come, when there would be no more wars, no more armaments, no more clashes between nations, and no more want. The actuality of the harsh compromises in the treaties, coupled with continued violence in eastern Europe, the Balkans, the Middle East, and Asia, mutual distrust among the victors, and a sharp recession following the immediate postwar boom, produced a widespread sense of disillusionment. Some felt that the peacemakers had not been sufficiently idealistic; others, that they had been impractical. Still others concluded that the outcome of the war had proved all governments incapable of acting in the interest of common men or had proved man's fate to be something altogether beyond man's own control. From these various moods emerged an increasingly strong pacifist movement; violent nihilist movements like that of the Nazis in Germany; an escapism that gave great popularity to esoteric poets, novelists, and painters; and a brooding fatalism that found reflection in such writings as those of Oswald Spengler and Søren Kierkegaard.

World War I had been modern civilization's most hideous experience. In some parts of Western Europe it had taken the life of one young man out of four, and, in the generations that matured in the 1920's and 1930's, few could understand for what reason it had been fought. The experience formed a trauma in the consciousness of most of the peoples who had taken part in it, and this fact is of cardinal importance for the understanding of the events that took place in the decades after it.

Appendixes

BY BRIGADIER GENERAL VINCENT J. ESPOSITO,
U.S.A. (RET.)

Appendix A. Chronology of the War

1870
July 19   Franco-Prussian War begins.
Sept. 2   French surrender at Sedan.
Oct. 27   French surrender at Metz.

1871
Jan. 18   William I is proclaimed German Emperor.
May 10   Treaty of Frankfurt; French lose Alsace and part of Lor-
                raine; vow war of revenge.

1878
July 13   Treaty of Berlin; Romania, Serbia, and Montenegro be-
                come independent, and Bulgaria partly independent;
                Russia acquires Bessarabia, Batumi, Kars, and Arda-
                han and Romania, Dobruja; Bosnia and Hercegovina
                are placed under Austrian administration.

1879
Oct. 7   Austro-German alliance is formed.

1881
June 18   Three Emperors' League (Germany, Austria-Hungary,
                Russia) is formed; lasts until 1887.

1882
May 20   Germany, Austria-Hungary, and Italy form Triple Alli-
                ance.

1883
Feb. 4   German colonial expansion begins with note to Great
                Britain on South West Africa.

1887
June 18   Reinsurance Treaty between Russia and Germany re-
                places Three Emperors' League; lasts until 1890.

1890
July 1   Great Britain cedes Helgoland to Germany.

1894
Jan. 4   Franco-Russian alliance is completed.
Aug. 1   Sino-Japanese War begins.

335

1895

Apr. 17   Treaty of Shimonoseki ends Sino-Japanese War after Chinese defeat.

May 8   Cession of Liaotung Peninsula to Japan is reversed in final Treaty of Shimonoseki as a result of intervention of the powers, particularly Germany, who arouses Japanese enmity.

1899

May 18   First Hague Conference opens; ends July 29.

Oct. 11   South African (Boer) War begins; there is an outbreak of German Anglophobia.

1900

June 12   German Reichstag passes bill to double fleet.

1902

Jan. 30   Anglo-Japanese alliance is formed.

May 31   South African War ends with Boer defeat.

Nov. 1   Italy and France secretly agree that the former will remain neutral if the latter goes to war with Germany as a result of a German attack on Russia.

1904

Feb. 8   Russo-Japanese War begins.

Apr. 8   Entente Cordiale is concluded by Great Britain and France.

1905

Schlieffen Plan is formulated for war against France.

Mar. 22   Emperor William II states at Bremen: "God has called us to civilize the world; we are the missionaries of human progress. . . . [We are] the salt of the earth."

Mar. 31   Visit of William II to Tangier precipitates Moroccan crisis.

June 6   German pressure forces removal of French foreign minister, Théophile Delcassé.

Sept. 5   Treaty of Portsmouth ends Russo-Japanese War.

1906

Jan. 16   Algeciras Conference on Morocco opens; ends Apr. 7 with an agreement favoring French position, which was supported by Great Britain.

1907

June 15   Second Hague Conference opens; ends Oct. 18.

Aug. 31   Anglo-Russian agreement completes Triple Entente.

1908
Oct. 5   Bulgaria becomes independent.
    6   Austria-Hungary proclaims annexation of Bosnia and Hercegovina. European crisis ensues; ends March, 1909.

1909
August   German Chancellor Theobald von Bethmann-Hollweg makes overtures to secure British neutrality in the event of a Continental war.
Oct. 24   Italy and Russia conclude a secret agreement on Balkans and other areas.

1911
July 1   German gunboat at Agadir provokes a new Moroccan crisis.
    15   Germany demands territorial compensation from France, including all of French Equatorial Africa and French pre-emptive rights to Belgian Congo.
    21   A speech by David Lloyd George in London serves as a warning to Germany.
Nov. 4   France cedes two strips of French Equatorial Africa to Germany in return for recognition of its protectorate in Morocco.

1912
March   Germany endeavors to obtain an unconditional pledge of neutrality from Great Britain during any war into which Germany "might be forced." British offer a naval holiday, but a new bill is published that increases the German Navy.
May–June   Italy occupies the Dodecanese.
Oct. 8   First Balkan War begins.

1913
May 30   Treaty of London ends First Balkan War; Turkey cedes territory.
June 1   Greece agrees by treaty to send troops to Serbia if the latter is attacked by Bulgaria.
    29   Second Balkan War begins; ends Aug. 10 with Treaty of Bucharest; Romania gains territory at expense of Bulgaria.
Aug. 7   Three-year military service bill is enacted in France.
Dec. 14   Gen. Otto Liman von Sanders arrives in Turkey as head of German military mission.

1914
June   28   Archduke Francis Ferdinand of Austria-Hungary and his
             wife are assassinated by a Serb at Sarajevo, Bosnia.
July   5   William II assures Austria-Hungary that he will support
             her and wage war against Russia and France if Russia
             aids Serbia.
        7   Austro-Hungarian Council of Ministers decides to send
             Serbia a 48-hour ultimatum.
       20   French President Raymond Poincaré and Premier René
             Viviani arrive in St. Petersburg; state visit ends July
             23.
       22   Germany warns Great Britain against outside interfer-
             ence between Austria-Hungary and Serbia.
       23   Austria-Hungary sends its ultimatum to Serbia.
       25   Conciliatory Serbian reply is rejected; Austria-Hungary
             breaks off relations with Serbia and orders partial mo-
             bilization.
       26   British propose a conference; proposal is rejected by Ger-
             many July 27.
       28   Austria-Hungary and Serbia are at war.
       29   Russia begins to mobilize.
       31   Russia orders general mobilization; Germany proclaims
             state of the danger of war; Austria-Hungary orders
             general mobilization.
Aug.   1   Germany mobilizes.
        2   Germany sends ultimatum to Belgium; secret treaty be-
             tween Germany and Turkey provides for subsequent
             entry of latter on side of Central Powers.
        3   Italy proclaims neutrality.
        4   Great Britain sends ultimatum to Germany.

DECLARATIONS OF WAR

1914
July   28   Austria-Hungary against Serbia.
Aug.   1   Germany against Russia.
        3   Germany against France.
        4   Great Britain against Germany at expiration of ultima-
             tum at midnight; Germany against Belgium.
        5   Montenegro against Austria-Hungary.
        6   Austria-Hungary against Russia; Serbia against Germany.
        9   Montenegro against Germany; Austria-Hungary against
             Montenegro.
       12   Great Britain against Austria-Hungary.
       13   France against Austria-Hungary.
       22   Austria-Hungary against Belgium (received Aug. 28).

Aug.	23	Japan against Germany.
	25	Japan against Austria-Hungary.
Nov.	1	Russia against Turkey.
	2	Serbia against Turkey.
	5	Great Britain against Turkey; France against Turkey.

1915

May	23	Italy against Austria-Hungary.
June	3	San Marino against Austria-Hungary.
Aug.	21	Italy against Turkey.
Oct.	14	Bulgaria against Serbia.
	15	Great Britain against Bulgaria; Montenegro against Bulgaria.
	16	France against Bulgaria; Serbia against Bulgaria.
	19	Italy against Bulgaria; Russia against Bulgaria.

1916

Mar.	9	Germany against Portugal.
	15	Austria-Hungary against Portugal.
Aug.	27	Romania against Austria-Hungary; Italy against Germany (to take effect Aug. 28).
	28	Germany against Romania.
	30	Turkey against Romania.
Sept.	1	Bulgaria against Romania.

1917

Apr.	6	United States against Germany.
	7	Cuba against Germany; Panama against Germany.
July	2	Greece against Germany, Austria-Hungary, Turkey, and Bulgaria.
	22	Siam against Germany and Austria-Hungary.
Aug.	4	Liberia against Germany.
	14	China against Germany and Austria-Hungary.
Oct.	26	Brazil against Germany.
Dec.	7	United States against Austria-Hungary.
	10	Panama against Austria-Hungary.
	16	Cuba against Austria-Hungary.

1918

Apr.	23	Guatemala against Germany.
May	8	Nicaragua against Germany and Austria-Hungary.
	23	Costa Rica against Germany.
July	12	Haiti against Germany.
	19	Honduras against Germany.

Breaking of Diplomatic Relations

1917

Feb.	3	United States with Germany.
Mar.	14	China with Germany.
Apr.	8	Austria-Hungary with the United States.
	10	Bulgaria with the United States.
	13	Bolivia with Germany.
	20	Turkey with the United States.
	27	Guatemala with Germany.
May	17	Honduras with Germany.
	19	Nicaragua with Germany.
Sept.	21	Costa Rica with Germany.
Oct.	6	Peru with Germany.
	7	Uruguay with Germany.
Dec.	7	Ecuador with Germany.

WESTERN FRONT

1914

Aug.	2	Germans invade Luxembourg.
	4	Germans invade Belgium.
	7	Germans enter Liége; French invade Alsace; British troops begin to land in France.
	8	Belgian Army falls back; limited French success is achieved in Alsace.
	9	French cavalry enters Belgium.
	10	French advance in Lorraine.
	20	Germans enter Brussels.
	21	Reverses force French from Alsace-Lorraine.
	22	French are defeated at Charleroi.
	23	Namur falls to Germans; Battle of Mons begins.
	24	British fall back from Mons; a general Allied retreat takes place.
	25	Gen. Joseph Joffre orders troops from the east to build up Sixth Army near Paris.
	26	Battle of Le Cateau; British are driven back.
	27	Lille and Mézières are occupied by the Germans.
	31	French Army falls back to line Aisne–Reims–Verdun.
Sept.	1	Germans take Soissons.
	2	Germans reach the Marne.
	3	French government moves to Bordeaux.
	5	Battle of the Marne begins.
	6	French Sixth Army attacks German flank from west in Battle of the Ourcq, with modest success.
	9	Marne battle ends; Germans begin retreat.
	14	First Battle of the Aisne begins (ends Sept. 28); this is the introduction of trench warfare.

Sept.	18	Stalemate on the Aisne; opponents begin series of attempts to outflank each other on the west, which develops into the Race for the Sea.
	23	Germans take Saint-Mihiel, forming salient.
Oct.	9	Germans take Antwerp.
	12	First Battle of Ypres begins (ends Nov. 11) as Germans try to break front; Allies hold.
	16	Battle of the Yser ends Race for the Sea; neither side succeeds in outflanking the other; this is beginning of the stabilized front.

1915

During the year the front remains essentially stabilized. There are local actions with few gains.

Jan.	8	Battle of Soissons begins (ends Jan. 15); French drive is repulsed.
Feb.	3	German attacks in Champagne are repulsed.
Mar.	10	Battle of Neuve-Chapelle; British achieve limited success in three-day battle.
	14	Battle of Saint-Éloi begins (ends Mar. 15); initial German gains are erased by British counterattacks.
Apr.	22	Second Battle of Ypres begins (ends May 24–25); costly and futile attacks are made by both sides; Germans introduce poison gas in war.
May	9	Second Battle of Artois begins (ends June 18); French make small gains at heavy cost.
	15	Battle of Festubert begins (ends May 25); Allies obtain limited successes.
June	20	German offensive in the Argonne begins (ends July 14); attempt to break French line fails.
Sept.	25	Allied offensives begin at Loos and in Champagne (end Nov. 6); good initial successes are obtained; fighting is violent, however, and final gains are limited.

1916

During the year only two major engagements take place, at Verdun and on the Somme; 38 air raids, mostly by zeppelins, are made over England.

Feb.	21	Battle of Verdun begins; Germans attack to deplete limited French manpower.
	25	Germans advance 3 miles at Verdun; capture Fort Douaumont.
Mar.	16	Five German attacks are repulsed at Verdun.
June	7	Germans take Fort de Vaux at Verdun.
July	1	Franco-British offensive begins Battle of the Somme.
	3	Allies obtain local successes on Somme.
	12	Battle of the Somme continues; British take Mametz Wood.

July	14	British capture Trônes Wood; first phase of Battle of the Somme ends.
	17	British capture German second Somme defense line.
Sept.	15	British introduce tanks in war on the Somme.
Oct.	5	British and French have limited successes on the Somme.
	13	40 Allied bombers raid factory in Oberndorf.
Nov.	13	Battle of the Ancre (part of Somme battle) begins (ends Nov. 18); British achieve success.
	18	Battle of the Somme ends; there are 650,000 German, 420,000 British, and 195,000 French casualties.
Dec.	12	Gen. Robert Georges Nivelle succeeds Joffre in command of the French.
	15	Great French attacks at Verdun make important gains.
	18	Battle of Verdun ends; there are 550,000 French and 450,000 German casualties.

1917

February		The Allies, now possessing superior manpower, plan offensive in Noyon salient.
Feb.	23	Apprised of coming offensive, Germans begin withdrawal from salient to Hindenburg Line.
Mar.	18	Following up the German withdrawal, the British occupy Péronne and the French, Noyon.
Apr.	5	Germans complete withdrawal.
	6	United States enters war.
	9	Battle of Arras begins (ends May 3); Canadians capture Vimy Ridge.
	16	Second Battle of the Aisne (ends May 9); Nivelle hurls French against impregnable defenses with staggering losses; French troops mutiny.
May	3	British break Quéant position; move on Cambrai.
	4	French take Craonne and Chemin des Dames on the Aisne.
	15	Gen. Henri Philippe Pétain replaces Nivelle in command of French.
June	7	Battle of Messines begins (ends June 8); British capture ridge.
	25	First American fighting troops land in France.
July	31	Third Battle of Ypres begins; British continue attacks until Nov. 6 to occupy Germans while French recuperate from Aisne debacle; there are tremendous casualties but meager successes.
Aug.	20	French make limited gains near Verdun.
Nov.	6	Canadians capture Passchendaele Ridge; Third Battle of Ypres ends.

Nov. 9   Allies form Supreme War Council.

20   Battle of Cambrai begins (ends Dec. 3); British first massed tank attack surprises Germans and breaks line; lack of reserves limits British success.

30   Germans counterattack at Cambrai (attack ends Dec. 1).

Dec. 4   British withdraw at Cambrai, losing much ground (withdrawal ends Dec. 7).

1918

Collapse of Russia permits transfer of German troops to west, giving the Germans numerical superiority; they plan supreme effort to win in France before United States can intervene.

Mar. 21   Somme offensive begins; the first German drive to split French and British, it achieves good initial gains.

22   German breakthrough at Saint-Quentin on Somme forces British retreat.

23   Germans reach Somme River; Big Bertha begins harassing firing on Paris from 74 miles away.

28   Germans are held up in north on Somme but advance in south.

Apr. 4   German Somme offensive runs down after gain of 30 miles for lack of reserves and supplies; Germans are left in salient.

9   Lys offensive begins; second German drive, designed to shatter British, wins 10 miles; it is stopped Apr. 29 by lack of reserves and Allied counterattacks, and Germans are left in salient.

14   Gen. Ferdinand Foch is appointed supreme Allied commander.

May 27   Aisne offensive (third German drive), designed to break French, reaches Marne in four days.

28   Battle of Cantigny; in first independent American operation, 1st Division captures Cantigny.

June 2   French hold on the Marne; Americans stop German crossings of the river at Château-Thierry.

6   Aisne offensive ends; Germans are left in salient.

9   Noyon–Montidier offensive begins; the fourth German drive, it is designed to threaten Paris; French hold with new defensive system, and drive ends June 13.

July 15   Champagne–Marne offensive (Second Battle of the Marne) begins (ends July 17); the last German drive, it is stopped by the French.

18   Foch begins to reduce German salients prior to launching general attack; Aisne–Marne offensive against

		Marne salient begins; eight American divisions participate.
July	27	Germans in Marne salient are in general retreat.
Aug.	6	Allies reach the Vesle and eliminate the Marne salient.
	8	British and French begin attacks to reduce Amiens salient.
	18	French advance between Oise and Aisne rivers in Amiens salient.
	21	British achieve success in Battle of Bapaume in Amiens salient (battle ends Aug. 31); German troops begin to break.
Sept.	3	Germans retreat to Hindenburg Line; the Amiens salient is reduced.
	6	Germans complete withdrawal from Lys salient.
	12	Newly created American First Army, aided by French, attacks Saint-Mihiel salient and gains five miles; Battle of Épehy, on Cambrai front, begins (ends Sept. 18); British obtain successes.
	13	Germans withdraw from Saint-Mihiel salient under American and French pressure.
	26	Foch's final general offensive begins; Americans and French begin Meuse-Argonne offensive and advance several miles; 1.2 million Americans participate.
	27	British start Second Battle of Cambrai and Battle of Saint-Quentin, piercing Hindenburg Line.
	28	Battle of Flanders begins with Anglo-Belgian success on 23-mile front.
Oct.	3	In the Meuse–Argonne offensive, there is stiff American fighting in the Argonne Forest.
	5	Second Battle of Cambrai and Battle of Saint-Quentin end; Germans fall back.
	8	A great British-French-American advance on Saint-Quentin–Cambrai front progresses three miles.
	9	Advance continues; British take Cambrai.
	10	British capture Le Cateau.
	14	Allies start Flanders offensive and advance five miles.
	17	Battle of the Selle; British-American attack on nine-mile front captures part of Selle position.
	19	Belgians occupy Zeebrugge and attack Brugge.
	25	Stiff American fighting occurs north of Verdun in Meuse–Argonne offensive.
	27	Gen. Erich F. W. Ludendorff, German supreme commander, resigns.
Nov.	3	Americans and French clear Argonne Forest and move into open country; French reach the Aisne.

Nov. 4   British-French offensive takes Oise–Sambre Canal.
      6   Germans are in general retreat; Americans and French
           reach river at Sedan; German armistice delegates leave
           Berlin for Western Front.
     11   Armistice is signed at 5 A.M.; firing stops at 11 A.M.;
           almost 2 million Americans are now in France.
     18   Belgians re-enter Brussels.
Dec. 1   British and American troops cross German frontier.
      8   Americans enter their occupation zone at Koblenz.
      9   French enter their occupation zone at Mainz.
     12   British enter their occupation zone at Cologne.

EASTERN FRONT

1914
Aug. 10   Austrians invade southern Russian Poland and aim for
           Lublin.
     17   Russian First Army invades East Prussia from the east;
           Germans attack it unsuccessfully in Battle of Stallu-
           pönen.
     18   Russians invade Galicia from the east.
     20   In East Prussia, Germans fall back in Battle of Gum-
           binnen; Russian Second Army moves into East Prus-
           sia from south to pinch off Germans; Germans move
           south to meet Second Army.
     23   Gen. Paul von Hindenburg and Maj. Gen. Erich F. W.
           Ludendorff take command in East Prussia; in Galicia,
           Russians are driven back in Battle of Kraśnik (battle
           ends Aug. 25).
     24   In East Prussia, Russian Second Army is repulsed in
           Battle of Frankenau.
     26   In Galicia, Austrians almost encircle Russians in Battle
           of Komarov but retire Sept. 1. South of Komarov,
           Austrians and Russians clash in Battle of the Gnila
           Lipa (battle ends Aug. 30); Austrians are put to rout;
           in East Prussia, Battle of Tannenberg begins.
     29   Battle of Tannenberg ends; Russian Second Army is
           surrounded and decimated.
Sept. 3   In Galicia, Russians occupy Lemberg.
     10   Germans drive Russian First Army from East Prussia
           back into Poland, beginning three-day First Battle of
           the Masurian Lakes.
     11   Austrians are severely beaten in Battle of Rawa Ruska in
           Galicia and withdraw to Carpathian Mountains 100
           miles to rear; Russians follow.
     27   Russians push toward Carpathians.

Sept.	28	German Ninth Army arrives in Galicia to bolster sagging Austrians; Austro-German advance begins.
Oct.	6	Russians fall back in Poland and Galicia.
	12	Germans advance to within 12 miles of Warsaw.
	16	Austrians reach line of San River.
	17	Russian reinforcements stop Germans at Warsaw.
	21	Germans retreat from Warsaw, and Austrians from the San.
Nov.	1	Germans and Austrians are back on their starting line.
	2	Russians drive Germans from Poland and re-enter East Prussia.
	4	German Ninth Army begins to move north from Galicia to attack Russian flank; in Galicia, Austrians are defeated at Jaroslau.
	10	Russians continue advance in East Prussia.
	11	German Ninth Army attacks Russian flank, beginning Battle of Łódź.
	14	Germans begin drive against Russians in East Prussia; Russians fall back.
	16	Russian line is pierced in Battle of Łódź; Russians fall back.
	21	Russian reinforcements trap Germans at Łódź.
	24	Germans extricate themselves from Łódź trap and draw back flank; Battle of Łódź ends.
Dec.	6	Russians fall back 30 miles from Łódź; Germans follow.
	25	All quiet on the Eastern Front.

1915
Jan.	4	Russians begin advance into Bucovina.
	17	Russians hold most of Bucovina.
	31	Germans attack Russians at Bolimów to divert attention from major offensive being prepared in north; tear gas is used for first time.
Feb.	7	Winter Battle of Masuria begins (ends Feb. 21); Germans encircle Russian Tenth Army near Nieman River and capture 100,000 prisoners; Austrians launch attack in Carpathians to assist German attack, but it fails.
	18	Austrians retake Czernowitz.
	28	Germans begin withdrawal from northern Poland.
Mar.	22	Przemyśl, under siege since Nov. 12, 1914, surrenders to the Russians.
Apr.	28	Field Marshal August von Mackensen's German Eleventh Army arrives on Carpathian front to save Austrian Army, threatened with destruction by the Russians.

May	2	Mackensen and Austrians launch huge offensive in Carpathians.
	4	Mackensen breaks Russian line between Gorlice and Tarnów; Russians lose 140,000 prisoners and 100 guns, and begin hasty retreat.
	11	Russians reach San River, 80 miles to rear.
	17	Russians are forced from the San and begin a 20-mile retreat.
June	2	Germans capture Przemyśl.
	12	Russian retreat continues; Germans follow it up.
	22	Austrians recapture Lemberg and Galicia.
July	16	Battle of Krasnotav begins (ends July 18); Russians are defeated.
	30	Germans occupy Lublin.
	31	Germans occupy Kholm.
Aug.	4–5	Germans enter Warsaw; Russians prepare to evacuate Riga.
	7	Germans are repulsed near Riga.
	25	Germans take Brest-Litovsk.
Sept.	5	Czar Nicholas II takes command of Russian armies.
	16	Germans take Pinsk.
	30	Great Russian withdrawal of almost 300 miles ends; Germans and Austrians, worn down, halt.
Oct.	3	Great battle for Dvinsk begins.
	10	German attack on Dvinsk fails.
Nov.	11	Russians drive Germans back from Riga.
1916		
Feb.	2	Austrians and Germans fight in Bucovina.
Mar.	18	Russians start strong attack at Lake Naroch and make good initial gains against Germans.
	26	Lake Naroch offensive bogs down in bad weather.
	30	Germans regain lost ground at Lake Naroch.
June	4	In an offensive led by Gen. Aleksei Brusilov, Russians launch massive surprise attack south of Pripet Marshes.
	6	Russians capture Lutsk.
	10	Russians pierce Austrian front to a depth of 50 miles.
	17	Russians capture Czernowitz.
	30	Russians win great victories at both ends of line; there are 700,000 Austro-German casualties.
July	4	A Russian attack in the north makes gains and is then halted by Germans; both sides rush to concentrate their forces on Southern Front; 15 German and 8 Austrian divisions are brought from other fronts to stop Brusilov offensive.

July	28	A series of bloody battles begins.
August		There are persistent attacks by both sides, with only small gains.
Sept.	20	Stiff opposition and heavy losses in men and materials halt Brusilov offensive.
Oct.	22	Russians sustain reverses in Galicia.

1917

Jan.	5	Russian offensive begins near Riga.
Feb.	1	Russian line is broken near Halicz.
	11	Germans are driven back near Halicz.
Mar.	12	Russian Revolution begins.
	15	Russian government is overthrown; Czar abdicates.
May	4	Russians attack in Romania; disorganization of Russian armies begins.
July	1	Brusilov begins offensive in Galicia.
	24	Counterattacking Germans drive Russians back in Bucovina.
Aug.	3	Germans take Czernowitz.
Sept.	3	Russians are driven from Riga.
Nov.	6–7	Bolsheviks seize power in Petrograd.
	8	Congress of Soviets calls for peace.
Dec.	2	Hostilities are suspended on Eastern Front.
	22	Peace negotiations are opened at Brest-Litovsk.

1918

Feb.	10	Leon Trotsky, dissatisfied with German terms, unilaterally declares war at an end.
	18	Germans renew fighting and drive eastward.
Mar.	3	Bolsheviks sign peace treaty at Brest-Litovsk.

ITALIAN FRONT

1915

Apr.	26	Secret Treaty of London is signed by Italy, France, Great Britain, and Russia; Italy is to enter war on Allied side in return for territorial gains in the Tirol, on the Adriatic coast, and elsewhere.
May	23	Italy enters the war; makes limited attacks up to June 16 to gain positions for offensive.
June	23	First Battle of the Isonzo begins (ends July 7); this is first of 11 battles launched by Italians against Austrians on the Isonzo River; attacks are made against Carso Plateau and Gorizia with small gains.
July	18	Second Battle of the Isonzo begins (ends Aug. 3); Italian attacks against the Carso make only small gains.

Oct. 18   Third Battle of the Isonzo begins (ends Nov. 3); attacks on the Carso and to outflank Gorizia make small gains.

Nov. 10   Fourth Battle of the Isonzo begins (ends Dec. 2); attacks on both sides of Gorizia fail; in these four Isonzo battles the Italians lose 275,000 men, and the Austrians 165,000.

1916

Mar. 9   Fifth Battle of the Isonzo begins (ends Mar. 17); attack is stopped by bad weather; there are no gains.

May 15   Asiago offensive begins (ends June 17); Austrians launch strong attack in the Trentino and capture Asiago, but end bitter fighting to send troops to meet Brusilov offensive on Russian front.

Aug. 6   Sixth Battle of the Isonzo begins (ends Aug. 17); Italians advance four miles and capture Gorizia and bridgehead over the Isonzo beyond the town.

Sept. 14   Seventh Battle of the Isonzo begins (ends Sept. 17); an attempt to enlarge the bridgehead makes negligible gains.

Oct. 10   Eighth Battle of the Isonzo begins (ends Oct. 12); a second attempt to enlarge the bridgehead also makes negligible gains.

Nov. 1   Ninth Battle of the Isonzo begins (ends Nov. 4); a third attempt is made to enlarge bridgehead; a small hold is gained on the Carso.

1917

May 12   Tenth Battle of the Isonzo begins (ends June 8); Italians widen hold on the Carso and make small gains beyond Plava.

Aug. 19   Eleventh Battle of the Isonzo begins (ends Sept. 12); Italians break Austrian position beyond Plava; Austrians retreat five miles.

Oct. 24   Battle of Caporetto begins (ends Nov. 12); Germans join Austrians on Isonzo front and launch strong surprise attack; Italians are routed and retreat 70 miles to Piave River; they lose 320,000 men.

Dec. 5   Austro-German offensive on Asiago Plateau makes limited gains.

24   Italians regain several positions on Asiago front.

1918

Jan. 29   Italians pierce enemy line near Asiago.

June 15   Battle of the Piave begins (ends June 24); a great Austrian attack across the Piave is beaten back by the Italians.

Oct. 24   Battle of Vittorio Veneto begins (ends Nov. 4); Italians
              shatter Austrian lines; Austrians flee, losing 500,000
              prisoners.
Nov. 3   Italians take Trento; armistice is signed for Italian front,
              effective Nov. 4.

COLONIAL AND JAPANESE CAMPAIGNS

1914

              There are British and German border raids in East
              Africa through the end of the year.
Aug. 7   British and French invade German Togoland.
      20–27   British and French invade German Cameroons.
      23   Tsingtao is bombarded by Japanese.
      26   Togoland is captured by British and French.
      29   New Zealand expedition captures Western Samoa.
September   Japanese occupy German islands north of the equator.
Sept. 17   Australians complete capture of northeastern New
              Guinea.
      19   Union of South Africa forces capture Lüderitz in Ger-
              man Southwest Africa.
      27   French and British amphibious force captures Duala in
              Cameroons.
Oct. 9   Rebellion breaks out in Union of South Africa.
Nov. 4   British fail in attempt to capture Tanga in German East
              Africa.
      7   Tsingtao is captured by Japanese.

1915

              British and German border raids occur all year in East
              Africa.
Feb. 3   Rebellion in South Africa is quelled.
May   12   Union of South Africa forces capture Windhoek in Ger-
              man Southwest Africa.
July 9   Germans in German Southwest Africa, cut off, sur-
              render.

1916
Jan. 1   Yaoundé, principal German base in the Cameroons, is
              captured by British.
Feb. 18   Last Germans in Cameroons surrender.
Mar. 5   Combined British-Belgian-Portuguese invasion of Ger-
              man East Africa begins.
July   British occupy northern half of German East Africa.
Sept. 3   Dar es Salaam, key port in German East Africa, is cap-
              tured by British.

1917
Nov. 28 Allies capture half of German forces in East Africa.
Dec. 1 Allies occupy all of German East Africa.

1918
Nov. 25 Last members of German East Africa garrison surrender to British in Northern Rhodesia after 1,600-mile chase.

TURKISH CAMPAIGNS

Dardanelles

1914
Nov. 3 British Navy bombards outer Dardanelles forts.

1915
Feb. 19 British begin naval attack to force straits.
Mar. 18 Naval attack fails, and fleet withdraws.
Apr. 25 British troops land on Gallipoli Peninsula; gain beachheads at Anzac Cove and Cape Helles.
May 6 Helles force attacks to enlarge beachhead (attack ends May 8); no gains are made.
June 4 Second Helles force attacks with minor success.
July 12 Third Helles attack begins; ends July 13 with little success; the total gain in all attacks is three miles.
Aug. 6 General British attack begins; troops land at Suvla Bay.
9 British are pinned down in all sectors.
15 A renewed British attack fails.
21 Another attack fails.
Dec. 20 British troops are evacuated from Anzac and Suvla Bay.

1916
Jan. 9 British troops are evacuated from Helles; campaign ends in complete failure.

Mesopotamia

1914
Nov. 7 British land in Mesopotamia opposite Abadan.
22 British occupy Basra.
Dec. 9 British move north to Al Qurna.

1915
Apr. 12 Turks attack British at Basra; attack fails, and they flee Apr. 14.
May 16 British occupy Ahwaz to protect oil pipeline.
June 3 British capture 'Amara on the Tigris.
July 25 British capture An Nasiriya on the Euphrates.
Sept. 22 British advance on Kut begins.
28 British rout Turks at Sannaiyat and enter Kut.

Oct.	5	British reach Al 'Aziziya.
Nov.	11	British start north for Baghdad.
	22	British attack Turks at Ctesiphon; capture front line.
	25	Turks hold firm; British withdraw southward.
Dec.	3	British halt retreat at Kut.
	7	Turks surround British in Kut.

1916

Jan.	21	First British attempt to relieve Kut fails.
Mar.	8	Second British attempt is beaten back.
Apr.	22	Third British attempt fails.
	29	British garrison at Kut surrenders.
Dec.	13	British advance toward Kut.

1917

Feb.	24	British force Turkish retreat; reoccupy Kut Feb. 25.
Mar.	5	British advance toward Baghdad.
	11	Turks evacuate Baghdad; British occupy city.
Sept.	29	British occupy Ramadi on the Euphrates.
Dec.	9	Turks are driven from Khanaqin.

1918

Mar.	9	British capture Hit.
Oct.	23	British begin advance to Mosul.
	30	Turks are surrounded and captured at Qal' a Sharqat; armistice is declared, effective Oct. 31.

Egypt and Palestine

1914

| Dec. | 18 | British proclaim protectorate over Egypt. |

1915

| February | | Turkish attempts to capture Suez Canal are repulsed. |

1916

June	5	Sherif Husein of Mecca proclaims Arab revolt against Turks.
Aug.	4–5	Turks are badly beaten at El Rumana; British start advance to Palestine border.
Dec.	21	British advance to El Arish.

1917

January		British arrive at Palestine border.
Mar.	26	First Battle of Gaza begins (ends Mar. 27); British attack Turks but are repulsed.
Apr.	17	Second Battle of Gaza begins (ends Apr. 19); British attacks are again repulsed.

Oct.	31	Third Battle of Gaza begins (ends Nov. 7); Turks are outflanked and forced to withdraw.
Nov.	13	Battle of Junction Station begins (ends Nov. 14); Turks are defeated.
Dec.	9	British capture Jerusalem.

1918

April		Five British divisions are transferred to Western Front and are replaced by Indian troops.
Sept.	19	Battle of Megiddo takes place; Turks are put to flight.
Oct.	1	British take Damascus.
	26	British take Aleppo.
	30	Armistice is declared, effective Oct. 31.

Caucasus

1914

Dec.	29	Turks, advancing on Kars, are badly defeated by Russians near Sarikamiş in battle ending Jan. 2, 1915.

1915

Russians push back Turks north of Lake Van.

1916

Jan.	17	Russian offensive on Lake Van–Black Sea front begins.
Feb.	12–16	Erzurum, Turkey, falls to Russians.
Apr.	17	Russians capture Trebizond (Trabzon).
July	25	Russians capture Erzincan; advance bogs down; front is stabilized for rest of the year.

1917

Mar.	12	Russian Revolution begins; Caucasus troops remain loyal.
April		Supplies to Caucasus army are cut off.
November		Troops begin to abandon front and return to Russia.

1918

Feb.	18	Turks begin advance to Baku oilfields.
	24	Turks reoccupy Trebizond.
Mar.	12	Turks reoccupy Erzurum.
Apr.	15	Turks reach Batumi.
	27	Turks capture Kars.
May–June		Armenians and Georgians oppose Turkish advance; Germans and Turks clash at Tbilisi.
Aug.	4	British detachment reaches Baku.
Sept.	14	Turks force British to evacuate Baku.
Oct.	30	Armistice is declared, effective Oct. 31.

BALKAN CAMPAIGNS

1914

July	29	Austrians bombard Belgrade; Serbs evacuate city.
Aug.	7	Serbs enter Bosnia.
	12	Austrians cross Drina River in first invasion of Serbia.
	16	Battle of the Jadar begins (ends Aug. 19); Austrians are defeated.
	20	Austrians retreat back across border.
Sept.	8	Second Austrian invasion begins; it makes little progress.
	16	Invasion is halted; Austrians retain bridgeheads.
	23	Serbs and Montenegrins approach Sarajevo.
Oct.	4	Advance is turned back in Sarajevo area.
Nov.	5	Albanian invasion of Montenegro is checked; Austrians begin third invasion of Serbia.
	11	Serbs are forced back from borders.
	15	Austrians capture Valjevo.
	29	Serbs evacuate Belgrade; Austrians occupy city Dec. 2.
Dec.	3	Serbian armies counterattack all along front.
	8	Austrians are defeated in Battle of the Rudnik Ridges.
	9	Austrians begin retreat.
	15	Austrians are driven from Serbia; invasion ends.

1915

Feb.	2	Montenegrins repulse Austrians in Hercegovina.
Aug.	16	Austrian attack on Montenegrin border is repulsed.
Sept.	6	Secret alliance is concluded by Bulgaria, Germany, and Austria-Hungary.
	22	Treaty whereby Turkey cedes territory to Bulgaria is ratified.
Oct.	1	Austro-German forces concentrate on Serbian border.
	3	Bulgarians mass on Serbian border; Anglo-French forces begin to land at Salonika, Greece.
	7	Austrians and Germans invade Serbia.
	9	Austrians occupy Belgrade.
	11	Bulgarians invade Serbia.
	14	Serbs are overwhelmed on all fronts.
	30	Allied Salonika force enters Serbia.
Nov.	5	Bulgarians capture Niš.
Dec.	2	Serbs withdraw from Bitolj; it is occupied by Bulgarians Dec. 5.
	9	Allied Salonika force retreats from Serbia.
	15	Remnants of Serbian Army begin to reach Albanian coast.

1916

Jan.	15	First Serbian troops are evacuated to Corfu; evacuation is completed Feb. 10.
	25	Montenegro accepts Austrian terms.
July	2	Skirmishes occur on Salonikan front.
	25	Serbs arrive at Salonika from Corfu.
Aug.	17	Secret Treaty of Bucharest, whereby Romania is to receive territory in exchange for attack on Austria-Hungary, is signed by Romania and Allies; Central Powers' offensive against Salonika is halted.
	27	Romania joins Allies; invades Transylvania Aug. 28.
Sept.	1	Field Marshal August von Mackensen's Danube Army crosses Romanian border.
	10	Allied Salonika offensive begins (ends Nov. 19); limited gains include capture of Bitolj.
	16	Mackensen's advance threatens Constanţa railroad.
	20	Russo-Romanian army halts Mackensen.
Oct.	7	Romanian advance in Transylvania is turned back.
	20	Mackensen resumes offensive in Dobruja.
	23	Mackensen captures key port of Constanţa.
	25	Mackensen captures Cernavodă and begins move westward to Svishtov.
Nov.	10	Romanians are ejected from Transylvania; Gen. Erich von Falkenhayn follows into Romania.
	23	Mackensen crosses the Danube and heads for Bucharest.
Dec.	1	Romanian counterattack fails; Mackensen and Falkenhayn drive for Bucharest.
	6	Bucharest and Ploeşti oilfields are captured; Russo-Romanian armies are put to flight.

1917

Jan.	7	Germans suspend operations against Romania.
May		Allied Salonika offensive is stalled; gains are limited.
June	12	Pro-German King Constantine I of Greece abdicates.
	27	Pro-Allied Eleutherios Venizelos resumes premiership.
July	2	Greece joins Allies.
Dec.	9	Romania signs armistice.

1918

Apr.	15	Greeks cross Struma River; occupy towns in Serrai area.
May	7	Treaty of Bucharest is signed by Romania and Central Powers; Dobruja is ceded to Bulgaria.
Sept.	1	British advance up Vardar Valley.
	14	French and Serbs advance in Serbia.
	17	Allied advance gains 20 miles.
	19	Allies cross the Vardar River; Bulgarians are in flight.

Sept.	26	British take Strumica; Serbs take Veles.
	29	Bulgaria signs armistice and surrenders.
Nov.	1	Serbs enter and occupy Belgrade.
	3	Austrians accept truce terms.

NAVAL OPERATIONS

1914

Aug.	2	Germans bombard Liepaja, Latvia.
	24	Allied warships bombard Kotor on the Adriatic.
	28	Battle takes place in Bight of Helgoland.
Oct.	29	Turkish warships raid Odessa, Sevastopol, Feodosiya, and Novorossisk.
Nov.	1	British squadron is defeated off Coronel, Chile.
	2	British declare North Sea a war zone; it is mined.
	3	German cruisers bombard Yarmouth and Lowestoft; British bombard outer Dardanelles forts.
	18	Russo-Turkish engagement occurs in Black Sea.
Dec.	8	Vice Adm. Maximilian von Spee's German squadron is destroyed in Battle of the Falkland Islands.
	16	German cruisers bombard Scarborough, Hartlepool, and Whitby, England.

1915

Jan.	24	Naval battle takes place in North Sea.
Feb.	4	Germans declare war zone around Great Britain, effective Feb. 18.
	10	United States protests German war zone.
	19	British bombard outer Dardanelles forts.
	25	Bombardment of Dardanelles forts is renewed.
Mar.	1	Allies establish undeclared blockade of Central Powers.
	4	Great naval attack on Dardanelles begins.
	18	Dardanelles attack fails; three British and French warships are sunk.
May	13	First United States note to Germany protests sinking of *Lusitania* on May 7 with loss of 128 American lives.
Aug.	16	Russo-German action occurs in Gulf of Riga.
	20	Russians defeat German landing operations on Gulf of Riga.
	21	Germans evacuate Gulf of Riga.
	23	Allied fleet bombards Zeebrugge.
Sept.	6	Allied fleet bombards Oostende.
Oct.	5	German government promises to avoid attacking passenger vessels.
	21	British bombard Bulgarian coast; United States protests undeclared Allied blockade.

1916

Jan.	18	Bulgarian coast is bombarded by Allies.
Feb.	6	Austro-Italian action occurs in Adriatic.
Mar.	25	British destroyers and seaplanes raid zeppelin sheds in Schleswig.
	31	British warship bombards Smyrna.
Apr.	18	United States demands assurances that Germans will not sink ships without warning.
	20	German auxiliary cruiser and submarine attempt to land arms in Ireland; cruiser is sunk.
	25	German squadron and zeppelins raid Lowestoft and Yarmouth.
May	4	Germany replies to United States that it has ordered submarine commanders to suspend operations against merchant shipping.
	31	Battle of Jutland begins between major British and German forces; ends June 1 in drawn battle.
Oct.	26	German destroyer attack is made in English Channel.
Nov.	4	Russian Fleet bombards Constanţa, Romania.
	10	Germans shell Baltic port near Tallinn; six to nine destroyers are sunk by Russians.
	26	German naval raid is made on Lowestoft.

1917

Jan.	23	German destroyers engage light British force off Netherlands.
	31	Germany announces resumption of unrestricted submarine warfare, effective Feb. 1.
Feb.	25	German destroyers bombard Broadstairs and Margate, England.
Apr.	20	Six German destroyers raid Dover; three are sunk.
	26	German naval raid is made on Ramsgate, England.
May	10	Eleven German destroyers sally from Zeebrugge, but are forced back by British.
	12	British air and naval bombardment is made on Zeebrugge.
Oct.	17	Two British destroyers and nine escorted ships are sunk off Shetland Islands by two German raiders.
Nov.	17	Light cruiser fight occurs off Helgoland.

1918

Apr.	22–23	British naval raids are made on Zeebrugge and Oostende, blocking Brugge Canal and Oostende harbor.
May	9–10	British again raid Oostende.
July	7	British naval air forces bombard Constantinople.
	19	United States cruiser is sunk by torpedo off Fire Island, N.Y.

Nov. 3   German sailors begin to mutiny.
      21   German High Seas Fleet surrenders to British.

1919
June 21   German crews sink most of the German fleet at Scapa
           Flow.

Peace Negotiations

1916
Feb. 22   Col. Edward M. House, President Woodrow Wilson's
           representative, and British Foreign Secretary Sir Ed-
           ward Grey initial agreement on peace terms (never
           effected).
Dec. 12   Germany calls for peace negotiations.
      18   President Wilson sends note to all belligerents, asking
           them to inform him confidentially of terms they
           would accept.
      26   In reply, Central Powers tell Wilson that any discussion
           should be held among belligerents.

1917
Jan. 10   Allies, in notes to Wilson, offer relatively mild terms.
      22   President Wilson calls on both sides to accept "a peace
           without victory."
February– Prince Sixte of Bourbon undertakes inconclusive peace
  May   talks with Austro-Hungarian government.
July 19   German Reichstag adopts peace resolution.
Aug. 1   Pope Benedict XV appeals to all belligerents to accept
           compromise peace.
      27   President Wilson stresses moral objections to negotia-
           tions with aggressive governments.
September Germans refuse to give pope guarantee on restoration of
           Belgium; negotiations lapse.
Dec. 3   German-Russian armistice negotiations open at Brest-
           Litovsk.

1918
Jan. 5   British Prime Minister David Lloyd George says Allies
           are fighting for just and lasting peace.
      8   President Wilson presents Fourteen Points.
Feb. 9   Central Powers and Ukraine sign peace treaty at Brest-
           Litovsk.
      18   German-Russian armistice is terminated after Leon
           Trotsky refuses to sign peace treaty and unilaterally
           proclaims peace.
Mar. 3   Bolsheviks sign Treaty of Brest-Litovsk, ceding much
           Russian territory, and agree to evacuate Finland.

Aug. 27   Russia signs treaty in Berlin, renouncing claims to Estonia and Livonia.

Sept. 14   Austria-Hungary sends note to belligerents, requesting exchange of views; it is rejected.

29   Bulgaria signs armistice; Gen. Erich F. W. Ludendorff asks that armistice be arranged on Western Front without delay.

Oct. 4   Austria-Hungary sends note to United States, requesting armistice on basis of Fourteen Points (including autonomy for peoples of empire); Germany, in similar note, also accepts Fourteen Points.

7   Council of Regency in Warsaw proclaims Poland an independent state.

8   President Wilson, replying to German note, questions whether it speaks merely for authorities that had thus far conducted the war.

12   German note states that it speaks for government and people; in reply, President Wilson sets four conditions for armistice.

14   Turks appeal for armistice.

18   United States informs Austria-Hungary that autonomy is no longer a sufficient basis for peace.

19   Serbs, Croats, and Slovenes assert sovereignty over South Slav portions of Dual Monarchy.

20   German note makes further concessions.

23   President Wilson agrees to take up question of German armistice with Allies.

27   Austria-Hungary offers to accept armistice on almost any terms; Germany advises United States that it awaits armistice proposals.

28   Czechs remove imperial officials in Prague.

30   Turks sign armistice, effective Oct. 31.

Nov. 1   Emperor Charles I releases Hungarians from vows of fealty.

3   Austrians sign armistice at Villa Giusti, effective Nov. 4.

5   German government receives President Wilson's fourth note, stating that Allies are prepared to receive German delegates.

9   Chancellor Prince Max of Baden announces that William II and his heirs have renounced German throne; Germany accepts Allies' armistice terms, agreeing to cease hostilities and to evacuate France, Alsace-Lorraine, Belgium, and Luxembourg in 14 days from signature of armistice, and left bank of Rhine and bridgeheads at Mainz, Koblenz, and Cologne in 31 days.

11   Germans sign armistice at Compiègne.

1919

Jan.	18	Peace conference opens in Paris.
Feb.	14	Draft Covenant of League of Nations is completed; President Wilson, chief United States delegate, returns to United States to secure support.
Mar.	4	Thirty-eight United States senators find Covenant unacceptable.
	14	President Wilson returns to Paris and begins work to secure revision of Covenant.
Apr.	24	Italian Premier Vittorio Orlando leaves conference over Fiume issue.
May	6	Peace conference delegates approve treaty providing for German cessions of territory (Alsace-Lorraine to France, Polish Corridor to Poland, plebiscites elsewhere) and reparations, creation of mandates from former German colonies, occupation of Rhineland, and limitations on German Army.
	7	German delegates receive peace terms.
	29	Germans present commentary on treaty; proposed changes are rejected by Allies.
June	28	Allied and German delegates sign Treaty of Versailles; United States, Great Britain, and France sign treaty of guaranty.
Sept.	10	Allied and Austrian delegates sign Treaty of Saint-Germain-en-Laye; Austria relinquishes claims to territory to be transferred to Italy, Yugoslavia, Czechoslovakia, Romania, and Poland.
Nov.	19	Treaty of Versailles fails of ratification in United States Senate.
	27	Allied and Bulgarian delegates sign Treaty of Neuilly; Yugoslavia and Greece receive terrritory at Bulgarian expense.

1920

Jan.	10	Treaty of Versailles is in effect.
Mar.	19	Treaty of Versailles fails of ratification in United States Senate.
June	4	Hungarian and Allied delegates sign Treaty of Trianon; Hungary cedes territory to Austria, Czechoslovakia, Romania, and Yugoslavia.
Aug.	10	Turkish and Allied delegates sign Treaty of Sèvres; because of its harsh terms, it is not ratified by Turks.

1921

Aug.	24	United States signs a separate treaty of peace with Austria at Vienna.

Aug.	25	United States signs a separate treaty of peace with Germany at Berlin.
	29	United States signs a separate treaty of peace with Hungary at Budapest.

1923

July	24	Allies and Turkey sign Treaty of Lausanne; Turks regain part of eastern Thrace.

Postwar Settlements

1919

May	14	War breaks out between Greece and Turkey.
Aug.	9	Treaty places Persia under British protection.

1920

Jan.	16	League of Nations begins functioning.
Feb.	2	Treaty of Tartu recognizes independence of Estonia.
Apr.	25	War breaks out between Poland and Russia; ends Oct. 12 with preliminary Treaty of Riga.
July	5	Reparations conference opens at Spa (ends July 16); protocol apportioning reparations is signed.
	12	Treaty of Moscow recognizes independence of Lithuania.
	28	Teschen is divided between Czechoslovakia and Poland.
Aug.	2	Italy recognizes independence of Albania.
	11	Treaty of Riga recognizes independence of Latvia.
Oct.	10	Plebiscite in Klagenfurt area results in its retention by Austria.
	14	Treaty of Tartu recognizes independence of Finland.
Nov.	12	Under terms of Treaty of Rapallo between Italy and Yugoslavia, Fiume becomes independent city.

1921

Feb.	21	Reza Khan Pahlavi triumphs in Persia; British 1919 treaty is denounced Feb. 27.
Mar.	16	Turkish possession of districts of Kars and Ardahan is recognized by U.S.S.R.
	18	Definitive Treaty of Riga delimits Soviet-Polish frontier.
	20	Plebiscite in Upper Silesia results in its partition between Poland and Germany.
Nov.	12	Washington Conference on disarmament opens; closes Feb. 6, 1922.

1922

Apr.	16	Treaty of Rapallo is signed by Germany and U.S.S.R.
Oct.	13	War between Greece and Turkey ends.
	28	Fascists come to power in Italy.

1923

Jan. 11   Because of German delay in reparations payments, French and Belgian troops begin to occupy the Ruhr.

July 24   Straits Convention is signed.

1924

Jan. 27   Yugoslavia agrees to cession of Fiume to Italy.

Apr. 9   Dawes Plan on reparations is presented.

July 16   London Conference on reparations opens (ends Aug. 16); adopts Dawes Plan.

1925

Aug. 25   French and Belgian troops leave the Ruhr.

Dec. 1   Locarno treaties, guaranteeing Franco-German and Belgo-German frontiers against aggression, are signed in London.

Appendix B. Costs of the War *

War costs are of two kinds—direct and indirect. Direct costs embrace all expenditures made by belligerents in carrying on hostilities. Indirect costs include the economic losses resulting from deaths attributable directly or indirectly to the war, the value of property damaged or destroyed, the loss of production arising from the transfer of men from civilian to military pursuits, expenditures for war relief work, the cost of war to neutral nations, and the like. The direct costs of World War I, based on the most reliable statistics, were $186,333,637,000; the indirect costs have been estimated at $151,646,942,560, making the total war bill $337,980,579,560. It has been possible to appraise the direct costs fairly accurately, but the indirect costs can only be estimated, for there is no unit of measurement by which they may be definitely fixed. Notwithstanding the many figures purporting to show how much money was spent to carry on the war, however, the fact is that it was fought mainly on credit, since the gold available at the outbreak of hostilities was not sufficient to have kept it going for more than 40 or 50 days. During the first three years of the war the average daily cost was $123 million, and in 1918 it rose to $224 million.

DIRECT WAR COSTS

Table 1 shows the net direct cost of the war to the belligerents. It allows credit for territory, shipping, and other material gains by the victors and assumes full repayment of loans and collections of indemnities.

* For details concerning the statistics given in Appendix B as well as for the derivation of the tabulations, consult Ernest L. Bogart, *Direct and Indirect Costs of the Great World War* (2d ed.; New York, 1920), a scholarly work published by the Carnegie Endowment for International Peace, from which these data have been taken.

Table 1. DIRECT COSTS OF THE WAR

Countries	Cost
Allied and Associated Powers:	
United States	$ 22,625,253,000
Great Britain	35,334,012,000
British Dominions and Colonies:	
Canada	1,665,576,000
Australia	1,423,208,000
New Zealand	378,750,000
India	601,279,000
Union of South Africa	300,000,000
Colonies	125,000,000
France	24,265,583,000
Russia	22,593,950,000
Italy	12,413,998,000
Belgium	1,154,468,000
Romania	1,600,000,000
Japan	40,000,000
Serbia	399,400,000
Greece	270,000,000
Other Allied countries	500,000,000
Total	$125,690,477,000
Central Powers:	
Germany	$ 37,775,000,000
Austria-Hungary	20,622,960,000
Turkey	1,430,000,000
Bulgaria	815,200,000
Total	$ 60,643,160,000
Grand Total	$186,333,637,000

INDIRECT WAR COSTS

Loss of Human Life

The average social value of an individual in the six leading belligerents at the time of the war has been estimated as follows: United States, $4,720; Great Britain, $4,140; Germany, $3,380; France, $2,900; Austria-Hungary, $2,750; and Russia, $2,020. Table 2 has been developed on the basis of these values and appropriate assumptions for the other belligerents.

Table 2. CAPITALIZED VALUE OF LOSS OF LIFE

Countries	Lives lost*	Value
United States	109,740	$ 517,972,800
Great Britain	839,904	3,477,202,560
Germany	1,997,365	6,751,093,700
France	1,654,550	4,798,195,000
Austria-Hungary	1,132,500	3,114,375,000
Russia	4,012,064	8,104,369,280
Belgium	272,000	788,800,000
Italy	1,180,660	2,397,053,200
Serbia†	757,343	1,529,832,860
Romania	397,117	802,176,340
Greece	37,500	75,750,000
Portugal	4,100	8,282,000
Japan	301	608,020
Turkey	488,789	987,353,780
Bulgaria	106,637	215,406,740
Total, armed forces	12,990,570	$33,568,471,280
Estimated loss resulting from civilian deaths‡		33,568,471,280
Total valuation of lives lost		$67,136,942,560

* Assumes that approximately half of those listed as missing or prisoners of war actually died.

† The figure of 757,343 lives lost by Serbia in this compilation is undoubtedly in error, for Serbia mobilized a total of only 707,343 men; a more valid figure would be 121,500.

‡ Such deaths are supposed to equal the number of those in the armed forces.

Property Losses

Estimating losses caused by destruction and damage to property in war is an exceedingly difficult task. One estimate, used in Tables 3 and 4, places total property losses in World War I at $36,760 million, of which $29,960 million was sustained on land and $6,800 million at sea. The merchant vessels sunk, aggregating 15,398,392 gross tons, represent a loss of $3,000 million, and their cargoes were valued at $3,800 million.

Table 3. PROPERTY LOSSES ON LAND

Countries or areas	Value
Belgium	$ 7,000,000,000
France	10,000,000,000
Russia (except for the Ukraine)	1,250,000,000
Poland	1,500,000,000
Serbia, Albania, and Montenegro	2,000,000,000
East Prussia, Austria, and the Ukraine	1,000,000,000
Italy	2,710,000,000
Romania	1,000,000,000
British Empire	1,750,000,000
Germany (except for East Prussia)	1,750,000,000
Total	$29,960,000,000

Table 4. LOSSES OF SEAGOING MERCHANT VESSELS
(In gross tons)

Countries of registry	Lost by enemy action	Lost by marine risk
Allies and Neutrals:		
United States	394,658	430,759
Great Britain	7,756,659	1,143,000
Norway	1,177,001	
Italy	846,333	
France	888,783	
Denmark	240,860	
Sweden	200,829	
Greece	345,516	
Russia	182,933	
Netherlands	203,190	
Spain	167,865	
Portugal	93,136	710,285
Belgium	83,819	
Japan	120,176	
Brazil	25,464	
Argentina	4,275	
Uruguay	6,027	
Peru	1,419	
Romania	3,973	
Persia (Iran)	758	
Total	12,743,674	2,284,044

Central Powers:		
Germany	187,340	86,265
Austria-Hungary	15,166	20,433
Turkey	61,470	...
Total	263,976	106,698
Total, all countries	13,007,650	2,390,742
Total, all sinkings		15,398,392

Loss in Production

One of the major indirect costs of World War I was the loss in production arising from the withdrawal of millions of men from commercial pursuits for service in the armed forces. In 1917 there were 38 million men under arms, and it is estimated that an average of 20 million men served in the armed forces during each of the four and one-half years of the war. If we ascribe to these men an average earning capacity of $500 annually, the estimated loss in production is $45 billion.

War Relief Costs

The relief work made necessary by the war is estimated to have cost $1 billion (Table 5), all of which was raised by voluntary subscriptions.

Table 5. WAR RELIEF EXPENDITURES

Countries	Contributions	
United States		$ 625,015,028
British Empire:		
Great Britain	$87,112,000	
Canada	91,750,000	
New Zealand	17,585,000	
Australia	36,000,000	
South Africa	10,000,000	
Newfoundland	3,000,000	
India	3,600,000	
		249,047,000
Other countries		125,937,972
Total		$1,000,000,000

Cost of War to Neutral Nations

As shown in Table 6, the estimated cost of World War I to the neutral nations is $1,750 million, which represents the sums that they expended in guarding their frontiers and in otherwise maintaining their neutrality.

Table 6. COST OF WAR TO NEUTRAL NATIONS

Countries	Expenditures
Netherlands	$ 672,000,000
Switzerland	250,000,000
Sweden	429,800,000
Norway	130,000,000
Denmark	90,000,000
Other neutral nations	178,200,000
Total	$1,750,000,000

TOTAL COSTS

In summary, the total of the direct costs and the various types of indirect costs of World War I is as follows:

Value of lives lost	$ 67,136,942,560
Value of property lost	36,760,000,000
Loss in production	45,000,000,000
War relief costs	1,000,000,000
Cost to neutral nations	1,750,000,000
Total, indirect costs	$151,646,942,560
Direct costs	186,333,637,000
Grand total	$337,980,579,560

WAR LOANS

During the war the United States and Great Britain made substantial loans to their allies, as shown in Tables 7 and 8. In addition, France advanced $1,547,200,000 to her allies, of which Belgium received $434,125,090; and Japan loaned $333 million to Russia.

Table 7. ADVANCES TO ALLIES BY THE
UNITED STATES

Countries	Loans
Great Britain	$4,316,000,000
France	2,852,000,000
Italy	1,591,000,000
Russia	187,000,000
Belgium	341,000,000
Serbia	27,000,000
Czechoslovakia	50,000,000
Greece	43,000,000
Romania	30,000,000
Cuba	10,000,000
Liberia	5,000,000
Total	$9,452,000,000

Table 8. ADVANCES TO ALLIES BY GREAT BRITAIN

Countries	Loans
France	$2,170,000,000
Italy	2,065,000,000
Russia	2,840,000,000
Belgium	435,000,000
Serbia	90,000,000
Other Allied countries	240,000,000
British Dominions	855,000,000
Total	$8,695,000,000

Appendix C. War Casualties

The number of casualties in World War I exceeded by far those of any other war before World War II, in which almost 17 million men of the armed forces perished. Civilian deaths from military action, massacre, starvation, and exposure in the war from 1914 to 1918 are estimated at 12,618,000. Tables 1, 2, and 3 include only casualties in the armed forces.

Table 1. ARMIES MOBILIZED AND CASUALTIES IN WORLD WAR I*

Countries	Total mobilized forces	Killed and died	Wounded casualties	Prisoners and missing	Total casualties	Percentage of mobilized forces in casualties
Allies and Associated Powers:						
Russia	12,000,000	1,700,000	4,950,000	2,500,000	9,150,000	76.3
France	8,410,000	1,357,800	4,266,000	537,000	6,160,800	73.3
British Empire	8,904,467	908,371	2,090,212	191,652	3,190,235	35.8
Italy	5,615,000	650,000	947,000	600,000	2,197,000	39.1
United States	4,355,000	126,000	234,300	4,500	364,800	8.2
Japan	800,000	300	907	3	1,210	0.2
Romania	750,000	335,706	120,000	80,000	535,706	71.4
Serbia	707,343	45,000	133,148	152,958	331,106	46.8
Belgium	267,000	13,716	44,686	34,659	93,061	34.9
Greece	230,000	5,000	21,000	1,000	27,000	11.7
Portugal	100,000	7,222	13,751	12,318	33,291	33.3
Montenegro	50,000	3,000	10,000	7,000	20,000	40.0
Total	42,188,810	5,152,115	12,831,004	4,121,090	22,104,209	52.3
Central Powers:						
Germany	11,000,000	1,773,700	4,216,058	1,152,800	7,142,558	64.9
Austria-Hungary	7,800,000	1,200,000	3,620,000	2,200,000	7,020,000	90.0
Turkey	2,850,000	325,000	400,000	250,000	975,000	34.2
Bulgaria	1,200,000	87,500	152,390	27,029	266,919	22.2
Total	22,850,000	3,386,200	8,388,448	3,629,829	15,404,477	67.4
Grand total	65,038,810	8,538,315	21,219,452	7,750,919	37,508,686	57.6

* As reported by the United States War Department in February, 1924.

Table 2. AMERICAN ARMY CASUALTIES
IN WORLD WAR I

Cause of death	Overseas	Domestic	Total
Killed in action	36,926	5	36,931
Died of wounds received in action	13,628	45	13,673
Died of disease	23,853	38,815	62,668
Died of accident	2,557	1,946	4,503
Drowned	328	399	727
Committed suicide	296	671	967
Murdered	159	159	318
Executed	11	25	36
Died of other causes	131	190	321
Total	77,889	42,255	120,144
Total wounded	198,059	...	198,059
Grand total, died and wounded	275,948	42,255	318,203

Table 3. AMERICAN WAR CASUALTIES
BY STATES AND TERRITORIES

State or territory	Total casualties	Killed or died
Alabama	5,160	1,251
Alaska	15	6
Arizona	557	150
Arkansas	2,658	883
California	6,650	1,747
Canal Zone	3	2
Colorado	1,759	537
Connecticut	6,625	1,265
Delaware	303	87
District of Columbia	773	202
Florida	1,171	467
Georgia	4,425	1,530
Hawaii	13	4
Idaho	1,351	409
Illinois	18,264	4,260
Indiana	5,766	1,510
Iowa	7,311	2,161
Kansas	5,182	1,270
Kentucky	5,380	1,436

Louisiana	2,160	823
Maine	2,090	518
Maryland	3,812	975
Massachusetts	13,505	2,955
Michigan	10,369	2,751
Minnesota	7,323	2,133
Mississippi	2,303	904
Missouri	10,385	2,562
Montana	3,443	934
Nebraska	3,041	855
Nevada	250	71
New Hampshire	1,535	358
New Jersey	10,166	2,367
New Mexico	860	228
New York	40,222	9,196
North Carolina	5,799	1,610
North Dakota	2,560	700
Ohio	16,007	4,082
Oklahoma	6,358	1,471
Oregon	1,577	512
Pennsylvania	35,042	7,898
Philippines	7	3
Puerto Rico	11	1
Rhode Island	1,562	355
South Carolina	3,919	1,138
South Dakota	1,867	554
Tennessee	6,190	1,836
Texas	10,133	2,722
Utah	1,006	302
Vermont	1,170	300
Virginia	6,130	1,635
Washington	3,070	877
West Virginia	4,018	1,063
Wisconsin	9,813	2,649
Wyoming	676	233

Bibliography

BY BRIGADIER GENERAL VINCENT J. ESPOSITO,
U.S.A. (RET.)

POLITICAL, ECONOMIC, AND SOCIAL WORKS

Prewar Era

The most up-to-date studies of the years 1871–1914, during which the seeds of war were sown, include Alan J. P. Taylor, *The Struggle for Mastery in Europe, 1848–1918* (London and Fair Lawn, N.J., 1954), and Pierre Renouvin, *Histoire des relations internationales* (8 vols.; Paris, 1953–58), Vol. VI: *Le XIXᵉ siècle: II, De 1871 à 1914, l'apogée de l'Europe*. Each of these volumes contains a full and critical bibliography, from which one may select books in practically all important languages.

Also to be recommended are: Raymond Poincaré, *The Origins of War* (London and New York, 1922); Herbert H. Asquith, *The Genesis of War* (New York, 1923); Karl Kautsky, ed., *Outbreak of the World War* (Washington, D.C., 1924), a translation of German official documents; John S. Ewart, *Roots and Causes of the War* (2 vols.; New York, 1925); German Foreign Office, *Die grosse Politik der europäischen Kabinette, 1871–1914* (40 vols. in 54 vols.; Berlin, 1922–27); Sidney B. Fay, *The Origins of the World War* (2 vols.; New York, 1930); William L. Langer, *European Alliances and Alignments, 1871–1890* (New York, 1931), and *The Diplomacy of Imperialism, 1890–1902* (2 vols.; New York, 1935); and British Foreign Office, *British Documents on the Origins of the War, 1898–1914* (11 vols. in 13 vols.; London, 1926–38).

Four excellent works covering this period are by Bernadotte E. Schmitt: *The Coming of the War, 1914* (2 vols.; New York, 1930); *Triple Alliance and Triple Entente* (New York, 1934); *The Annexation of Bosnia, 1908–1909* (New York, 1937); and his article "July 1914: Thirty Years After," *Journal of Modern History*, XVI (Chicago, 1944), 169–204, which is reprinted in *The Making of Modern Europe*, ed. Herman Ausubel (New York, 1951), Bk. 2, pp. 942–91.

Of great value are the works of the English historian George P. Gooch, whose impartiality has long been recognized: *Before the War: Studies in Diplomacy* (2 vols.; New York, 1936–38); *Recent Revelations of European Diplomacy* (4th ed.; New York, 1940); and *Studies in Diplomacy and Statecraft* (New York, 1942).

For the crisis of July, 1914, the best book is Luigi Albertini, *The*

Origins of the War of 1914 (3 vols.; London and Fair Lawn, N.J., 1952–57), Vols. II and III.

Diplomacy in the War

George F. Abbott, *Greece and the Allies, 1914–1922* (London, 1922); Harry N. Howard, *The Partition of Turkey: A Diplomatic History, 1913–1923* (Norman, Okla., 1931); Charles N. Spinks, "Japan's Entrance into the World War," *Pacific Historical Review*, V (Berkeley and Los Angeles, 1936), 297–311. Frank P. Chambers, *The War Behind the War, 1914–1918* (New York, 1939), is the best general account of the relations between the nations at war and of their domestic policies. Wolfram W. Gottlieb, *Studies in Secret Diplomacy During the First World War* (London and Fair Lawn, N.J., 1957) deals in detail with Turkey's and Italy's entrances into the war.

Neutral Nations

Percy A. Martin, *Latin America and the War* (Baltimore, 1925); Montagu W. W. P. Consett and Octavius H. Daniel, *The Triumph of the Unarmed Forces, 1914–1918* (rev. ed.; London, 1928); Marius J. van der Flier *et al.*, *The Netherlands and the World War* (4 vols.; Oxford, 1923–28); Eli F. Hecksher *et al.*, *Norway, Sweden, Denmark, and Iceland in the World War* (New Haven, 1930); R. H. Gibson and Maurice Prendergast, *The German Submarine War, 1914–1918* (London and New York, 1931); Charles Seymour, *American Diplomacy During the World War* (Baltimore, 1934); Thomas E. La Fargue, *China and the World War* (Palo Alto, 1937); Marion C. Siney, *The Allied Blockade of Germany, 1914–1916* (Ann Arbor, Mich., 1957); Ernest R. May, *The World War and American Isolation, 1914–1917* (Cambridge, Mass., 1959).

Termination of the War

Humphrey J. T. Johnson, *Vatican Diplomacy in the World War* (Oxford, 1933); John W. Wheeler-Bennett, *Brest-Litovsk: The Forgotten Peace* (New York, 1957); Kent Forster, *The Failures of Peace: The Search for a Negotiated Peace During the First World War* (Washington, D.C., 1941); Harry R. Rudin, *Armistice, 1918* (New Haven, 1944); Leonid I. Strakhovsky, *Intervention at Archangel* (London and Princeton, N.J., 1944); John A. White, *The Siberian Intervention* (Princeton, N.J., 1950).

Victor S. Mamatey, *The United States and East Central Europe, 1914–1918* (Princeton, N.J., 1957), despite its focus on American policy, gives the best account of the breakup of the Austro-Hungarian Empire.

Peace Conferences and Peace Treaties

Harold V. W. Temperley *et al.*, *A History of the Peace Conferences of Paris* (6 vols.; London, 1920–21); Carnegie Endowment for International Peace, *The Treaties of Peace, 1919–1923* (2 vols.; New York, 1924); Paul Birdsall, *Versailles: Twenty Years After* (New York, 1921); Thomas A. Bailey, *Woodrow Wilson and the Great Betrayal* (New York, 1945). Bailey's *Woodrow Wilson and the Lost Peace* (New York, 1941) gives the liveliest account of the peace conference and of the defeat of the treaty in the United States.

Postwar World

John M. Keynes, *The Economic Consequences of the Peace* (London and New York, 1920); Louis Fischer, *The Soviets in World Affairs* (2 vols.; New York, 1930); Geoffrey M. Gathorne-Hardy, *A Short History of International Affairs, 1920–1938* (London, 1938); Hugh M. Seton-Watson, *Eastern Europe Between the Wars, 1918–1941* (2d ed.; New York, 1946); Edward H. Carr, *The Twenty Years' Crisis, 1919–1939* (2d ed.; New York, 1946); George Lenczowski, *The Middle East in World Affairs* (Ithaca, N.Y., 1952); Ingvar Svennilson, *Growth and Stagnation in the European Economy, 1913–1945* (Geneva, 1954).

MILITARY WORKS

Official Histories

The best sources of information on the military aspects of the war are the multivolume national official histories. Outstanding among these is the British *History of the Great War Based on Official Documents*, brought out by the Imperial Defence Committee (79 vols.; London, 1920–49). The German history, *Der Weltkrieg, 1914 bis 1918*, compiled by the Reichsarchiv (16 vols. in 27 vols.; Berlin, 1925–39), remains incomplete. The French counterpart, *Les armées françaises dans la grande guerre*, published by the État-Major de l'Armée (11 vols. in 75 vols. and 20 atlases; Paris, 1922–39), is excellent. The American *The United States Army in the World War, 1917–1919*, issued by the Historical Division of the Department of the Army (17 vols.; Washington, D.C., 1948) is primarily a collection of orders and correspondence. The Italian work is *L'esercito italiano nella grande guerra, 1915–1918*, prepared by the Ufficio Storico della Stato Maggiore (6 vols. in 19 vols.; Rome, 1927–54); the Austrian is *Österreich-Ungarns letzter Krieg, 1914–1918*, brought out by the Bundesministerium für Landesverteidigung (7 vols.; Vienna, 1930–38).

General Histories

Two one-volume general histories stand out among the many published: Cyril B. Falls, *The Great War* (New York, 1959), a fine general survey, and Sir James Edmonds, *A Short History of World War I* (London and Fair Lawn, N.J., 1951), which covers and emphasizes the military campaigns splendidly. Both authors prepared many of the volumes of the British official history.

Other good publications include: John A. Buchan, *A History of the Great War* (4 vols.; Boston, 1922); Victor Corda, *La guerre mondial (1914–1918)* (Paris, 1922); Winston Churchill, *The World Crisis* (rev. and abbr. ed.; New York, 1931); Max Schwarte (ed.), *Der grosse Krieg, 1914–1918* (10 vols.; Leipzig, 1921–33); Charles Robert Mowbray Fraser Cruttell, *A History of the Great War* (London and Fair Lawn, N.J., 1934); Basil H. Liddell Hart, *A History of the World War, 1914–1918* (New York, 1935); Girard L. McEntee, *Military History of the World War* (New York, 1937); and Cyril B. Falls, *A Hundred Years of War* (London, 1953).

An excellent French human-interest work by André Ducasse *et al.* is *Vie et mort des français, 1914–1918* (Paris, 1959). For a quick survey of military operations of the war on annotated maps, consult Vincent J. Esposito (ed.), *The West Point Atlas of American Wars* (2 vols.; New York, 1959).

Western Front

Events on the Western Front are covered in detail in the British, French, and German official histories and in adequate summary form in the general works. The volumes listed below go deeper into specific phases of the operations.

The plans and objectives of the German High Command are well told in the accounts of two of their principal leaders: Erich von Falkenhayn, *The German General Staff and Its Decisions, 1914–1916* (New York, 1920), and Erich F. W. Ludendorff, *Ludendorff's Own Story, August 1914–November 1918* (2 vols.; New York, 1920). Gerhard Ritter, *The Schlieffen Plan* (New York, 1958), gives a good account of the German initial plan for the war on the Western Front.

Joseph F. Revol, *Le plan XVII: étude stratégique* (Paris, 1920), and Charles Lanrezac, *Le plan de campagne français et le premier mois de la guerre* (Paris, 1921), deal similarly with the French plans.

Edward L. Spears, *Liaison, 1914* (London, 1930), covers the opening operations. Émile J. Galet, *Albert, King of the Belgians, in the Great War* (Boston, 1931), tells of the Belgian operations in 1914 and is particularly good on the defense of Liége. The Battle of the Marne is described vividly and accurately in the scholarly work of Sewell T. Tyng, *The Campaign of the Marne, 1914* (New York, 1935). Alexander von Kluck, commander of the crucial German First Army, gives his account of the battle in *The March on Paris and the Battle of the Marne* (New York, 1920); and his able chief of staff, Hermann J. von Kuhl, gives his version in *The Marne Campaign, 1914* (Fort Leavenworth, Kan., 1936). Barbara W. Tuchman, *The Guns of August* (New York, 1962), gives an excellent description of the beginning of the war.

Henri Philippe Pétain, *Verdun* (New York, 1930), and Henry Dugard, *La victoire de Verdun, 21 février, 1916–3 novembre, 1917* (Paris, 1918) describe this historic bloody siege. Leon Wolff, *In Flanders Fields* (New York, 1958), covers the British offensive in Flanders in 1917. Edward L. Spears, *Prelude to Victory* (London, 1939), tells of the 1917 Arras operations and Robert Georges Nivelle's disastrous offensive in the Second Battle of the Aisne. Alistair Horne, *The Price of Glory: Verdun, 1916* (New York, 1963), is perhaps the best book on this great battle.

The last German bid for victory in the spring of 1918 is covered in Hermann J. von Kuhl, *Entstehung, Durchführung und Zusammenbrach der Offensive von 1918* (Berlin, 1927); and Louis Koeltz, *La bataille de France (21 mars–5 avril 1918)* (Paris, 1928). Alexander H. C. Kearsey, *The Battle of Amiens, 1918* (London, 1950), is the best account of this Allied offensive. Sir Frederick Maurice, *The Last Four Months* (Boston, 1919), covers the final Allied general offensive on the Western Front.

Sir John French, *1914* (Boston, 1919), is the account of the first commander of the British Expeditionary Force (BEF); Sir Hubert Gough, *The Fifth Army* (London, 1931), deals with the operations of that British army as told by its commander, a fine soldier made a scapegoat. Sir Archibald Montgomery, *The Story of the Fourth Army in the Battles of the Hundred Days* (London, 1920), describes that British army's activities in the final offensive. *Sir Douglas Haig's Despatches*, ed. J. H. Boraston (New York, 1919), and *Douglas Haig's Private Papers, 1914–1919*, ed. Robert Blake (London, 1952), present the reports, opinions, and convictions of the last commander of the BEF. John Terraine, *Ordeal of Victory* (Philadelphia and New York, 1963), is an excellent biography of Haig.

The participation of Commonwealth contingents is covered in Sir John Monash, *The Australian Victories in France in 1918* (London, 1920); Harwood Steele, *The Canadians in France, 1915–1918* (London, 1920); Sir Arthur Currie, "Interim Report on the Operations of the Canadian Corps During the Year 1918," *Report of the Ministry, Overseas Military Forces of Canada, 1918* (London, 1919); George F. G. Stanley and Harold M. Jackson, *Canada's Soldiers, 1604–1954* (New York, 1955); Sir James Willcocks, *With the Indians in France* (London, 1920); H. T. B. Drew, ed., *The War Effort of New Zealand* (Auckland, 1923); and John Buchan, *The History of the South African Forces in France* (New York, 1920).

Sir Arthur Conan Doyle, *The British Campaigns in Europe, 1914–1918* (London, 1928), is a general account. The volumes of William H. Marsily (pseudonym Willy Breton) in *Pages d'histoire* (Paris, 1914–19) are a semiofficial account of the operations of the Belgian Army. Barthélemy E. Palat, *La grande guerre sur le front occidental* (14 vols.; Paris, 1917–29) is an exhaustive French account. Richard L. Thoumin, *La grande guerre* (2 vols.; Paris, 1960), is a collection of colorful eyewitness accounts. Joseph J. C. Joffre, *1914–1915: la préparation de la guerre et la conduite des opérations* (Paris, 1920), presents the recollections of the first commander in chief of the French armies in the war.

American participation on the Western Front is well covered in the following: Jacques A. de P. Chambrun and Charles de Marenches, *The American Army in the European Conflict* (New York, 1919); Frederick Palmer, *Our Greatest Battle (the Meuse–Argonne)* (New York, 1919); John J. Pershing, *Final Reports of General John Joseph Pershing, the Commander-in-Chief American Expeditionary Forces* (Washington, D.C., 1919); Johnson Hagood, *The Services of Supply* (Boston, 1927); Hunter Liggett, *A.E.F.: Ten Years Ago in France* (New York, 1928); James G. Harbord, *The American Army in France, 1917–1919* (Boston, 1936); and American Battle Monuments Commission, *American Armies and Battlefields in Europe* (Washington, D.C., 1938). Lawrence Stallings, *The Doughboys* (New York, 1963), is a gripping, prideful story of the A.E.F.'s battles. In addition, there are many biographies, autobiographies, and memoirs of the principal leaders on the Western Front; these are contained in the section *Biographical Works*.

Eastern Front

There is no Russian official history of the war; most of the military writings on the Eastern Front are by other nationals. The best general works are: Sir Alfred Knox, *With the Russian Army, 1914–1917* (New York, 1921); Max Hoffmann, *The War of Lost Opportunities* (New York, 1925); Yuri N. Danilov (Russian chief of staff), *La Russie dans le guerre mondiale (1914–1917)* (Paris, 1927); Aleksei A. Brusilov (Russia's best general in the war), *A Soldier's Notebook, 1914–1918* (London, 1930); Winston Churchill, *The Unknown War: the Eastern Front* (New York, 1931); and Nicolai N. Golovine, *The Russian Army in the World War* (New York, 1931).

The classic campaign in East Prussia, which ended in the Battle of Tannenberg, is well covered in the works of two of the German leaders: Hermann K. B. von François, *Tannenberg: das Cannae des Weltkrieges in Wort und Bild* (Berlin, 1926), and Max Hoffmann, *Tannenberg wie es wirklich war* (Berlin, 1926); also in Sir Edmund Ironside, *Tannenberg: the First Thirty Days in East Prussia* (Edinburgh, 1925), and Alexander H. C. Kearsey, *A Study of the Strategy and Tactics of the East Prussian Campaign, 1914* (London, 1932).

Other works of limited scope are Basil Gourko, *Memories and Impressions of War and Revolution in Russia, 1914–1917* (London, 1918); Hermann K. B. von François, *Gorlice, 1915* (Leipzig, 1922), which deals with the great German breakthrough on the Gorlice–Tarnów front; Yuri N. Danilov, *Russland im Weltkriege, 1914–1915* (Jena, 1925); Nicolai N. Golovine, *The Russian Campaign of 1914* (Fort Leavenworth, Kan., 1933); John W. Wheeler-Bennett, *Brest-Litovsk: The Forgotten Peace* (New York, 1957); and David Footman, *Civil War in Russia* (New York, 1962).

Allied operations against the Bolsheviks after the collapse of Russia are treated by a "Chronicler" in *Archangel: the American War in Russia* (Chicago, 1924); Sir Charles Maynard, *The Murmansk Venture* (London, 1928); William S. Graves, *America's Siberian Adventure, 1918–1920* (New York, 1931); Richard E. Dupuy, *Perish by the Sword* (Harrisburg, 1939); Leonid I. Strakhovsky, *Intervention at Archangel* (London and Princeton, 1944); and John A. White, *The Siberian Intervention* (Princeton, 1950).

Italian Front

The Italian, Austrian, and German official histories give the best detailed accounts of operations on the Italian front. Max Schwarte (ed.), *Der grosse Krieg, 1914–18* (10 vols.; Leipzig, 1921–33), Vol. V., contains excellent accounts by direct participants and is good on Austrian strategy. Some excellent general works are: Amadeo Tosti, *La guerra italo-austriaca, 1915–1918: sommario storica* (Milan, 1925); Aldo Valori, *La guerra italo-austriaca, 1915–1918* (2d ed.; Bologna, 1925); Gaetano Ettore Giardino, *Rievocazioni e riflessioni di guerra* (3 vols.; Milan, 1929–30); Luigi Villari, *The War on the Italian Front* (London, 1932); Luigi Segato, *L'Italia nella guerra mondiale* (4 vols.; Milan, 1935); Girard L. McEntee, *Italy's Part in Winning the World War* (Princeton, N.J., 1937); Roberto Bencivenga, *Saggio critico sulla nostra guerra* (5 vols.; Rome, 1930–38), the fundamental work for the Cadorna period of the war; and Piero Pieri, *La prima guerra mondiale, 1914–1918: problemi di storia militare* (Turin, 1947), a fine analysis of the tactical and strategic problems of the Italian front in the light of World War I as a whole.

The much-debated Italian disaster at Caporetto is covered in detail in the official report of the Commission of Inquiry on Caporetto, *Dall'Isonzo al Piave, 24 ottobre–9 novembre 1917* (3 vols.; Rome, 1919), and is dealt with in Konrad Krafft von Dellmensingen, *Der Durchbruch am Isonzo* (2 vols.; Berlin, 1926); Enrico Caviglia, *La dodicesima battaglia (Caporetto)* (Milan, 1933); Aldo Cabiata, *La battaglia dell'ottobre 1917* (Milan, 1934); and Alfredo A. P. P. Conquet, *La Bataille de Caporetto* (Paris, 1936). Enrico Caviglia, *Le tre battaglie del Piave* (Milan, 1934), deals with the Italian revival on the Piave, as does the Italian Supreme Command report *The Battle of Piave* (London, 1919).

The final 1918 operations are covered in the Italian Supreme Command's *Report on the Battle of Vittorio Veneto* (Rome, 1919), and Adriano Alberti, *L'Italia a la fine della guerra mondiale* (2 vols.; Rome, 1924). Adolfo Omodeo, *Momenti della vita di guerra (dai diari e dalle lettere dei caduti* (Bari, 1934), is a classic documentation of the spirit of the common man under arms. Edmund Glaise von Horstenau, *Die Katastrophe* (Vienna, 1930), is rich in facts and data. Field Marshal Count Luigi Cadorna, the victim of Caporetto, gives his views in *La guerra alla fronte italiana, fino all'arresto sulla linea della Piave e del Grappa* (2 vols.; Milan, 1921), and *Altre pagine sulla grande guerra* (Milan, 1925). Field Marshal Count Franz Conrad von Hötzendorf (Austrian commander against Italy) gives his account in *Aus meiner Dientzeit, 1906–1918* (5 vols.; Vienna, 1921–25).

Colonial and Japanese Campaigns

The best references are two volumes of the British official series: Charles Hordern (ed.), *Military Operations, East Africa* (London, 1941), and Frederick J. Moberly, *Military Operations, Togoland and the Cameroons, 1914–1916* (London, 1931). Troops of the Union of South Africa played major roles in the operations against German Southwest and East Africa; their exploits are told in the official history of the Department of Defence, South Africa, *The Union of South Africa and the Great War, 1914–1918* (Pretoria, 1924). Brian Gardner, *On to Kilimanjaro* (Philadelphia, 1963), is a good popular history of the long East African campaign.

The *Official History of Australia in the War of 1914–1918* (12 vols.; Melbourne, 1921–42) covers Australian operations against the German Pacific islands. Similar operations of New Zealand are described in H. T. B. Drew, ed., *The War Effort of New Zealand* (Auckland, 1923), Vol. IV of the *Official History of New Zealand's Efforts in the War*.

The Belgian official history, brought out by the État-Major de l'Armée, is *Les campagnes coloniales belges, 1914–1918* (2 vols.; Brussels, 1927–32). A general account is Edmund Dane, *British Campaigns in Africa and the Pacific* (London, 1919).

Other works of value are: Angus Buchanan, *Three Years of War in East Africa* (London, 1919); Sir Hugh Clifford, *The Gold Coast Regiment in the East African Campaign* (London, 1920); Charles P. Fendall, *The East African Force, 1915–1919* (London, 1921); and Edmund H. Gorges, *The Great War in German West Africa* (London, 1930). Accounts of French operations in Togoland and the Cameroons

are contained in their official history. The best German work is Paul
E. von Lettow-Vorbeck, *East African Campaigns* (New York, 1957);
the author is the German general who conducted brilliant guerrilla-
type operations against the British, Portuguese, and Belgians, and
eluded them throughout the war.

Other German accounts are: Heinrich Schnee, *Deutsch Ostafrika im
Weltkriege* (Leipzig, 1916), Richard Henning, *Deutsch-Südwest im
Weltkriege* (Berlin, 1920); Waldemar Vollerthun, *Der Kampf um
Tsingtau* (Leipzig, 1920); and Hans Oelhafen von Schoellenbach, *Der
Feldzug im Südwest, 1914/1915* (Berlin, 1923).

Turkish Campaigns

The British official series contains three excellent works on the Turk-
ish campaigns: Cyril B. Falls, *Military Operations, Egypt and Palestine*
(2 vols.; London, 1930); Cecil F. Aspinall-Oglander (ed.), *Military
Operations, Gallipoli* (2 vols.; London, 1929–32); and Frederick J.
Moberly, *The Campaigns in Mesopotamia* (4 vols.; London, 1923–27).
Two general histories give good accounts: Sir James Edmonds (ed.),
A Short History of World War I (London, 1951), and Cyril B. Falls,
The Great War (New York, 1959), which contains scarce material on
the Turko-Russian fighting in the Caucasus. William E. D. Allen and
Paul Muratoff, *Caucasian Battlefields* (Cambridge, Eng., 1953), is also
good in this area.

Other general works of value are Maurice Larcher, *La guerre turque
dans la guerre mondiale* (Paris, 1926); Otto Liman von Sanders, *Five
Years in Turkey* (Annapolis, Md., 1927), the account of the chief of
the German military mission in Turkey; Winston Churchill, *The
World Crisis: the Eastern Front* (London, 1931); Max Schwarte (ed.),
Der grosse Krieg, 1914–1918 (10 vols.; Leipzig, 1921–33); and Carl
Mühlmann, *Das deutsche-türkische Waffenbündnis im Weltkriege*
(Leipzig, 1940). Among the best of the many volumes on the contro-
versial Dardanelles and Gallipoli operations are: the Dardanelles Com-
mission's *Final Report* (London, 1919); Sir Charles Callwell, *The
Dardanelles* (Boston, 1919); Sir Ian Hamilton, *Gallipoli Diary* (New
York, 1920), the account of the commander of the ill-fated expedition;
Sir Roger Keyes, *The Fight for Gallipoli* (London, 1942), an assess-
ment by a senior naval officer; and Alan Moorehead, *Gallipoli* (New
York, 1956), an excellent definitive account.

Sir Charles Townshend, *My Campaign in Mesopotamia* (London,
1920) is the story of the British commander in Mesopotamia who was
forced to surrender his army to the Turks. Sir Archibald Wavell, *Allenby, a Study in Greatness* (London and Fair Lawn, N.J., 1941), is a
fine character study of the British commander in Palestine. Cyril Falls,
Armageddon (New York, 1964), is an excellent account of Allenby's
final campaign in Palestine. T. E. Lawrence, *The Seven Pillars of Wis-*

dom (Garden City, N.Y., 1938), presents a fascinating narrative of the Arab uprising against the Turks.

Balkan Campaigns

Cyril B. Falls, *Military Operations, Macedonia* (2 vols.; London, 1933–35), of the British official series, is a fine work on the Balkan operations. The French and German official histories contain sections dealing with these campaigns. Luigi Villari, *The Macedonian Campaign* (London, 1922), is a good reference, as is Maurice Larcher, *La grande guerre dans les Balkans* (Paris, 1929).

Several worthwhile works on operations in Serbia are: Gordon Gordon-Smith, *Through the Serbian Campaigns* (London, 1916); W. H. Crawford Price, *Serbia's Part in the World War* (Garden City, N.Y., 1920); Fernand Feyler, *Les campagnes de Serbie, 1914 et 1915* (Paris, 1926); and John C. Adams, *Flight in Winter* (Princeton, N.J., 1942). The tribulations of the Allied Salonika Army are told in G. Ward Price, *The Story of the Salonika Army* (New York, 1918); Arthur J. Mann, *The Salonika Front* (London, 1920); and Maurice P. E. Sarrail, *Mon commandement en orient (1916–1918)* (Paris, 1920).

Naval Warfare

No comprehensive general history of the war at sea in World War I has been published; nor have analytical studies been made of the official publications of Great Britain and Germany, which were completed in 1949 and 1939, respectively. Great Britain's *History of the Great War Based on Official Documents* has three series devoted to the war at sea: Charles Ernest Fayle, *Seaborne Trade* (3 vols. and atlas; London, 1920–24); Sir Archibald Spicer Hurd, *The Merchant Navy* (3 vols.; London, 1921–29); and Sir Julian Corbett and Sir Henry Newbolt, *Naval Operations* (5 vols.; London, 1920–31).

The German official naval work is Eberhard von G. Mantey and Kurt Assmann, *Der Krieg zur See, 1914–1918* (18 vols.; Berlin, 1920–38).

Thomas G. Frothingham, *The Naval History of the World War* (3 vols.; Cambridge, Mass., 1924–26), is the comprehensive American work. Another American work of merit, although biased toward Admiral William S. Sims, is Tracy B. Kittredge, *Naval Lessons of the Great War* (Garden City, N.Y., 1921). Sir Henry Newbolt, one of the official British historians, produced the one-volume *Naval History of the War, 1914–1918* (London, 1920). The latest, and excellent, material is contained in Elmer B. Potter and Chester W. Nimitz (eds.), *Sea Power, a Naval History* (New York, 1960).

The blockade of Germany is well treated in two works: Louis Guichard, *The Naval Blockade, 1914–1918* (New York, 1930), and Marion C. Siney, *The Allied Blockade of Germany, 1914–1916* (Ann Arbor,

Mich., 1957). There are no comparable works for the most critical part of the war at sea: the German submarine campaign and Allied counter-measures. The best available are: Andreas Michelson, *Der U-Bootskrieg, 1914–1918* (Leipzig, 1925), by the former commander of the submarine forces, which was translated and published for official use in 1926 by the United States Navy Office of Naval Intelligence; André Laurens, *Histoire de la guerre sous-marine allemande (1914–1918)* (Paris, 1930); R. H. Gibson and Maurice Prendergast, *The German Submarine War, 1914–1918* (New York, 1931); and Edmond Delage, *La guerre sous les mers* (Paris, 1934). David D. Lewis, *The Fight for the Sea: the Past, Present, and Future of Submarine Warfare in the Atlantic* (Cleveland, 1961), is the work of an American naval officer.

Air Warfare

Henry A. Jones and Sir Walter Raleigh, *The War in the Air* (6 vols.; Oxford, 1922–37), is a special British official history devoted to aviation in World War I. The French, German, Italian, and Austrian official histories previously listed clearly outline the role of the air forces in each operation.

An authoritative review of American air operations in World War I is contained in the United States Air Force official history: Wesley F. Craven and James L. Cate, *The Army Air Forces in World War II* (Chicago, 1948), Vol. I. Edward M. Earle *et al.* (eds.), *Makers of Modern Strategy* (Princeton, N.J., 1943), contains particularly helpful chapters on individuals who shaped the concepts of air strategy and policy.

John C. Slessor, *Air Power and Armies* (London, 1936), is a complete restudy of air power in World War I by an enthusiastic British airman. Arsène M. P. Vauthier, *Le danger aérien et l'avenir du pays* (Paris, 1930) is a French survey of the World War I performance of air power and a prophecy of its future. Giulio Douhet, *The Command of the Air* (New York, 1942), is a translation of the principal writings of the first prophet of air warfare. William Mitchell, *Our Air Force* (New York, 1921), is the work of the colorful and controversial leading airman of World War I.

Peter Gray and Owen Thatford, *German Aircraft of the First World War* (London, 1962), is a very complete and detailed book, lavishly supplied with photographs, diagrams, and specifications. George W. Haddow and Peter M. Grosz, *The German Giants* (London, 1962), gives the story of the largest bombers ever to raid London. Douglas H. Robinson, *The Zeppelin in Combat* (London, 1962), is a thorough and impartial study of the subject.

Strategy, Tactics, and Weapons

Valuable works on strategy in the war are: Douglas W. Johnson,

Topography and Strategy in the War (New York, 1917); Joseph F. Revol, *Le plan XVII: étude stratégique* (Paris, 1920); Herbert H. Sargent, *The Strategy on the Western Front* (1914–1918) (Chicago, 1920); Edmond A. L. Buat, *Hindenburg et Ludendorf stratèges* (Paris, 1923); Philip Neame, *German Strategy in the Great War* (London, 1923); Wolfgang Foerster, *La stratégie allemande pendant la guerre, 1914–1918* (Paris, 1929); Charles R. M. F. Cruttwell, *The Role of British Strategy in the Great War* (New York, 1936); and Gerhard Ritter, *The Schlieffen Plan* (New York, 1958).

Three works dealing with air power are: Oliver Stewart, *The Strategy and Tactics of Air Fighting* (London, 1925); Edgar J. Kingston-McCloughry, *War in Three Dimensions: the Impact of Air-Power upon the Classic Principles of War* (London, 1949); and Irving B. Holley, *Ideas and Weapons: the Exploitation of the Aerial Weapon by the United States During World War I* (New Haven, 1953).

In the field of tactics there are: Edward G. D. Liveing, *Attack: an Infantry Subaltern's Impressions of July 1st, 1916* (New York, 1918); Charles Baux, *Études sur le combat* (Paris, 1921); William Balck, *The Development of Tactics—World War* (Fort Leavenworth, Kan., 1922); and Wilhelm J. F. von Leeb, *Defense* (Harrisburg, Pa., 1943).

In the field of analysis, consult: Sir George Aston, *War Lessons, New and Old* (London, 1919); Friedrich von Bernhardi, *The War of the Future in the Light of the Lessons of the World War* (London, 1920); and Jean Bourget, *Gouvernement et commandement; les leçons de la guerre mondiale* (Paris, 1930).

On the introduction, development, and employment of the tank there are a number of very good works: John F. C. Fuller, *Tanks in the Great War* (London, 1920); Victor W. Germains, *The "Mechanization" of War* (London, 1927); George M. Wilson (ed.), *Fighting Tanks: An Account of the Royal Tank Corps in Action, 1916–1919* (London, 1929); Giffard L. Martel, *In the Wake of the Tank* (London, 1931); Sir Ernest Swinton, *Eyewitness* (Garden City, N.Y., 1933), which deals primarily with the origin and development of the tank; and Ralph E. Jones, *The Fighting Tanks Since 1916* (Washington, D.C., 1933).

By far the best and most complete work on the machine gun, which played such an important role in the war, is George M. Chinn, *The Machine Gun* (2 vols.; Washington, D.C., 1951–55).

Statistics and Logistics

Good references in the area of statistics are: Ernest L. Bogart, *Direct and Indirect Costs of the Great World War* (2d ed.; New York, 1920); and Samuel Dumas and Knud Otto Vedel-Pederson, *Losses of Life Caused by the War* (London and New York, 1923).

The home-front efforts in support of the war are described in: Benedict Crowell, *America's Munitions, 1917–1918* (Washington, D.C., 1919); George A. B. Dewar, *The Great Munition Feat, 1914–1918* (London, 1921); and Peyton C. March, *The Nation at War* (Garden City, N.Y., 1932).

The great construction feats in France are treated in Robert K. Tomlin, *American Engineers Behind the Battle Lines in France* (New York, 1918), and Institution of Royal Engineers, *Work of the Royal Engineers in the European War, 1914–1919* (9 vols.; Chatham, Eng., 1921–27).

Notes on the Contributors

ANDRÉ DUCASSE, the son of a Protestant clergyman, was born in 1894 in Clemenceau's Vendéan village, Mouchamps. A student at the Ecole Normale Supérieure, he abandoned plans for an academic career to fight in World War I as an infantry officer (Chemin des Dames, Salonika). From 1924 to 1960 he was a professor at the Lycée de Marseille. Since his retirement, he has been living at Sanary-sur-Mer (Var) on the Azure Coast. Mr. Ducasse's books include *La Grande Mademoiselle, Les Négriers,* and *La Guerre des Camisards. La Guerre des Camisards* was crowned by the French Academy, as was the best seller *Vie et Mort des Français, '14–'18,* of which he was co-author. He has written two other books on World War I, *La Guerre de '14 racontée par les Combattants* and the recently published *Balkans '14–'18.* In addition, he is the author of a novel on World War II, *Si bleu, si calme, ou Mars et les Marseillais.*

IRA C. EAKER, Lieutenant General U.S.A.F., (Ret.), chairman of the Advisory Board of Hughes Aircraft Company, was born in Llano County, Texas, in 1896. Appointed 2d Lieutenant of Infantry in the Regular Army in October, 1917, and promoted 1st lieutenant the following July, he received an Air Force captaincy in 1920. Twenty years later he attained colonel's rank. Promoted brigadier general, U.S.A., in 1942, he received his final promotion, to lieutenant general, the following year. During World War II, in England, he commanded the 8th Bomber Command (1942) and the Eighth Air Force (1943); in Italy, he commanded the Mediterranean Allied Air Forces (1944). He was Deputy Commanding General, Army Air Forces, and Chief of Air Staff (1945–47). He flew on many European missions, including the first heavy bomber raid on German-occupied Europe in August, 1942. General Eaker retired in 1947 and, for the ensuing decade, was vice-president of the Hughes Tool Company, then vice-president of Douglas Aircraft (1957–61). With the late General H. H. Arnold, he is co-author of *This Flying Game, Army Flyer,* and *Winged Warfare.*

GEORGE FIELDING ELIOT, military analyst, born in Brooklyn, N.Y., in 1894, moved with his family to Australia in 1902. He served with the Australian Imperial Force as an infantry officer in World War I; thereafter, he returned to the United States, where from 1922 to 1930 he was a captain, then major, in the Military Intelligence Reserve, U.S. Army. He began his writing career in 1926. During World War II, Major Eliot was military analyst for the *New York Herald-Tribune* and the Columbia Broadcasting System. In 1950, he initiated a syndicated article on military subjects. He has contributed extensively to the periodical press and has been a guest lecturer at the National War College and other service schools and colleges. His books include *The Ramparts We Watch, Bombs Bursting in Air, If Russia Strikes, Caleb Pettengill, U.S.N., Victory Without War, Sylvanus Thayer of West Point*, and *Reserve Forces and the Kennedy Strategy*.

VINCENT J. ESPOSITO, Brigadier General, U.S.A. (Ret.), was appointed from the Army in 1921 to the U.S. Military Academy, from which he was graduated sixteenth in the class of 1925. Transferring from the Air Corps to the Engineers, he served as an engineer officer from 1926 to 1938. During this period, he received the B.S. degree from M.I.T. and also attended the Engineer School and the Command and General Staff College. He was an instructor in the Military Academy's Department of Civil and Military Engineering from 1939 to 1942. A three-month tour with the 4th Amphibian Brigade preceded service in the Operations Division, War Department General Staff (April, 1943–June, 1945), in which position he was a member of the Joint and Combined Chiefs of Staff Logistics agency and logistics adviser at international conferences. He was promoted brigadier general in June, 1945, and next year became a faculty member of the National War College. In 1947, he returned to West Point as Professor of Military Art and Engineering, heading the department in 1956. When placed on the retired list, effective November 1, 1963, after almost forty-five years of military service, Brigadier General Esposito was awarded the D.S.M. Co-editor of *A Short Military History of World War I* and *A Military History of World War II*, he is chief editor of *The West Point Atlas of American Wars, The West Point Atlas of the Civil War*, and co-author of *A Military History and Atlas of the Napoleonic Wars.* A prolific writer on military subjects, he has contributed to many standard reference works and has been for nearly a decade the Encyclopedia Americana's Advisory Editor on Military Affairs.

CYRIL FALLS, born in 1888, was educated at Bradfield College, Portora Royal School, and London University. He served throughout World War I, receiving the *croix de guerre* with two citations, and two mentions in Haig's dispatches. Between wars he wrote several official histories. During World War II he was Military Correspondent of the London *Times*, and later Chichele Professor of the History of War, Oxford University. Among Captain Falls' twenty books is *The Great War*.

GERALD FREUND, born in 1930, was educated at Haverford College (B.A.) and Oxford University (Ph.D.). He has assisted George F. Kennan at the Institute for Advanced Study, held a fellowship at the Council on Foreign Relations, taught at Haverford College, and now serves in the Humanities and Social Sciences Program of the Rockefeller Foundation. He has published two books: *Unholy Alliance* (1957), and *Germany Between Two Worlds* (1961).

JOHN DANIEL HAYES, Rear Admiral, U.S.N. (Ret.), is a native New Yorker who lives in Annapolis, Maryland. An Annapolis graduate of 1924, he was chief engineer of the heavy cruiser *Astoria* when she was lost in battle at Savo Island in World War II; he served during the remainder of the war in the Amphibian Forces in the Pacific. A Naval War College and Armed Forces Staff College graduate, he was teaching at the Industrial College of the Armed Forces when he retired in 1954. He is a writer on professional subjects. His article "Peripheral Strategy, Littoral Tactics and Limited War" (*Army*, September, 1954) has often been reprinted as most representative of this concept of American military policy.

ERNEST R. MAY is Professor of History at Harvard University. He is the author of *The World War and American Isolation, 1914–1917, Imperial Democracy: The Emergence of America as a Great Power*, two volumes in the LIFE *History of the United States*, and, with John W. Caughey, *A History of the United States*. He has edited *The Ultimate Decision: The President as Commander in Chief* and the four-volume *The American Image*.

PIERO PIERI, born in 1893 at Sondrio, Lombardy, of a Tuscan family, fought in World War I as an officer of mountain troops (Alpini) and was twice decorated for valor. After teaching in high schools in Naples from 1922 to 1935, he became Professor of History at the School of Education of the University of Messina. Since 1939, he has been Professor of History at the School of Education of the University of Turin. He has also frequently served both schools as dean of the faculty. Since 1930, Professor Pieri has devoted himself almost exclusively to military history viewed in relation to political history. His principal works are: *Il Rinascimento e la crisi militare italiana* (1934; 2d rev. ed., 1952), *La Prima Guerra Mondiale—Problemi di storia militare* (1947), *Guerra e politica negli scrittori italiani* (1955), and *Storia militare del Risorgimento* (1962).

Index

Index

(References in italics are to maps.)